D1600766

The Afterlife of John Fitzgerald Kennedy

In his new book, Michael J. Hogan, a leading historian of the American presidency, offers a new perspective on John F. Kennedy, as seen not from his life and times but from his afterlife in American memory. *The Afterlife of John Fitzgerald Kennedy* considers how Kennedy constructed a popular image of himself, in effect, a brand, as he played the part of president on the White House stage. The cultural trauma brought on by his assassination further burnished that image and began the process of transporting Kennedy from history to memory. Hogan shows how Jacqueline Kennedy, as the chief guardian of her husband's memory, devoted herself to embedding the image of the slain president in the collective memory of the nation, evident in the many physical and literary monuments dedicated to his memory. Regardless of critics, most Americans continue to see Kennedy as his wife wanted him remembered: the charming war hero, the loving husband and father, and the peacemaker and progressive leader who inspired confidence and hope in the American people.

Michael J. Hogan is Distinguished Professor of History at the University of Illinois, Springfield, and Emeritus Professor of History at Ohio State University. Past president of the Society for Historians of American Foreign Relations, Hogan served for fifteen years as editor of *Diplomatic History*, the journal of record for scholars of American foreign relations and national security studies. He is the author and editor of ten books, notably his prize-winning history *The Marshall Plan: America, Britain and the Reconstruction of Western Europe, 1947–1952* (Cambridge University Press, 1987) and *A Cross of Iron: Harry S. Truman and the Origins of the National Security State, 1945–1954* (Cambridge University Press, 1998), his book on the origins of the national security state. He has written numerous essays and articles in leading professional journals, including *The American Historical Review* and *The Journal of American History*.

The Afterlife of John Fitzgerald Kennedy

A Biography

MICHAEL J. HOGAN

University of Illinois, Springfield
The Ohio State University, Emeritus

CAMBRIDGE
UNIVERSITY PRESS

CAMBRIDGE
UNIVERSITY PRESS

One Liberty Plaza, 20th Floor, New York, NY 10006, USA

Cambridge University Press is part of the University of Cambridge.

It furthers the University's mission by disseminating knowledge in the pursuit of education, learning, and research at the highest international levels of excellence.

www.cambridge.org
Information on this title: www.cambridge.org/9781107186996
10.1017/9781316911945

© Michael J. Hogan 2017

First published 2017

Printed in the United States of America by Sheridan Books, Inc.

A catalogue record for this publication is available from the British Library.

Library of Congress Cataloging-in-Publication Data
Names: Hogan, Michael J., 1943– author.
Title: The afterlife of John Fitzgerald Kennedy: a biography / Michael J. Hogan, University of Illinois, Springfield.
Description: New York, NY: Cambridge University Press, 2017. |
Includes bibliographical references and index.
Identifiers: LCCN 2016041860 | ISBN 9781107186996 (hardback)
Subjects: LCSH: Kennedy, John F. (John Fitzgerald), 1917–1963 – Public opinion. |
Kennedy, John F. (John Fitzgerald), 1917–1963 – Influence. | Presidents – United States –
Biography – History and criticism. | United States – Politics and government –
1961–1963 – Historiography. | Collective memory – United States. |
Public opinion – United States.
Classification: LCC E842.1.H64 2017 | DDC 973.922092 [B]–dc23
LC record available at https://lccn.loc.gov/2016041860

ISBN 978-1-107-18699-6 Hardback

To My Granddaughters, with Love
Cameron
Marley
Madigan
Jessica
Ella
Reese
Brady
Joie
Lillian
&
Eleanor

Trí na chéile a thógtar na cáisléain
In our togetherness, castles are built
(Irish Proverb)

Contents

Acknowledgments

I've had more support than I deserved in writing this book. I've been blessed with a patient family, including my wife, Virginia, who endured my obsession with the Kennedys, read a good deal of the manuscript, and offered helpful advice on how it might be improved. Similar assistance came from Chris Zacher and Martha Garland, both friends from Ohio State University, where I'm an emeritus professor of history, and from three research assistants: Jacob House, who spent a good deal of time tracking down published sources, particularly magazine and newspaper articles, which he photocopied for my use; Dr. Melissa Steinmetz, who read every line of the manuscript, proofread the notes, and assembled the bibliography; and Sarah Iler Pfeffer, who helped locate and identify the photographs that appear in the following pages. I am also indebted to two former colleagues and collaborators. Dr. Lisa Troyer saved me from numerous computer problems and provided expert advice on research strategies and sources, including some of the relevant literature in her field of sociology. Professor Mary Ann Heiss of Kent State University critiqued much of the manuscript, was incredibly helpful in locating published sources, and aided my research at the Kennedy Library and the National Archives.

I also want to thank my editor at Cambridge University Press, Deborah Gershenowitz, and her editorial assistant, Kristina Deusch, for their help in preparing the manuscript for publication. I am indebted as well to the University of Illinois, which provided me with a home on the Springfield campus, where I could teach online, and with substantial research support throughout the project. That support covered almost all of my research expenses, including the cost of three research assistants, and enabled me to devote considerable time to research and writing. When it came to gathering sources for this volume, I am grateful for help rendered by the staff of the National Archives in Washington, DC, although my biggest debt in this regard is to the John F. Kennedy Presidential Library in Boston. This acknowledgment may seem ironic, because the history told here is often critical of the library administration. Nevertheless, I will be the first to praise the archivists and staff who worked hard on my behalf, not to open records still sealed, but to access those already available. I also commend the Kennedy Library for digitizing its holdings, which made my research much easier and much less expensive. A careful examination of my notes will show the reader how much I depended on these records and how much help I had from the staff.

Thanks as well to Jessica C. E. Gienow-Hecht, a professor at the Free University of Berlin, for guiding me to some of the most useful literature in the field of theater and performance studies; to Professor Emeritus Emily S. Rosenberg of the University of California, Irvine, who reviewed an abstract for this project and whose work on Pearl Harbor in American memory served as something of a model for my own book; and to Professor Holly Kent of the University of Illinois, Springfield, who endured more than one conversation on Jacqueline Kennedy's wardrobe and who led me to some of the best literature on the history and sociology of fashion. Finally, I owe very special debts to Professors Edward Linenthal of Indiana University and Robert Mason of the University of Edinburgh, both of whom invested considerable time and energy in my manuscript. Reviewing manuscripts for a university press can sometimes be a thankless job. But to them I give "thanks" in abundance. This book is better for their attention.

Although I have benefited from the work of many other scholars, the list is far too long to acknowledge in this space. Instead, I urge the reader to peruse my notes, where I try to express the debt I owe to each of them. I am especially grateful for the many works in history, sociology, and cultural studies dealing with memory and nostalgia, collective cultural trauma, and performance in the theater of everyday life. The authors of these impressive works have helped me organize my narrative and give it meaning. This has been a difficult book to write, in large part because it deals with a subject vastly different from anything I've tackled before. I chose the subject, and my approach to it, partly because they were new to me, and therefore more challenging. Others will have to decide if I rose to the occasion, but if so, it is due in no small part to the guidance of scholars far more able than I.

Finally, and most importantly, I express my appreciation and give my love to my granddaughters. They will wonder why I'm thanking them. After all, the youngest is only three and none of them has read a single word of this book or offered a single piece of advice. But like my children, not to mention my own parents and siblings, they have given me constant joy and a sense of purpose, both of which have added meaning to my work and to my life. This book is dedicated to all ten of them.

Abbreviations

AMSPP	Arthur M. Schlesinger Jr. Personal Papers, JFK Library
CHPP	Chet Huntley Personal Papers, JFK Library
DFPPP	David F. Powers Personal Papers, JFK Library
FPK	Historical Studies Division, Historical Office, Bureau of Public Affairs, Department of State, *The Funeral of President Kennedy and United States Government Actions, November 22–25, 1963*. Research Project no. 662, March 1967, DOS Record Number 1191001710094, Record Series Lot 71D411, S/S Files, National Archives II, College Park, MD
JBKOPP	Jacqueline Bouvier Kennedy Onassis Personal Papers, JFK Library
JFKPOF	Papers of John F. Kennedy, Presidential Papers, President's Office Files, JFK Library
JFKWHP	Papers of John F. Kennedy, Presidential Papers, White House Photographs, JFK Library
JFKWHSF	Papers of John F. Kennedy, Presidential Papers, White House Social Files, JFK Library
OHC	Oral History Collection, JFK Library
RFKPSP	Robert F. Kennedy Papers, Senate Papers, Series: Correspondence: Personal File, 1964–1968, JFK Library
RSSPP	R. Sargent Shriver Personal Papers, JFK Library
THWPP	Theodore H. White Personal Papers, JFK Library
WWPP	William Walton Personal Papers, JFK Library

The Afterlife of John Fitzgerald Kennedy

An Introduction

The president woke up in a good mood on November 22, 1963. His back hurt more than usual, so he reinforced the corset he normally wore with a bandage-wrap for extra support. The discomfort did not darken his spirit, however; nor did the news of continued wrangling among leaders of the Democratic Party in Texas, particularly a squabble between conservative Governor John Connally and liberal Senator Ralph Yarborough that even Vice President Lyndon Johnson had been unable or unwilling to resolve. Despite this annoyance and his aching back, the president seemed more impressed by the large crowds and thunderous welcome that he and his wife had experienced during the first leg of their Texas trip. Even First Lady Jacqueline Kennedy, who normally disliked campaigning, was thrilled by their reception, and she and her husband had no reason to expect anything less from the day ahead. On the contrary, another enthusiastic crowd was already forming in the street below their hotel window. "I'll go anywhere with you," said the first lady, as she watched a smile flash across the handsome face of her husband.[1]

Nor was their mood darkened by a newspaper advertisement just published in the conservative *Dallas Morning News*. It began with sarcastic words welcoming President John F. Kennedy to the Lone Star State, but then launched a scurrilous attack, concealed in a series of leading questions, on the president's liberal policies at home and his supposedly soft stand on communism abroad. The ad revealed a degree of hostility toward the Kennedy administration that had been building for some time. Right-wing groups had physically and verbally assaulted Vice President Johnson and his wife when they campaigned in the state three years earlier, and similar groups had roughed up UN ambassador Adlai

Stevenson during his visit to Dallas only a month before the president arrived. Stevenson was the darling of the liberal wing of the Democratic Party, a status that did not endear him to the increasingly conservative voters of Texas, who also viewed Johnson, a Texas native, as a traitor to his state for supporting the president's progressive agenda, especially on civil rights for African Americans.[2]

All this was well known to Kennedy, as was the politics of the *Dallas Morning News* and its publisher and board chairman, E. M. Dealey. Dealey was a leading figure in Dallas and a member of its Citizens Council, a private group of local elites that acted like an unofficial city council and was sometimes called the "White" Citizens Council. He had made the *Morning News* a strong defender of states' rights and segregation, and an arch-critic of the federal government, liberal social programs, civil rights, foreign aid, the United Nations, the Supreme Court, northern cities, and the Catholics, Jews, blacks, and Democrats who inhabited them. He had personally confronted Kennedy at one of the president's regular meetings with newspaper publishers, editors, and columnists, accusing the president of surrounding himself with "weak sisters" who were soft on communism. What the people needed, he said, was "a man on horseback," but what Kennedy gave them was a man barely adept at riding his daughter's tricycle. Under the circumstances, it came as no surprise to see the scurrilous ad in the *Morning News* – nor that it had been paid for by the local John Birch Society, an extremist right-wing group, and by Nelson Bunker Hunt, son of ultra-conservative oil magnate H. L. Hunt. Together, these men and others like them, including other members of the Citizens Council, had made Dallas the epicenter of an aggressively right-wing movement that was spreading through a good portion of the South, much to the detriment of the Democratic Party and Kennedy's reelection prospects.[3]

Still, the president was undaunted, even jocular, teasing his wife that they were now entering "nut country."[4] He seemed to make light of any threats against him, perhaps because he had met similar challenges in the past and had triumphed time and again. His bad back and other ailments had led him to death's door more than once, each time receiving the last rites of the Catholic Church and each time bouncing back, like Lazarus arising from the grave, with renewed life and vitality. He had survived the Second World War as well, serving as a PT boat commander in the Pacific and saving most of his crew when a Japanese destroyer rammed their ship. The incident, which made him a decorated war hero, was celebrated in a best-selling work by the author, John Hersey, and more recently in a popular movie that President Kennedy and friends had just screened in the White House theater. Nor were these the only examples of his success against the odds. His bid for the Democratic Party nomination in 1960 and his subsequent victory over Republican candidate Richard M. Nixon in the fall election had both overcome significant obstacles, the greatest being his young age, inexperience, and the widespread prejudice, especially in the South, against a Catholic politician whose decisions were supposedly guided less by the U.S. Constitution than by religious doctrine. He had dealt with these issues directly and successfully during the Democratic Party primaries, especially the West Virginia primary, and in a major address to a gathering of Protestant ministers in Texas.

Few could doubt that Kennedy led a charmed life. Harvard-educated scion of a wealthy Irish family, he was a hero of the Pacific War with the medals to prove it, and a published author of some distinction, having won a Pulitzer Prize for his book *Profiles in Courage*. Blessed with Hollywood good looks, he was also a man of enormous personal charm, quick intelligence, and a self-deprecating sense of humor, whose public appearances and televised press conferences had made him the most popular politician in the country. And if all that were not enough, he was married to a beautiful and intelligent woman and the father of two attractive children. Kennedy himself must have felt fortunate as he began laying the groundwork for his reelection bid just one year away, including his trip to raise funds as well as votes in Texas, mend fences in the state's Democratic Party, and calm the ferocious spirit of an ascendant conservatism.

Enthusiastic receptions by large crowds in San Antonio, Houston, and Fort Worth had exceeded expectations, and the last stop was to be a brief, overnight visit to Vice President Johnson's ranch outside of Austin. Only a three-hour campaign in Dallas remained, and that part of the trip began with another exuberant crowd welcoming the Kennedys when Air Force One landed at Love Field. Teeming throngs waved and screamed wildly as the president's motorcade wound its way through Dallas to the Trade Mart, where he was to deliver remarks and enjoy lunch with a large group of local businessmen and party donors. For the Kennedys, and for Governor Connally and his wife, the trip to that point had been a resounding success. "You sure can't say that Texas doesn't love you," Mrs. Connally told the president as she and the governor rode with the Kennedys to the luncheon. "No you can't," he replied, a broad grin breaking across his face just before rifle bullets pierced the back of his neck and exploded the right side of his head. The president of the United States was dead.[5]

But was he really? Or would John F. Kennedy somehow transcend death to occupy a special place in the living memory of the nation? If so, how would this happen and who would decide how Kennedy was remembered? How would they define his identity and delineate his legacy, and what would their constructions have to say about the nation's sense of itself – about what it meant to be an American? As these questions suggest, this is not another book about the life and times of John F. Kennedy. It says little about his presidency or, for that matter, his assassination. It presents instead a new perspective on the president, as seen not from his life but from his afterlife in American memory.[6] That being said, the following introduction briefly surveys Kennedy's domestic and foreign policies. It provides background for what follows in the text and notes why so many people saw the president as a liberal champion whose identity was defined less by his achievements than by what he appeared to represent, what he tried to accomplish, and what conservatives had to say about him.

Similarly, the second chapter goes into some detail about the so-called style on display in the Kennedy White House. It uses the words "style," "brand," and "image" more or less interchangeably and draws for its argument on sociological theories dealing with performance in the theater of everyday life. Kennedy's style was in many ways a self-constructed representation of the parts that he and his wife played as president and first lady. Much like any commercial brand, moreover, it concealed some aspects of their real selves, featured other more appealing attributes, and was designed to popularize or promote a particular product or personality – namely, the president and his policies. Style and substance thus went hand in hand in the Kennedy White House. By conjuring up an idealized image of what it meant to be an American, Kennedy's style, or the style of his presidency, added enormously to his popular appeal and political effectiveness. It was widely admired at the time of his death and remained central to the social construction of his memory in the years that followed. This explains why I devote so much attention to how the Kennedys presented themselves. Doing so establishes the Kennedy style as a central theme in the chapters that follow and helps to account for the visceral public reaction to the president's brutal murder.

That reaction is described in Chapter 3. Borrowing again from sociological theories, this time dealing with cultural trauma and collective memory, it describes how Kennedy's assassination triggered widespread feelings of grief, shock, and insecurity, as well as a tendency, typical in moments of great national trauma, to idealize those who lost their lives in the tragedy. In this case, the trauma led most Americans to burnish the image of the president that he and his wife had already constructed, turning it into a sacred symbol of mythical proportions and lodging it deep in the collective memory of the nation. The assassination thus began the process of transporting Kennedy from history to memory. It set the stage for a long struggle over how he would be memorialized, who would own or control his memory, and how his legacy would be defined. In many ways a struggle over what would be remembered and what would be forgotten, it highlights the persistent tension between history, memory, and heritage that runs throughout the story of Kennedy's afterlife.[7]

These themes open one upon the other, like the folds of an expanding accordion, in the remainder of this book. Using the metaphor and language of the theater, Chapter 4 describes the president's funeral. It tells how Jacqueline Kennedy staged one of the most dramatic events in American history, largely with an eye to reproducing her husband's presidency as she wanted it remembered, and how, in doing so, she, too, became a symbol of what it meant to be an American. Chapters 5 through 8 show how the former first lady and her allies worked in subsequent years to nourish and protect the popular image of the president, as he had played his part in the White House. Their goal was to make the president worthy of remembrance, which they largely achieved in the decade following his death, when artists, poets, and musicians commemorated his life more or less as the former first lady wanted him remembered. This was also true of the many mementos that would bear his name and of the great monuments erected in his honor. These chapters treat the Kennedy monuments and memorabilia as text and try to discern the message they conveyed, especially when the former first lady was involved, which was the case, for example, with the Kennedy Center for the Performing Arts in Washington, DC, the president's memorial gravesite in Arlington National Cemetery, and the Kennedy Presidential Library and Museum in Boston, Massachusetts.

In all of these endeavors, as with her careful scripting of the president's funeral, Jacqueline Kennedy became the chief guardian of her husband's memory. She devoted herself to what had become, in her mind, his inviolable image and to embedding that image in the approved version of his life and presidency. This was evident not only in the physical monuments to his memory, but also in the literary monuments erected by the first generation of Kennedy scholars, some of whom, like Theodore Sorensen and Arthur M. Schlesinger Jr., had been close colleagues of the former president. There were critics, of course, but not many, in part because

Jacqueline Kennedy, her friends and family, were largely successful in blocking alternative narratives and controlling the way history remembered her husband.

By the mid-1970s, however, frustration over the Vietnam War and the Watergate scandal, among other things, had created a new political culture in the United States, out of which came a wave of revisionist historians whose views were decidedly at odds with those of their predecessors. Unlike Schlesinger and Sorensen, revisionist scholars pictured Kennedy as a cautious and mediocre president with little success to his credit and a private life, including poor health and extramarital affairs, that betrayed his public persona and the way his family wanted him remembered. At that point, as discussed in Chapters 7 and 8, Kennedy's identity became contested terrain in a memory war that engaged not only historians but the media as well, not to mention the Kennedy family and officials at the Kennedy Library, who did what they could to protect the sanctified image they had helped to construct in the first place. As we will see, the memory wars raged through the 1970s and 1980s before eventually producing a more balanced, postrevisionist history of Kennedy and his administration.[8]

This is hardly the whole story, however. Although postrevisionism eventually gained the upper hand among professional historians, it had little appeal to the nation at large, where views once typical of the founding generation of Kennedy scholars seemed to prevail over time. This was evident in the many sympathetic books about Kennedy that flew from the bookstores every time the nation commemorated his assassination. It was also evident in the respect he garnered over the years from so many in the mainstream media and from the inexorable tide of Hollywood movies, TV specials, and documentaries recounting his life. It was evident as well in the deference he claimed from the many politicians who tried to appropriate his memory, not to mention his famous style, for themselves and their party. And it was evident in the high ratings he received in one public opinion poll after another in the years following his death.

It was as if historians made no impression on the American mind, except perhaps, when mainstream cultural institutions and the so-called heritage industry translated historical scholarship for public consumption. And because that process could obscure as much as it revealed, it tended to preserve the Kennedy brand as a vital part of the nation's heritage, if not always its history. For the heritage industry, in fact, including the makers of mementos, popular books, movies, TV specials, and museum exhibits, the past was a product and the Kennedy brand a boon to business. For this reason, it reinforced the image that Kennedy had constructed of himself, and in the process contributed to how Americans would remember the late president. This is one of the many reasons why Kennedy still has such an enduring grip on the American imagination – now more than fifty years after his assassination.[9]

II

All of this will become clear in the following chapters, but first, a brief introduction to the politics and policies of the Kennedy administration. This will spare us the need to repeatedly explain these subjects at different points in the text and help us understand why so many people viewed the president, or at least his brand, as a noble reflection of their own values – of who they were or aspired to be as Americans. When he traveled to Texas in November 1963, Kennedy knew that deep racial, regional, and partisan divisions in Congress and across the country had made it difficult to deal effectively with the pressing economic and social issues of the day. International issues were no less partisan, contentious, and apparently intractable, even though the Cold War seemed to be reaching its most dangerous point. All of this had been evident already in the 1960 campaign. Aware that Republican Party leaders had earlier accused the Truman administration of "losing China" to the communists, Kennedy had decided in 1960 to protect his own prospects by turning the tables on his Republican opponents. During the course of the campaign, he charged President Dwight D. Eisenhower and Vice President Richard M. Nixon with losing the space race to the Soviet Union and creating a "missile gap" in the nation's defense posture – a charge that later proved to be unfounded. He also accused them of weakness in Europe, where West Germany faced the constant threat of Soviet aggression, and of giving ground to communism in Asia, Africa, Latin America, and especially Cuba, where Fidel Castro's communist government had just come to power. Kennedy promised to close the missile gap and reverse the communist tide, partly by spending more on defense and partly by stressing the deterrent power of conventional forces, including Special Forces like the Green Berets, which could fight and win guerrilla wars in the underdeveloped world.

Kennedy did not ignore domestic issues entirely. On the contrary, he called for a war on poverty, more aid to education, a more lenient policy on immigration, health care for the elderly, a higher minimum wage, and civil rights for minorities, notably African Americans. On these issues, however, he knew that progress would be difficult, if not impossible, in the face of a powerful congressional coalition of Republicans and conservative southern Democrats. This prospect, together with the global dangers confronting the nation, helps to explain Kennedy's emphasis on foreign rather than domestic policy during the course of his campaign.[10]

Nor did the election change things. Winning with only 49.7 percent of the vote, Kennedy's majority was not strong enough to throttle the conservative bloc and secure his domestic agenda in Congress. On the international front, moreover, he still faced a potentially deadly arms race with the Soviet Union, new challenges from communist China, and major crises in Europe, Latin America, and Asia. Under the circumstances, it's not surprising that national security issues dominated his famous inaugural address, or that he spent most of his time in office dealing with these issues. He increased spending for the space program and added to the defense budget. He also established new foreign aid programs like the Peace Corps and the Alliance for Progress to encourage economic development, foster democracy, and contain communism in developing countries around the world. Just three months into office, moreover, he threw his weight behind a wildly reckless plan to topple Fidel Castro's communist government in Cuba.[11]

Poorly conceived by the Central Intelligence Agency (CIA) and previously approved by President Eisenhower, the plan called for Cuban exiles, trained by the CIA, to invade Cuba at the Bay of Pigs in April 1961. The CIA expected the invasion to trigger a popular uprising against Castro's government, which would then be replaced with a pro-American administration. The outcome instead was an unmitigated disaster. Ambivalent about the plan to begin with, Kennedy refused to be drawn deeper into the conflict when the exiles failed. He would not use American air power to rescue the invaders or oust Castro, as many of his advisors suggested, and came away from the experience deeply suspicious of both the CIA and the Joint Chiefs of Staff. The results were evident in the many crises that followed, including the Berlin crisis in the second half of 1961.[12]

Just months after the Bay of Pigs, Kennedy and his wife traveled to Europe to meet with leaders from Great Britain, France, and the Soviet Union. The first two meetings went more or less as expected, but the conference in Vienna with Soviet Premier Nikita Khrushchev sparked a heated confrontation that nearly ended in disaster. Kennedy had hoped for productive discussions on a range of issues, including a nuclear test ban agreement, but his most pressing concern was the future of Berlin. After the Second World War, Germany had been divided into Eastern and

Western occupation zones; the former became a Soviet protectorate while the United States and its allies supported the latter. When the two sides could not agree on a treaty that would reunify Germany and recognize its sovereignty, the zones eventually hardened into separate East and West German states, with the city of Berlin, also divided into separate jurisdictions, located in the Eastern Zone. Always a sore point in East–West relations, the divided city became a particular embarrassment for the Soviets when a large number of East Germans and others from Eastern Europe began fleeing through Berlin to freedom in the West.

Anxious to halt the exodus, Khrushchev and the Soviet delegates in Vienna renewed earlier threats to negotiate their own treaty with East Germany, thereby making permanent what was supposed to be a temporary arrangement. The proposed treaty would recognize East Germany's sovereignty over a unified Berlin, including its right to limit western access to the city and staunch the flow of its own citizens from East to West. Kennedy rejected the proposal, as did the allies, and the Vienna Conference ended with fruitless ideological exchanges and threats of war on both sides. Privately, however, Kennedy worried about the sanity of those, including some of his own military advisors, who talked of nuclear war if the Soviets did not back down. He looked for a way to resolve the crisis short of national suicide, as he called it, and found the solution in August 1961, when the communists closed the border between East and West Berlin and began building what came to be known as the Berlin Wall. Because this solution appeared to rule out the reunification of Germany, nationalists in West Germany and hawks in the United States denounced the president as an appeaser, which forced him to reassure Americans and their allies by adding still more to the defense budget. At the same time, however, Kennedy dismissed his critics as extremists. He said the Berlin Wall, though deplorable, was preferable to a nuclear war and reminded everyone that Khrushchev and the communists had blinked first – and with a solution that made them look like jailers who imprisoned their own people behind a concrete barrier.[13]

Twice in less than a year – his first year in office – Kennedy had managed two major crises short of war. He admitted his personal culpability for the Bay of Pigs fiasco, but pulled back in time to prevent an even greater disaster; he acknowledged his failure in Vienna, but seized on a solution that ended the Berlin crisis without a nuclear exchange. There were other challenges and some triumphs as well. To deal with a civil war in the small, Southeast Asian country of Laos, and to prevent it from becoming another site of superpower confrontation, Kennedy managed to engage the Soviets in a negotiated agreement that neutralized the little country under a shaky coalition government. He was also cautious when it came to the civil war in Vietnam, which he considered the most serious problem in Southeast Asia. Although he increased the number of American military advisors training South Vietnamese troops in their fight against the communist Viet Cong and their North Vietnamese allies, he clearly preferred a political to a military solution. He urged progressive political and social reforms on President Ngo Dinh Diem and his government in Saigon, thinking that such reforms could win the hearts and minds of the Vietnamese people and undercut popular support for the Viet Cong. When reforms were not forthcoming, he blamed Diem, sanctioned a military coup that toppled his government, and hoped for more success under a new regime. He did not authorize Diem's assassination, however, and was reluctant as well to commit American troops to the battle. On the contrary, he began talking toward the end of his life about decreasing the number of American military advisors and disengaging from the struggle altogether.[14]

Something similar can be said of Kennedy's Cuban policy after the Bay of Pigs. Because of that reckless effort, not to mention subsequent plans to destabilize the Cuban economy and assassinate the Cuban leader, it's not surprising that Castro would seek economic aid and military protection from the Soviet Union. Nor is it surprising, given the Berlin crisis, that Khrushchev would try to right an unfavorable balance of power with the United States in Europe, which included American missiles in Turkey, by seeking a foothold in the Western Hemisphere. So it was that in October 1962, less than two years after taking office, Kennedy learned from U-2 reconnaissance photos that Soviet leaders were installing offensive nuclear missiles in Cuba. He immediately convened a task force of national security advisors to review the situation and recommend a course of action. The president himself came to favor a naval blockade, or embargo, that would stop Soviet missiles from reaching the Caribbean island and allow time for a negotiated resolution of the crisis. The Joint Chiefs and other advisors criticized this approach as tantamount to appeasement. It would make the United States look weak, they argued, and undermine its credibility with allies who counted on American protection against communist aggression. They wanted an immediate military response, notably a preemptive attack on Cuba, including, if necessary, a full-scale air bombardment and ground invasion.

Their recommendation reminded Kennedy of Japan's surprise attack on Pearl Harbor. He thought it would alienate the United Nations as well as the South American countries he was trying to court, prompt the Soviets to respond with similar action against Berlin, and lead inevitably to a nuclear war. Although the president had few allies at the moment of maximum danger, he prevailed nonetheless. Without renouncing the military option altogether, he established a naval blockade of Cuba and opened negotiations with the Soviets. The combination led to compromise in a final settlement that avoided World War III. The Soviets agreed to remove the missiles from Cuba and the Americans pledged never to invade the island. In a private arrangement revealed years later, they also agreed to dismantle the American missiles in Turkey, which were outdated in any event and already scheduled for removal.[15]

It's impossible to excuse Kennedy for earlier American efforts to destabilize Cuba and plans to assassinate Castro. These actions, together with the US-sponsored invasion at the Bay of Pigs, almost certainly set the stage for the Cuban Missile Crisis in the first place. In the end, however, Kennedy's judgment was sober and his actions restrained. He showed considerable strength in standing up to the many advisors, including military advisors, who were aligned against him, and to the conservatives and war hawks in both parties who urged a reckless response to the equally reckless policy of the Soviet Union. He survived the political damage they promised to inflict on him and emerged from the crisis, not only more popular than ever before but also more convinced that only some kind of accommodation with the Soviets could bring a dangerous nuclear arms race under control. This realization set the stage for two of his most remarkable speeches.

The first was a major address at American University in Washington, DC, on June 10, 1963. In the background were ongoing talks between the United States and the Soviet Union over how to control the proliferation of nuclear weapons and limit or ban nuclear tests in the atmosphere and underground. The talks began shortly after the Cuban Missile Crisis and faced the daunting task of satisfying critics in both countries, including, in the United States, the Joint Chiefs of Staff and their allies in Congress. This was the background to Kennedy's speech, which aimed to move the negotiations forward to a treaty that public opinion could support and the United States Senate could ratify.

But so, in a way, was the president's second great speech of the summer, the famous "I am a Berliner" address he delivered during his visit to Berlin in June 1963. Kennedy spoke before a throng of almost hysterical German citizens who cheered wildly when they heard the president's implacable promise to defend Berlin against Soviet aggression. Delivered in the classic, almost hyperbolic, language of the Cold War at its most dangerous moment, the speech appeared to belie his hopes for a modest détente with the Soviet Union and successful conclusion of a test ban agreement. Yet at the same time, the president's remarks, however over-heated, served several related purposes. Besides assuaging the Germans, who were still miffed about Kennedy's apparent willingness to live with the Berlin Wall, it increased his standing in Europe, where he was eas-ily the most popular American president since Franklin Roosevelt, and added to his already enormous popularity in the United States. Most importantly, it mollified his critics at home and abroad, made it easier for them to tolerate the sweet reasonableness of his pleas for détente with the Soviet Union, and led to favorable action on his Limited Test Ban Treaty – which passed the Senate with flying colors in late September 1963.[16]

Kennedy also had at least some success when it came to other parts of his agenda. He secured funding for a space program that would put an American on the moon by the end of the decade and restore the coun-try's position as the global leader in science and technology, which had supposedly been lost to the Soviet Union when it launched the Sputnik satellite a half decade earlier. He scored another victory when he forced the big steel companies to rescind a major price increase. The compa-nies immediately branded the president as anti-business, but public opin-ion praised his strength and his resolve to protect the nation against the dangers of inflation and the rapacious power of big business. In addi-tion, Kennedy managed to raise the minimum wage slightly, gain modest increases in Social Security payments and federal aid to education, and win congressional approval for a major trade expansion act. As we will see, moreover, he and his wife did more to advance the arts in American life than most of his predecessors, and what they did gave the admin-istration an air of elegance and sophistication – a sense of style – that captured the American imagination.

Larry O'Brien, who headed the president's congressional relations staff, later assembled a long list of the president's legislative triumphs, only to have most liberals discount the list as inconsequential. The gains were too small, they said; the list was too short and did not include the major reforms they wanted. In truth, while Democrats held a majority in both houses of Congress, Kennedy could not muscle the votes he needed to overcome opposition from conservatives in both parties, who threw one roadblock after another in front of his agenda. They forced him into budget bills that left little room for the programs he wanted, including a tax cut to stimulate the economy and health insurance for the elderly, which critics denounced as socialized medicine. His proposal for a new Department of Housing and Urban Development, the centerpiece of a planned attack on urban poverty, also fell victim to congressional conservatives, especially southern conservatives who saw no need to address the problem of poverty in northern cities.[17]

Nor did Kennedy receive much support for civil rights legislation, either in Congress or in public opinion polls. He did move, though cautiously, to end discrimination in publicly financed housing and took other steps when executive action, rather than congressional legislation, made modest gains possible. However reluctantly, he also sent federal officials to protect the Freedom Riders when their efforts to integrate interstate transportation met violent resistance from bands of southern segregationists. He did the same when white segregationists in Georgia and Mississippi burned black churches and attacked civil rights protesters in a series of confrontations that came to a head when the governor of Mississippi refused to comply with a federal court order to enroll James Meredith, a black air force veteran, as a student at the University of Mississippi. Kennedy denounced the violence and sent federal marshals to protect Meredith, much as he did when police officers and firemen in Birmingham, Alabama used dogs and water cannons to assault young black protesters and when Governor George Wallace promised to defy a federal court order integrating the University of Alabama. In the midst of ongoing violence and continued defiance of the law, Kennedy forced Wallace to back down and appealed once more for peace and civil rights, which he now defined as a moral as well as legal issue.

Over the objections of some of his key advisors, including Theodore Sorensen, the president also asked Congress to enact a strong civil rights bill that would guarantee African Americans the right to vote and equal protection under the law. That bill, as well as Kennedy's tax proposal, was on its way to passage when the president was gunned down in Texas.[18] To be sure, Kennedy had acted too slowly, too cautiously, to satisfy Martin Luther King Jr. and other black leaders who rightly viewed civil rights as a moral imperative that could not wait any longer. When pushed by their protests, however, and by the violent defiance of federal law, the president did step forward, and with the strongest piece of civil rights legislation the country had ever seen. Whatever the leadership thought, black citizens generally applauded his actions and considered him the greatest champion of civil rights since Abraham Lincoln. What is more,

Kennedy took action knowing it could stall other parts of his legislative agenda, divide the Democratic Party along sectional lines, and risk his own reelection in 1964.

That's what brought the president to Dallas in November 1963. As noted earlier, Dallas was a city increasingly under the sway of conservatives, many of them extremists and segregationists, who were tearing the state's Democratic Party apart. Many were leaving the Democratic for the Republican Party, which appeared more sympathetic to their concerns about racial integration, the spread of global communism, and the growth of big government, with its support for business regulations and welfare legislation that amounted, in the conservative mind, to a socialist assault on free enterprise and states' rights. In his visit to Texas, Kennedy hoped to counter conservative fears and bring Democrats together under the banner of the New Frontier, which now added an aggressive defense of civil rights to the more familiar liberal platform of higher wages and aid to education, the elderly, the ill, and the poor.[19]

On the eve of his assassination, then, Kennedy's identity was taking shape and starting to coalesce in the public mind at home and abroad. To some extent, Kennedy had defined himself by what appeared to be a strong commitment to peace and social justice and by his efforts, evident in his Texas trip, to reconcile the many differences that divided his party and the nation. To some extent, however, he was defined by his critics: those who denounced him for being "soft" on communism in Cuba, Berlin, and Southeast Asia; those who accused him of appeasement when he negotiated the Test Ban Treaty and talked of détente with the Soviet Union; and those who called him a reckless big spender and socialist when he proposed tax cuts, new social programs, and civil rights for black Americans. Opposition from his critics, especially conservatives in both parties, may have limited Kennedy's legislative success. But it also defined him as different from his critics, as a man of courage and compassion, the great reconciler and peacemaker, the champion of democracy and reform at home and around the world.

Seen in this light, Kennedy's successes reached beyond the legislative arena; it was not what he accomplished in Congress that mattered so much as what he represented. Judging by opinion polls, at least, he had come to symbolize what was best in America – the ideal American whose many attributes and virtues, so far as they could be seen, were those to which all Americans should aspire. He promised Americans a New Frontier of economic justice, democratic progress, and enlightened leadership of a world at peace. He inspired in them a faith in the future, a conviction that all good things were possible, and a confidence in the American way as the best way. He made them feel good about themselves as Americans, which is why, as we will see, so many of them would think of him as a martyr to democracy, a man of faith and strength who had risked his life in Dallas, as the ancient Christians had faced death in the Colosseum, for his own deeply held convictions. It's why they would compare him to Lincoln, Moses, and Jesus. For many, he became the hero in a national morality play that pitted good against evil in the long struggle for peace and democracy.

As we will see in the chapter that follows, Kennedy's vaunted style only added to his image. It went deeper than his attractive and youthful appearance, his rhetorical skills, sense of humor, and practical intelligence. It went beyond the White House restoration, the famous state dinners hosted by the Kennedys, their elaborate costumes and orchestrated entertainments, and their support for the arts, broadly defined. In the eyes of his admirers, Kennedy's style was also his substance. It embraced his liberal vision, to be sure, as well as the postwar aspirations of the American people. It signified an American brand of royalty and the country's new position as both a world power and as the rightful, though benevolent, heir to a long western tradition of global leadership. All of this helps to explain both the intense reaction to his death and why his image has become fixed in the deep memory of the nation.

2

All the World's a Stage

Constructing Kennedy

If all the world's a stage, as William Shakespeare suggested, only a few people have played their parts on a stage so grand as the White House, let alone cast themselves in the lead roles, written their own scripts, and directed their own performance. Yet this was the case with President John F. Kennedy and his wife, First Lady Jacqueline Kennedy, after they came to the White House in January 1961. Despite the barbs of latter-day critics, their nearly three-year run scored positive reviews at the time, set the benchmark against which subsequent performances would be measured, and still resonates in the popular imagination today. Indeed, it would become central to the approved story of the president's life, as later framed by his wife and family, and would be embedded forever in the many monuments to his memory, from his state funeral, to his gravesite at Arlington National Cemetery, to his presidential library and museum in Boston. When we remember John F. Kennedy, in other words, we are likely to remember the performer, as much as the person, and not only the part he played as president in his own White House productions but also the part his wife and others reproduced in the years following his death.

Comparing the Kennedys to stage performers or Hollywood stars is hardly a novel analogy, but the parallel has not been explored with an eye to its political content or to the way we remember the slain president. As they drafted the script for their productions, however, and as they directed the staging and played their parts, the Kennedys were also embellishing the office of the president, the authority of its occupant, and the prestige of the United States around the world. They were performing not just the presidency but the nation, defining not only the identities of the characters they played but that of the country as well. In these and

16

other ways, their presentation of the presidency went beyond entertainment, or mere "style," as some historians have described it. They created what marketers would call a "brand," basically a positive representation of themselves and their country, and in the process, transformed performance into power, style into substance for an audience that seemed hungry for what their production had to say, not only about the president but also about themselves as Americans.

In their roles as president and first lady, as this suggests, the Kennedys did not always appear as themselves. Their identities were carefully constructed idealizations that exemplified the highest qualities of American life, including personal qualities that neither the president nor the first lady always displayed when backstage at the White House. On the contrary, when it came to their celebrated restoration of the Executive Mansion, their famous parties and state dinners, or other aspects of the Kennedy brand, they tried at every turn to minimize or conceal any element of personality that would contradict their constructed selves or call into question the sincerity of the roles they played. They harnessed other members of the production to the same illusion, and used costumes, scenery, staging and other theatrical devices to convince their audience that actor and act were synonymous. As far as possible, they revealed themselves in images of their own making, in settings of their own choosing; and because their performance was so artfully staged, it was often difficult to distinguish between the real Kennedys and the characters they played. To most Americans, they came to embody the nation as they wanted to see it; their brand became the American brand – which is why Kennedy's style, not just his public policy and diplomacy, is so important to any study of his enduring hold on American memory.[1]

II

If she had her way, a young Jacqueline Bouvier once confessed, she would be the "Overall Art Director of the Twentieth Century." As it turned out, of course, she did have her way, more or less. Jacqueline Bouvier grew up in socially prominent families with homes in Manhattan; East Hampton, Long Island; McLean, Virginia; and Newport, Rhode Island. Educated, for the most part, at elite private schools, at Miss Chapin's in Manhattan, Miss Porter's in Connecticut, and Vassar College in New York, she came out as "Debutante of the Year" in 1947, traveled abroad, became an expert horsewoman, and spoke fluent French, as well as passable German and Spanish. Yet, despite these and other advantages, there was a backstory to this apparently picture-book life. Her father, known to all as "Black Jack" Bouvier, drank to excess, squandered the family fortune on ill-advised investments, and was such a reckless womanizer that his wife, the former Janet Lee, filed for divorce when Jackie was only eleven years old.[2]

Thereafter, Jackie spent most of her time with her mother and her mother's second husband, Hugh D. Auchincloss, a wealthy Wall Street investor and heir, through his mother, to a share of the Standard Oil fortune. A large, clumsy, and somewhat eccentric man, Hughdie, as he was called, spoke with a stutter, collected pornography, and pinched every penny that came through the doors of Hammersmith Farm, his seventy-five-acre estate on Narragansett Bay just outside of Newport, Rhode Island, or Merrywood, his second, terraced estate perched on a hill high above the Potomac River in McLean, Virginia. Always a gentleman, extremely proud of his WASP-ish background and club memberships, Hughdie enjoyed a comfortable relationship with his stepdaughter, though one more like that of a fictive uncle than a loving father.

Jackie, for her part, never lost touch with Black Jack, whom she adored, and who showered her with affection and a good deal of his dwindling reserves, including funds to board her horse at stables in Manhattan and at Miss Porter's school in Connecticut. By contrast, Jackie was always somewhat distant from her mother. An attractive, slender, energetic, and meticulously organized woman – all traits that Jackie would inherit – Janet Lee Bouvier Auchincloss was also an ambitious social climber and society woman who could muster good humor and great charm when necessary. But she could also be cold, demanding, and temperamental, all of which made for a family environment that was more volatile than serene. Intensely critical and controlling of her children, she resented the affection that Jackie bestowed on her father but not on her, and was in no position to give her daughter the security of an inheritance that could sustain anything like the lifestyle she enjoyed at Merrywood and Hammersmith Farm.

Torn between her parents, and with no long-term security she could count on, Jackie struggled to build her own identity and find her own way in the world. Often critical of her appearance, with large feet, big hands, and eyes set unusually far apart, she nonetheless managed to style herself in ways that concealed her flaws and revealed instead a uniquely beautiful woman. The emotional turmoil and insecurity of her family life left her uncomfortable with intimacy and reluctant to share her inner life with others. She nurtured a persona that was detached and guarded, sometimes even aloof and secretive, preferring always to be the skilled observer or clever mimic of everything and everyone around her. An avid reader, she buried herself in books on art, literature, history, and architecture, favoring above all else a contemplative life with as much solitude as she could manage. Perhaps most importantly, she learned from an early age to identify with European, especially French, culture and with the fashionable lifestyle of French aristocrats.[3]

As a child, Jackie had been told that she descended from French aristocracy. This had been the theme of *Our Forebears*, a family genealogy published in 1927 by her grandfather, John Vernon Bouvier. "Grampy Jack," as he was called, claimed to trace both sides of his family back to ancient and illustrious French families and did all he could to cultivate a sense of French tradition, even grandeur, in his household. He distributed copies of *Our Forebears* to every member of the family, insisted that French be spoken at the lunch table at least once a week, and employed a French chauffeur. In truth, Jackie was only one-eighth French, through her father's side, while her mother actually descended from humble Irish immigrants – although she, too, claimed to be the offspring of aristocrats, in her case, southern aristocrats, whom she identified as the Lees of Maryland.

On both sides, then, Jackie's family history was something of a fiction, which she probably discovered no later than 1949–50, when she spent her junior year in college as a study abroad student in France. By then, however, the fantasy of a noble French heritage had become part of her imagined identity. If not what she was but what she wished to be, it added strength and purpose to a life that had been shaken by marital strife and divorce, by her father's financial ruin and alcoholism, and by the cold manipulation of her mother. From this wreckage, she fashioned a new role for herself, marked by a particular attachment to French literature and art, as well as French fashion and the decorative arts more generally, both of which became particular passions for the rest of her life. Already sophisticated and cosmopolitan by the time of her college graduation, she was not interested in being a mere housewife, as she told her school yearbook. Her vision ran more to a life like those of the influential literary women who organized the great salons of Paris in the seventeenth, eighteenth, and nineteenth centuries. This vision, combined with her background, education, and cultural interests, helped to shape the part she would play as first lady of the United States, including her restoration of the White House as a stage on which the drama of her husband's presidency would unfold.[4]

III

The White House had gone through several renovations since it was first occupied in 1802 and then reconstructed following the War of 1812. Nevertheless, Jackie considered it a drab and dreary place when she first toured the mansion with her mother in 1941. Nor did her assessment change when Mamie Eisenhower led her on a second excursion shortly after her husband's election in November 1960. Having enjoyed the genteel elegance of Merrywood and Hammersmith Farm, the White House reminded her of a "big, drafty hotel," much like a "Statler" that had been "decorated by a wholesale furniture store during a January clearance." Her husband felt the same way, describing the White House furnishings as strictly "Sears Roebuck." The food was terrible, the carpets worn, the colors gloomy, and the rooms cold, due in part to an antiquated heating system and fireplaces that had not been stoked in years. At a small dinner party for friends less than a week after the inauguration, both the president and the first lady were already talking excitedly about their plans to give the old mansion a new look.[5] For their performance, the White House had to be properly staged.

In fact, Jackie had been studying the architecture and furnishings of the White House for more than a month before the inauguration. The president kept abreast of her thinking and was quick to endorse her plans, as long as they were shielded from the kind of criticism that had greeted President Harry S. Truman's decision to add a second-floor balcony to the South Portico of the White House in 1948. With this in mind, they both agreed that costs had to be covered as far as possible through private funds and that the project had to be more than a mere redecoration. It had to be a full restoration of the public rooms, supposedly to their historic beauty, and had to be guided by the highest standards of historical scholarship.[6] This explains the initial difference between the refurbished family quarters on the second floor of the White House and the imposing style eventually evident in the state rooms below.

With the aid of her decorator, Mrs. Henry Parish II, Jackie launched the White House restoration just as soon as the new administration took office. "Sister" Parish, as her friends called her, was a well-known society decorator who had worked with Jackie on earlier projects, notably the Georgetown home she shared with her husband prior to moving into the White House. Famous for her warm, chintz-filled, almost country interiors, she had decorated the Georgetown house in this fashion, and both she and Jackie had something similar in mind for the White House. The two proceeded with their plan in the family quarters on the second floor, making allowances for several rooms, such as the Lincoln Bedroom and the Treaty Room, whose functions and historic significance dictated a more formal style. It took them less than a month to complete this part of their work, at a cost of $50,000, whereupon they turned their attention to the public rooms, including the state rooms, on the ground and first floors of the White House. Whether in the family quarters or the public rooms, the first lady devoted herself to the task at hand; nothing escaped her attention, which would also be the case, as we will see, when it came to scripting her husband's funeral or managing his memory in literature and art.[7]

Sister Parish expected to play a significant role in restoring all the public rooms, but as the restoration progressed, she found her advice increasingly ignored and her role diminished, to the point that even her earlier work would be substantially revised.[8] The change reflected Jackie's penchant for constantly redoing her interiors – apparent in her redecoration of the Georgetown house – but also her evolving sense of the important part the White House would play in her husband's presidency and how he would be remembered. Not just a family home or even a showcase of American culture, the White House became, in her mind, the center of the nation's executive authority and symbol of American power. To her way of thinking, the restoration should cast the White House in this light. It should convey the nation's rise to power, the many achievements of its great presidents, and its role as champion of democracy worldwide. This kind of historical and political sensibility, which squared with advice Jackie received from some of her experts, increasingly informed the aesthetic she brought to bear on the restoration.[9] Specifically, she began to emphasize the more formal, luxurious, and grand style evident in the great European, especially French, palaces she had known, though never to the point of overrunning her American themes altogether.

When it came to the state rooms, President Kennedy directed Clark Clifford, a family friend and influential Washington, DC, attorney, to draft a legal framework that would safeguard this part of the project from public criticism and facilitate private fundraising. The result was Public Law 87–826. Passed by Congress in September 1961, the law gave the White House a museum-like status, making its contents inalienable and barring the door against any deviation from the historic character of the restored rooms. As further protection against public – especially political – criticism, the Kennedys created the Fine Arts Committee of the Fine Arts Commission, as well as various subcommittees, to advise on the restoration, raise funds, and authenticate furnishings and other decorative aspects.[10] Although most accounts make clear that Jacqueline Kennedy reserved final decisions to herself, she did staff the committee and its satellites with a number of experts in the field of historic restoration as well as prominent people of wealth and social standing. Again, her strategy aimed to mute any criticism of the restoration and advance its fundraising goals, both through the financial contributions of committee members and through the gifts they solicited from their network of wealthy friends.[11]

Most committee members happily deferred to the first lady's leadership, including her decision, taken on the advice of experts, that her restoration include furnishings from the whole of the eighteenth and nineteenth centuries through the early part of the twentieth century, as opposed to the original plan, which looked to restoring the White House as it had appeared under Presidents Thomas Jefferson and James Monroe, both keen collectors of fine French furniture.[12] This decision notwithstanding, Jackie's aesthetic also ran to expensive French furnishings, including French Empire furniture, wall coverings, draperies, light fixtures, and other decorative pieces. These furnishings dovetailed with her sense of the White House as a symbol of American power and stage for the performance of her husband's presidency, in all of its grandeur. Much like Jefferson and Monroe, she wrapped American themes in this style, even when it led to squabbles between key members of the Fine Arts Committee.

Of all the committee members, including those on the satellite committees dealing with paintings, publications, and the White House library, four members merit special mention as the principal set decorators in the first lady's staging of the Executive Mansion. The first was its chairman, Henry Francis du Pont, an immensely wealthy eighty-five-year-old blue blood who was an acclaimed expert on early Americana, an avid collector, and founder of the famous Winterthur Museum outside Wilmington, Delaware. Once the family home on a lush nine-hundred-acre estate, Winterthur housed both Du Pont's immense collection of antiques, eventually gathered in approximately two hundred period rooms, as well as the Winterthur Program in Early American Culture, established in 1952 as the first graduate program of its kind in the United States. All of this made Du Pont not only a premier collector of early American antiques but also perhaps the nation's most eminent expert in the field of American historical decoration.[13]

Du Pont's appointment had been suggested by Jayne Wrightsman, another influential member of the committee. A friend of Jackie's and a

Palm Beach neighbor of her father-in-law, Joseph P. Kennedy, Wrightsman was married to the irascible oil tycoon, Charles B. Wrightsman. Over the years, she and her husband had furnished their homes in Palm Beach and New York with spectacular pieces of eighteenth-century French furniture, a collection they later donated to the Metropolitan Museum of Art. Like Du Pont, Jayne Wrightsman had acquired a high degree of expertise in antique furnishings and had the ability to contribute her knowledge and financial resources to the work of the committee. Much the same was true of Rachel Lambert Mellon, heiress to the Listerine fortune and wife of the billionaire founder of the National Gallery of Art. "Bunny" Mellon was a self-taught expert in interior floral design and exterior landscaping, most famous for her redesign of the White House Rose Garden for President Kennedy and for the creation of what became the Jacqueline Kennedy Garden outside the East Wing of the White House.[14]

Sister Parish, the last of the four committee members to be mentioned, assumed from the start that she would be the principal designer in the White House restoration. As noted earlier, however, she was soon shut out of key decisions regarding the state rooms on the first floor. It was Wrightsman's job to negotiate this transition, and a similar transition in the family quarters, where much of what Parish had accomplished was later recast at the direction of Stéphane Boudin, a French society designer and friend and mentor to Jayne Wrightsman. Famous for his restoration of many European palaces, including Josephine Bonaparte's Malmaison in France and Lady Olive Baillie's Leeds Castle in England, Boudin's client list read like a *Who's Who* of wealthy collectors, including the Duke and Duchess of Windsor, the shah of Iran, and Jayne Wrightsman herself, whose Palm Beach house Boudin reimagined as a French chateau.[15]

Although he emerged as the most important influence on Jacqueline Kennedy's aesthetic, Boudin, who donated all of his services to the restoration, never served as a member of the Fine Arts Committee, lest it appear that a Frenchman led much of the White House restoration or that Jackie's taste ran more to French than to American design. He came to Jackie's attention in part through Jayne Wrightsman, the great go-between who connected most of the major personalities involved with the restoration, and in part because he had done some modest work on Jackie's Georgetown home. Boudin became Jackie's tutor during the White House restoration. His Paris-based firm specialized in historical interpretation, especially in translating the French style of the eighteenth and nineteenth centuries to residences around the world. More than anything else, it was this specialization that endeared him to the first lady.[16]

When Jackie told a reporter that she had seen great palaces abroad and wanted something similar for the American president, it was the great European, mostly French, palaces she had in mind. One of these was Malmaison, the French Empire–style chateau of Josephine Bonaparte outside of Paris. Boudin had contributed to its redecoration and had urged the first lady to study the chateau as prelude to her restoration of the White House. Jackie toured the palace during her husband's state visit to Paris in the summer of 1961. The visit, hosted by French President Charles de Gaulle, also included an elaborate reception and state dinner at the Palace of Versailles, followed by a presentation of the Paris Opera Ballet in the restored Louis XV Theater. Surrounded by the French Empire furnishings she loved, Jackie thought she was "in heaven," and both she and the president came away with a strong sense of how such elaborate, theatrical settings could inspire a sense of national power and grandeur.[17]

Although Jackie insisted publicly that her goal was to make the White House a showcase of American history and culture, the historical interpretation she and Boudin favored tended to blend democratic themes with an imperial aesthetic. It was as much European, especially French, as it was American; as much about America's place in the western imperial tradition, as it was about the nation's democratic past. "When it is done," she once declared, the restoration should make even de Gaulle "ashamed at Versailles." But it should also embody all "the ideas on which American democratic institutions are based," as she said of the restored White House library. Like the great French Impressionist painters she so admired, her idea was to go beyond a literal reading of American history and create instead an impression of the past that was not wholly bound by museum standards. In her mind, history would be as much feeling as fact, as much imagined as real, as much about the future as the past.[18]

The restored Blue Room is a case in point. One of the great state rooms on the first floor of the White House, it was to be restored to its appearance during the presidency of James Monroe, who had decorated it with some of the French Empire furnishings that Jackie adored. The trouble began when Maxine Cheshire of the *Washington Post* learned that in the first lady's plan, the Blue Room was not going to be blue at all, as it had been for years, but cream colored, as it was when James Madison occupied the White House. Making matters worse, Boudin and the first lady wanted to replace the crimson curtains, upholstery, and carpets in Monroe's original design with blue fabrics, similar to those that had been used since the Van Buren administration. In the end, the room seemed to reflect Madison and Van Buren as much as Monroe, who was supposed to have been its inspiration. Because the changes seemed indifferent to the original conception, if not to history altogether, Cheshire's story sent the first lady scrambling for advice from her husband. It could not be known for sure, they now argued, if the room had actually been painted or papered in blue during Monroe's presidency. Under the circumstances, it was best to go with something more cream colored, as this had been the room's shade during the administration of Monroe's predecessor. As for the crimson carpets, curtains, and upholstery in Monroe's design, they clashed with colors in the redesigned Red Room next door and had to be replaced with blue accessories selected by the first lady – which, at least, made it possible to still call it the Blue Room.[19]

No matter what Maxine Cheshire had to say, and no matter how grounded in history the Blue Room turned out to be, Jacqueline Kennedy loved the room and considered it Boudin's "masterpiece." Dominated by a French Empire theme, it resembled a formal reception room like those in a great European palace. Looked at in theatrical terms – in terms of the message and mood that any stage and its scenery seeks to convey – Boudin's Blue Room, as the first lady noted, presented its audience with "a sense of state, ceremony, arrival, and grandeur." It was, in this sense, much like the room that President Monroe had hoped to create with his numerous purchases of fine French furniture. In fact, Jackie rediscovered some of Monroe's original furnishings in White House storage and used them to lend a sense of historical gravitas to the renovated room that in other respects was lacking.[20]

The restoration of other rooms conveyed the same impression, the most notable being the Red Room. The first of the state rooms to be redecorated, it personified the first lady's preference for French design, as reflected in the early nineteenth-century American style known as American Empire. The restoration incorporated as props some authentic American originals in that style, including a French Empire mantelpiece purchased by James Monroe and an Empire sofa once owned by Dolley Madison. These and other furnishings gave the room the same combination of aesthetic and authenticity that Boudin and the first lady favored in the Blue Room. Much the same can be said of the room's red silk-upholstered wall covering and the decision to fill the walls with spectacular paintings, including portraits of the first seven American presidents. The overall result again blended American themes with French design, history with aesthetic, while also capturing the sense of drama, ceremony, and majesty later evident in the Blue Room – all to the chagrin of Sister Parish, who came close to resigning in this round of the designer wars.[21]

The Yellow Oval Room is another case in point. Used for many purposes over the years, it became, with the Kennedys, a warm but somewhat formal drawing room dominated by French Empire design and Louis XIV furnishings. It was, in the end, the most French of all the White House rooms. Widely used for private as well as formal entertainment, it stood with the Red and Blue Rooms as Jackie's favorites. Even in cases in which the French influence was muted, the sense of an imperial setting remained. This was the case with the Green Room, for example, which was restored as an American parlor of the Federal period. Boudin's influence was minimal but still sufficient to capture the drama and grandeur that he and the first lady sought to convey. Something similar can be said of the State Dining Room, to give one last example. Other than some gilded embellishments, fresh paint, and white marble additions, Jackie made few changes to the previous renovation engineered by President Theodore Roosevelt. One of Kennedy's favorite presidents, Roosevelt viewed the renovated dining room as a symbolic reflection of America's early-twentieth-century emergence as a world power, just as Jackie's White House restoration aimed to announce America's mid-century arrival as a great imperial nation.[22]

Taken as a whole, the White House restoration captured the country's progress from the rebirth of independence after the War of 1812 to imperial hegemon after the Second World War. As such, it called attention not only to the power of the United States but to that of its president as unrivaled leader of the free world, the youthful champion of "a new generation of Americans," as the president put it in his famous inaugural address, "born in this century, tempered by war, disciplined by a hard and bitter peace, proud of our ancient heritage."[23] As these words suggest, the president shared his wife's view of the symbolic content of the restoration. Although he could not muster the degree of expertise she brought to bear on the project, he followed its progress, sometimes helped to select from samples presented, gave personal tours to visiting friends or guests, defended his wife against criticism, and took pride in the results.[24] All this became clear from the remarks he offered in a cameo appearance at the end of his wife's "Tour of the White House," a network television broadcast aired on Valentine's Day 1962.

Walking with CBS correspondent Charles Collingwood through the state rooms, as well as the Lincoln Bedroom and other historic rooms on the second floor, the first lady described in a whispery voice and expert detail the restoration that had taken place to that point. She commented on the building's history, related charming anecdotes about its previous occupants, noted the many gifts received, and thanked important donors. At the end of the tour, the president joined his wife to praise the good work she and others had done. In a not-so-subtle reference to the nation's ongoing greatness as captured in the restoration, he also alluded to its preeminence as the last in a long line of empires. "When we were founded," he said, "there was a king in France, a czar in Russia, an emperor in Peking. Today, all of that's been wiped away – and yet this country continues." The picture of "American historical life" captured in the restoration was a dramatic presentation of the "great story of the United States," the president concluded. While other empires had come and gone, the United States was just reaching the pinnacle of its power and there was every reason to believe that its success would "continue in the future."[25]

The restoration had its critics, to be sure, including *Washington Post* reporter Maxine Cheshire. Cheshire ran an eight-part exposé revealing, among other things, Boudin's key role and the evident French influence on Jackie's thinking. The series earned Cheshire and her editor a cold shoulder from the first lady and a rebuke from the president.[26] Divisions on the restoration team were more difficult to deal with, notably those between Du Pont and his allies, on the one hand, and Boudin and Jackie, on the other. Du Pont brought all of his formidable authority to bear on the restoration. He traversed every room in the White House, offered suggestions on everything from wall colors to fabrics, floor coverings, draperies, furniture, and more, and supported his recommendations with research undertaken by experts at his Winterthur Museum. Nevertheless, his suggestions were often at odds with those coming from Boudin, whose approach, in Du Pont's opinion, ran more to interior decoration than historical restoration. The first lady, with help from Jayne Wrightsman, tried to mediate these differences, but in the end, her interests, like Boudin's, were "more aesthetic than historical." This is the assessment of James A. Abbott and Elaine M. Rice in their account of the White House restoration. Indeed, Jackie was drawn to Boudin precisely because he used antiques not as artifacts displayed for their own sake, but as props to "evoke a feeling of the past," in the words of Abbott and Rice. In this sense, they functioned, much like the scenery in a stage play, to convey the symbolic significance of the space rather than its museum quality.[27] They branded the United States not simply as a great power but as a cultural center, with a president whose global authority derived as much from the nation's cultural accomplishments as from its economic and military power.

The battleground for these differences became the White House curator's office, which Jackie established in March 1961 to organize and authenticate the mansion's collection of historic furnishings. On Du Pont's recommendation, the first lady appointed Lorraine Waxman Pearce as the first White House curator. A graduate of the Winterthur program, Pearce considered Du Pont to be her mentor and shared his concerns about Jackie's preference for aesthetics over accuracy. What is more, Pearce took advantage of her position to publish articles and give speeches dealing with the restoration, leading the first lady to see her as an opportunist who put her professional advancement ahead of her White House assignment. Still worse, she often turned to Du Pont rather than Jackie for direction and reinforced his critique of Boudin's work with reservations of her own. All of this led the first lady to see her as disloyal, an impression that Pearce appeared to confirm when she allowed herself to be interviewed by Maxine Cheshire for her exposé in the *Washington Post*. That was the final straw. It convinced Jackie to ease Pearce out of the curator's position, replacing her with William Voss Elder, who lasted longer but was no less dismayed when Boudin or the first lady ignored museum standards at odds with their own tastes. Boudin, Elder once complained to a sympathetic Du Pont, "may be all right as a decorator but he has absolutely no knowledge or respect for American furniture or paintings."[28]

Despite his disappointment, Du Pont never spoke publicly of his concerns, perhaps because the White House restoration remained more or less immune to media criticism and incredibly popular with the American people. For them, the "great story" of American history captured in the restoration and retold in the first lady's televised tour was a source of enormous pride. It imagined the White House as a great symbol of the nation's power and global purpose, matching in its restored beauty the soaring rhetoric of the president's inaugural address. According to historian Barbara Perry, three-quarters of the American population, or approximately eighty million people, watched Jackie's television tour de force, which was subsequently rebroadcast in more than one hundred countries around the world. Jackie herself received ten thousand letters from enthusiastic fans, as well as an Emmy for her performance, and media reviews were nearly as breathless as the first lady's voice. Nor do these facts give full measure to her success.

Having enshrined the restoration in Public Law 87–826, Jackie also established the White House Historical Association, which immediately published, under her direction, a White House guidebook. *The White House: An Historic Guide* recounted the mansion's history, including its architectural and decorative features. The first lady expected that book sales would help finance the ongoing restoration, as well as the acquisition and preservation of historic furnishings in the years ahead. What is more, she and the president made sure that all who wanted to see the mansion had ample opportunity to do so, raising an earlier limit on the number of touring visitors from less than one million in 1960 to approximately two million by the end of 1963. Already by the end of 1962, an average of forty-five hundred visitors were touring the White House each day, compared to three thousand per day during the Eisenhower administration.[29] Many of these visitors purchased at least one copy of the guidebook, so that sales increased exponentially. The first printing of 250,000 copies sold out within three months of its publication in June 1962, as did two more printings by the end of 1963, at which point more than a million copies were in print. The White House Historical Association launched an aggressive marketing operation to sell as many copies as possible, and did what it could to prevent potential competitors from infringing on its market. The book became a best seller, and its success encouraged the first lady to lay plans to publish a brief history of the presidents, which, in turn, would lead to a matching volume on the first ladies.[30]

Neither the first lady's nor the president's vision could be contained in the White House, nor even within the mansion's lawns and gardens, which they also restored and expanded. It crossed the street to Lafayette Square and the lovely, historic townhouses that surrounded it, which they saved from a demolition previously approved by the Eisenhower administration; to Blair House, the president's guest house, which the Kennedys slotted for its own restoration; and even up Pennsylvania Avenue to the Capitol, as part of a long-term plan to transform Washington, DC, into a grand capital befitting the nation's new prominence as a world power. This same vision also led the Kennedys to put their weight behind plans to build a modern performing arts center, similar to those that existed in the great capitals of the world – what would later become the John F. Kennedy Center for the Performing Arts.[31]

In all of these initiatives, power and culture, style and substance were linked in a set of dramatic symbols that celebrated the superiority of the United States, its civilized beauty, its distinguished past, and its still-youthful strength and vitality. It was this same kind of thinking that led the president to stop meeting visiting dignitaries at Union Station and driving them through urban blight to the White House. Better to meet them at National Airport and helicopter to the White House lawn, where they would be welcomed in a formal ceremony as grand as any they might receive elsewhere in the world. It was also this kind of thinking that led the president and the first lady to present visiting dignitaries with gifts that were often original designs and works of art in their own right, and to commission Air Force One, the first jet available to an American president. With its slick exterior and interior designs and its jet-powered engines, Air Force One became a modern but dignified symbol of the global reach of American power and culture.[32]

The goal throughout was to manage impressions, to create an American brand of national and presidential leadership that conveyed not simply the vast superiority of American power but linked that power to its democratic values, so that culture became its own version of power in the Cold War. Writing about Blair House in a letter to Du Pont, the first lady captured this message in words her husband might have uttered. The house made the wrong impression, she said, with its "peeling walls – wire coat hangers, stuffed furniture and a ghastly television set." What must visiting dignitaries think? "All during their visits here, we are telling them that they should choose to go with us and not the Russians," yet they "have probably just slept in gilded beds and eaten off Ivan the Terrible's gold plates in the Kremlin." That's why, she concluded, it was so important "how you first affect them when they reach this country."[33]

The restored White House thus became a stage not only for the performance of Kennedy's presidency but also for the performance of the nation. The two, in fact, shared the same identity, the same "brand," as Jessica Gienow-Hecht might put it.[34] The restoration represented the nation as a blend of New World democracy and Old World elegance, of youth and tradition, of power and culture, with a president whose blend of style and substance reflected the virtues and attributes embedded in the very fabric of American life. As such, both were prepared for the role that history had thrust upon them – as the enlightened guardian of western civilization, leader of the free world, ambassador of democracy. It did not matter that Kennedy knew little about interior design, or that his wife blended her presentation of American history with a French aesthetic, or that the nation's glorious past had sometimes been diminished by its failures. Judging by the many markers of its success – by the millions of tourists who flocked to see the new White House, the large audience for the first lady's TV tour, her successful campaign to raise funds for the restoration, or the best-selling status of her White House guidebook – this was the image of the president that most Americans wanted to see, in part because it mirrored the country they wanted to believe in. As will become clear, moreover, it was also how Jacqueline Kennedy wanted her husband remembered, and why she would embed that image, time and time again, in the many monuments to his memory.

IV

The hard work behind the White House restoration was backstage to the actual performance, just as the wall coverings, antiques, paintings, and more made up the props and scenery on display. All of it was important, but nothing was more important than the performance itself, as revealed in the magnificent events hosted by the Kennedys, the costumes they wore, and the entertainment they offered. The president dressed impeccably, of course, which was far different from the casual, rumpled, often ill-fitting clothing he wore before becoming a presidential candidate. Something similar can be said of the first lady. Happiest and most comfortable in her riding gear, or in the casual slacks, jeans, and sweaters she wore when free of official obligations, Jacqueline Kennedy nonetheless set a standard for haute couture when performing her duties as first lady.[35]

So much has been written about the first lady's wardrobe and accessories – the costumes she donned for her public performances – that little need be added here. It's enough to remember that fashion has been used historically to signify one's identity as a member of a particular culture, country, class, or religion, and at the same time to differentiate oneself within the group without repudiating it altogether. In the case of political figures and national leaders, fashion can be an unmistakable sign of position and authority within the hierarchy they inhabit. It can signal the part to be played on the political stage and the message to be conveyed, both about themselves as actors and about the nation they represent, its values, and its role in the larger world. This was the case with the Kennedys. For them, especially Jacqueline Kennedy, fashion became another form of representation, another way to brand themselves and the nation.[36]

The first sign of this came on Inauguration Day. The president – in top hat, tails, and waistcoat – struck a formal, almost aristocratic pose that departed from the dark business suits his predecessor had worn on similar occasions. At the inauguration itself, however, the coldest in years, he discarded the top hat and heavy winter overcoat, so that his overall appearance combined elements of American youth and vigor with

European grandeur and glamor. Together with Jackie's wardrobe, it reinforced the message of his inaugural address, that a "new generation" had taken center stage in American political life. At the inauguration, the first lady wore a light-colored wool coat trimmed with a sable collar and topped with what came to be known as a pillbox hat, while at the inaugural balls she dressed in a sleek, light-shimmering gown of unqualified elegance. Not only did her wardrobe announce a new and youthful standard in American fashion; it also distinguished her from the older women with whom she shared the stage. Most of them, as her designer noted, wore colorful cloth coats, traditional hats, and bulky furs that made them look "like a bunch of bears."[37]

The first lady's inaugural creations had been inspired, for the most part, by Oleg Cassini, who remains to this day the most insightful source on her personal fashion. What Boudin was to Jackie's decorative style, Cassini was to her wardrobe. A handsome, Paris-born couturier, with jet-black hair and a Clark Gable mustache, Cassini had become a US citizen and popular Hollywood designer, well known for his European charm, aristocratic pretense, and love affairs with Hollywood starlets, including a marriage to Gene Tierney and a romance with Grace Kelly. He came to the first lady's attention through her father-in-law, Joseph P. Kennedy, with whom he shared a casual friendship, not to mention a Hollywood background and mutual love of beautiful young women. He met with Jackie shortly after the 1960 election in her Georgetown hospital room where she was recovering from the birth of her son John F. Kennedy Jr. and thinking about the wardrobe she would fashion for herself as first lady. Jackie was a clothes horse, much to the chagrin of her husband, who had complained for years about her lavish spending on expensive, especially French, designs. The same habits had been the subject of critical media commentary during the 1960 campaign, and the president-elect was anxious to avoid similar criticism once he entered the White House. With this in mind, Jackie decided, with her father-in-law, to send her clothing bills to the elder Kennedy, thereby hiding them from the public, and to limit herself to less expensive clothes by a single American designer. Cassini was an improbable choice for such a constricted assignment, which neither he nor the first lady took seriously in any event, but in other ways, his selection was positively inspired.[38]

Jackie realized almost immediately that Cassini's vision of her wardrobe squared with the role she imagined for herself as first lady of the United States. After his work with Paramount Pictures, as Cassini explained, he could easily envision himself as the designer for a Hollywood star playing the queen in a court drama. In his interpretation of how Jackie might "play the role of First Lady," he imagined her "as an ancient Egyptian princess, dressed cleanly, architecturally," with her "head in profile, broad shoulders, slim torso, narrow hips, long neck, and good carriage." He spoke to her about the "message her clothes could send" to others and how they "could reinforce the message of her husband's administration." She had an opportunity, he said, mixing his metaphors, to create "an American Versailles." The allusion must have appealed to the young Francophile, who told Cassini that she wanted a wardrobe like the one she would wear "if Jack were President of France." But not quite. As with her plans for the White House restoration, the concept Jackie and her new couturier had in mind would blend culture with power, a French, even a royal, aesthetic with American principles. "Sumptuous fabrics" and "magisterial elegance" would be mixed with a plain, "simple and youthful" American look, with little in the way of jewelry and other frills that might "detract from the monastic simplicity of her wardrobe." Cassini called it the "A Look," others the "Jackie Look." And while the first lady wanted all of her "dresses to be original in style and fabric," with no "fat little women hopping around" in them, her A-line dresses and pillbox hats, medium-heeled pumps and bouffant hair soon appeared on women of all shapes and sizes the world over.[39]

President Kennedy paid close attention to his wife's appearance, sometimes selecting her wardrobe for a particular occasion or giving his approval for a bold new design. This was the case, as Cassini recalled, when the president gave his blessing to a one-shouldered evening gown before the first lady could wear it, and later, to a strapless gown that left both shoulders bare. Although the gowns seemed daring at the time, they soon became part of the "Jackie Look" popular everywhere. Most importantly, both Kennedys understood the role that fashion could play in branding the president's diplomacy and in making Washington, DC, not only the political but also the social and cultural capital of the world.[40]

The earliest examples came with their official visits to Canada in May 1961, and then to Europe, specifically France, later in the summer. The first lady researched the history and culture of each country she visited, and then used her wardrobe, as well as her remarks, to pay tribute to what she had learned. Her hosts, in turn, noticed her every gesture and cheered her courtesy. In Canada, for example, although she dressed for dinner in an A-line evening gown of lush fabric, the high point came when she inspected the horses of the Royal Canadian Mounted Police. On that occasion, she wore a red wool suit in military cut that paid compliment to the color and style of the uniformed troops who escorted her. The gesture did not go unnoticed in the American media, where *Life* magazine featured a photo of the first lady in her colorful garb, nor in Canada, where the press and people alike showered praise on her thoughtful performance.

The reaction was similar in Paris, where the first lady dazzled the French people and captivated President Charles de Gaulle. She conversed with him in near perfect French, translated for her husband, and displayed a knowledge of French history and culture that surpassed that of de Gaulle's own countrymen. Once again, moreover, her costume and accessories had a diplomatic strategy of their own. Forsaking Cassini on this occasion, not to mention her pledge to buy only American, the first lady wore an elegant gown by the exclusive French designer Hubert de Givenchy when she and the president dined with their hosts at a state dinner in the Hall of Mirrors at the Palace of Versailles. Her gown included colors matching those in the French flag, while her hair was coiffed by a famous Paris hairdresser and topped with a small tiara that gave her appearance a royal look appropriate to the occasion. These careful details, not to mention a television interview in French, made her an instant hit with the French people, who hailed her as the American "queen" and swarmed to see her. When it came to US prestige, according to American ambassador David Bruce, the first lady was worth more than ten divisions.[41] Presidential aide Arthur Schlesinger later made a similar point. The French response to the first lady, he recorded in his history of the Kennedy administration, "had the air of a startled rediscovery of America as a new society, young and cosmopolitan and sophisticated, capable of aspiring to the leadership of the civilized peoples."[42]

This kind of fashion diplomacy continued through the rest of the Kennedy administration, conveying the image of the first lady as queen of a new American empire, as elegant as any of her European predecessors but less ornamental, pretentious, and old. In this sense, her performance on the global stage also performed the nation as the Kennedys wanted to show it. Their brand was the American brand. On every occasion, the first lady tried to present in her fashion a democratic agenda that was youthful and progressive, straightforward and unaffected. In a White House dinner for the shah of Iran and his wife, the first lady stole the show in a modified A-line gown of pink-and-white silk, adorned only with her signature elbow-length gloves and a small diamond starburst in her hair. Her look of sheer simplicity contrasted sharply, and favorably, with the mink and bejeweled appearance of the shah's wife, who also wore a large and heavily jeweled crown.

In trips to South America, Mexico, India, and Pakistan, all critical bat-
tlegrounds in the struggle for hearts and minds in the Cold War, the first
lady wore simple, unadorned day dresses and shifts in yellow, apricot,
light blue, and other vibrant colors popular with people living in warm
environments. In Mexico, she donned a large straw hat vaguely reminiscent of a Mexican sombrero. In India, her wardrobe borrowed from
Indian book illustrations, including a "princess" coat inspired by the traditional Raja wrap and later converted by Cassini into his popular Nehru
jacket for men. In these and other ways, the first lady's self-constructed
presentation captured how Americans saw themselves. She was "the
physical embodiment of the New Frontier," noted Hamish Bowles of
Vogue, simple and straightforward, elegant but unpretentious, youthful
and progressive.[43]

V

Something similar can be said about how the Kennedy's performed their
official duties at home, where they used the first lady's wardrobe, the
restored White House, and other symbols of American power and culture to represent themselves and the nation as modern embodiments of
enlightened democracy in an embattled world. The president and first
lady hosted about seventy events each year. The list included a large
number of state dinners for world leaders, particularly those from developing countries whose support was so critical to American victory in
the Cold War. In their first two years alone, as Barbara Perry notes, they
entertained four heads of state from African countries, two from South
Asia, and one each from South America, the Middle East, and Puerto
Rico.[44]

The Kennedys favored a more relaxed and informal style of entertaining than their predecessors. Whenever possible, they abandoned the
formal receiving line, introduced alcoholic beverages, permitted smoking,
and used candlelight, fireplaces, floral arrangements, light wall colors,
and other theatrical devices to create a warm and welcoming environment. At the same time, however, they were often criticized for a style that
seemed pretentious and cosmopolitan, if not altogether un-American. In
truth, both descriptions are correct. While they abandoned the starchy,
military style of their predecessor, the Kennedys kept many old habits
as well, particularly when it came to state dinners and other occasions
in which they entertained foreign leaders. The president still arrived to
ruffles and flourishes and "Hail to the Chief," which he loved, and he still

enjoyed a formal presentation of the colors. In other words, a good deal of the traditional pomp and circumstance remained, to which the president and the first lady added elements of their own, including a French-born chef, menus printed in French, and wine selected by a New York connoisseur. What is more, while their entertainment could easily include Broadway show tunes, it could just as easily feature poetry readings, symphonic selections, Elizabethan plays, and other displays of high culture, for which they were sometimes criticized. Critics, as the president put it, complained constantly that White House entertainment was becoming "too frenchy and too international." They were always asking why "nobody could read or understand the menus" and why the White House was not "more American."[45]

In the final analysis, the Kennedy brand might be described as an elegant informality that combined a relaxed American style with European grandiosity. What is more, the Kennedys favored each honored guest with unique and special attention, particularly foreign dignitaries whose support the president needed for his foreign policies. They entertained the duchess of Luxembourg with selections from Shakespeare and matching musical interludes because she had a particular fondness for poetry and music from the Elizabethan period. Similar selections honored the president of Sudan's Armed Forces Council, another fan of the Bard. The shah of Iran heard a selection from Jerome Robbins' *Ballets: U.S.A.*, and the king of Morocco was thrilled with a performance of *Brigadoon*. A selection from the ballet *Billy the Kid* delighted a visiting head of state who was enamored of romantic stories about the famous American outlaw; and the king of Afghanistan, a military man, was flattered with an imposing military parade, complete with an amazing display of fireworks on the White House lawn.[46]

As this suggests, more was involved than mere entertainment, as evident in the White House dinner for André Malraux, the French minister of state for cultural affairs and one of Jacqueline Kennedy's idols. The event included some of the brightest lights in American arts, not to mention the famous violinist Isaac Stern, who provided the evening's entertainment. Intended, in part, to repay Malraux for his courtesy when the president and first lady visited Paris the previous summer, it served important political goals as well. It helped her tease the French into lending the *Mona Lisa* for display at the National Gallery, added distinction to the American presidency, and reminded the world that the United States was as sophisticated and cultured as any of the great nations in history, and thus entitled to the global leadership it now enjoyed.[47]

This blending of performance and power, style and substance, so typical of how the Kennedys branded themselves and the nation, could be seen even more clearly when the president of Peru visited the White House. On this occasion, the Kennedys had the famous G. P. A. Healy portrait of Abraham Lincoln moved to the State Dining Room. There, it could serve as a prop to remind the Peruvian that another American president had waged war to free the slaves and bring modernity to the American South, just as Kennedy's Alliance for Progress, Peace Corps, and other initiatives would supposedly promote economic development and social reform in Latin America. As Barbara Leaming has noted, the gesture might also counter criticism, especially sharp after the Bay of Pigs debacle, that Kennedy was just as reactionary and imperialistic as any of his predecessors.[48]

Similar themes emerged at a state dinner, the first held outside the White House, to honor the president of Pakistan, Mohammed Ayub Khan. In selecting George Washington's Mount Vernon estate as the site, the president and first lady again revealed their remarkable talent for using dramatic settings, including elaborate ceremonies, costumes, and other props, as backdrops to American diplomacy. Khan was a key ally in the Cold War struggle against communism in Asia. He had contributed Pakistani troops to aid American policy in Laos, among other helpful initiatives, and Kennedy was anxious to repay him. Beyond this courtesy, moreover, Mount Vernon provided a stage on which the Kennedys could enact the pageant of American history, revealing its cultural superiority and democratic ideals and convincing the Pakistani leader that an American alliance would put his country on the right side of history. After all, the United States, once a collection of struggling colonies, had thrown off the shackles of empire to become, in Kennedy's words, "the greatest revolutionary country on earth." It had set itself on a path to democratic progress that started at Mount Vernon, home of the first American president, and had now ascended to new heights under President Kennedy, the youngest American elected to that office. This was the future that awaited Pakistan and other Third World countries if they followed the American road to revolution and modernization, rather than the course laid out by the communists.[49]

The evening began with guests traveling by boat down the Potomac from Washington, DC, to the pier below Mount Vernon, from which point they were escorted by marine guards in rippling salute up the hill to Washington's mansion. Once there, they mingled on the pillared piazza or on the great lawn overlooking the Potomac, sipping mint juleps made from Washington's own recipe and served in silver cups, much as they had been at the start of the Republic. Guests gathered for dinner at tables for eight under a marquee lit by chandeliers from Tiffany's and decorated with floral arrangements selected by Bunny Mellon. René Verdon, the Kennedys' French chef, prepared a menu of French cuisine with just a hint of the early American offerings that Martha Washington had once served. Entertainment included a military drill and rifle volley by the Colonial Color Guard and Continental Fife and Drum Corps, decked out in red coats and tri-cornered hats as they had been in Washington's day. Designed to impress the guest of honor, himself a general in the Pakistani army, this display of military pageantry preceded a concert of classical music, including selections from Mozart, Gershwin, and others, all performed by the National Symphony Orchestra on an acoustical stage constructed especially for the occasion. As was the case with her costume selections in Canada, Paris, and elsewhere, the first lady wore a gown that captured the overall theme of the evening, in this case, the link between past and present in the march of American civilization. She looked "authentic," as Cassini put it, in a full-length, sleeveless gown of white lace and organza tucked at the waist with a sash of silk chartreuse. Designed by Cassini to the first lady's specifications, the gown had a "romantic antebellum look, in keeping with the pillared elegance and historical setting of Mount Vernon."[50]

Such a performance did not always require the presence of a dignitary from abroad. On the contrary, the American audience had an apparently insatiable appetite for displays of glamor and grandeur that celebrated the nation's many virtues and its new role as leader of the free world. One such display was the first-ever reception for recipients of the Medal of Honor, by all accounts a moving and memorable evening, and another was the famous dinner honoring forty-nine Nobel Prize winners. The first honored American wartime heroism and surely reminded everyone of the president's own military service as hero of the Pacific; the second gave him another opportunity to celebrate American excellence in science, the arts, and government service, all themes that were recognizable standards in the president's official rhetoric. At the Nobel dinner, the president resorted again to these themes, linking his White House guests and himself to a long history of American distinction. Never before, he told his guests, had the White House hosted such an "extraordinary collection of talent," except perhaps "when Thomas Jefferson dined alone." Together, the president and his wife conjured up an image of America as the new Athens, an image reinforced by the first lady's gown, an off-shoulder, pale-green Cassini gathered into simple Grecian lines with only white gloves as adornment. The guests were enraptured, if also a little inebriated, by the evening's splendor, so much so that it became one of the most celebrated in the history of White House entertainment.[51]

On such occasions, the Kennedys played idealized versions of themselves on the White House stage. They were the happy couple and loving parents who communicated a message of hope and progress, youth and beauty, charm and intelligence. They enacted an American version of royalty that was wealthy, sophisticated, and cosmopolitan, but also pragmatic and idealistic; an American brand of elegance that was still unadorned, straightforward, and democratic. For most of their countrymen, the Kennedys apotheosized the American dream. They embodied everything good about a nation that was wealthy, powerful, and cultured, that had progressed from colony to empire, and that was now leading the world to a bright and shining future. In this sense, the Kennedys were a mirror of the nation as most Americans saw it. They captured in their brand the pride that Americans took in their national life, their democratic progress, and their new world standing. As we will see, moreover, this is how Jacqueline Kennedy wanted her husband to be remembered; and indeed, we remember him in part because he and the first lady were so good at reflecting what Americans believed about themselves and their country – and to a degree that no subsequent president has been able to match.

VI

As the intoxicated guests at the Nobel dinner remind us, these Kennedy constructions differed in some ways from the personal style revealed backstage at the White House. Not every event radiated the same sophistication. After the Nobel dinner, for example, about a dozen guests, some already "pleasantly looped," retreated to the Yellow Oval Room upstairs, where they smoked and drank to the wee hours.[52] Many such parties took place in the family quarters or at retreats elsewhere. They were usually fun loving, even rowdy affairs, involving family and friends and resembling nothing so much as a college fraternity party. Oleg Cassini, for example, might give dance instructions for the Twist or the Hully Gully and the president would demand impromptu remarks from his guests, or command push-ups if they fell short. On one occasion, following a dinner for the Indian ambassador, Cassini paraded around the Yellow Oval Room in a bathrobe with a towel wrapped like a turban around his head, wielding a fireplace poker as his sword and giving his imitation of a Mogul Indian emperor.[53]

Other events were more raucous, if not raunchy. At a party to celebrate the president's forty-sixth birthday, for example, Jackie arranged a long sail down the Potomac on the *Sequoia*. It took no time for the guests, mostly family and friends, with a splash of Hollywood celebrity, to turn the party into a boozy affair with a three-piece band and more "Twisting," boisterous toasts, broken furniture, and a presidential proposition of Tony Bradlee, whose husband, Ben Bradlee, was the editor of *Newsweek* magazine. On another occasion, a White House dinner and dance in honor of the first lady's sister, Lee Radziwill, and Giovanni Agnelli, the wealthy Italian who headed the Fiat motor company, the alcohol again flowed freely. The guests did the Twist to pop music, though it was still considered such a lascivious dance that Pierre Salinger, the president's press secretary, later denied that it had been part of the evening's entertainment. At one point, Vice President Lyndon Johnson fell flat on the dance floor; at another, author Gore Vidal, a relative by marriage to the first lady, exchanged insults and nearly came to blows with the president's brother, Attorney General Robert Kennedy; and at still another point, the president supposedly disappeared from public view long enough to proposition Tony Bradlee's sister, Mary Meyer, who would later become one of his many lovers.[54]

News of these parties seldom reached the public in full detail. As suggested when Salinger censored reports about Twisting in the family quarters, the Kennedys made every effort to conceal behavior that might be at odds with the roles they played as president and first lady. In other words, the Kennedys who lived their real lives behind the scenes had to appear, or be made to appear, as close as possible to the Kennedys who performed on the White House stage – lest any gap between representation and reality undermine the image they had constructed of themselves and the nation. Few were as prepared or as skilled as the Kennedys when it came to managing the illusions sometimes involved, and fewer still could count on the help of friends and staff from whom absolute loyalty was required.

Kennedy and his siblings grew up in front of the camera. Hardly a family event went by that was not recorded for posterity in photographs or motion pictures. His father, Joseph P. Kennedy, was one of the first to make home movies, and his many children seldom missed an opportunity to ham it up for posterity. They grew up feeling at ease on film, especially the future president, who also had the benefit of his father's experience in Hollywood, where he owned a major motion picture studio and socialized with Hollywood elites, including producers, directors, and the stars themselves. His son would be exposed to all of this over the years. He would become a cinema buff himself, forge his own connection to Hollywood stars, and bring many of them into his political and personal life. He would also develop an acute appreciation, from the start of the television age, of the political power of visual images.

If the elder Kennedy might be construed as a Hollywood impresario, the agent and producer of his son's performance on camera, he was equally familiar with the print media and used it as well, not to mention his own financial resources, to make and market his son's brand and political ambitions. No stone was left unturned, not even Kennedy's marriage to Jacqueline Bouvier, which his father made into a major media spectacle with an archbishop presiding, a message from the pope, and a guest list straight from *Who's Who*. With massive press coverage and more than three thousand gawking spectators, the wedding looked less like the sacrament of holy matrimony than the gala premier of a major motion picture. "Old Joe," as he was sometimes called, was similarly instrumental in the publication of his son's Harvard thesis, using his friend Arthur Krock, Washington bureau chief for the *New York Times*, to review and edit the work and persuading Henry Luce, publisher of *Time* magazine, to write the introduction for what became *Why England Slept*. He also guaranteed wide circulation of "Survival," John Hersey's account of Kennedy's wartime heroism as the captain of PT 109, originally published in the *New Yorker*. He subsequently paid to have the same account reproduced as a campaign document for his son, and then republished again in *Reader's Digest*, a popular magazine with enormous circulation. He was even instrumental in the publication of Kennedy's Pulitzer Prize–winning book, *Profiles in Courage*, and in securing the prize itself. Most importantly, perhaps, he used his skills in advertising and marketing, polished during his Hollywood days, to promote his son's political ambitions and various campaigns. As historians John Hellmann and Mark White have argued, these and other interventions by the elder Kennedy were instrumental in the construction of his son's public identity as a serious intellectual and prizewinning author, as war hero and statesman, as a devoted husband and father, and as handsome leading man, as much a matinee idol and sex symbol as any Hollywood star. Taken together with his charm and good humor, his support for liberal social programs and his search for peace and nuclear disarmament, these were the very attributes that would come to mind when people learned of

Kennedy's assassination – by which time he had become, in the American mind, the person he played on camera and on television.[55]

In the interval, Kennedy had learned to buff his own popular image. Much of Joe Kennedy's talent for self-promotion and media management rubbed off on his second son, who brought all of it to bear on his handling of the media, not to mention a relaxed self-confidence that came, no doubt, from years of exposure to the camera. He understood the importance of television in contemporary politics, and of his own physical appeal to the TV audience. He also cultivated newspaper people, as a farmer cultivates his field. During the 1960 campaign, he flattered their egos and pandered to their needs; he pampered major publishers and their star reporters; and he used photographers, such as Jacques Lowe, to capture in pictures the campaign narrative that he wanted told. Indeed, Kennedy gave a select number of reporters, photographers, and filmmakers special access during the campaign, a favor they repaid with commentary and pictures that recounted the story of Kennedy's life as loyal son in the bosom of a large Irish clan, as war hero and prizewinning author, as forward looking and progressive, as loving husband and doting father.[56]

By the time the campaign came to an end, these images had been firmly fixed in the public mind, and both the president and the first lady took every opportunity to protect and nourish them after they entered the White House. Not everything went their way, of course. At one point, Kennedy appeared to blame press coverage for the Bay of Pigs disaster and later earned criticism for too closely controlling the news during the Cuban Missile Crisis. He was criticized as well for playing favorites among reporters, for canceling subscriptions to the *New York Herald Tribune* when it blasted his handling of the steel companies, and for urging the *New York Times* to chastise David Halberstam, one of its correspondents in Saigon, for his critical reporting on the president's policy in Vietnam.[57] The first lady had her own issues. Besides Cheshire's exposé on the White House restoration, and occasional stories about her lavish White House entertainment and expensive wardrobe, she and the president had to contend with critical press coverage of her personal vacation travel.

This was the case when she vacationed in Greece following the president's European trip in the summer of 1961. The press reporters and photographers who pursued her everywhere found their reward in photos of the first lady tripping the light fantastic at a local night club and racing about Greece with Crown Prince Constantine in his upscale Mercedes – all while her husband, nearly paralyzed with back pain, suffered alone in the White House. Her Greek vacation produced its share of unfavorable commentary in the media and among Republicans in Congress, though nothing like the criticism that accompanied a subsequent vacation along the Amalfi coast of Italy, where she stayed mostly with friends, including Giovanni Agnelli, the handsome Italian auto manufacturer. She went sailing on Agnelli's yacht, danced with him at a nightclub in Capri, and looked relaxed in a trim, black-and-white swimsuit, tanning with her host on the beach. The press had a field day with pictures of this excursion and again criticized the first lady for ignoring her husband and for her nightclubbing, beachwear, and cavorting with the wealthy Italian. Similar criticism accompanied a vacation to Greece in October 1963, when she and her sister sailed the Greek islands on the luxurious yacht of Aristotle Onassis. Once again, she was seen living the high life, sunbathing in sleek swimwear, and sharing company with a wealthy tycoon, this time a shipping magnate who had earlier been indicted and fined for tax evasion in the United States.[58]

Still, criticism of this sort faded fast in a media otherwise enamored of the Kennedys. The president continued to dazzle reporters with his smart and witty press conferences, much as he had during the 1960 campaign. The first president to do regularly televised press conferences, Kennedy used them to speak directly to the American people in a way that his predecessors had not. The sessions, for which he prepared assiduously, gave him ample opportunity to show his mastery of public policy and foreign affairs, and to reveal, as well, a personality full of wit, charm, and good humor. Called the "best matinee" in town, the press conferences were popular with most of the media and with the American people, for whom Kennedy became a friendly presence, much like a member of the family, who appeared regularly in their living rooms.[59]

At the same time, Kennedy continued to polish the media strategies that had worked so well during the campaign. He flattered reporters with praise for their work and with friendly intimacies, much as he did with Hugh Sidey of *Time* magazine, who interviewed the president while the two were skinny-dipping in the White House pool. The first lady did something similar when she invited Sidey to interview her for a story in *Life* magazine on the White House restoration, and when she appealed to *Newsweek* for a story that would counter the criticism coming from Maxine Cheshire of the *Washington Post*. As a general rule, the Kennedys spoon-fed the press as much good news as they could and played to their fascination with celebrities by parading Hollywood stars and other distinguished guests through the White House lobby in full view of reporters and photographers. In addition, the president continued to cultivate publishers and select newsmen. He gave them scoops when it helped the White House, provided almost unfettered access to other officials in the administration, asked them to private meetings in the Oval Office, included them more often than any other group in White House lunches and dinners, and invited a select few to share his friendship.

All this was contingent on favorable reporting, however. When the president read reports he didn't like, the invitations and flattery were quickly replaced with snubs, scolding telephone calls, and restricted access. The administration also used threats of an FBI probe to preempt the publication of information it considered classified and illegal CIA wiretaps to spy on reporters and track the sources they consulted. Even friendship was contingent when reporting fell short of the president's expectations. This happened to Arthur Krock, whom Kennedy came to despise, and to Ben Bradlee, a Kennedy friend since the 1960 campaign. Friend or not, Bradlee got the cold shoulder when he implied that Kennedy was too sensitive to criticism, only to be redeemed later when he helped the president rebut rumors that Jackie was actually his second wife.[60]

The president and first lady also took pains to regulate press access to the White House and to control any stories or photographs released to the public. Jackie was especially adamant on this score, some say because of her craving for privacy and concern for her children, but also because she understood the need to manage her image and that of her family. This explains why she selected Mary Van Rensselaer Thayer to write her first biography. Thayer was a family friend who basically allowed Jackie to coauthor the final manuscript, which naturally came as close as possible to telling her story as she wanted it told.

The president and the first lady also appointed the first White House photographer, Cecil Stoughton, and worked more closely with some press photographers than with others. The list included Jacques Lowe, Stanley Tretick, Mark Shaw, and others, many of whom worked for the influential photo-magazines of the day, especially *Look* and *Life*. The first lady's strategy was to bring this select group to the White House for periodic photo sessions, because that way "we'll have an okay on it." In other words, Stoughton's appointment, the release of selected photos, and their close collaboration with Lowe worked well for the Kennedys, who had enormous exposure while at the same time controlling how and where their images were displayed. The first lady's photograph, to give one example, appeared on the cover of *Look* magazine a remarkable seventeen times during her White House years, and the president had similar success with his own image, as when he invited Stanley Tretick of *Look* magazine to capture what became iconic family photographs of the president and his wife sailing or of his children romping beside him in the Oval Office. Much the same was true with television, where they tried at every turn to set the ground rules before giving interviews, as they did, for example, with the first lady's televised tour of the White House or with the president's interviews with television news anchors.[61]

If in all these ways, the Kennedys functioned like the script writers, directors, and stars of their own performance, members of the White House staff were expected to play the part of loyal stagehands or face the consequences. Soon after the inauguration, the Kennedys asked members of their staff to sign a confidentiality agreement promising never to reveal what they saw or heard backstage at the White House. This was one way to make certain that no gap appeared between the image the Kennedys constructed of themselves as president and first lady and the way they lived their lives behind the scenes. The request had to be abandoned when news of it threatened a public scandal, with J. B. West, the chief White House usher, forced by the president to take responsibility for the supposed faux pas. Nevertheless, top aides would be reluctant over the years to publish anything without prior permission of the former first lady or the Kennedy family – and for good reason. After all, Letitia Baldrige, the first lady's social secretary, found herself out of a job when she complained once too often about Jackie's dereliction of her official duties; and the first White House curator, as we have seen, lost her position after criticizing Jackie's plans for the White House restoration and allowing herself to be quoted in Cheshire's exposé on the subject.[62]

It was well known in the West Wing that the president functioned more or less as his own press secretary, though less well known that the first lady adopted a similar strategy when she appointed Pamela Turnure to handle her press affairs. "My press relations will be minimum information given with maximum politeness," she instructed Turnure. She had no intention of holding regular press conferences or providing any photographs of herself or her family except those of which she approved. As for Turnure, she was to be neither seen nor heard. She should avoid talking about the first family while out and about, give no interviews of her own without permission, and generally remain "fairly anonymous."[63] Cassini got the same instructions. Having a single designer was one way for the first lady to control information about her wardrobe. She expected to be "so much more of fashion interest than other First Ladies," but did not want her husband "plagued by fashion stories of a sensational nature" or to become, herself, "the Marie Antoinette or Josephine of the 1960s." Accordingly, her "Fashion Mistress," as she called Cassini, could only make information available to the newspapers with her prior approval, and even then, "there just may be a few things we won't tell them about."[64]

Together with the traditional rules of reporting in what was then a male-dominated professional culture, all of these efforts helped the Kennedys to project the images they liked and conceal those they did not. More than anything else, their carefully crafted constructions would become what so many Americans remembered about the president and first lady, not as media representations, however, but as the real Kennedys. People saw few photographs of the president on crutches and none of the first lady smoking, even though back pain could leave him near paralysis and she smoked at least a pack of cigarettes a day. They learned next to nothing about the many other physical ailments that bedeviled the president, some very serious, or about the many drugs he took, including the amphetamines to which he and his wife were practically addicted. His romantic affairs, too many to permit an exact count, were concealed as well, as were her lavish expenditures on interior decorations and clothing. Other than Cassini, few knew that she purchased nearly three hundred designer pieces during her brief White House years, or that her personal expenditures in 1961 and 1962 would average, at today's value, approximately $110,000, about half of which went toward clothing. No one knew that she used surrogate shoppers to buy European designs she could not acknowledge in public, or that she returned or sold items she did not like, using the proceeds, in some cases, to cover a constant deficit in her household accounts, or that she kept for herself or traded away many of the gifts she received as first lady. All of this and more the Kennedys carefully concealed from public view in order to protect the constructed images they revealed on the White House stage.[65]

VII

In their restoration of the White House, famous state dinners, elegant costumes, and skillful management of the media, the Kennedys represented themselves as idealized versions of president and first lady. They embodied in their performance all that was good in American life, and in the process, idealized the nation itself. They were young and vigorous, hopeful and optimistic, idealistic and pragmatic, beautiful and sophisticated, cosmopolitan and confident, rich and powerful. To most Americans, all of these attributes came to life in Kennedy's foreign aid programs, his creation of the Peace Corps, and his call for service and sacrifice, not to mention the many progressive elements in his domestic agenda. As we will see next, these were the things that so many people recalled about the president at the time of his assassination. Together with his charm and wit, his status as a public intellectual and war hero, his movie-star looks and loving family, they would define the lost president for those who mourned him.

So would the sense of style that he and his wife brought to their lives in the White House. In later years, some historians would claim that Kennedy was all style and no substance, while others, more favorably disposed, would simply see his style as inspirational but clearly subordinate to his achievements in domestic and foreign policy. In Kennedy's mind, however, style was substance. He and the first lady appreciated the connection between performance and power – how culture, in effect, could be its own form of power and how theatrical settings could inspire a sense of awe and admiration. In their restored White House, they presented traditional American themes of economic progress and democratic achievement wrapped in elements of drama and grandeur reminiscent of a European palace – an "American Versailles," as Cassini called it. They revealed themselves in costumes that blended a royal aesthetic with an American touch that was straightforward and simple, youthful and unadorned. They performed on the White House stage in entertainments that were young and old, American and European, relaxed and sophisticated, all at the same time. They showcased ballet and opera as well as Broadway show tunes, Shakespearian theater and modern drama, as if enacting an American version of royalty that combined the best of the Old World and the New, that was deserving of its global responsibilities and capable, as Schlesinger put it, "of leading the civilized people" in the ongoing struggle between Russia and the West, between slavery and freedom.

In short, the Kennedys made every effort to portray themselves and the presidency as they wanted them presented – and, perhaps, as most Americans wanted to see them – and to conceal any evidence to the contrary, any signs of weakness or moral ambivalence, of frivolity or bourgeois vulgarity. Carefully, self-consciously, they constructed what I have called a Kennedy "brand," what others have called Camelot. Nor did these efforts end with their days in the White House. On the contrary, as we will see, the assassination launched the Kennedy brand from history to memory, as did the president's funeral. One of the most dramatic and heartfelt events in recent history, the funeral was the first of many efforts to preserve in American memory the image of the president that he and his wife had crafted in their White House years. It's to these parts of the story that we now turn.

3

From History to Memory

Assassination and the Making of a Sacred Symbol

As we have seen, Kennedy's thirty-five months in office, notably the policies he pursued and the way he and his wife comported themselves, had shaped his public identity. In fact, he and his wife had fashioned their own brand, basically a positive representation of themselves and the nation that most Americans found enormously appealing. That brand, moreover, would survive the president's death and become even more appealing, as evident in the way most people reacted to his assassination and what they said about his life. Indeed, it's impossible to understand Kennedy's commanding role in American memory without understanding the terrible shock of his death, both in the United States and around the world. People were shamed by what had happened. They felt a profound sense of guilt and personal loss, as if they had lost a friend as well as a champion who wanted to bring the blessings of liberty to those who did not enjoy them. These feelings account, in part, for why people would remember Kennedy so fondly and why their memories would long endure.

But this is not the whole story. In the United States, the assassination triggered a dark psychic state that contrasted sharply with the joyful exuberance, confidence, optimism, and hopefulness that most Americans associated with Kennedy's politics and personal style. The contrast alone made his remembrance more compelling. What is more, most people identified Kennedy with what was best in American life and his murder with a dangerous trend toward hatred and violence that was tearing at the nation's political fabric, destroying its social cohesion, and calling into question the shared identity of its citizens. As they saw it, the president had given his life trying to staunch the violence and heal divisions, which meant that his sacrifice could only be redeemed by honoring his memory and completing the unfinished work of his presidency. All of this explains why Kennedy's murder added luster to the image that he and his wife had constructed of themselves, why he would emerge from death as a larger-than-life figure, and why his brand, now overlaid with the sanctified mantle of a martyr, would become so deeply embedded in the collective memory of the American people.

II

News of the assassination shot like a thunderbolt across the country. The major American news agencies – the Associated Press and United Press International – also sent the news to more than one hundred nations around the world, and foreign news agencies quickly followed suit. According to the National Opinion Research Center, 68 percent of adult Americans learned of the assassination within thirty minutes of the president's death, and nearly 100 percent had heard the news within six hours.[1] The reaction was nothing short of astonishing. From the moment the news broke until the president's funeral three days later, people everywhere followed developments almost minute by minute, many of them recording their thoughts at the time or in subsequent reflections. The effect was a national fellowship of grief, what political scientist Larry Sabato has described as a "communal town hall" or what sociologists have called a collective cultural trauma of the sort brought on by a great national tragedy.[2] Together with deep-seated feelings of insecurity and fears for the future, such traumas are marked by a strong sense of collective responsibility, calls for atonement, and hopes of redemption. There is also a general tendency to ennoble those who lost their lives in the tragedy, to feel their loss as acutely personal, and to see in them all the virtues identified with the nation itself, and thus with their own sense of national identity, now shaken by the tragedy.[3]

Not surprisingly, in light of this definition, polling data taken within days of the assassination showed large numbers of people worried about the security and stability of the American political system.[4] At Parkland Hospital, where Kennedy was pronounced dead, everyone from Secret Service agents and the president's staff to Lady Bird Johnson feared a vast conspiracy against the government. For some, it was a Soviet conspiracy, a by-product of the Cold War and retaliation for Kennedy's victory over the Soviets in the Cuban Missile Crisis. One newsman wondered if Kennedy's assassination marked the start of World War III. Military personnel, especially those stationed abroad, shared this alarm, and the Joint

Chiefs of Staff, taking every precaution, ordered American forces to stand ready. For others, it was not a Soviet but a Cuban conspiracy, plotted by Fidel Castro in retaliation for the Kennedy administration's repeated attempts to kill him and overthrow his government. Still others, including the new president and Attorney General Robert Kennedy, suspected to their dying days that President Kennedy had been murdered, if not by Castroites, then by anti-Castro Cubans who thought the president had not done enough to topple the Cuban dictator; by mobsters who resented the administration's war on organized crime; or by CIA agents who were angry because the president had little confidence in their abilities and had refused to follow through on their plans for the Bay of Pigs invasion.[5]

As concerns about the mob suggest, many people looked inward for the cause of their anxiety. Senator Paul H. Douglas of Illinois wondered aloud if the United States was becoming more like a Latin American country where political disputes were settled through violence and coups d'état. Given the growing racial strife of recent years, one in five questioned whether anyone could feel safe in American society.[6] "No one knows yet who the killer is," Arthur M. Schlesinger Jr., one of Kennedy's special assistants, recorded in his journal the night of the assassination, "whether a crazed Birchite or a crazed Castroite."[7] Almost everyone agreed that it was an extremist of one stripe or another. "Look what the Birchers have done!" exclaimed a man in Washington, DC, while the former mayor of Birmingham saw Kennedy's death as just the latest "episode in the long and sordid history" of communist "control by revolution and assassination."[8]

Although some people, particularly in the South or among Republicans, put responsibility on one or more fanatics, others went further, blaming what they saw as a collective culture of extremism that spawned hatred and violence everywhere. "This is a legacy of the hate that has arisen" in recent years, said a Los Angeles public relations man about the president's murder.[9] Columnist James Reston of the *New York Times* wrote about Kennedy as a peacemaker who had tried to reconcile factions, mitigate their hatred, and defuse their violence. The president, he reminded readers, had traveled to Texas to "pacify the violent politics of that state" and to Florida the week before to "pacify the businessmen" whose extremist rhetoric pictured Kennedy as virulently anti-business, if not a socialist altogether. Besides restraining those "extremists on the right" who urged violence in the civil rights struggle at home, Reston said that Kennedy had also sought to calm those "who wanted to be more violent in the cold war overseas." He found it sad that a man who had tried so hard to heal divisions and curb violence had now become their victim.[10] No American, the *New York Times* editorialized, could "escape a share of the fault for the spiral of unreason and violence" that had scarred the country and had now claimed the life of "our martyred president."[11] For Chief Justice Earl Warren, burdened by grief at the death of a man he loved and admired, murders of the sort that had claimed the president's life were "commonly stimulated by forces of hatred and malevolence, such as today are eating their way into the bloodstream of American life."[12]

The same themes surfaced in countless sermons by priests, rabbis, and ministers, and in commentaries by ordinary people all over the country. Time and again, they attacked what they saw as a culture of hatred and violence. Dean Francis Sayre of Washington Cathedral cited as evidence the recent murder of Medgar Evers and four black children in Birmingham, not to mention more "ancient injustices." All of this had set the stage for the president's assassination, as had the abuse heaped earlier on Lyndon Johnson and Adlai Stevenson. Many also denounced the rhetoric of disrespect, if not hate, used by business leaders in their diatribes against the president and by anticommunist crusaders who found Kennedy too anxious to disarm and too eager to appease the Soviet Union. It was not enough to blame left- or right-wing groups, moreover, let alone a single fanatic. Both blame and guilt were collective. They belonged to everyone who had encouraged or even tolerated the growth of a political culture rooted in hatred and violence. Americans must "face up to their share of the guilt," Dorothy DeLomel wrote to NBC news anchor Chet Huntley. Oswald may have pulled the trigger, "but did we not all ... set the stage" for the president's assassination? "May God have mercy upon us," she concluded, "and help each member of his family to forgive us." Nor was it enough to express guilt or cast blame. If hatred and violence were the problems, love and peace were the solutions. Americans needed to confess the error of their ways. They needed to atone for their sins and seek redemption by honoring the president's legacy and moving forward with the programs he supported.[13]

Most of those who recorded their reaction to the assassination spoke less about the country's political culture or fears of conspiracy than about their own sense of personal loss and loneliness. "Why, why, why," asked Mrs. Dale Petus of Ohio. "Why ... this terrible feeling of shock and loss?" It was as if "something had been taken from me."[14] More than anything else, such responses tell us a good deal about how deeply, and personally, the president had touched the American people, and thus about his standing with them in the decades following his death. People everywhere would remember where they were and how they felt when they heard the news of the president's assassination. These "flashbulb memories," as they are called, became so deeply imprinted on the mind that even the passage of time could not erase them.[15] Thirty years later, Abigail Van Buren, author of the famous syndicated column, "Dear Abby," received over three hundred thousand letters and cards when she asked her readers where they were when President Kennedy was shot. Some recounted the day as their first childhood memory; others reflected back on a memory still indelible after eighty years of life; and still others remembered exactly what they were doing at home, work, or school.[16] One man was diving a hundred feet below the ocean off the California coast when the news came to him over the diver's radio. Another recalled being in Chicago with the same friend he had been with when President Franklin D. Roosevelt died eighteen years earlier. "We have to stop meeting like this," his friend declared. A woman in Florida remembered sitting under a hair dryer in a New Jersey beauty shop, the same place she would be when she learned of Robert Kennedy's assassination five years later. In Phoenix, a woman heard the news in the grocery store and rushed home to tell her husband, only to find him dead from a heart attack, the radio beside him still blasting the shocking news from Dallas. Another woman heard the news on a car radio just as her husband announced that he was leaving her for a girlfriend in Alaska. Years later, she still found it ironic that both she and Jacqueline Kennedy had lost their husbands on the same day.[17]

Countless people had birthday celebrations ruined, perhaps forever, by news of the president's death, while others associated the day with a bit of good news. An autograph dealer in New Jersey saw his LBJ signatures automatically appreciate; a man in Pennsylvania remembered an Internal Revenue Service auditor dismissing his case; a group of people in California had their traffic fines waived; and a patrol officer, also in California, recalled putting his citation book away as he watched dozens of motorists, driving in a state of shock, violate "virtually every section of the vehicle code." In California as well, a recent immigrant recalled waiting to be sworn in as a US citizen, only to have the judge announce the tragic news and abbreviate the ceremony. "Please raise your right hand," the judge declared. "Welcome to the United States."[18]

A woman in New Jersey returned home from her husband's funeral, learned of the president's death, and grieved again as if she had lost another member of her family. This reaction was surprisingly common. People everywhere talked of Kennedy as a member of the family, and felt as badly about his death as they did about the death of a parent, brother, or close friend.[19] A young Peace Corps volunteer in West Africa wept "as if my brother or close relative had died." Jimmy Carter, then working on his peanut farm in Plains, Georgia, felt a "grievous personal loss" and cried openly "for the first time since the day my father died."[20] Senator Claiborne Pell of Rhode Island made the same point. Rona Barrett, a society columnist, remembered how she and those around her reacted as if they, too, had lost a "member of their immediate family." Legendary football coach Lou Holtz recalled his feelings in almost the same words, as did Jules Bergman and Sam Donaldson, both of ABC News. "It was as if a loved one of my own had been killed," wrote Donaldson.[21]

Having considered Kennedy like a father, brother, or son, many people marked his death by adding the president symbolically to their family, as if an act of imagined reincarnation would preserve the spirit of the man for another generation. One woman, a receptionist for a doctor in Sedan, Kansas, found a stray cat, took him into her home, and named him Fitzgerald. Another decided that day to conceive a child, who would be born nine months later and named John. Still other women who delivered baby boys on November 22 named them John, Fitzgerald, or Kennedy. "The nurse told me later," one reported to "Dear Abby," "that eighteen boys were born in her hospital that day, and at least half were named after the deceased president."[22]

Reports of almost uncontrollable weeping were commonplace after the assassination, and while opinion polls showed that many people wanted to be left alone in their grief, more typical was a need for the comforting embrace of others.[23] A surprising number of witnesses recount wandering the streets as if in a state of shock, huddling with strangers, and crying together "for one of our family." A woman in New Orleans ran compulsively from her apartment into the street just because she "needed someone to talk to." Shoppers in a New York department store "clustered instinctively," and in one case, "prayed together."[24] Others shared their misery over the telephone to such an extent that phone lines quickly jammed, while still others found togetherness through radio and television. "Someone found a radio and we all clustered around waiting for the next piece of news," said actress Donna Reed. Film director Billy Wilder, along with his wife and partner, "just sat in [the] office and watched TV," as did the cast members of TV's popular *Dick Van Dyke Show*.[25] Everyone kept close to a radio or TV, as one expectant mother put it, "trying to comprehend the awful truth." Many reported being "glued to the television" from the president's assassination through his funeral three days later. In some households, the whole family – parents, grandparents, and other relatives – watched events unfold on television. Peace Corps volunteers abroad listened to the news on the Voice of America or whatever radio station they could tune in, while college students gathered in dorm rooms that had a TV set or at campus locations where televisions were provided.[26]

The news media, particularly television, became a great social adhesive, bonding people together in a national family. "The death of President Kennedy was a death in all our families," explained a married couple in California, and television enabled them "to participate, as we needed and as was appropriate, in the private tragedy of a loved one's dying." For those who could not be part of the official mourning in Washington, television enabled them "to pay our respects in a more deeply personal way than otherwise would have been possible." They could "share in the sorrow of the President's family" and feel "very much a part of everything." In addition, knowing that millions of others were watching the same events unfold on television "seemed to unite the entire country," gave all viewers a sense of great comfort, and helped them come to terms with the terrible tragedy.[27] They were grateful to those who brought them the news. "You have helped a gravely troubled public find some strength," one couple wrote to Chet Huntley, "and gain some inspiration from all of the confusion." In a time of such "personal loss," a New Yorker confessed to Huntley, "I have come to you as an old friend looking for answers ... and even consolation."[28]

As this suggests, in a period of acute cultural trauma, many people needed the warmth of family, friends, and faith. The actor Gene Kelly canceled a television appearance in New York to rush back to his wife in California. The playwright Edward Albee, in the Soviet Union at the time, felt "more homesick" than ever before. College students away from their families thought only to "call home," as one put it. Another student remembered how his classmates walked, "without exception and from all directions," to the campus chapel to console each other and pray for the president's soul.[29] A woman shopping in Los Angeles when she heard the news went straight to the nearest church, where she soon noticed how quickly the pews filled with others who wanted company and a place to pray for the president and his family.[30] Indeed, church attendance increased in the days following the assassination; substantial numbers of people recalled praying quietly to themselves; and national leaders were more likely than ever to invoke God in their public pronouncements.[31]

As Edward Albee's remark points out, Americans abroad felt a particularly acute sense of "isolation and desolation" when they learned of Kennedy's assassination. Most "longed to be back home."[32] "Dear Abby" herself, along with other Americans vacationing in Tokyo, "just wanted to go 'home' and be with our people." Short of that, they rushed for comfort to the Americans around them. A couple in Mexico gathered with other Americans to watch the TV news in their hotel lobby, as did a group of Americans at a hotel in Tokyo. A military couple living in England found the British very sympathetic, though "it would have been better to be at home." An air force couple in Paris gathered with their American neighbors to share their shock and sadness "so far away from the U.S.A." The Americans were "pulling together in a foreign land," is how another soldier put it.[33]

Peace Corps volunteers were especially devastated by the death of a president who had inspired in them a strong sense of service to humanity. They, too, wished for nothing more than to share their sorrow with fellow Americans. Unable to get home, they collected their Peace Corps friends around them and listened to radio reports with "heavy hearts" and "blank looks." "I needed to be with other Americans," recalled a volunteer in Bangkok, Thailand, who went immediately to a restaurant favored by American travelers and spent most of his time with other Peace Corps volunteers. Two volunteers in Morocco traveled sixty miles to Tangier where they joined their colleagues from across that country. "Feelings ran very deep that weekend," one later wrote, as "we tried to console each other," in part by celebrating high Mass at a Catholic church on Sunday.[34]

For some, in fact, even the streets had become a solemn place, almost church-like, where all sound stopped, as if the world itself had paused in sacred silence. A young woman spending her honeymoon night in Dallas remembered the city as a "tomb." A New Yorker recalled walking down a busy Fifth Avenue, when suddenly "taxis, cars, buses, trucks – everything froze in place" as radios announced the devastating news. Another writer told "Dear Abby" how the "normally active downtown" of Knoxville, Tennessee, became "like a funeral procession. Everyone on the buses simply stared out the windows." Still another recalled hearing the news on her car radio while stopped at a traffic light in Cleveland, Ohio. When the light turned green, no one budged. Drivers just buried their heads in their steering wheels and cried "for a good half hour."[35]

For these witnesses, wherever they were, it seemed as if all sound had been muted and time stood still. The nation itself had become a church; the hustle and bustle of normal life stopped and people everywhere prayed in "stunned silence."[36] A student in the sports center at Boston College remembered how an eerie "quiet fell over all within earshot." Another student, at the University of Delaware, found the "usual garble of voices" in the student union suddenly replaced by a hushed silence."[37] It was "like in a dream," said a New Yorker about the streets of Manhattan; "everything got real quiet."[38] To actor Cliff Robertson, whose movie *PT 109* had just been released, it seemed as if "the entire community had been struck down." Driving alone through the Pacific Palisades, he found it shrouded in silence without a "single horn honking." In Robertson's memory, time seemed to wind down as if in slow motion. Others, making the same point, described the "zombie-like" state of those around them, or recounted walking aimlessly about, feeling frozen in time, or having a "mystical experience."[39] Indeed, 57 percent of those interviewed at the time felt dazed or numb after hearing the news from Dallas.[40]

As the public reaction suggests, Kennedy's death touched off widespread feelings of fear, anxiety, and disorientation, all feelings associated with a period of collective cultural trauma. It led many people to blame themselves or others for what had happened. Some looked inward, seeking solace in silent reflection. Some rushed to the company of family and friends, huddled in small groups on quiet streets, or gathered in churches where they often found spiritual union with complete strangers. Together, they prayed for the president's soul, examined their own consciences, and considered how they might atone for such a terrible calamity. As often happens in moments of great national tragedy, they shared a profound sense of personal loss and a tendency, as we will see, to idealize the victim. In Kennedy's case, they would slight his shortcomings, exaggerate his virtues, and bury more deeply in American memory the image that Kennedy had constructed of himself as a man of style and substance, a peacemaker at home and abroad, a crusader for social justice, a champion of civil rights. This was the beginning of the Kennedy cult, the cult of the dead, to paraphrase Conrad Cherry – a devotion so burdened by the shock of the president's murder that people would begin to canonize him as an exemplar of American ideals, as a martyr to the American cause, as a hero whose death could only be redeemed by taking up the important work to which he had devoted his life.[41]

III

There was a similar reaction abroad, where the sorrowful response to Kennedy's death far exceeded that of any other American president. Not even the deaths of Abraham Lincoln and Franklin Roosevelt struck such a deeply discordant note. This was particularly true in the European democracies, where, as historian Frank Costigliola has shown, people had come to see Kennedy not only as the leader of the free world, but as their leader too. He was the very symbol of what was best in American life and culture. His youth and charm, his optimism, confidence, and idealism, all gave hope of a better life and a more secure future for Europeans as well as Americans. Indeed, most thought he was a martyr to the good causes he had championed, such as civil rights, arms control, and care for the poor, the ill, and the old. Not surprisingly, given these feelings, Kennedy's tragic death triggered a prolonged period of intense public mourning and devout expressions of regret, not only in Europe, but across the world.[42]

National leaders sent their heartfelt sympathies, of course. They laid immediate plans to attend the president's funeral in Washington and rushed to sign condolence books at the US embassies in their countries. In France, President Charles de Gaulle was "stunned" to see people crying in the streets, as if Kennedy "were a Frenchman, a member of their own family." He immediately ordered the French flag lowered to half-staff and declared a period of official mourning.[43] In Ireland, ancestral home of the Kennedys, grief was especially overwhelming and made worse because of the president's recent visit to the family homestead in Wexford. It was as if there had been "a death in every family in Ireland," mourned a radio commentator in Dublin.[44] "Ah," said a Fitzgerald of Limerick, we "cried the rain down that night."[45]

The reaction was the same in Italy, as it was in the United Kingdom, where Kennedy's father had served as US ambassador to the Court of St. James's, where his younger sister had been buried after a tragic air crash, and where his older brother was stationed when he lost his life in the Second World War. According to former prime minister Harold Macmillan, sorrow was at once universal and individual. The bells of Westminster Abbey began tolling, the Union Jack came to half-staff, and the queen ordered a week of court mourning. The American embassy in London had to put out twelve tables and add six staff to accommodate the thousands of people who stood in long lines to sign the official condolence book.[46] A similar scene unfolded in West Germany, especially West Berlin, where Kennedy had recently declared himself a citizen of the city and promised the protection of the United States against Soviet aggression. Here, too, more than a quarter million mourners stood in long lines to sign condolence books, and Willy Brandt, the mayor of West Berlin, declared that Kennedy's death had struck the German people like that of a brother.[47]

In other parts of Europe, governments and their people responded the same way, as they did in countries across the globe. In India, Thailand, and Taiwan, in Argentina, Brazil, and Mexico, in Egypt, Israel, and throughout Africa, governments proclaimed official periods of mourning. They issued formal eulogies, staged mock funerals, and placed the dead president's photograph on prominent display, while at the same time, churches filled to capacity and vigil candles appeared in storefront windows and family homes everywhere.[48] In Tokyo, Crown Prince Akihito and his wife, though Buddhists, led a procession of three thousand mourners into a Catholic church to celebrate a memorial Mass for the fallen leader. In Lima, Peru, the House of Representatives voted to recommend Kennedy for the Nobel Peace Prize. Even in the Soviet Union, Premier Nikita Khrushchev hurried to sign a condolence book at the American embassy and ordered Soviet television to broadcast the president's funeral.[49] In Cuba, meanwhile, Castro told a visiting French journalist that Kennedy's death was "bad news," a comment, perhaps, on the president's recent flirtation with the possibility of a rapprochement between the United States and Cuba.[50]

Americans living abroad at the time provided particularly poignant descriptions of their reactions to the assassination. Taken together, they reveal how touched Americans were by the enormous admiration and personal affection that Kennedy had inspired around the world, and by the widespread respect thereby accorded the United States and its citizens. Even in death, Kennedy made Americans feel good about themselves. They were proud of their country, its standing in the world, and the personal esteem they commanded in the reflected glory of their fallen leader. "It was as if the sky had fallen," recalled an American living in Ankara, Turkey. Officials there ordered all flags lowered to half-staff and quickly proclaimed a day of complete silence for the whole city. In Istanbul, too, flags were lowered, only classical music played on the radio, and Americans were treated "as though we had lost a member of our immediate family." It was the first time, according to two Americans, that Turkish officials had publicly mourned the death of a foreigner. In Nicaragua, the whole country went into official mourning, stores and banks closed, and the Catholic Church in Managua held a mock state funeral. In Sweden, too, public facilities were closed and windows were decorated with the American and Swedish flags, while in Amsterdam, another American reported, the government turned off all holiday lights and organized a large memorial for the president, which more than one hundred thousand people attended.[51]

There were other reports of this sort, but what touched most Americans abroad were the personal expressions of sympathy. To be sure, many found their hosts confused by what had happened. In Amsterdam, for example, some people worried that Kennedy's death would mean another European war or the collapse of the US government. In Saudi Arabia, they could not understand why Kennedy's assassin had not been executed on the spot. And in Barcelona, Spain, people wanted to know what was "wrong with you Americans? Are you all crazy?"[52]

Declarations of support were far more typical, however, as were spontaneous tributes to the dead president. In West Berlin, a group of university students organized a torchlight procession in honor of their American hero. The procession swelled to more than seventy-five thousand people who marched to city hall, where Kennedy had delivered his famous "I am a Berliner" speech the previous June. In Portugal, men put on black ties to commemorate the president's death. In Moscow, the staff at one hotel wept openly with their American guests, as did the Japanese staff at a hotel in Tokyo. For days after Kennedy's death, people in London were still stopping Americans on the street to extend their condolences. The same thing happened in Paris and in Berlin, where American residents opened their mail to find condolence cards from complete strangers. In Belfast, Northern Ireland, one American was amazed to find strangers ringing his doorbell to extend their sympathy or stopping him on the street to shake hands and say a few words. Another American, a concert pianist touring Sweden, saw his entire audience stand in a show of respect when he played a special number in honor of the late president.[53] And when an American business consultant in Scotland entered a hotel pub on the day of the assassination, local customers stood with bowed heads in complete silence. He could not buy his own drinks that day or for as long as he stayed in the hotel. "To all the Scots, Brits, and Europeans there," he wrote, "I represented the only available American to whom they could express their sorrow."[54] "It was a dramatic experience," said one commentator of the sorrow he witnessed, and it brought to his attention just "how much the world loved John F. Kennedy."[55] Another, talking about the reaction in West Berlin, wrote later that he "had never seen or experienced such an outpouring of emotion from so many people in such a few short minutes."[56]

Such expressions of personal sympathy were not confined to Europe. People in other parts of the world responded the same way, as a few examples will suffice to show. An American teaching in West Pakistan the day Kennedy was killed soon had neighbors, students, and colleagues calling at his home, bringing gifts of food, and extending their condolences. One wept over the death of a president whose picture hung in his house and whose wife had visited the local bazaar during her trip to Pakistan the previous year. Even more extraordinary was the story of an American military attaché with the US embassy in Somalia. He came home to find friends, both Somalis and members of the international community, anxious to provide emotional support and share their own grief with him. Somali tribesmen learned of the president's death through the "bush telegraph," he recorded, and many of them walked miles across the desert "to make their mark" in the condolence book at the US embassy and to pack a local church where a requiem Mass followed the next day.[57] In Egypt, where young men and women had taken to imitating the first lady's fashion and the way President Kennedy styled his hair, thousands simply walked into the street in search of more news of the day's events. In Kenya, youth leaders made a wreath of seventeen hundred flowers to send for the president's funeral, and three thousand tribesmen stood in silent vigil.[58] In Bolivia, people everywhere wept openly. They loved Kennedy, who was Catholic like they were and who had been "helping Bolivia with the Point Four Program and Peace Corps."[59] The Bolivian people "really felt our sorrow," recorded another American on the scene.[60]

IV

In the wake of Kennedy's assassination, as this suggests, expressions of shared sorrow were heartfelt and commonplace. Although Kennedy had enemies, too – particularly in the American South and in communist countries like China – and while some detractors celebrated his death, loving admirers seemed far more in evidence in the months following the assassination. In a poll taken after his death, 64 percent of respondents claimed to have voted for the late president in the 1960 election, even though he had garnered less than half the ballots cast.[61] The discrepancy in these numbers might be explained if we remember that Kennedy, once elected, became extremely popular with the American people. Public opinion polls often showed his approval rating above 70 percent. And while this number declined in the last months of his life, particularly after his controversial speech on behalf of civil rights, it still hovered around 60 percent, with three-fourths of those surveyed convinced that he would be reelected easily against any Republican contender.[62]

What was it about Kennedy that drew so many people to him? What did he represent to most Americans, and others, at the time of his death? Why did his death seem like a personal loss to so many, as if they were mourning the death of a friend or relative? Why did they see him as the ideal American, whose public policies and personal style, not to mention his assassination, made him a hero worth remembering? Several themes emerge from comments made at the time, some already noted, or when people later reflected on the president's assassination. For many, the answers were to be found in his appealing amalgam of personal traits and moral character, at least so far as they were revealed in the carefully framed image he had constructed of himself. This included his support of the arts and his positive presentation of himself and the nation, evident in the White House renovation that he and his wife had engineered, their costumes, and their elaborate entertainments. Kennedy, it seemed, embodied in himself what most Americans thought best about themselves. He personified the nation and made them feel proud to be Americans, even in the wake of his assassination, when they reveled in the way people everywhere shared their sorrow and paid tribute to their president.

Other aspects of the Kennedy brand were mentioned in this connection as well, including the president's physical attractiveness and the glow of his personality, his intelligence and good humor, his incredible charm and charisma, all of which were on regular display in the media. Others noted his upbeat tempo, positive attitude, and eloquent and uplifting rhetorical style, which had supposedly encouraged the nation to tackle its problems and move forward. For others, it was his apparent compassion for the ill, the aged, working people, and the poor, as revealed not only in his support for a higher minimum wage and more funding for education, health care, and Social Security, but also in his foreign aid programs, including the Peace Corps and the Alliance for Progress. "Many Americans have lost an idol," wrote F. J. Bode of Phoenix, "but the great and real loss has been to the 'downtrodden peoples,' especially the 'little people' in the far lands, for they have, in truth, lost a great champion." Others admired his courage, as revealed in his war record, his efforts to overcome the debilitating aliments that afflicted him, and his decision to stand up to the Soviets during the Cuban Missile Crisis and face down his critics, in Texas and elsewhere, who attacked his religious faith, his plans to control nuclear weapons, and his support, however late, for the cause of civil rights.[63] These traits help to explain why the president was "so well liked," as a woman in St. Louis put it, and why a black woman riding a bus in Oakland, California, cried out in despair when she learned of Kennedy's death: "No, Lord. I loved that man so much!"[64]

Another appealing aspect of Kennedy's image was his identity as a family man – a devoted husband and father. For many people, this was the image that came to mind when they heard the news from Dallas. James Farmer, then working for the Congress of Racial Equality, "immediately recalled pictures of Kennedy sitting on the lawn with his children." Others thought of the iconic photo of the president and his son that appeared on the cover of *Look* magazine just days after his assassination. For a mailman in Ohio, Kennedy was a family man who "had young children just like we do."[65] And with his death, people thought not only of the murdered president, but also of the "lovely lady" widowed and the two children who had lost a father. Together, they appeared to be the ideal American family and had set a "happy tone" and admirable example of "family life" in the White House.[66]

Almost everyone commented as well on the appeal of Kennedy's youthful leadership. Compared to the older presidents who preceded him, Kennedy seemed "so alive and vibrant," so "youthful" and "vigorous." "Youth," in fact, became something of a metaphor for a whole set of appealing attributes, all of which made Kennedy the symbol for what he and others called a new generation of leadership.[67] These attributes included his enthusiasm, optimism about the future, and confidence that the new generation could get things done. A related attribute, also associated with Kennedy's youthful leadership, was his sense of adventure, which had supposedly "rekindled" the country's "pioneering tradition." The space program and the president's call to put a man on the moon became favorite pieces in this corner of the Kennedy mosaic. But they were easily connected to others by the familiar themes of self-sacrifice, public service, and voluntarism that Kennedy so often invoked when talking about the Green Berets; the Peace Corps and its domestic counterpart, VISTA; and other parts of his program. He asked us to solve problems, said one American who had been a college student at the time, and gave us hope that all things were possible.[68]

Next to his youth, in fact, the word most commonly associated with Kennedy's leadership was "hope." With him, so many believed, there was

more hope that seemingly intractable problems could be solved, especially the problems of racial inequality, poverty, and war.[69] This helps
to explain why so many people, particularly young people, who considered Kennedy "our hero," saw his murder in Dallas as "the passing of an
era."[70] A young co-ed measured the transition in personal terms, from
youthful innocence to sober adulthood, from worries about her weekend
dates to new concerns about the state of the nation. Kennedy's murder
"was a turning point," recalled another commentator, for whom the "sixties" began on November 22, 1963. "Not the Beatles or the Stones," he
said, "but President Kennedy's death started it."[71]

As he and others saw it, Kennedy's assassination ended an age of hopeful innocence that would never come again.[72] It instilled in them a sense of
despair, as if there had been a break in time, with the Kennedy years being
nothing more than a brief and shining interlude in the dreary march of
history, a brilliant shaft of light squeezed between two pillars of darkness.
For those who recorded their thoughts in hindsight, the assassination had
planted the seeds for a harvest of hopelessness. "Dreams were cancelled
that day," recalled a former student at the University of Oregon. "It was
all over, the dreams and the hopes," said a Peace Corps employee.[73] Some
predicted a new age of social conflict, others, a collapse of the civil rights
movement, and yet others, a heightening of Cold War tensions.[74] All that
remained for them was to ask: "what might we have become if ... ?"[75]

But if Kennedy's death turned dreams to dust for some, others
remained faithful to the image they had formed of him, including his
hope for a better future. For them, Kennedy and his memory helped
to inspire an ongoing struggle for peace, civil rights, and social justice.
This was the legacy he bequeathed, and it made him not only a force
for change in his own day but an inspiration for generations to come.
Although it was not limited to them, this sentiment seemed especially
strong among African Americans, and even Africans. It helps to explain
why they were so drawn to him in life, why they suffered so at his
death, and why images of the fallen leader could still be found, years
later, adorning the walls of their homes. They and others saw Kennedy
as a champion of civil rights, in the tradition of Abraham Lincoln, and
compared his death to Lincoln's assassination. "This is what it was like
in 1865," is how one put it.[76] Others agreed that Kennedy was "the
new Lincoln" or the "second Emancipator" whose "place in history,"
as A. Philip Randolph explained, "will be next to Abraham Lincoln."
Some preferred to think of Kennedy as another Moses, leading his people out of the desert and into the Promised Land; some went even

further, comparing Kennedy's murder to the crucifixion of Christ. For most, however, Lincoln was the natural referent.[77]

Like Lincoln, Kennedy was a man who "gave hope to black people after so many years of hopelessness." These were the words of Vivian J. Malone-Jones, one of the two black students who integrated the University of Alabama in the summer of 1963. The president's defense of her admission and his subsequent decision to draft a major civil rights bill for congressional action "brought a new sense of self-worth to our lives," she said, and a "fresh beginning" for African Americans. Myrlie Evers-Williams made the same point when recalling Kennedy's famous civil rights speech on June 11, 1963, the very day her husband, civil rights leader Medgar Evers, was murdered in Jackson, Mississippi. "Never in my lifetime," she said, "had I ever heard a President of the United States make such a poignant and eloquent speech on behalf of the civil rights of black Americans." She and others like her "began to believe a new day was coming, one that would give us our legitimate place in American society." Although such hopes appeared to be "broken against the rocks" of Kennedy's assassination, they actually lived on in those who took up his cause and in the legislation his death inspired.[78]

To be sure, many prominent civil rights leaders, including James Farmer, were less enthusiastic in their assessment of Kennedy's record on civil rights, believing that he was slow to act and reluctant to go as far as they wanted. But even Farmer had to concede that Kennedy gave people, especially black people, hope of a better life. This explained why he was so "popular with rank-and-file blacks throughout the country" and in Africa as well, and why they continued to display his photograph years after the assassination.[79] For black Americans, Kennedy was one of them. He "loved our people," as one said, and made their cause his own. In their view, moreover, he did more for black people than any president since Lincoln, even sacrificing his life for their welfare. He was heaven-sent, wrote Marzell Swain of Newark, New Jersey. "He was water in dry places. He was shelter in the time of storm."[80]

Kennedy's image as a champion of civil rights folded naturally into a larger portrait of him as a crusader for peace and justice broadly conceived. Here, the comparison was often to Franklin Roosevelt, another president who believed in peaceful coexistence and "a one world nation." Like Roosevelt, moreover, Kennedy was seen as a humanitarian who cared for the working class and the downtrodden, the hill people of West Virginia, the sick, the elderly, and the "average American" with "limited opportunities and without a voice in government." With VISTA and the

Peace Corps, moreover, and with his call for sacrifice on behalf of the greater good, the murdered president had supposedly inspired a whole generation of people to enter public service and had set the stage for the progress achieved in the decades following his death. Had he lived, one writer believed, he would have continued to be a "voice for the poor, the oppressed, the dispossessed," and for peace. As it was, his legacy was to be found in the many reforms he conceived for later generations to achieve.[81] Because of this legacy, one man reflected, "we will always remember and miss him."[82] In short, Kennedy was a man worthy of remembrance.

V

In the final analysis, then, the Kennedy brand was an attractive blend of personal attributes and moral character. On the one hand, people spoke of his handsome appearance and charismatic personality, his cool non-chalance, his wit and good humor, his rhetorical flourish, his can-do spirit and breezy self-confidence – all of which endeared him to people across the country and around the world. They made him one of the most popular presidents ever and helped to sustain his popularity more than a half-century after his death. As Paul R. Henggeler has shown, they even impressed his political opponents and virtually every president who followed him to the Oval Office, most of whom tried, without much luck, to project the same personal attributes that appeared to come so naturally to Kennedy.[83] These attributes, on the other hand, reinforced the virtuous aspects of the president's image, including his courage, hopefulness, and compassion; his loyalty to family, friends, and nation; and his sense of duty and capacity for self-sacrifice, even, if necessary, the heroic sacrifice of his own life for the betterment of others. These virtues appeared to inspire his call to public service and his support for arms control and détente, civil rights and social justice, including foreign aid and aid to the poor, the aged, and the ill. Taken together, they seemed to make Kennedy the ideal American, the very embodiment of all that Americans should aspire to be.

The Kennedy image, of course, had been fashioned in part by the Kennedys themselves, both of whom were amazingly adept at how they presented themselves to the public, and thus at how others would remember them. The president's brutal assassination and the profound cultural trauma it induced, only added luster to the brand they had constructed and buried it even more deeply in American memory. Thereafter, as we will see, the Kennedys and their allies made every effort to further enhance and jealously guard what the president had fashioned, beginning with his funeral. Indeed, Jacqueline Kennedy scripted, staged, and directed her husband's funeral, as she had so many White House productions, so that when we look back on that drama what we see is what she wanted revealed, and to an audience that still admires the enormous, enduring success of her performance.

4

Ritual and Remembrance

Cultural Trauma, Collective Memory, and the Funeral of John Fitzgerald Kennedy

As we have seen, people felt close to President Kennedy, or at least to the persona he projected, so close that his death struck them as a personal loss. They reacted with shock and dismay, a vast outpouring of grief, a profound sense of guilt for whatever part they may have played in the tragedy, and deep-seated fears and doubts about the future, including doubts about their own identity as a people and their ability to cohere as a nation. Much of this reaction was spontaneous and highly emotional, though it later became more controlled and organized as the period of mourning moved from the president's assassination through the funeral planning and burial that followed. The same period, moreover, witnessed a general tendency to ennoble the slain president. In a nation wounded by guilt, its faith in the future shaken, Kennedy assumed heroic status. His already popular image was polished in ways that enabled Americans to feel whole again, proud of their place in the world and of the values both they and their fallen leader seemed to personify.[1]

This is not an unfamiliar process. According to the great French sociologist Emile Durkheim, not to mention his many followers over the generations, most cultures have funeral rites of passage that aim to move the dead from the world of the living to whatever lies beyond. But the same rituals are about the living as well, and are designed to serve important social purposes. If mourning the death of a loved one is an obligation imposed on the family, which feels diminished by its loss, it is no less a duty imposed on the whole community when death strikes down a head of state whose life seemed to embody elements of character identified with the nation itself. Just as a family reacts to its loss by coming together in the shared sorrow of a funeral, and just as this process can spur renewed hope and family spirit, so the nation is summoned to mourn the death of the hero-patriot in a collective grief that can inspire a resurgent sense of strength, shared identity, and common purpose.[2]

In Kennedy's case, much of this inspiration derived from the theatrical elements that marked his funeral, which resembled in many ways a dramatic rendering staged by the state in active collaboration with the president's widow, family, and friends. The funeral procession became a mournful pageant and the burial a performance in profound bereavement, both directed by a grieving widow who had managed so many elaborate productions in her role as first lady. Of course, great public rituals, including the inauguration of a president or his burial, always take on the air of a spectacle. As deliberately calculated compositions, they use the techniques of theater to arouse in their audience a set of intense feelings, usually of a patriotic nature. Symbols of state and nation are deployed to invoke these emotions, including the American flag and such musical scores as the national anthem, "Hail to the Chief," and "God Bless America." In Kennedy's funeral, these symbols expressed an American civic religion. They were embedded in a sacred ceremony that honored the nation, notably its God-given mission to preserve and protect democracy, but also the fallen leader whose virtues were those of the nation in whose service he had perished. All of this, in turn, overlaid Catholic religious rituals that carried their own symbolism, such as the use of holy water and blessing of the casket.[3]

Although many of these civic and religious rituals are typical of state funerals and will be noted here, the focus in these pages is also on the way Jacqueline Kennedy personalized the funeral for her own purposes. This was the beginning of the memory work that would occupy the rest of her life. Combining style and substance once again, she transformed the funeral into a stage for the reproduction of her husband's presidency, much as she would later do with the Kennedy Library and Museum. She introduced her own symbols of the president's life and its meaning. She used the funeral to remind the nation of her husband's accomplishments and the values that guided him, and she encouraged her audience to honor his memory, follow his example, and complete the unfinished work of his presidency. Much the same was true of the many political leaders and editorial writers who eulogized the dead president. In effect, they joined the former first lady in reinforcing the messages and images that she and her husband had worked so hard to create in their White House productions. Following her lead, they added powerfully to the emotional content of the funeral, elevating it above all other state funerals in American history, and creating a living memory – basically an afterlife for the former president – that has lasted more than half a century.

In the process, moreover, and with Jacqueline Kennedy's help, the media also transformed the former first lady into a symbol, like her husband, of what it meant to be an American. She as well as her husband now appeared to personify core values at the heart of American life, so much so that those who witnessed her performance responded with a degree of gratitude, admiration, and adulation that bordered on hero worship. In all of these ways, the funeral of John Fitzgerald Kennedy helped to spark a renewed sense of social cohesion and collective purpose in the face of an acute cultural trauma. It became easier for people to cope with the fears, anxieties, and doubts that wracked the country on November 22, 1963, and to overcome, at least temporarily, the personal animosities and political divisions, the national and international crises, that might have deepened the trauma, rather than repaired it.

II

As this suggests, Kennedy's funeral took place in a turbulent political context. His had been a crisis presidency, although not in the sense of Lincoln's presidency, nor that of Franklin Roosevelt, both of whom died at the end of a long and bloody war. The Kennedy administration had been marked instead by a series of crises, including the debacle at the Bay of Pigs, which was an American humiliation; the Berlin crisis, when the world averted another war only at the expense of dividing Germany; the Cuban Missile Crisis, which brought the United States to the brink of nuclear annihilation; and the civil rights crisis, which provoked deep social and political divisions and growing domestic violence. These crises followed one upon the other so quickly that it seemed as if Kennedy's entire administration had been engulfed in a single crisis of substantial proportions. Although his shrewd manipulation of the media, his personal charm and attractiveness, and his clever staging of the presidency all contributed to Kennedy's popular appeal, and thus to the sense of loss that followed his assassination, these crises, as Barry Schwartz has noted, also made his presidency seem more conspicuous, his policies more substantial, and his death more consequential. They intensified not only the sense of loss that most Americans felt when the president died but also the insecurity and anxiety that his death provoked. The widespread worry that Kennedy's killer was but one spoke in a wider wheel of conspiracy further intensified these feelings, as did media, particularly television, coverage of the three-day period of mourning. Most Americans spent approximately twenty-seven hours watching TV broadcasts of the president's assassination and funeral, with results that were mixed at best. Media coverage could encourage a spirit of shared sorrow and common identity, thus reconstructing a social cohesion that had been fragmented by Kennedy's death; but it could also aggravate already widespread feelings of dislocation, vulnerability, and doubt, as was the case when Jack Ruby murdered the president's assassin on national television.[4]

This explains why Kennedy's successor, Lyndon Baines Johnson, was so anxious to close ranks with the president's widow, retain as many members of his cabinet and staff as possible, and take other initiatives to emphasize national stability and continuity as the country moved abruptly from one president to the next under difficult circumstances. Although he had clearly become president some time earlier, Johnson refused to acknowledge his new status or even to leave Parkland Hospital until Kennedy had been officially declared dead. In his mind, anything less would appear presumptuous, if not unconstitutional. Similarly, he would only leave Dallas with the former first lady in tow, the two sharing space with the dead president on board Air Force One as it sped back to the nation's capital. He also insisted on taking the oath of office before departing Love Field, and he wanted Jacqueline Kennedy at his side during the brief ceremony, even though she was clearly in a state of shock and still wearing the same pink wool suit, now soaked in blood, she had been wearing when her husband was shot. News of the ceremony and photographs of the president's oath, with the widow beside him, were immediately released to the media, again with a view to assuaging the American people. So, too, did Johnson take every opportunity in subsequent meetings with the White House staff, congressional leaders, and the media, as well as in his first address to Congress, to stress his commitment to the foreign and domestic policies of the late president. In every way possible, he tried to reassure his countrymen that any apprehensions were unfounded. The government was on guard against a conspiracy, the administration was stable, and important strands of continuity would bind Johnson's presidency to that of his predecessor.[5]

Despite these efforts, not everything went as Johnson had hoped. Seen in hindsight, Texas politics in 1963 portended a major political realignment in the United States and a long-term struggle for control of both political parties. Indeed, the increasingly conservative politics in Texas pointed ultimately to shifting party loyalties in the South, as Democratic voters moved their allegiance to an increasingly conservative Republican Party, especially when it came to issues of civil rights and social justice. Regional realignment led in turn to a more conservative transformation of the Republican Party at the national level, which in turn contributed ultimately to the poisonous politics and polarized political deadlock so evident by the end of the century. Much of this would be revealed in the years ahead, though even the early signs were enough to add weight to the widespread nervousness and sense of foreboding that followed Kennedy's assassination. More obvious in the short term were tensions within the Democratic Party, which was already dividing into liberal and conservative, northern and southern wings. This division, basically a struggle for control of the party, had been the inspiration behind Kennedy's trip to Texas in November 1963. It was a division, moreover, that Johnson's rhetoric of unity and continuity could not easily overcome, not least because he and Robert Kennedy were already on the edge of a major battle for party leadership and the presidency.[6]

This battle had a personal as well as a party dimension. To say that Robert Kennedy and Lyndon Johnson were vastly different personalities would be an understatement. They were not so much polar opposites as repelling opposites. Johnson was almost a stereotype of the tall Texan. Six feet three inches in height, with broad shoulders, a thick upper body, and hands the size of bear paws, he was more like a force of nature than a mere human. He used his large hands and substantial body as weapons in any conversation, so aggressively that his demeanor could seem threatening, even to old friends. Full of hyperbole and tall tales, usually told with language foul enough to wither a witness, he would swarm over his company, his hands flailing, his body looming large above theirs, and his face so close they could have felt the spit from his mouth. A master tactician and manipulator as Senate majority leader, he was ever the pragmatic politician with enormous authority and a solid record of achievement. Not surprisingly, he felt utterly bored, unappreciated, and underutilized as vice president, and he blamed his fate on Robert Kennedy, the attorney general whom everyone considered the real vice president.

Kennedy's style was much different. Small framed and much younger than Johnson, he was also more passionate about his convictions, more a moralist than a pragmatist, and more a power broker than a politician. He spoke with a hard New England accent rather than Johnson's Texas twang, and abhorred Johnson's coarse language, his long-winded tall tales, and every inch of his Texas style, from the ten-gallon hat on his head to the boots on his feet. His humor ran to sarcasm rather than storytelling and his style could be abrupt to the point of rudeness. Whereas Johnson was full of bombast, Kennedy was shy, almost withdrawn, and liked to keep a fair amount of space between himself and those around him. Like his older brother, moreover, Robert Kennedy was easily bored and obviously uncomfortable with physical contact of the sort that Johnson lavished on just about everybody. Perhaps the only attributes the two men had in common were those that actually drove them apart. Both had tempers that flared easily; both were impatient; both were thin-skinned when it came to being criticized; and both suffered from an inner insecurity and fear of losing. President Kennedy had tried with some success to harness the mutual animosity that divided his vice president from his attorney general. But with his death in November 1963, the president's restraining hand was gone and the field was thrown open to the kind of unbridled rivalry that followed.[7]

That rivalry dated back at least to the 1960 primary campaign for the Democratic Party's presidential nomination, particularly the party's nominating convention in Los Angeles. There, Kennedy and Johnson vied for party delegates, one representing the northern liberal wing of the party, the other its increasingly conservative southern wing. Trailing in the delegate count, Johnson's backers tried to undercut Kennedy's lead by attacking his integrity and the honor of his family. They claimed that Kennedy suffered from Addison's disease and was therefore medically unfit for the highest office, a claim that was right on the first count but not on the second. They also impugned Kennedy's record as a US senator and then, for good measure, denounced his father as a Nazi appeaser in the 1930s, not to mention a ruthless capitalist who was trying to buy the presidency for his son. Although Kennedy could roll with these punches, and would ultimately prevail, his brother and campaign manager could not. Nor could Robert Kennedy tolerate his brother's decision to offer Johnson the vice presidential slot on the party ticket; indeed, he may have conspired against that decision with the help of northern liberals and labor leaders who considered Johnson too southern and too conservative to trust.[8] After the new administration took office, moreover, Robert Kennedy, together with many of his friends and allies in government, lost no opportunity to belittle the new vice president, denigrate his contributions to the president's programs, and question whether he should remain on the ticket in the next election – the very election that brought the president to Texas in hopes of uniting the party and raising funds for the 1964 campaign.[9]

The same personal animosities and political divisions surfaced almost immediately after President Kennedy was killed. Robert Kennedy, as well as the Kennedy staffers who traveled with the president to Texas, thought it presumptuous of Johnson to return to Washington on Air Force One, the president's plane, instead of the more or less identical plane that normally accommodated the vice president. They were equally disturbed when Johnson wanted Kennedy's remains, as well as his widow, to travel with him; when he decided to take the oath of office while still in Dallas; when he asked the former first lady to stand by his side; and when he rushed Evelyn Lincoln, Kennedy's secretary, to vacate her Oval Office perch. Johnson returned at least some of the venom, poking fun at Robert Kennedy's diminutive stature, high-pitched voice, and Harvard friends. He also complained when the attorney general, boarding Air Force One at Andrews Air Force Base, failed to acknowledge him as the new president, and when Kennedy staffers, on the plane and later, found it hard to conceal their contempt for the man they had once called Senator Cornpone. Johnson was especially irked when Kennedy appeared to frustrate the early exercise of his constitutional rights and responsibilities, as when his late entrance disrupted Johnson's first cabinet meeting, or when he tried to thwart the president's plans to move into the Oval Office and address Congress as quickly as possible.[10]

If Kennedy saw these plans as insensitive to the family's personal tragedy, the new president saw them as necessary to reassure his fellow citizens that their government was working and the new administration had legitimacy. As noted earlier, Johnson suspected that a Cuban, Soviet, or CIA conspiracy lay behind Kennedy's murder, and this was one reason for his decision to take the oath of office as soon as possible. He must have thought of President Lincoln's assassination, which had been part of a broad conspiracy that included plans to assassinate other government officials, especially Vice President Andrew Johnson and Secretary of State William Henry Seward, who was actually wounded. Two other presidents had been assassinated since Lincoln – James Garfield and William McKinley – and still others, including Harry Truman, had been the targets of attempted assassinations. In almost every case, the incident had provoked widespread, if unfounded, fears of a broader conspiracy. Seen in this light, Johnson's fears were not without precedent, although they went much further than his colleagues knew at the time.

Always a bit paranoid, he apparently suspected that Robert Kennedy wanted to stall the new president in the exercise of his authority, maybe even challenge his constitutional right to the office and thus pave the way for another Kennedy in the White House. His suspicions may have stemmed from what had long been some confusion regarding the constitutional provisions governing succession when a president dies in office. The question was whether or not the vice president filled the remainder of the dead president's term or simply remained vice president, exercising presidential authority, until a new president could be selected, perhaps by special election. The issue first arose following the death in office of President William Henry Harrison, whereupon Vice President John Tyler assumed the presidency for the remainder of Harrison's term, virtually the entire four years. No one challenged Tyler's right to do so, despite the constitutional confusion, which would not be fully clarified until 1967, when Congress passed the Twenty-Fifth Amendment. Given these circumstances, and in light of the bitter animosity between the two men, it would not be surprising if Johnson suspected Robert Kennedy and his allies of conspiring against his presidency.[11]

In any event, if rushing the oath of office was part of a larger plan to steady the country's nerves in the midst of a major cultural trauma – and this was surely the goal – Johnson was not altogether successful. His rivalry with Robert Kennedy, reflecting as it did a wider struggle within the Democratic Party, divided the new administration and defied his efforts to stabilize emotions in a country shaken by the assassination. To achieve this goal, Johnson needed to supplement his own efforts with help from Kennedy's family and friends, especially from Jacqueline Kennedy, whose staging of the president's funeral did more than anything else to sooth a suffering nation.

III

As president and commander in chief, Kennedy was entitled to a state funeral. And in state funerals, most of the mourning and burial rituals are prescribed by tradition and codified in a manual titled *State, Official, and Special Military Funeral Policies and Plans*. The Military District of Washington, then commanded by Major General Philip C. Wehle, had general responsibility for such funerals. Founded in the Second World War as part of a larger plan to defend the capital city, it was headquartered at Fort Meyer and included an army unit known as the "Old Guard," which not only protected the Tomb of the Unknowns at Arlington National Cemetery but also conducted state funerals as well as somewhat similar military funerals for deceased officers above a certain rank. The Old Guard was as ready for Kennedy's funeral as it could be, given the circumstances. Although Franklin Roosevelt was the last president to be so honored, the Military District of Washington had revised its plan for state funerals as recently as 1958. It had used the new plan for the burial of the Unknowns that year, and had been anticipating another state funeral for some time. After all, former presidents Truman and Eisenhower were of advanced age, as were retired general Douglas MacArthur and former president Herbert Hoover. Indeed, Hoover, at eighty-nine years of age, was near death in New York and the Old Guard had recently rehearsed for his funeral. So it was that all preparations for a state funeral were in place, although no one could anticipate that it would be the funeral of the youngest man ever elected to the highest office and the only president whose parents would outlive him.[12]

Given their preparations, it was not surprising to see the Old Guard snap into action as soon as it learned of the president's death. The body bearers were selected almost immediately, as were members of the so-called Death Watch. Reminiscent of an ancient military tradition, the Death Watch would stand guard at each corner of the president's casket, wherever it was, until he was finally laid to rest. Other commands also acted quickly, including the Army Band at Fort Myer, the Air Force Pipe Band, which cancelled a scheduled performance in New Orleans, and the Old Guard's famous Fife and Drum Corps, which had entertained President Kennedy and his guests during the famous state dinner at Mount Vernon in 1961. At the same time, several casket teams and Honor Guards raced to Andrews Air Force Base where they quickly formed into different details, one as an Honor Guard for the new president, one to move the former president's casket from Air Force One to the tarmac, and one to accompany the president's remains to Joseph Gawler's Sons Funeral Home for autopsy and embalming. This is where the Death Watch assembled, according to Jim Leeke, and where it was using the space reserved to rehearse, over and over again, the silent, slow-motion drill it would execute when the guards changed every thirty minutes.

Not all went as planned. The friends and Secret Service agents who had traveled with the president to Texas, having battled the Texas state coroner's office almost to the point of a fist fight in order to remove the president's remains for autopsy in Washington rather than Dallas, now muscled out the military casket team as it tried to move the president's body from Air Force One to the tarmac. They were "like a mother holding a dead child to her breast," Major General Wehle said of the president's entourage. Once on the ground, moreover, Jacqueline Kennedy decided to forgo Gawler's and take her dead husband, a former navy man, to Bethesda Naval Hospital for autopsy, forcing the Death Watch at Gawler's to abandon its drills and rush to the new location, where it arrived just in time to receive the former president.[13]

While all this was underway, the Military District of Washington also dispatched its ceremonies officer to establish contact with the former president's staff in the White House.[14] The goal here was to coordinate its efforts with those of the Kennedy family. Only forty-two years old when he entered office, Kennedy had not thought to write his own funeral instructions, as other presidents had done. In fact, when Kenny O'Donnell and others complained about the choice of Johnson as a running mate in 1960, Kennedy said they had nothing to worry about. After all, Johnson was several years older and had already suffered a major heart attack, whereas he was much too young and far too healthy "to die in office."[15] Accordingly, when Kennedy was killed, important decisions, such as his burial site, religious rites to be observed, musical pieces to be performed, and more were left to his widow and family, all of whom were mired in a grief so profound it seemed frozen to their faces. Adding to their burden, moreover, was the Catholic practice of burying the dead within three days of passing. This left the family with no more than seventy-two hours to make all arrangements, some of which would have to be determined almost immediately.

Not only did Jacqueline Kennedy muster the strength and composure to handle the difficult task before her, she had a platform on which she could build. Her own sense of history now combined with her experience in staging the presidency to produce a period of mourning and a funeral that blended civic traditions with Catholic convictions, personal expressions with rituals of state. The final performance, which was nothing short of magnificent, struck a deep emotional chord in the American people, further enshrined the president's legacy in American memory, and helped to mend, at least temporarily, the social fabric torn by his assassination. In this production, moreover, the first lady served not only as director and producer of what was basically a national drama. She also took center stage as a principal actor whose audience on hand and through the media once again took great pride in what she had to offer and what it said, not only about her late husband but also about themselves.

Her contributions began to unfold as Air Force One raced home from Dallas with President Kennedy's casket tucked securely into a rear compartment. Sitting next to the casket, the widow found herself surrounded by some of her husband's closest friends, notably members of the so-called Irish Mafia that had come to the White House from Boston in

1961. At one point, the little compartment resembled a sacred space, a winged chapel soaring skyward with the former first lady keeping vigil over her husband's body. One by one, his former colleagues came forward, dropped to one knee, and whispered prayerful words of comfort in her ear, much as the Virgin Mary had been sustained by her son's apostles. At other points, the gathering resembled an Irish wake, one of several that would take place over the next three days. The widow sipped two glasses of scotch, a whisky she had never tasted before, and remembered, among other things, how her husband had enjoyed the singing of Luigi Vena, a Boston tenor who performed at their wedding. Kenny O'Donnell, Dave Powers, and Larry O'Brien, trying desperately to anesthetize their own pain, had much more to drink and spent even more time reminiscing about their dead friend, as was customary at an Irish wake. O'Donnell and Powers recalled the president's last visit with his father in Hyannis Port, as well as the visit he had made to his son's grave in Brookline, Massachusetts. Together with the former first lady, they also recalled his recent trip to Ireland, where he fell in love with Celtic music, Irish ballads, and bagpipes.[16]

It was in this setting that Jacqueline Kennedy made her first decisions about the period of mourning and the funeral that would follow. She vowed that Luigi Vena would sing Schubert's "Ave Maria" at her husband's funeral Mass. Inspired by her own memories and those of the Irish Mafia, she also decided to incorporate into her husband's funeral a group of Irish military cadets whose drill performance had impressed him during his trip to Ireland, as well as a band of pipers from the Black Watch of the Royal Highlanders, whose recent White House concert had drawn rave reviews from the president. More importantly, she decided to reunite her husband with their dead children in a common burial plot, what would become a family plot, wherever it might be. These decisions, all symbolic and some highly theatrical, would begin to link the funeral to the president's Catholic religion, his Irish ancestry, his love of family, and his personal preferences. In effect, they would lend emotional weight to the funeral and personalize it in ways that most Americans would appreciate. After all, they were burying a president, to be sure, but also a man of the people, a man of faith, like other men, who loved his family and honored the ways of his ancestors.[17]

It was also on Air Force One that Jackie made other decisions about how she would present herself and her husband in the days ahead. Of these, her decision to witness Johnson's oath of office was one of the most important. Many Kennedy advisors thought Johnson both selfish and callous for demanding her presence. But she disagreed. "In the light of history," she told Kenny O'Donnell, "it would be better if I was there." As this remark suggests, Jackie clearly understood the role she was playing in a moment of great historical significance, though her view of the moment may have been different from Johnson's. If Johnson saw her presence as affirming the continuity of history under the new administration, she may have seen it as one more scene in a dramatic performance of her life and the afterlife of her husband. In this first agonizing moment of public exposure, she revealed not only the strength and dignity that would be so evident, and so inspiring, in the days ahead, but also the themes of duty, service, and sacrifice that had been key elements in her husband's political rhetoric and public image.[18]

This also helps to explain her dress, which became yet another symbol with a similar message. While she managed to remove fragments of her husband's brain tissue from her face and hair, she refused to change her blood-stained dress, which now became a costume in the drama of her husband's funeral, a theatrical prop sure to stir emotions in her audience. She wanted the American people to see what they had done, as she put it. Though later surprised to learn that Kennedy had been murdered by a self-proclaimed communist rather than a right-wing segregationist, she was nonetheless convinced, at the time and later, that his assassination was a brutal byproduct of the increasingly violent political culture that her husband was trying to moderate with his trip to Texas and efforts to reconcile the two wings of the Democratic Party. The bloody dress symbolized that culture, and her decision to keep it on should be read as part of the message she wanted the president's funeral to convey, and Americans to remember – that of her husband as a heroic peacemaker who had sacrificed his life trying to calm a roiling nation.[19]

A similar message followed in her decision to take the president's remains to the United States Naval Hospital in Bethesda, Maryland, rather than Gawler's Funeral Home in Washington, DC. Gawler's was a well-known establishment. It had handled funeral arrangements for many leading citizens, including William Howard Taft, Franklin Roosevelt, James Forrestal, and John Foster Dulles. Nevertheless, Jackie declined to use it. She consistently sought to protect her husband's damaged appearance from public view, as she had done at Parkland Hospital when she covered his shattered head with the suit jacket of Secret Service agent Clint Hill. She wanted him remembered as he was in life. Initially, this meant opposing a formal autopsy and rejecting any involvement by a private funeral home. And when these conditions proved impossible, it meant limiting the number of people who could view the president's remains and using facilities such as the naval hospital over which she and her family had greater control. At the same time, moreover, Jackie did not want an autopsy to reveal her husband's medical problems, which he had consistently denied, or the drugs he had been taking. What is more, Kennedy was a navy veteran whose wartime heroism as the captain of PT 109 had been central to his popular image and success in politics. By selecting Bethesda Naval Hospital instead of Gawler's, Jackie was asking everyone to recall her husband's heroic service and previous sacrifice on behalf of the nation.[20]

Similar thinking would ultimately inform her decision about where the president would be buried, which also began to take shape as Air Force One raced his remains back to the nation's capital. For members of the Irish Mafia, there was really no decision to make. It was axiomatic in their minds that President Kennedy would be buried in Boston. That was his native ground, where he could be laid to rest with his son Patrick, whom he had buried there just months before. A similar choice had the early endorsement of the president's mother, Rose Kennedy, as well as other members of the family when they discussed the subject as Air Force One was en route to Washington. There was even some talk of a large tomb in the center of Boston Common – perhaps, one imagines, something like Grant's Tomb in New York City. It seemed a natural choice, if not an inevitable one, to many friends and relatives, but not to the former first lady.

When the subject came up on Air Force One, she hesitated to agree with the Irish Mafia, recalling instead a conversation she had with her husband near the end of his first year in office. Returning to the White House after a funeral, she wondered aloud where they might be buried. The president found it difficult to take the subject seriously. After casually suggesting the Kennedy family compound in Hyannis, he made some joke about a large mausoleum or perhaps a tomb like that of the pharaohs, whereupon Jackie suggested Arlington National Cemetery in Virginia as the most appropriate choice. After all, she said, as president, he belonged to the whole nation, not just to Massachusetts. Although Kennedy's friend Ben Bradlee and Secretary of Defense Robert McNamara were formulating similar arguments in Washington, Jackie decided to postpone a decision in light of the pressure coming from other directions. Nevertheless, it is clear from her exchange with O'Donnell and Powers that in her mind, more was involved than a family funeral and burial in the family plot. Where she buried her husband had important symbolic significance and the symbolism should convey a message consistent not only with the other decisions she was making but also with the many policies he had pursued and with his popular image, as both he and his wife had framed it on the White House stage.[21]

The gesture of greatest symbolic significance, of course, was her decision to model her husband's funeral after that of Abraham Lincoln, which meant decorating the White House with appropriate props, scenery, and other theatrical devices. This decision was made at Bethesda Naval Hospital, as she was looking for some guidance on how to stage her husband's burial. While the manual of the Military District of Washington provided operational details, there was no model for the personal and emotional side of a state funeral. Officials at the State Department were scrambling for some description of FDR's funeral, the last to be held in Washington, but at the hospital, all Jackie had in mind was a sketch of Lincoln's body lying in repose in the East Room of the White House. She had seen the drawing, she thought, in an early issue of the White House guidebook, and linking her husband's legacy to that of the sixteenth president must have appealed to her as consistent symbolically with the message she wanted his funeral to impart. Accordingly, she asked the White House staff to find whatever they could on Lincoln's funeral.[22]

By that time, a group of Kennedy's aides, friends, and family members had begun to assemble in the White House office of presidential assistant Ralph Dungan. They convened there almost constantly over the next three days, working red-eyed through the nights in order to plan all aspects of the president's funeral. Leadership fell to Sargent Shriver, President Kennedy's brother-in-law, who had been a top manager at the Merchandise Mart – the vast retail enterprise that Joe Kennedy owned in Chicago – and was now director of the newly established Peace Corps. Shriver was a man of enormous organizational and management skills, surpassing those of any other member of the Kennedy family, and he put them to use in a race to prepare the funeral and burial in the very short time available. His principal liaisons were Robert and Jacqueline Kennedy, especially Jackie, who intervened as necessary to put her own stamp on the proceedings.

Once decisions were made, Shriver handed out assignments to those around him. He used Lieutenant Colonel Paul Miller, the ceremonies officer for the Military District of Washington, to coordinate the family's wishes with its own well-established arrangements for handling state funerals, including arrangements for the president's lying in repose in the

East Room of the White House and lying in state in the Capitol Rotunda. He collaborated with Angier Biddle Duke, the State Department's chief protocol officer, on how to handle international leaders and diplomats who might attend the funeral. Although a Catholic Mass would be celebrated in the White House for the benefit of the Kennedy family, Shriver, self-conscious of the line between church and state and aware of the role that religion had played in Kennedy's 1960 campaign, met with religious leaders to make sure that all denominations could share in vigil services for the dead president. He asked Adlai Stevenson to review the protocol for international guests, made initial arrangements for a funeral Mass with Richard Cardinal Cushing, and set a variety of colleagues to work fixing schedules and drawing up list after list of those who would be included in the rituals of mourning and burial. He asked Richard Goodwin, at that time one of his top aides in the Peace Corps, to explore Lincoln's lying in repose, and Goodwin enlisted the help of Arthur Schlesinger Jr., the historian in the White House, who worked with others to scour the Library of Congress for whatever they could find.[23]

With that information in hand, Shriver asked others to locate the catafalque on which Lincoln's casket had been placed for lying in state, and William Walton to decorate the East Room before the president's casket arrived, just hours away. A Kennedy friend, former newspaper correspondent, and now an artist living in Washington, Walton had worked with the president and his wife on their plans to save Lafayette Square and on the construction of a new center for the performing arts in the capital city. His artistic temper told him immediately that it would be a mistake to make the East Room look exactly as it did for Lincoln's funeral. So he made changes, though always changes he knew the first lady would appreciate as consistent with the story she wanted the funeral to elaborate. He placed kneelers where the casket would lie, so that religious leaders from a variety of faiths could take turns praying over the dead president's remains. Lanterns would line the White House drive when the ambulance conveying the president's body arrived from Bethesda Naval Hospital. Honor Guards, a casket team, and the Death Watch would be ready to perform their dreary duties. Working with the White House staff, Walton found enough black crepe to cover the door and window frames, as well as the chandeliers in the East Room and the grand entrance under the North Portico of the White House. The idea came from what he had learned of Lincoln's lying in repose, though Walden's arrangement was less heavy and more eloquent, and thus very much in keeping with Jacqueline Kennedy's taste in fashion. Similarly, the original plans for heavily ornate candlesticks and a lavish five-foot crucifix, both reminiscent of Lincoln's funeral, gave way to plain wooden sticks borrowed from St. Stephen's Church in Washington and a beautiful Benedictine cross confiscated from Shriver's bedroom wall. Walden put the cross at the foot of the president's casket, as he did flowers, some of which came from the White House garden. What is more, his team finally located two catafalques. One was the original on which Lincoln's remains had rested; the other was a duplicate used in 1958 for the interment of the Unknowns who had died in the Second World War and the Korean conflict. As the Kennedy team worked it out, the original, which was stored in the Capitol, would remain there to receive the president's body when it lay in state in the Rotunda, while the other would serve a similar purpose in the East Room.[24]

At 4:30 A.M. on Saturday, November 23, the fallen leader and his wife arrived home for their last official appearance on the White House stage where they had given so many splendid performances in their roles as president and first lady. The frantic work of the last hours, finished just moments before their arrival, seemed to pay off. Having staged so many spectacular events herself, Jacqueline Kennedy must have been more than satisfied with what William Manchester called "a scene of indescribable drama: the flame lit drive, the deep black against the white columns, the shrouded door way, the East Room in deep mourning, the catafalque ready to receive the coffin."[25] It could not have escaped her notice that over the next three days, her husband's body would rest first on a catafalque used in honors to the fallen heroes of the Second World War and then on the catafalque that had once held the remains of Abraham Lincoln. When it left the White House, moreover, Kennedy's body would be carried on the same gun caisson that had carried Franklin Roosevelt's remains to the Capitol Rotunda for lying in state. Symbolically, these three props now linked the dead president back to the war that had made him a national hero and then to two of the great reform presidents in American history. After all, this had been her intention, the message she wanted embedded in the symbolism of her husband's funeral and in the memory of the American people.

One more decision remained. After the casket had been moved to the East Room and placed on the catafalque, and after the widow had prayed beside it, she and Robert Kennedy had to decide whether it would be opened for public viewing, both at the White House and in the Rotunda. Despite the shattering wound to the head, the president's face had not been damaged and the wound itself would not be apparent to viewers.

McNamara and others argued strenuously for an open casket when the subject first came up at Bethesda Naval Hospital, and then again at the White House, when Robert Kennedy asked for their views. Whatever the family wanted, McNamara said, could not override the need of the people to view the remains of their deceased leader and pay their respects. Others who viewed the body in the East Room came to a different conclusion. "It's a wax dummy," Bill Walton said in a harsh verdict. Arthur Schlesinger also considered the remains "too waxen, too made up," and others, sharing the same opinion, thought the former president simply did not look like himself.

As in so many things, it was the former first lady who had to decide. From the start, she had considered an open casket grotesque, no matter how her husband might appear. But more importantly, perhaps, she did not want the last costume he wore on the White House stage to look like a "rubber mask," as Chuck Spalding put it, or like the waxen figure in a Madame Tussaud exhibit, as the first lady herself would later explain. Her thinking was the same as it had been when she covered her husband's head at Parkland Hospital and when she turned to the naval hospital rather than Gawler's to perform his autopsy. She wanted people to remember him as he was in life – attractive, animated, and full of expression – and to hold that memory forever. The coffin would be closed. In this decision, as in others, the former first lady was staging her husband's funeral, as she had so many events in the White House, with a view to protecting and preserving the image he had cultivated as president.[26]

With this decision behind them, the Kennedy family and friends retired to the first of two Irish wakes over the next forty-eight hours. These occasions saw the usual reminiscing and storytelling. There was plenty to eat and drink and a fair amount of wicked humor, often typical of an Irish wake and of the Kennedys in particular. At the first, Robert Kennedy's wife, Ethel, suffered the embarrassment of having her wig pulled from her head and passed around the room like a rag mop for all the laughing guests to model. At the second, Aristotle Onassis, a late invitee to the funeral and close friend of Jackie's sister, had to endure the ridicule of Robert Kennedy and others poking fun at his enormous wealth and soliciting a false promise that he would donate half of his fortune to charity.[27]

Wakes like these might have helped to staunch, if only temporarily, the great burden of grief that mourners felt, particularly family members or those who were close friends of the deceased. Other traditions, also invoked, could provide some comfort as well, though never joy, as was the case when Jacqueline and Robert Kennedy looked last upon the late president. In this case, they were enacting the ancient ritual, dating back more than six thousand years, of leaving grave goods with the dead. On the morning of November 24, they stepped into the East Room, opened the casket for the last time, and left the dead president their parting gifts. Jackie placed letters from herself and each of her children inside the casket, along with a pair of gold cufflinks and a piece of carved scrimshaw, both of which she had given as gifts to her husband. Robert contributed his PT 109 tie clasp and a silver rosary, whereupon Jackie clipped a tuft of her husband's hair and shared it with her brother-in-law.[28]

In times long past, grave gifts, such as food, weapons, tools, and money, had been intended to pacify the spirits of the dead or aid their passage to the next life. More recently, as in Kennedy's case, they were tokens of affection and appreciation for a lost loved one. These and other rites formed parts of a funeral that most people took for granted, not always knowing their ancient origins and sober meaning. So it was with the thousands of floral bouquets on display through the lying in state and the burial, the water used to bless the casket and the gravesite, the candles that burned everywhere. All of these were life cycle rituals used widely in different cultures to symbolize the death and hopeful rebirth of the deceased and the cleansing of his soul before passage to the next life.[29]

Obvious throughout Kennedy's funeral, even if not always understood, these ritual practices and their symbolic significance complemented the civic traditions embedded in the funeral manual of the Military District of Washington. These included the riderless horse with empty boots reversed in the stirrups. This ancient ritual, symbolizing a fallen leader, was widely used in other cultures, dating back, some say, to the Roman Republic and first used in the United States during Lincoln's funeral. The playing of "Taps" at the gravesite, another much noted feature, was also well established in American custom, as common in state and military funerals as rifle and cannon salutes, including the twenty-one gun salute reserved for deceased presidents. Standard procedure also governed the order of march in what was fundamentally a military procession, as appropriate for a president who was also commander in chief of the armed forces. Together with the riderless horse, the marchers escorted the president's remains from resting in repose in the White House to lying in state in the Capitol, and from there on November 25 to a requiem Mass in St. Matthew's Cathedral before proceeding to Arlington Cemetery for the burial. The procession included nearly two thousand members of the armed forces, most notably the Joint Chiefs of Staff, all parading in unison to the sound of beating drums, another standard practice, with state, federal, and presidential flags on display and, at one point, a flyover of fifty military aircraft, one for each state of the union.

The heavy symbolism embedded in the procession, especially the flag presentations, displays of military might, and a good deal of patriotic music, not to mention the ordered ranking of the participants, were typical of state funerals, as they were of nineteenth-century civic parades, which historian Mary Ryan has described as collective and ritualized cultural performances. They were also familiar expressions of an American civic religion that transcended sectarian differences, and were particularly important in the case of Kennedy's funeral, where they could reassure a country still reeling from the tragic death of a popular leader who seemed to personify American ideals.[30] All carried emotional content and symbolic meaning, though none more so than the symbols contributed by the former first lady.

IV

Prior to the president's lying in repose in the East Room, for example, family and friends assembled for the first of two Masses to be held in the White House. Although a Catholic Mass, it was not part of the official program and Jackie was careful to invite friends and colleagues from a variety of different religions. Besides recalling the president's pledge to respect the separation of church and state, which he made in the 1960 campaign, the brief ceremony also recalled his commitment to the principle of inclusiveness, which would be evident in the rest of the day's program as well. For the repose itself, to cite a further example, the first lady went beyond the formal protocol as outlined in the official manual of the Military District of Washington. The manual allocated time for each branch of government to say farewell to the president, with members of the executive branch, including White House staff, cabinet members, and other presidential appointees moving through first, then members of the Supreme Court, followed by members of Congress and state governors, and concluding with the heads of diplomatic missions in Washington. Symbolizing the traditional hierarchy of government authority, the progression reminded a nervous nation that the normal order of things remained intact and helped, in this way, to restore the sense of stability and security disrupted by the assassination. In this case, as in others, however, Jackie made a contribution of her own. She invited members of the press to pay their respects, which they did in large numbers, and she included as well a long line of butlers, maids, doormen, gardeners, and other members of the household staff. Both gestures were surely intended to remind everyone of the president's popularity with the media and of his concern for the lives of ordinary people.[31]

She conveyed a similar message in other decisions, including her choice of the gun caisson that would carry the president's casket to the Capital Routunda. Plain and simple by comparison with the ornate funeral wagons that bore Lincoln's remains, it suited Jackie's personal taste and the democratic ideal she wanted the funeral to convey, particularly since it was the same caisson that had been used in FDR's funeral. Something similar could be said of the simple candlesticks and the small but dignified cross that surrounded the president's casket as it rested in repose in the White House. In addition, Jackie confirmed her decisions to include the Irish cadets and their drill of mourning in the funeral arrangements. She made sure the Old Guard's Fife and Drum Corps and the Black Watch of the Royal Highlanders also had a place, and then added the Air Force Pipe Band as well. She also approved Robert Kennedy's wish to add Green Berets to the Honor Guard and made important decisions about the music that would accompany the funeral processions. These included, famously, her decisions to play "Hail to the Chief" at a much slower tempo than was typical and to have only the haunting sound of muffled drums on the procession to the Capitol. Some of these decisions recalled the president's fondness for military drills and the music of bagpipes; some reminded witnesses of his commitment to the Army Special Forces, which he had established; some added a particularly theatrical note to a solemn occasion. Nothing escaped her attention, including the design of funeral invitations and Mass cards; floral selections for the East Room, the Capitol Rotunda, St. Matthew's Cathedral, and the gravesite; and the use of matching gray rather than black horses to pull the president's caisson. Even the smallest detail was important to her, especially if it added emotional force to the drama of the president's funeral or personalized the event with symbols and theatrical staging that went beyond the rule book of the Military District of Washington.[32]

Most importantly, Jackie finally came to the conclusion that her husband would be buried in Arlington National Cemetery. She had been leaning strongly in that direction since flying back to Washington on Air Force One. The Irish Mafia still favored a Boston burial, as did some members of the Kennedy family, but it took only one trip to Arlington Cemetery to harden her initial inclination into a firm resolve. Secretary of Defense Robert McNamara, who had always leaned toward the Arlington site, visited several possible locations in the early hours of November 23. He then brought others, including Robert Kennedy and his sisters, to review his selections and won their support. The decision was still the widow's to make, however, and while the approval of her in-laws made the decision easier, other considerations weighed more heavily on her thinking, especially after making her own visit to Arlington. She remained convinced that her husband, as president of the whole nation, not just his home state, should be laid to rest at a national site. But cementing the decision in her mind was the discovery made by her friend Bill Walton that the Arlington site lay on a direct line from the Custis-Lee Mansion to the Lincoln Memorial on the other side of the Potomac River. As with the catafalque and other efforts to imitate Lincoln's funeral, the former first lady no doubt found the symbolism of the Arlington site irresistible. It conveyed again the message she wanted her husband's funeral to forge in the memory of the American people, namely, that he had inherited Lincoln's legacy and, like Lincoln, had sacrificed himself to the principles of national unity, freedom, and civil rights that both he and the sixteenth president shared.[33]

The decision on a burial site did not end Jackie's intervention in the funeral plan, which was adjusted in still other ways to capture the meanings she had in mind. She agreed that Cardinal Cushing, a Kennedy friend, should preside over the funeral Mass, but battled the cardinal and others over who would assist in the proceedings. She wanted Bishop Philip Hannan to assist Cushing, rather than Archbishop Patrick O'Boyle of Washington, who would have been the normal choice. A former paratrooper, Hannan was friendly with the Kennedys and was younger and more attractive than O'Boyle. What is more, he reminded the widow of her assassinated husband, was an excellent speaker, and would deliver the formal eulogy. This was to be the only eulogy in the funeral Mass and would consist of President Kennedy's favorite quotes from scripture and excerpts from his inaugural address. The entire eulogy would be prepared under her close supervision, showing again her painstaking attention to detail and how she used every opportunity to affirm her husband's commitment to the values embedded in his faith and in the policies and programs of the New Frontier.[34]

Bishop Hannan would deliver his eulogy in St. Matthew's Cathedral in Washington, where the funeral Mass would be held over the stiff opposition of Catholic prelates and many of those working in the White House. They much preferred the Shrine of the Immaculate Conception. A vast, imposing edifice on the campus of Catholic University in northeast

Washington, the shrine was richly decorated and perhaps the only Catholic church in the country large enough to handle the substantial crowd that would attend the service. Nevertheless, the former first lady rejected it out of hand. She hated its name, considered it too ornate, and neither she nor her husband had attended services there. They had attended the more humble St. Matthew's Cathedral, which was located in the heart of the city not far from the White House. No doubt the less ostentatious setting of St. Matthew's appealed to her as consistent with the democratic message she wanted to send on her husband's behalf, and with her own preference for simple rather than ornate designs. But the key factors appear to have been its distance from the White House, only six blocks, and her decision to walk behind her husband's casket in the funeral procession on Monday, November 25. Almost everyone opposed that decision as well, not least because it would pose an enormous security risk to her and to all who walked with her. That list would include President Johnson, leading officials in the American government, and heads of state from all over the world, notably French President Charles de Gaulle, who had several times been the target of would-be assassins. In addition, while such walks were not uncommon in the history of state funerals, it was unusual for them to be led by the widow, or to include women at all.[35]

Still, the former first lady would not be deterred, with results that produced one of the most theatrical and poignant moments in the president's funeral, if not in modern American history: the young and beautiful widow, the mother of two fatherless children, dressed in mourning black, including full veil, striding with admirable dignity and purposeful resolve, just two steps ahead of her husband's brothers, as she lead the nation and the world in somber mourning. There can be little doubt about the symbolism of this moment in her mind, revealing, as it did, her own determination to display the courage, sense of duty, and strength of purpose she wanted everyone to associate with her husband, not to mention his role as president of all the people, as peacemaker to battling political factions, as champion of the downtrodden, as leader of the free world. Cabinet officers, congressional leaders, Supreme Court justices, state and city officials, party functionaries and others had come to honor him in a ceremony of national unification. International leaders paid tribute to him as the champion of democracy worldwide, and in doing so, recognized the great power and important role of the United States in global affairs. All fell into line behind his casket and the marching widow who had, with her husband, come to represent, for so many, everything that was to be admired in American life.[36]

As this suggests, the former first lady had become, by this point, more than the scriptwriter, director, and choreographer of her husband's funeral. She now took center stage in that drama and in the process made herself, as much as her husband, an iconic figure in the American mind. Her new role began to reveal itself on the morning of November 24, when she followed her husband's casket out the North Portico of the White House to the caisson that would carry it to the Capitol, where his remains would lie in state throughout the day. This was the first time she had appeared in public since the assassination, and the scene was dramatic, to say the least. She moved forward, holding steady the hands of her two young children, and then paused, standing in silent dignity for a moment on the White House steps, as if inviting the world to observe her dark and sorrowful presence. It was much like her photograph with Lyndon Johnson as he took the oath of office, except that her costume had changed from a blood-soaked dress to mourning black. Otherwise she seemed to be asking her audience to witness again her terrible loss and to see in her quite dignity the great strength, sense of duty, and determined resolve supposedly rooted in American character and reflected as well in the constructed image of her late husband.[37]

An hour later, after the president's casket had been placed on the Lincoln catafalque in the Capitol Rotunda, she delivered the message for a second time. She and her daughter Caroline walked slowly forward and kneeled at the bier, whereupon the former first lady touched the flag that covered her husband's casket, and the little girl, moving her hand under the flag, appeared to console the father inside. This gesture of forlorn love and loneliness brought those in the Rotunda almost to their knees in convulsions of uncontrolled grief. It once more reminded the audience on hand or watching on television of the awful sacrifice the president and his family had made on their behalf, even as it revealed the strength, composure, and dignity of the dutiful wife and mother who had been first lady to the nation. Then, yet another dramatic scene, one destined like the others to become iconic, as Jacqueline Kennedy and her children emerged from St. Matthew's Cathedral following the funeral Mass. Again, the dramatic pause as she stopped center stage on the church steps, a child in each hand, and asked her young son to say farewell to his father. No one who witnessed what followed would ever forget John F. Kennedy Jr. delivering a near-perfect salute, the result of much practice with presidential aides over the past year.[38]

With these gestures, including her determined march behind the caisson to St. Matthew's Cathedral, Jacqueline Kennedy became the central figure in an American sacred service that canonized her husband and assuaged the nation in the wake of a great tragedy. She signaled to the world not only the virtues that she and her husband supposedly embodied but also the virtues that presumably inhered in the American character: a sense of duty to the nation; a willingness to sacrifice for the common good; the importance of family; and the need to act with dignity, courage, strength, and composure. By doing so, she was reminding everyone of what the American people were like at their very best. They could take pride in her example, not to mention the nation's great power, its important role as the defender of freedom world wide, and the respect it inspired from international leaders who gathered to pay their respects to the slain president. In these and other ways, they could feel a renewed sense of well-being, confidence, and unity; reclaim old values for the nation; and calm the storm of confusion and uncertainty that had gripped the country in the aftermath of the assassination.

Nothing else could explain what became a silent celebration of Kennedy and the country as the president's remains progressed from the White House to the Capitol, then to St. Matthew's Cathedral for the funeral Mass, and finally to Arlington National Cemetery for burial. More than one hundred thousand mourners lined the streets over the eighteen blocks between the White House and the Capitol. Looking out of place in the formal procession was a large, somewhat ragtag bunch of rumpled newspaper reporters who had Jacqueline Kennedy's permission to march in honor of the president, whose company they had clearly enjoyed. As the procession passed by, hundreds of heartbroken bystanders, stacked several deep on sidewalks, moved into the street behind the reporters and made themselves part of what became, in effect, a civic parade. Much like the household staff and news people who were invited by the first lady to pay their respects as the president lay in repose, this trail of ordinary people and reporters gave the formal and ordered procession a more open, spontaneous, and democratic appearance, much as Jacqueline Kennedy had intended. In the Rotunda, as Kennedy's body lay in state on the Lincoln catafalque, thousands upon thousands walked past his bier. By nine o'clock Monday morning, when the Rotunda was closed, more than a quarter million people had braved bitterly cold weather and a line that stretched upwards of three miles in order to pay their respects to the dead president. At least twelve thousand had to be turned away, though many of them simply joined more than a million other mourners who positioned themselves along the procession route to St. Matthew's Cathedral and Arlington Cemetery.

The solemn dignity and near-perfect cadence of the marchers, the riderless horse, the muffled drums, the awesome drama of the procession,
inspired perfect silence from the grief-stricken mourners who lined the
streets along the procession route. Even more impressive than the size
and silence of the crowds was their vast diversity: young and old and
everything in between, men and women, people of all ethnic, racial, and
religious backgrounds. It no longer seemed to matter if the president was
a Democrat, if he came from the North, if he was a Catholic. He was
the president of the United States, and everyone seemed to agree that the
attack on him had been an attack on the nation. This conviction added
weight to the sense of renewed solidarity and national pride that Jackie's
performance inspired.[39]

It all came to a conclusion with the burial at Arlington National
Cemetery. This, the last act in the drama of the president's funeral, indeed
of the Kennedy presidency, had all the martial spectacle, all the theatrical displays, and all the symbolism associated with the burial of a head
of state: the twenty-one gun salute in his honor; the last rendition of
"Hail to the Chief"; the national anthem and "God Bless America"; the
mournful wail of "Taps"; the fifty air force jets streaking above the burial
site; Air Force One in its own flyover, bowing its wing to the lost leader;
the last member of the Honor Guard folding the American flag that had
draped his coffin and presenting it to the grieving widow. Other symbols, largely religious, played their part as well: the vast spray of flowers
arranged by Bunny Mellon that ran up the hill behind the grave and symbolized, as had been the case in many cultures for many years, a faith in
life reborn; the blessing of the grave with holy water, yet another symbol
of life renewed; and most importantly, the eternal flame that Jackie and
the Kennedy brothers lit at the end of the hillside service.

This important theatrical device was the last and most enduring symbol contributed by the former first lady. The idea had come to her a
day earlier and, like many of her personal contributions, encountered
substantial opposition. For some it was inappropriate, since there was
already a similar flame honoring the war dead at the Gettysburg battle-
field; some worried that it would appear un-American, reminiscent as
it was of the eternal flame at the Tomb of the Unknown Soldier at the
Arc de Triomphe in Paris; some just considered it impractical over the
long run and impossible to accomplish in the hours ahead. Some suggested alternatives – a rose arbor, for example, or a fountain of bubbling
water. But Jackie batted down every objection and alternative. To her, the
symbolism of the flame must have seemed obvious. Fire, in the form of

candles or incense, had long been typical in religious observances, particularly funerals. In Catholicism, and for Christians generally, it signified the purifying force of Christ and his victory over the forces of darkness. Jackie was probably aware of this particular symbolism, and had certainly observed the presence of candles in religious rituals over the years. But she was no doubt moved even more by the civic symbolism of an eternal flame. After all, it recalled her husband's inaugural address, when he talked about the torch being passed to a new generation of Americans, of which he was both member and leader. The torch, in this case, was the torch of freedom, much like the one atop the Statue of Liberty in New York Harbor. By calling forth this imagery, Jackie was recollecting for all Americans the spirit that had supposedly guided her husband. She was linking his memory to American purpose, his core values to those at the heart of American life, and his policies and principles to a legacy that would light the path to enduring progress. To make the point even more clearly, she would inscribe portions of the president's famous inaugural address on the granite wall that eventually bordered the gravesite.[40]

V

If these were Jackie's intentions, and they clearly were, they were more than fulfilled, judging at least by the public opinion polls taken at the time (and since) and by the eulogies and editorial commentary that appeared in Congress and in the press. As noted earlier, Kennedy's approval ratings in the monthly Gallup polls were consistently above 70 percent, with a high of 83 percent, during his time in office. They seldom dropped below that range, and only twice below 60 percent – the result, no doubt, of his forceful call for new civil rights legislation. What is more, even this decline appeared to be a temporary setback, as his approval rating was on the rebound at the time of his murder. After the assassination, of course, his ratings soared to new heights and remained high in the decades that followed, so much so that he is still cited as one of the most popular of American presidents.[41]

Editorial commentaries and other eulogies gave further evidence of the president's popularity and how widely shared the Kennedy brand had become by the time of his death. They paid tribute to the successful staging of both his presidency and his funeral, in part by reinforcing the messages and images that had marked his performance on the White House stage. By celebrating his character and citing his example, they, like the former first lady, reminded all who would listen what it meant to be an American. They helped to reassure their distraught readers, restore their faith in themselves and the country, and reassemble the pieces of their national identity. This was the way to honor the president's memory, or so they said; but as we will see, it would also have the effect of embellishing Kennedy's emerging status as an American hero of almost mythical proportions.

The amalgam of personality traits and heroic virtues frequently mentioned in these political and editorial eulogies were largely the same as those noted by the many Americans who wrote to Jackie after her husband's death, or who recorded their thinking in subsequent reminiscences about where they were and what they were doing when the president was assassinated. Foremost among them was the president's courage. Time and time again, this virtue topped the list of those mentioned. It could be seen in Kennedy's decision to take a different path from the one traveled by his forceful father, who was far more conservative than his son and more inclined toward isolationism than internationalism. It could be seen in the fortitude and strength of character he displayed in coping with life-threatening illnesses and war injuries, never wallowing in self-pity and never allowing almost constant pain to dampen the ambition he had for himself and the country. Nor do these examples exhaust the list of those cited by commentators and eulogists. Kennedy's courage could also be seen in his heroism as captain of PT 109, his resolve in standing up to anti-Catholic bias during the 1960 election, his confrontation with the Soviets in the Cuban Missile Crisis, and his fight for civil rights and world peace. Kennedy, they agreed, had bravely confronted the most challenging issues of the day, even when it threatened his life, as it did when he traveled to Texas against the advice of many colleagues.[42]

This aspect of the president's character was something he, his wife, and colleagues had quietly lauded throughout his career, and sometimes not so quietly, as when they distributed PT 109 tie clasps at every possible opportunity. For those who eulogized him, however, the president's unflinching courage and fearless devotion to duty were only two of the things that made him the quintessential American. Joseph Alsop, a Kennedy friend, eulogized the president as an intelligent, idealistic, but practical man, a man of grace and good humor with a boundless love of country and confidence in its future.[43] Others noted his sense of history, his tolerance for the views of others, and his relentless pursuit of excellence. Still others praised his devotion to the large Kennedy family, especially his own wife and children, as well as his religious convictions and faith in God. His commitment to the arts drew special notice, too, as did his belief in public service and self-sacrifice, both of which he tried to inspire in others, especially those who came, as he had, from privileged circumstances. And then, of course, there were repeated references to his restless energy, his quick wit and self-deprecating humor, his intellectualism and soaring rhetorical style, his physical attractiveness and unmatchable charm. Taken together, all of these attributes, also celebrated in the personal reminiscences and letters that Jackie received after the president's death, constituted what many saw as Kennedy's personal style.[44] By stressing his many virtues, with barely a word of criticism, eulogists and commentators pictured him in real life as basically identical to the idealized version of the president he had played on the White House stage. Indeed, as Steven R. Goldzwig and Patricia A. Sullivan have pointed out, they made him larger than life itself. He became not so much the archetypal American or the American everyman, but rather the American superman – in effect, a mythical figure whose life could reach beyond the grave if only others followed his example.[45]

These personal attributes, big and small, had supposedly made possible a successful presidency with its share of achievements. The list included such highlights as the Peace Corps, the space program, the Trade Expansion Act, and the Limited Test Ban Treaty, which some saw as Kennedy's crowning achievement. Many commentators were even prepared to give him credit for legislative achievements that were not yet law at the time of his death, notably the major tax cut and the Civil Rights Act that would follow over the next year. They were pleased when the new president pledged to advance these and other items on Kennedy's legislative agenda. In doing so, Johnson was acknowledging the inspiration that Kennedy had provided and recognizing that his death, perhaps more than anything else, had made his goals achievable. What is more, political observers added, these legislative successes would honor the memory of the late president and evince a continuity of leadership and policies, a sense of unity and common purpose that could help the American people transcend the crisis brought on by the president's assassination.[46]

This, too, was a major theme in most editorial and political eulogies. It was important, all agreed, that Americans examine their own culpability in the president's death. They had not done enough to resist the hatred and violence that was surging across the country, like mighty swells rolling inexorably toward some distant and dangerous shore. The result was a shot aimed not only at the president but also at the nation and the government he represented. At the same time, however, it was important to avoid violent recriminations or do anything that might further divide the nation. According to these commentaries, what the country needed now was not simply an admission of collective responsibility but also a new spirit of collective action. "The Republic must go forward," as the *Los Angeles Times* put it. It was time for Americans to unite, not divide, to recommit themselves to the faithful performance of their duties as citizens, and to bring to bear on the nation's problems the same virtues that Kennedy had displayed in life.[47]

Kennedy, they seemed to be saying, exemplified what was really a cluster of virtues at the core of the nation's identity: the love of family and nation; the confidence, courage and compassion to address the challenges of the day; and the spirit of public service and sacrifice, not to mention the optimism and strength of character, that made progress possible. The American people needed to mobilize these same virtues and come together in efforts to aid the poor, end discrimination, negotiate world peace, and promote economic development at home and abroad. This was Kennedy's agenda, they said, and bringing it to fruition would extirpate the guilt, despair, and anxiety that Americans felt at the time of his death. It would replace those feelings with what Joseph Alsop called, paraphrasing Lincoln, "a new birth of hope."[48] If the nation honored Kennedy's memory by completing his unfinished work, what the *Washington Post, Times Herald* described as "eulogy by action," it could transcend the crisis brought on by his death.[49] Indeed, the president would not have died at all. He would live "beyond the grave," as Eugene Patterson wrote in the *Atlanta Constitution*, not only in the nation's collective memory, nor even in his many accomplishments, but also in a "new sense of direction, a new admiration for excellence, a new moral concern."[50]

What is more, many of the same eulogists who celebrated the president's life also celebrated his wife's performance in the drama of her husband's funeral – and for many of the same reasons. She, too, displayed the virtues seemingly evident in her husband's life and so much a part of the nation's aspirational identity. Like her husband, moreover, she, too, became an icon of Americanism and thus an example of how others should live their lives, manage their grief, and move beyond the current crisis. "The performance of Jacqueline Bouvier Kennedy throughout her longest day," intoned the *Cleveland Plain Dealer*, "will be awesomely remembered after many of the events connected" with her husband's assassination have been forgotten. "The ordeal of supporting the President" on the ride to Parkland Hospital "was enough to make strong men collapse." But not Jacqueline Kennedy, who actually helped medical attendants remove her husband's body from the bloody backseat of the presidential limousine. She stood bravely by his side at Parkland until "her worst fears were confirmed," and then sat by his casket as Air Force One traveled back to Washington and as the ambulance carried his remains from Andrews Air Force Base to Bethesda Naval Hospital. She was not paralyzed by her grief, the newspaper added, even doing her duty by standing witness as Lyndon Johnson took the oath of office. "Call it courage, or any of the things that hold thoroughbreds together in the face of massive personal disaster." But whatever it is called, the world will forever "stand in awe of a magnificent performance by a remarkable woman" who "had the perseverance to tend to every detail of her final day with her husband."[51] Preston McGraw, writing for the *Atlanta Constitution*, made the same points, noting as well how the first lady fell to the car floor to hold her wounded husband and managed then, and throughout the day, to meet her obligations and maintain her composure.[52]

Helen Thomas used her syndicated column to describe Jacqueline Kennedy "as ever erect, never faltering, her head high even in grief." Often a critic of the former first lady, Thomas, in this case, was overwhelmed by the way she transformed the tragedy of Dallas into "the grandeur of Washington with a majestic state funeral that assured" her husband a place on the honor roll of American history. She went on to describe the "dignified ceremonies" and cite some of the most symbolic and emotionally charged gestures in Jackie's theatrical performance: her exit from the North Portico of the White House with her two children in hand; her prayers with her daughter before her husband's casket in the Rotunda; her march behind his caisson to St. Matthew's Cathedral; her son's prompted salute to his father; the eternal flame. Thomas was aware that all of these and other gestures had been part of a carefully orchestrated drama produced, directed, and performed by the former first lady. She "called most of the dramatic signals," Thomas concluded, and "enthralled" the world with a flare and decorum that few other women could muster, particularly under such difficult circumstances.[53] Others made the same points about the widow's performance, adding to the list her decision to include the Black Watch, the Irish Guard, the Green Berets, and more to the funeral procession. Still others considered her performance all the more remarkable in light of her young age and the simultaneous need to meet her maternal responsibilities, especially her plans to carry through with birthday parties for her two children.[54]

Louise Hutchison, writing in the *Chicago Tribune*, described the new widow in words often reserved for her husband, and in the process somewhat offset the paternalistic language of praise that marked so many other comments. Jackie was a woman "of courage and steel," she wrote, a figure of "towering strength" who wears "her mourning black like regal trappings" and "who has told the nation by her actions that even in despair there must be dignity, and even in sorrow, composure." Quoting a woman she interviewed on the street, Hutchison said the widow had "'gained stature equal to her husband's.'" She was her own profile in courage, and had given Americans, in the words of the *London Evening Standard*, a sense of "majesty" they had always lacked.[55] The same themes appeared over and over again in congressional tributes to the late president and in the nation's press. Senator Albert Gore of Tennessee called the former first lady an "American heroine" who comported herself with grace and courage throughout the ordeal of her husband's death and funeral. Senator Ralph W. Yarborough of Texas spoke paternalistically of how her demeanor "gave the nation a new pride in woman's courage." Representatives John W. McCormack and Edward P. Boland of Massachusetts made similar points, as did Representative Charles McC. Mathias Jr. of Maryland. None of the three had ever seen such a display of courage and "grace under pressure," which McCormack, at least, thought the finest example ever witnessed by the nation.[56] The *Christian Science Monitor* called the former first lady an "example of fortitude and strength" and a model of what should be our "own devotion to the demands of the future."[57] Mary McGrory, writing in the *Boston Globe*, said her "gallantry" had become "legend."[58] And the *Los Angeles Times* called her "a model of supreme courage, ... matchless nobility," and "sheer bravery." She was not only the perfect example of "American womanhood," according to this newspaper; she was an inspiration to the nation as a whole.[59]

Stressing the need for unity, continuity, and shared purpose, so evident in eulogies to the dead president, the *Los Angeles Times* cited the widow's ability to "carry on after a staggering blow" as one of "our republic's basic strengths." Its readers, the paper concluded, should follow her lead, pull themselves together, and go about their "daily tasks as Americans dedicated to creating a finer America."[60] Paul Coates, a writer for the same newspaper, carried this theme further. Noting the "sick feeling of despair" and the "epidemic of disbelief" that gripped the country in the wake of Kennedy's assassination, he wondered if the American people would ever awake from the "awful nightmare" to find some degree of reassurance. Would there be "something to restore our pride and our unity," he asked, "something of value to retain from the vicious martyrdom" of the president? The answer, he said, was "yes." There was "something of which we can be proud" in the "astonishing courage of the woman" widowed by the assassination. "None of us could fail to get strength from her strength." History might have a special place for John Kennedy but it would also have one for his wife. "Because of her," Coates concluded, "our great-grandchildren will know that there is a nobility in this Democracy ... not of class, but of person."[61]

Even religious leaders joined the chorus of praise, including top Protestants. Meeting in Philadelphia, the National Council of the Churches of Christ praised the widow's "dignity and poise under the most shattering circumstances," her "sensitive response to the feelings of others," her "loving concern for her children," and her willingness to share her Christian faith with them. They praised as well her resolve to avoid any "excess of sentimentality, self-pity, political and national aggrandizement" and to present in her demeanor "the majesty and the solace of a Christian commitment." The former first lady, they said, embodied the grace that "enables the Christian not merely to endure but to transform tragic sorrow into triumph."[62]

VI

In the theater of death, as it is sometimes called, Jacqueline Kennedy's performance of her husband's funeral, with its robust symbolism and theatrical rituals, recapitulated the couple's performance on the White House stage, where their restoration of the stage itself, their careful attention to costume, their spectacular state dinners, and their skillful management of the media had created an American brand of royalty, beautiful not only in form but in virtue as well. With guidance from the president and first lady, the media had helped to polish this brand during the couple's White House years and had then followed the widow's lead in reading the same image into the president's funeral, including, as an encore, her return to the White House from Arlington in order to receive, on behalf of the nation, Charles de Gaulle and the many other international leaders who had come to pay their respects to the late president. Here again was the very personification of strength and grace under pressure, of dignity, nobility, and majesty, of gallantry and composure, of duty and self-sacrifice. Although editorialists and eulogists seemed to understand that Jackie's part in her husband's funeral was, in fact, a performance, a staging of herself and the nation, it was still a role that inspired them to rave reviews almost devoid of criticism.

For these editorialists and eulogists, the goal was that of most state funerals held under tragic and destabilizing circumstances, which was to reassure the nation in a time of travail and inspire a resurgent sense of collective identity and common purpose. As such, their words reinforced what President Johnson was trying to accomplish by pledging his support for Kennedy's goals at home and abroad, and by carefully cultivating Kennedy's family, staff, and cabinet. In the long run, these efforts would stumble and fall on the rocks of party divisions, personal animosities, and competing ambitions. But in the short term, Johnson's efforts and Jackie's staging of her husband's funeral did their healing work, though at a cost that not everyone appreciated at the time. By celebrating Kennedy's life and virtuous character, by calling upon the American people to follow his example, and by doing all of this with less than a critical eye, they forged a narrative that forgot as much about the late president as it recalled. By leaving some things out and exaggerating others, they made Kennedy into a mythic character whose influence on the country would transcend his tragic death. Something similar happened to Jacqueline Kennedy. Her careful management of the president's funeral provided much of the script for the commentaries and eulogies that followed, but it was her own performance as the dutiful widow that transformed her, not just her husband, into an idealized representation of what was best in the American spirit.

So it was that for most Americans, the slain president and his widow emerged from the great trauma of his assassination and the sorrowful pageantry of his funeral as larger-than-life figures who supposedly revealed in more or less perfect form the best attributes of American character. Both events would reinforce in American memory the image of the president and the first lady as they had played their parts in so many White House productions. As we will see, moreover, Jacqueline Kennedy, her family, and friends would devote themselves to cultivating the same image in the years following the president's death. Indeed, they would nourish and protect it, like guardians at the gates of history, and seek to inscribe it in every remembrance of the late president, his life and administration. This part of the story comes to life in the great historiographical battles of the 1960s and later, in the many monuments erected to the late president, in the regular commemorations of his life and death, and in the work of the presidential library that bears his name.

FIGURE 1 President-elect John F. Kennedy and Jacqueline Kennedy, 1960.
Source: Mondadori, Getty Images, Image 141566405.

FIGURE 2 Lieutenant John F. Kennedy in the cockpit of PT 109, 1943.
Source: Photographer unknown, JFKPOF-132-012-p0113, JFK Library.

FIGURE 3 President John F. Kennedy and Astronaut John Glenn look inside
Friendship 7 space capsule, February 23, 1962.
Source: Bettman, Getty Images, Image 515024430.

FIGURE 4 President John F. Kennedy signs the Nuclear Test Ban Treaty, October
7, 1963.
Source: Keystone/Staff, Hulton Archive, Getty Images, Image 2641522.

FIGURE 5 President John F. Kennedy addresses the nation on the Cuban missile crisis, October 22, 1962.
Source: Bettman, Getty Images, Image 515512470.

FIGURE 6 State dinner at Mount Vernon in honor of Muhammad Ayub Khan, president of Pakistan, July 11, 1961.
Source: Abbie Rowe, JFKWHP-AR6687-I, JFK Library.

FIGURE 7 The Shah and Empress of Iran arrive at the White House for dinner in their honor, April 11, 1962.
Source: Abbie Rowe, JFKWHP-AR7165-K, JFK Library.

FIGURE 8 First Lady Jacqueline Kennedy shakes hands with violinist Isaac Stern at the White House state dinner for Andre Malreaux, the French minister of state for cultural affairs, May 11, 1962.
Source: Bettmann, Getty Images, Image 515029572.

FIGURE 9 President John F. Kennedy plays with his children in the Oval Office, October 10, 1962.
Source: Cecil Stoughton, JFKWHP-ST-441-10-62, JFK Library.

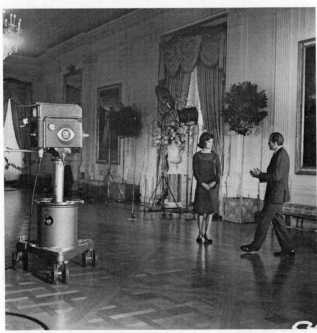

FIGURE 10 First Lady Jacqueline Kennedy tours the White House with CBS newsman Charles Collingwood, January 15, 1962.
Source: CBS Photo Archive, Getty Images, Image 51154808.

FIGURE 11 First Lady Jacqueline Kennedy with members of the White House Fine Arts Committee, December 5, 1961.
Source: White House Photographs, JFKWHP-1961-12-05-K, JFK Library.

FIGURE 12 Fashion designer Oleg Cassini, who designed much of Jacqueline Kennedy's White House wardrobe.
Source: Jack Tinney, Getty Images, Image 541497801.

FIGURE 13 A group listens to news of President John F. Kennedy's assassination, New York City, November 22, 1963.
Source: Agence France Presse, Getty Images, Image 51238732.

FIGURE 14 Jacqueline Kennedy watches President Lyndon B. Johnson take the oath of office aboard Air Force One, November 22, 1963.
Source: Universal Images Group, Getty Images, Image 113493550.

FIGURE 15 President John F. Kennedy lies in repose in the White House, November 23, 1963.
Source: Bettmann, Getty Images, Image 515512404.

FIGURE 16 First Lady Jacqueline Kennedy and her daughter Caroline kneel beside the President's coffin in the Capitol Rotunda, November 25, 1963.
Source: Bettmann, Getty Images, Image 515514010.

FIGURE 17 Jacqueline Kennedy leading her husband's funeral procession as it arrives at St. Matthew's Cathedral.
Source: Bettmann, Getty Images, Image 515553698.

FIGURE 18 John F. Kennedy Jr. salutes his father's casket as it is carried from St. Matthew's Cathedral.
Source: Bettmann, Getty Images, Image 517330220.

FIGURE 19 The eternal flame at President John F. Kennedy's gravesite in Arlington National Cemetery.
Source: Loop Images/Universal Images Group, Getty Images, Image 566439159.

FIGURE 20 President John F. Kennedy and Arthur M. Schlesinger Jr., April 1, 1962.
Source: Art Rickerby. The LIFE Picture Collection, Getty Images, Image 50548171.

FIGURE 21 Special Counsel to the President Theodore C. Sorensen, the White House, January 25, 1961.
Source: Abbie Rowe, JFKWHP-AR6295-1H, JFK Library.

FIGURE 22 Author William Manchester, holding a copy of his book, *The Death of a President*, 1967.
Source: Library of Congress, New York World-Telegram & Sun Collection, Image LC-USZ62-109632.

FIGURE 23 The Kennedy gravesite, Arlington National Cemetery, with a view across Memorial Bridge to the Lincoln Memorial.
Source: Tim Sloan/AFP, Getty Images, Image 103205499.

FIGURE 24 Architect John Warnecke, who designed the Kennedy gravesite in Arlington National Cemetery.
Source: Francis Miller, The LIFE Picture Collection, Getty Images, Image 50657695.

FIGURE 25 The John F. Kennedy Center for the Performing Arts in Washington, DC. *Source*: Carol M. Highsmith/Buyenlarge. Getty Images, Image 564118277.

FIGURE 26 The John F. Kennedy Space Center at Cape Canaveral, Florida. *Source*: Mark Wilson, Getty Images, Image 79617159.

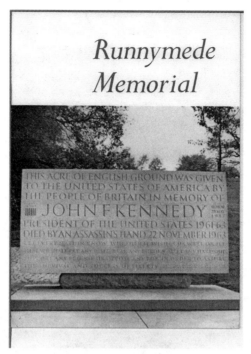

FIGURE 27 Program cover for dedication of the John F. Kennedy memorial at Runnymede in Great Britain.
Source: Photographer unknown, JBKOPP-SF075-088, JFK Library.

FIGURE 28 Robert F. Kennedy places the family flag atop Mt. Kennedy in Canada on July 7, 1965.
Source: William Albert Allard/National Geographic, Getty Images, Image 81188339.

FIGURE 29 John F. Kennedy Presidential Library and Museum in Boston, Massachusetts designed by I. M. Pei.
Source: Alan Goodrich, NLJFK93-C52:29, JFK Library.

FIGURE 30 First Lady Jacqueline Kennedy looks on as architect I. M. Pei speaks. Pei designed the JFK Presidential Library and Museum in Boston.
Source: Bettmann, Getty Images, Image 515493606.

FIGURE 31 Future president Bill Clinton meets then president John F. Kennedy at a White House gathering on July 24, 1963.
Source: Arnold Sachs, Getty Images, Image 2717010.

5

In Death There Is Life

Monuments of Paper and Pen

As we have seen, President Kennedy's assassination and funeral marked a period of acute cultural trauma notable not only for its widespread feelings of grief, shock, and insecurity but also for its many "flashbulb" memories – of a child's adoring salute to his father, of a daughter's loving embrace of his casket, of a widow's strength and courage, of the eternal flame.[1] For those on hand, not to mention the millions watching on television, these individual memories quickly folded into a collective memory that would last a lifetime. In this sense, the president's funeral served not only to calm a nervous nation, or even to burnish further the idealized image of the president and first lady as both had performed their parts on the White House stage. It also served as a frame of reference through which so many Americans would remember John F. Kennedy in the years following his tragic death.

Memories of the late president would quickly take on a sacred quality; his character would be ennobled and his virtues celebrated as those at the heart of the nation's identity. Here was the president as hero, the larger-than-life figure who was one of us, as Arthur G. Neal put it, but also the best of us. Here was the ideal American president, the man of charm and good humor, the optimistic and confident leader who inspired hope in the American people and the conviction that they could do anything. Here was the devoted husband and loving father, the tolerant and pragmatic idealist, the seeker of peace through security, the champion of social justice and human rights. Here was the decorated navy veteran who had given his life in service to the nation and from whose death would spring a new birth of American democracy.

This basically conventional narrative of national redemption through the blood sacrifice of a fallen leader became, for the Kennedy family and most Americans, the approved story of the president's life.[2] It was the frame through which they remembered John Fitzgerald Kennedy as he performed his presidency on the White House stage; it was the tale told ceaselessly by so much of the media, both in print and in the relentless television coverage of the president's life and death; it was the script, drafted by the former first lady, by which they recalled her husband's funeral, her homage to Abraham Lincoln, and her conviction that both men had given their lives so that others might enjoy the blessings of liberty. It was the Kennedy brand; and like many successful brands, it concealed some aspects of the president's life – his serious medical problems, for example, or his drug addictions and reckless philandering – while highlighting those that had made him so appealing at the time, and so deserving of remembrance later.

Keeping this narrative embedded in the nation's memory required careful attention of the sort that both the president and the first lady had lavished on their White House productions. As Barry Schwartz has noted in another context, it required the constant enterprise of family, friends, and admirers whose job it was to make the late president worth remembering. They would have to nurture the idealized representation of John F. Kennedy and guard against its erosion in a social and political environment that changed over time. They would have to remind Americans how to remember him – as the heroic leader who embodied their most noble virtues and democratic ideals. They would have to redeem his sacrifice by repudiating his enemies and celebrating his legislative triumphs, both real and potential.[3] And because constructed memories can be contested, even deconstructed, they would have to use all of the "vehicles of memory" at their disposal in a relentless war against countermemories or alternative narratives that might challenge what had become, in their eyes, the venerated image of the slain president.[4]

II

Just weeks after her husband's funeral, in a meeting with journalist Theodore White, Jacqueline Kennedy set about the task of sustaining her husband's image in the collective memory of the nation. White had been a favorite of the former president. His book on the 1960 presidential campaign had helped to fix the public perception of the young candidate that Kennedy would polish over the next three years – that of the attractive and charismatic man, the prizewinning author and war hero, the intelligent and progressive politician with a young and beautiful family. By his own admission, White let the former first lady dictate the terms of the interview and much of the story he later published in *Life* magazine. Aware that other journalists – notably Arthur Krock, whom her husband detested – were planning to publish stories assessing the dead president's life and legacy, Jackie wanted to beat them to the punch by conveying her own view in one of the nation's most successful mass-circulation magazines.

It was in this interview that she associated her husband's administration with King Arthur's court at Camelot, thereby giving the Kennedy brand its most popular label. She recounted his fondness for one of the songs in the popular Broadway musical of that name, which ended with the line, "Don't let it be forgot, that once there was a spot, for one brief shining moment, that was known as Camelot." The metaphor left Arthur Schlesinger sputtering with the righteous indignation of a professional historian; he claimed that even the former president, himself something of a historian, would have found the comparison not only bad history but entirely ridiculous. Maybe so, but Jacqueline Kennedy was not interested in historical accounts as such, which she thought focused too narrowly on a narrative of presidential achievement and could not fully capture what her husband had meant to the nation. Nor did she care much for historians, whom she characterized as the "bitter old men" who wrote "dusty" and "bitter histories." She was interested in memory. Her husband liked romantic history, she told White, a history full of heroes, and she wanted him remembered that way. As White later recounted in a conversation with one of Jackie's many biographers, the former first lady thought her husband's life "had more to do with myth, magic, legend, saga, and story than with political theory or political science." For her, in other words, it was what her husband represented, as much what he accomplished, that was important, and even White, who claimed to know bad history when he saw it, found her remembrance of the former president compelling.[5]

Jacqueline Kennedy would spend her whole life concealing any blemish on the idealized image of her late husband and promoting instead the romantic and heroic representation she had shared with White. Her staging of Kennedy's presidency as a White House drama had pointed in this direction. So had her careful management of the media and her decision, following the president's death, to cover his shattered head as he was carried into Parkland Hospital. For similar reasons, she and her brother-in-law Robert Kennedy had decided to place his remains in a closed casket, secure his autopsy records, and lock up all of the files that remained in the White House at the time of his death. According to Seymour Hersh, these files included White House logs that registered visitors to the mansion; tape recordings of the president's meetings and phone calls; and anything having to do with his romantic liaisons, drug use, and health record.[6]

Her protective reach extended to recorded history itself. As noted earlier, she and her husband had tried to prohibit members of the White House staff from publishing their impressions of life with the Kennedys. Although this attempt at preemptive censorship failed at the time, she would later be unforgiving, even vindictive, toward former colleagues who published their White House recollections without her prior approval. The list included Maud Shaw, the Kennedy's English nanny, whose memoir mentioned that she, not the first lady, had informed the Kennedy children of their father's death. It included Mary Gallagher, Jackie's personal secretary, whose account revealed the president's constant concern with his wife's lavish spending, among other things. It included Paul "Red" Fay, a navy friend and undersecretary of the navy who played the role of court jester in the Kennedy administration. In Fay's case, the Kennedys intervened to cut a large amount of personal detail from his proposed book on life with the late president. And when the published volume still included some unflattering particulars, especially about strains in the president's marriage, Robert Kennedy refused to speak to him again, as did his sister-in-law, who returned Fay's personal contribution to the John F. Kennedy Memorial Library Fund. The list included Ben Bradlee as well. Although Jackie had once referred to Bradlee and his wife, Tony, as her best friends, she refused to exchange greetings with them – or even to acknowledge their presence – after Bradlee published his book *Conversations with Kennedy* in 1975. A dozen years had passed since the assassination, but Jackie still could not forgive Bradlee for revealing that her husband swore like a sailor and had an eye for beautiful women, not to mention other revelations that, in her mind, desecrated the memory of the former president.[7]

The Kennedys, as one source explained, thought "they had a right to review" what others wanted to write about them.[8] The most notable example was the journalist and historian William Manchester, whom Jacqueline and Robert Kennedy commissioned in the first months of 1964 to publish an authorized history of the president's assassination. Writing such accounts threatened to become a cottage industry in the months after the president's funeral, with one such endeavor being a volume by writer Jim Bishop, who had earlier published a book on the shooting of President Lincoln. Jacqueline Kennedy had no tolerance for Bishop. She worried that he would sensationalize the president's death and tried unsuccessfully to discourage his project. As he recalled in the introduction to the book he eventually published, *The Day Kennedy Was Shot*, both she and Robert Kennedy spoke disparagingly of the project to Bennett Cerf and some of his colleagues at Random House, the famous publishing company that was considering Bishop's book for publication. At the same time, Bishop began hearing from Cardinal Cushing and George Thomas, President Kennedy's valet, that Jacqueline Kennedy had warned them against giving interviews to the author. Shortly thereafter, the former first lady delivered the news herself, telling Bishop in a letter that she had asked all of the people connected with the assassination not to speak to him. The Kennedys, Bishop concluded, "were trying to copyright" history.[9]

It was up to William Manchester to file that copyright for the Kennedy family. He was to control the Kennedy narrative on their behalf and pre-empt Bishop, much as the former first lady had wanted Theodore White to preempt Arthur Krock. Manchester alone would have access to the "people connected with November 22," including personal interviews with the former first lady and other members of the late president's family. He was to be her "hired" historian and write as she directed. She did not want to censor history, she said, but to "protect President Kennedy and the truth," which meant that she alone would decide how this part of the president's life and death would be remembered. Otherwise, Manchester's manuscript would never see the light of day.[10] Nothing of this sort discouraged Bishop, as the Kennedys had hoped, but it did set the stage for a major controversy between the Kennedys and Manchester, who decided, in the end, not to play the part of court historian.

Manchester had earlier published a small but flattering biography of John F. Kennedy, which may be one reason the Kennedys chose him to write a history of the president's assassination. Surely he would recount events in a way that accorded with the inviolable memory of the president, as they wanted it constructed. And surely his book would quickly become the definitive account, further inscribing the president's idealized image on the collective memory of the American people. For his part, Manchester was a great fan of the late president. In his mind, as Gore Vidal once put it, the sun went down "when John Kennedy died." Surely he felt comfortable in the conviction that his account would meet their expectations, which may explain why he accepted a contract that gave them the right to review the manuscript and required their permission prior to its publication, either as a book or as a serialization in a major magazine.[11] Whatever his thinking, Manchester soon came to regret his decision.

Taking leave from his appointment as writer-in-residence at Wesleyan University, Manchester moved his family to Washington, DC, where he nearly worked himself to death in order to finish his book before Bishop finished his. At Robert Kennedy's urging, he also agreed to put the book under contract to Harper & Row rather than Little, Brown and Company, his usual publisher. In the battle to determine how the president would be remembered – in effect, to decide who would control that memory – this decision turned out to be critical. In the publishing world at that time, as Manchester understood, Harper & Row was well known as the publisher of works by Democratic Party politicians; Republicans went elsewhere, usually to Doubleday. Harper had previously published President Kennedy's *Profiles in Courage*, Robert Kennedy's *The Enemy Within*, and Theodore Sorensen's *Kennedy*. Harper's executive vice president, Evan Thomas, who took charge of Manchester's manuscript, oversaw all of these projects, and Cass Canfield, the president of Harper & Row, knew Jacqueline Kennedy through social circles and the one-time marriage of his son to her sister. If the Kennedys thought that such a web of relationships would give them more control over Manchester's book, Evan Thomas soon proved them right. Almost from the outset, he wanted to censor the manuscript of anything that might "tarnish the memory of the late President Kennedy," embarrass Kennedy's wife, or damage the political prospects of his brother, who was then a US Senator with presidential ambitions.[12]

These were the concerns of everyone involved, including Jacqueline Kennedy. They insisted, to give just two examples, that Manchester remove from his manuscript any mention of the president's critical comments regarding Texas and its residents, as well as any reference to Maud Shaw's role in breaking the news of Kennedy's death to his children. In other words, how Kennedy was remembered depended not only upon what Manchester included, but upon what he left out as well. Beyond such "personal details," moreover, Thomas wanted to excise anything that might alienate President Lyndon Johnson, a potential author in the Harper stable and the one man, more than any other, who could hamper Robert Kennedy's political prospects. This meant eliminating what Thomas saw as an anti-Johnson bias in Manchester's manuscript, including references to President Kennedy's somewhat critical view of his vice president and to the poor relationship Johnson had with Robert Kennedy and the late president's staff. Because memory is as much about forgetting as remembering, these details would have to go unreported in the narrative of Kennedy's life sanctioned by his family and friends.[13]

Not normally part of an editor's purview, Thomas's excisions quickly gave the editorial process political wings and eventually sent Manchester's book flying into court. The first draft of his manuscript garnered positive comments from a number of readers, including Arthur Schlesinger, Richard Goodwin, and both Edwin Guthman and John Seigenthaler, newspaper editors who had once worked for Robert Kennedy in the Justice Department. Unwilling to relive dreadful memories, Jacqueline Kennedy had refused to read the draft. She delegated her authority to Robert Kennedy, who, for similar reasons, delegated his authority to Guthman, Seigenthaler, and Thomas. Thomas was the holdout. He demanded revisions that addressed the issues noted earlier, usually by eliminating key words, phrases, and passages. Each time Manchester made one set of revisions, however, Thomas demanded another. At one point, Robert Kennedy, speaking for the Kennedy family, appeared to approve a draft for publication, but Thomas and others pushed back, Jacqueline Kennedy raised new concerns, and the deal was off. According to Manchester, Thomas even gave copies of the manuscript to various politicians who wanted to make revisions of their own. He discussed the controversy with reporters, often in terms calculated to put the author on the defensive, and tried, along with other members of the Kennedy camp, to undermine Manchester's credibility, in part by claiming that he was emotionally unstable – if not actually suffering a nervous breakdown.[14]

In truth, Manchester had worked himself into a state of mental and physical exhaustion. He was emotionally tortured by the assassination story he was reporting, lost his appetite, and had difficulty sleeping, all symptoms of severe distress that only grew worse as he battled the Kennedys over the book and his plans to serialize the manuscript in *Look* magazine. Before the struggle was over, he ended up on the critical list of a Connecticut hospital suffering from acute pneumonia and what must have been a profound sense of disillusionment. Like most authors, Manchester was accustomed to working with editors who championed the author's cause rather than amplifying the personal and political critiques of interested third parties. He was heartsick as friends such as Richard Goodwin, Theodore Sorensen, and Arthur Schlesinger abandoned him, sided with the Kennedys, and questioned his character. Like the Kennedys, they aimed to control how the late president would be remembered. No doubt they wanted Manchester to align his story with their own accounts rather than offer an alternative narrative of his own. But Manchester must have wondered if they also wanted something more, perhaps a positive relationship with the Kennedy family or a prestigious position in another Kennedy administration.[15]

The great affection and admiration that Manchester once had for the Kennedys turned to cynicism that he could not conceal in subsequent comments about his experience. He recalled one meeting with Robert Kennedy, ostensibly to seek Manchester's help with a speech on academic freedom – that most precious of all university values – only to have Kennedy try to censor his manuscript. At another meeting, according to the author, "Bobby was at his most abrasive." He threatened to sue *Look* magazine if it serialized any portion of Manchester's book and demanded that Manchester give a larger share of his royalties to the Kennedy Library, all the while assuring everyone "that he wanted the book published."[16]

Turning to Jacqueline Kennedy, Manchester described, with barely disguised sarcasm, how she skillfully metamorphosed into different characters. Depending upon the dramatic needs of the moment, she could be the carefree seductress, lighthearted and feminine, or the angry widow, dark and menacing. Earlier, Manchester had called her a "tragic actress." He considered this a compliment – or so he said – but was soon comparing her to Marie Antoinette and recounting reports of her romantic engagements, worldwide travels, cruise adventures, horseback rides, dance parties, and preference for a couture that made her photograph the ideal cover for *Women's Wear Daily*. For Manchester, the former first lady could no longer present herself as the suffering widow. On one occasion, meeting Manchester on Cape Cod, she "looked stunning" in bright-colored casual wear, including a miniskirt; gave a great performance as a world-class water skier while leaving the famous author to babysit her son in the backseat of the towing boat; and nearly drowned her guest as the two of them swam to shore, she wearing flippers while he struggled without them. When this performance failed to beguile Manchester into revising his manuscript, a more aggressive second act followed suit. Having refused to read the manuscript herself, she had others do it for her, including her secretary, Pam Turnure, who compiled a long list of changes that Jackie demanded. Manchester was shocked that he was being asked to accept revisions suggested by a secretary with no experience in the publishing world. When he asked Jackie for a reasonable review of the facts, however, he was confronted with "tears, grimaces, and whispery cries of 'Jesus Christ!' " Sometimes sobbing, running in and out of the house in search of composure and Kleenex, she denounced *Look* magazine for planning serialized segments of Manchester's book, blasted Arthur Schlesinger because he had not made all the revisions she wanted before publishing his recent book on President Kennedy, and threatened "savagely" to fight every publication she did not like. "Anyone who is against me," she told Manchester, "will look like a rat, unless I run off with Eddie Fisher," a reference to the popular singer who had recently left his wife, actress Debbie Reynolds, for an affair with Elizabeth Taylor.[17]

She was equally high-handed in a meeting with Gardner Cowles, the publisher of *Look* magazine, when he refused to make the changes she demanded before serializing Manchester's book.[18] Meanwhile, Robert Kennedy and his advisors, including Dick Goodwin, Arthur Schlesinger, and Evan Thomas, continued to sharpen their editorial pencils, largely under pressure from Jackie and out of concern for Robert Kennedy's political prospects, not to mention their own. Although Kennedy, like his sister-in-law, had still not read the manuscript, he nonetheless approved as his colleagues, meeting over dinner in New York, compiled another list of changes in the third and fourth installments of *Look*'s serialization. Ever accommodating, Manchester made some but not all of the prescribed changes, left the revised manuscript with Harper & Row, and prepared to board the *Queen Mary* for a European vacation. Shortly before boarding, however, he met Evan Thomas, who was waiting for him in the lobby of his hotel, along with others who seemed especially anxious to stay on the good side of Jacqueline and Robert Kennedy, particularly Manchester's one-time friend, Richard Goodwin. Much to the author's surprise, they demanded still further changes on behalf of the Kennedys. Manchester balked at the idea, fled to his suite, and refused to open the door when an agitated Robert Kennedy, arriving on the scene, seemed ready to break it down. "You have to see him," Thomas exclaimed. "The hell I do," shouted Manchester. "I didn't invite him, and have nothing to say to him." Besides, he asked Thomas, "Do you really think a former Attorney General of the United States is going to break down a door?"[19] The editor gave no answer.

A similar pattern prevailed over the following weeks: further changes were demanded; some but not all were made; threats and ultimatums were exchanged. Finally, in the last month of 1966, almost all parties to the dispute, now thoroughly exhausted, reached an agreement on both the book manuscript and the last round of serialization for *Look* magazine.

They recommended the agreement in letters to Jacqueline Kennedy, who read them carefully and then, in Manchester's clipped prose, "phoned her lawyer, and told him to sue."[20]

Manchester was confident of his case, as were his publishers, including Harper & Row, which had finally decided to take a stand on behalf of its beleaguered author. He had given the Kennedys the right of final approval, to be sure, but he had also been accommodating throughout, had been told that Robert Kennedy would make the final decision on behalf of the family, and had documents from Kennedy that appeared to grant his approval. Although Kennedy was not enthusiastic about a court battle, and would not join his sister-in-law in her suit, nor would he abandon her. On the contrary, he rallied to her defense throughout a process that even Guthman, who had been one of Kennedy's field marshals in the battle of the book, thought "undignified" and "demeaning" to everyone involved, including Kennedy and his sister-in-law.[21]

By the time the controversy came to an end, it had generated an enormous amount of media commentary, much of it critical of the Kennedys at a time when Robert was contemplating a presidential campaign. *Newsweek* magazine captured the tone in an article titled, "JFK Censored?" Citing columnists Drew Pearson and Jack Anderson, *Newsweek* revealed how the Kennedys had sought to squelch Jim Bishop's proposed book, had censored the memoirs of Paul Fay and Maud Shaw, and were now trying to do the same with Manchester's manuscript. Tom Wicker, writing for the *New York Times*, attacked Jacqueline Kennedy for issuing a public statement impugning the accuracy of a manuscript she had not read and the integrity of the author she had commissioned to do the work. As he saw it, much of what she and her brother-in-law deplored about the book, namely its treatment of President Johnson, had more to do with political calculations than with any concern for historical accuracy. Other critics were even harsher. The *Cincinnati Enquirer*, for example, accused the former first lady of "treating a chapter of U.S. history as her private memoir" and compared her unfavorably to Eleanor Roosevelt, who had continued her public work in quiet dignity following the death of her husband. By comparison, the paper judged, Jacqueline Kennedy had spent much of her time gallivanting around the world with jet-setting friends – when she was not busy throwing a tantrum over Manchester's book. Manchester came in for his share of criticism, too, so that in the end, all parties were prepared to settle.[22]

Robert Kennedy must have concluded that nothing in Manchester's manuscript could be worse for him than the steady barrage of newspaper criticism. Given the press onslaught, even Jacqueline Kennedy became more flexible. Among other things, she finally worked her way through the last of the serialization segments and then through the book manuscript. Surprisingly, she liked what she read, asked for just a few more changes, and the deal was done. Some of the changes were insignificant, such as substituting the word "vanished" for the word "disappeared." Others were personal and political, including Manchester's discussion of the dress Jackie wore in Dallas, which her husband had selected in order to "show up those cheap Texas broads." Manchester lost seven more pages of what became a 710-page book, most in an effort to assuage the former first lady, who was engaged, as Gore Vidal put it, "with legend if not history." The Kennedy lawyers also wanted the author's promise that he would never write another book about the Kennedy family. Manchester declined to promise, but then again, he didn't have to.[23]

Although Manchester had clearly had enough of the Kennedys, his book, which turned out to be a smashing commercial success, did well by him. In the four years following its publication, *The Death of a President* sold 1,685,232 copies. Manchester became a rich man, and the Kennedy Library did well too. Under the terms of the contract Manchester had negotiated with the Kennedys, the library received $750,000 as its share of the royalties from the sale of the book in its first year of publication, and more than $1 million by late 1969, the last time following publication that he received an accounting from the library. Much to his chagrin, he did not receive a single note of appreciation from the library nor, unsurprisingly, from the Kennedy family. On the contrary, old friendships, like flowers trampled in a late summer storm, never bloomed again. These included Robert Kennedy's relationship with Evan Thomas and Harper & Row. Thomas would leave the publisher for W. W. Norton, and Harper & Row would lose the publication rights to Kennedy's next book, which went to Doubleday instead. They also included Manchester's relationships with Richard Goodwin, Pierre Salinger, and Arthur Schlesinger, among others, all of whom had taken the author to task during the controversy, not to mention Ted Sorensen, who had drafted the press statement that Jacqueline Kennedy used to announce her lawsuit and attack Manchester's integrity. The Kennedys suffered as well. A Harris Poll taken after the Manchester debacle showed that 20 percent of those surveyed had a lesser opinion of Robert Kennedy – and for his sister-in-law, the news was even worse. Although one poll, taken in December

1966, ranked her as the most admired woman in the world for the fifth consecutive year, another poll, taken the following month, showed her reputation declining by more than 30 percent, the first real decline in her popularity since her husband's funeral.[24]

Jacqueline Kennedy seemed less concerned with her own reputation, however, than with the idealized image of her husband. This was the image that she and the president had cultivated on the White House stage, now overlaid with the blessed mask of a martyr who had given his life for the nation. She hovered over his memory, much like a museum curator hovers over a mannequin, styling every aspect to make it as much like the idealized image as possible. She commissioned allies, such as Theodore White and even William Manchester, to tell the narrative of Kennedy's death as she wanted her husband remembered. She did everything possible to discourage those, like Arthur Krock and Jim Bishop, who could not be trusted to bend to her wishes. She tried, with considerable success, to preview every word that friends and former colleagues wrote about the late president. In effect, she established herself as the owner of her husband's representation and tried, in every way, to control how he would be remembered, in part by concealing aspects of his life and death that she did not want recalled.

III

Although the Manchester controversy titillated the press and undermined Jacqueline Kennedy's standing in the polls, it did nothing to damage the sacred memory of President Kennedy. Polls showed no decline in the respect, admiration, and affection people still felt for their fallen hero. Perhaps it was because the book dealt only with his assassination and funeral, perhaps because the controversy focused on other members of the Kennedy family, or perhaps because Manchester's uniformly positive treatment of the former president was all that remained in the minds of millions of people who read his book. Besides, Manchester was not the only one writing at the time, and much of what others had to say did a good deal to shore up the idealized image of the late president in the collective memory of the American people. These included a number of Kennedy aides – more or less the shock troops in the war over Kennedy's memory – as well as sympathetic voices in the American press. Their works reinforced the larger-than-life image of the late president that his wife sought to nourish, in effect, sculpting a paper monument to the Kennedy brand that would stand without serious challenge for nearly a decade after his death.

The list of aides included "Red" Fay and Maud Shaw, whose books, ironically, Jacqueline Kennedy had challenged. Shaw's memoir treated the Kennedys with respect and admiration, while Fay's fun-loving and playful account, *The Pleasure of His Company*, humanized Kennedy and captured, as the title suggests, the deep affection he inspired in those he befriended. The list also included the admiring recollections of Evelyn Lincoln, who served as Kennedy's secretary for twelve years. Jacqueline Kennedy had allowed Lincoln special access to the president's records, which were otherwise sealed from the public, and she did the same for Joan Meyers, whose book, *John Fitzgerald Kennedy: As We Remember Him*, featured flattering photographs of the late president along with equally flattering commentary. Two members of the Irish Mafia, Kenneth O'Donnell and David Powers, published another admiring and sentimental account in *"Johnny, We Hardly Knew Ye,"* as did Pierre Salinger, Kennedy's rotund press secretary, who published his memoir of the Kennedy administration, *With Kennedy*, and then cooperated with newsman Sander Vanocur on *A Tribute to John F. Kennedy*. Most of these books were best sellers, with the Salinger-Vanocur volume selling more than six hundred thousand copies. The same was true of Rose Kennedy's book of family reminiscences, *Times to Remember*, which appeared later.[25]

All of these works enjoyed a degree of credibility as insider accounts by authors who could claim to speak with the authority of people who knew or worked with Kennedy. But none of them spoke with the authority of Arthur M. Schlesinger Jr. and Theodore Sorensen. Schlesinger was actually a marginal figure in the administration, more a gadfly than anything else. But if he lacked authority on that score, he made up for it with his standing as a Harvard historian and prizewinning author of major books on Presidents Andrew Jackson and Franklin Roosevelt, not to mention his almost sycophantic relationship with Jacqueline Kennedy. Something similar can be said of Sorensen, who was the silent voice behind so many of Kennedy's famous speeches but never a member of his social circle or active participant in policymaking. Nevertheless, Jacqueline Kennedy gave both men privileged access to government and personal records denied to other scholars. Both submitted their manuscripts for her approval, and both made revisions she demanded. As with Theodore White, not to mention William Manchester, at least at the outset, both Salinger and Sorensen agreed to serve as scriptwriters for Jacqueline Kennedy's dramatic production of her late husband as a hero worth remembering. Even so, she was never fully satisfied with Schlesinger's book, at least not until its critical acclaim, including a Pulitzer Prize, finally allowed a happy rapprochement.[26]

Neither writer found much to criticize in Kennedy or his policies. On the contrary, when it came to remembering the president, they were inclined, much like the Kennedys themselves, to conceal or slight aspects of their subject that might be interpreted critically. These parts of Kennedy's past would be forgotten. For them, Kennedy was still the man behind the brand: the incandescent personality whose personal attributes and many virtues were those described by ordinary citizens and newspaper commentators at the time of his death. He was handsome and charming, full of wit and good humor, courage and grace, a man of high ideals, to be sure, but also realistic and tough minded. In their accounts, Kennedy was a brilliant man, the most brilliant of all the brilliant men in his administration, a real intellectual to be compared with Jefferson, an idealist in the tradition of Lincoln, a pragmatist like FDR, always inclined toward action but reluctant to waste his credibility and power on lost causes. Most importantly, perhaps, was what they saw as the spirit of the man: his confidence in the future, his conviction that all things were possible, and his sense of adventure – all attributes evident in the space program and the Peace Corps – not to mention his call to service and self-sacrifice for the greater good, including better prospects for the poor, the uneducated, the ill, and the old. It was this spirit that suffused the nation during his administration and inspired young people with renewed pride in their country and hope for the future.

It was also this spirit, not to mention his many other virtues, that animated Kennedy's foreign and domestic policies. Other than the Bay of Pigs, or his failure to energize the State Department, Kennedy made few mistakes, at least in their view, and always learned from his setbacks. He had a long list of accomplishments to his credit, including a revolutionary turn toward Keynesian fiscal policy; a victory over Khrushchev in the Cuban Missile Crisis; the Test Ban Treaty and tilt toward détente with the Soviet Union; and a brave commitment to civil rights, despite the threat it posed to his political standing and prospects for a second term. For Schlesinger and Sorensen, even the legislative successes that followed his death had sprouted, like Jack's giant beanstalk, from the magic seeds planted in the fertile soil of the Kennedy administration.[27]

The books by Sorensen and Schlesinger were paper "monuments," to borrow a phrase from Hans Morgenthau, to Kennedy's greatness, both real and potential. Taken together with the works by Salinger and Shaw, O'Donnell and Powers, Lincoln and other "fierce Kennedy partisans," as Rexford G. Tugwell called them, they constituted "a really formidable defense" of the president's administration.[28] Not surprisingly, given her hand in much of this work, both books reinforced the sanctified image of the fallen leader that Jacqueline Kennedy sought to inscribe on the collective memory of the American people. Nor were they the only vehicles of memory at work in this process. On the contrary, their works were at the core of a liberal consensus that quickly formed around Kennedy and was nowhere more evident than in the special issues of two liberal journals: the *New York Review of Books*, published in December 1963, and *Current*, published in January 1964.

Both issues featured brief essays by leading intellectuals of the day, with some commenting on the assassination itself, others deploring the violence in American society, and still others focusing on Kennedy's remarkable personality. Some contributors complained that Kennedy's economic policies were too conservative and that he had not done enough when it came to civil rights or aid to the poor. He was not a great president, they concluded, but they also agreed that his failures were not necessarily his own but those of a political and congressional system bitterly divided along party, ideological, and regional lines. Given these constraints, some insisted, he had done more than most presidents, especially in view of the short time allotted him.[29]

Most contributors were more positive. Kennedy, they said, had not shied away from the commanding issues of the day. Before his administration, historian William Leuchtenburg reminded his readers, "no American had yet orbited the earth" and "no American president had identified himself with ... the struggle of the Negro for full equality." Kennedy had also revitalized the office of the president and had fixed its place once again at the center of American government. This was Leuchtenburg's view and also that of Richard Rovere, who said that Kennedy had "made thinking respectable in Washington" and had motivated a whole generation of public servants. He was cut down before achieving his full agenda, concluded Rovere, but would still be remembered for the "things he set in motion, the energies he released, the people and ideas he encouraged, and the style he brought to the Presidency."[30]

For many contributors, Kennedy's international achievements were equally impressive, the Bay of Pigs notwithstanding. According to Leuchtenburg, Kennedy had restored "a sense of direction in foreign affairs" that had been lost under the previous administration. Zbigniew Brzezinski went even further. To his way of thinking, Kennedy "achieved something which no political leader had ever achieved before: acceptance as a global leader." Roosevelt and Churchill had always remained regional leaders, but the worldwide reaction to Kennedy's death revealed to Brzezinski the extent to which Kennedy "symbolized, dramatized, and articulated the hopes of the new generation," not only in the United States but the world over. Historians Richard Hofstadter and Arthur S. Link agreed. Hofstadter, who was in England at the time of the assassination, was "impressed by the desperate immediacy this event had for people there," by how quickly they had "adopted Kennedy as their own statesman, and by the realization of how much he had done in Europe to abate or dispel the mindless anti-Americanism of the past fifteen years." Assessing Kennedy's future standing among historians, Link thought they would rank him as one of the century's best, in the company of Theodore Roosevelt, Woodrow Wilson, and Franklin Roosevelt, and not only because of the "spirit and tone" he brought to the office but also because of his "commanding mastery of the art of diplomacy."[31]

Not surprisingly, it was Kennedy's "spirit and tone," his style, that captivated so many of these writers, as it did the American people, who agreed with Jacqueline Kennedy that her husband should be remembered as less the subject of political science than the stuff of myth and legend. Historian William Carleton considered Kennedy one of "history's romantic heroes" whose death had in it "the stuff of religious epic." David Bazelon thought the president's assassination would turn out to be "one of the greatest cultural events of the modern period." But it was Gerald W. Johnson, a veteran journalist, who captured better than anyone else why the sacred image of the slain president, already deeply rooted in the memory of most Americans, would withstand the test of time and the criticism of historians. Whatever charges they might level against him, Johnson wrote, would pale "into insignificance by comparison with what the nation feels about him now and will continue to feel through the predictable future." "Dr. Dryasdust" and other historians, Johnson argued, in words reminiscent of Jacqueline Kennedy, "will have about as much effect on his position in history as Mrs. Partington's mop had upon the Atlantic tide." This was so because a man "once touched by romance is removed from all categories and is comparable only with the legendary." Now Jack Kennedy, the "young chevalier," had joined "Washington the god-like" and "Lincoln the saintly" as an "epic" figure for whom legend "overwrites the page of history." Americans were at a moment in time when a symbol was worth more than a sage, Johnson concluded.

Dr. Dryasdust might complain, but wiser men "will weigh the wisdom of him who, if he were allowed to write the songs of a nation, cared not who wrote the laws."[32]

Other journalists were also busy adding height to the spiraling edifice that scholars and memoirists were erecting to the memory of the former president. Memory makers in the mainstream media repeated, as if reading from the same script, the late president's many virtues. The usual list included his courage, common sense, and strength of character; his devotion to duty, as a public figure and private man; the spirit of service and sacrifice he brought to public life; his romantic faith in American greatness, his confidence in the basic goodness of the American people, and his optimism about the future. These characteristics, virtues all, had inspired the progressive political agenda that his death helped to advance.[33]

The *Cleveland Plain Dealer* remembered the president as "a great reformer, a great humanitarian, and a dreamer."[34] J. K. Saunders, writing in the same paper, celebrated Kennedy's support of the arts and the "breadth of character" that he and his wife "projected from the showcase of the White House."[35] Herb Kenny of the *Boston Globe* and Tom Wicker of the *New York Times* wrote glowing accounts of the president's wit and good humor, both of which gave the great man a human dimension not always evident in other political figures.[36] Joseph Alsop considered Kennedy's foreign policy a success and his domestic policy on the right track, if only fulfilled after his death. But the most important thing about him, according to Alsop, was that "he was loved" by the American people as no other president before.[37] Although James Reston, writing in the *New York Times*, lamented Kennedy's timidity on certain issues, notably civil rights, and was certainly aware of the bleak outcome at the Bay of Pigs, he nonetheless found something "vaguely legendary" about him. He was "a story-book president," not only young and handsome but "graceful, almost elegant, with poetry on his tongue and a radiant young woman at his side."[38]

Even notable journalist Walter Lippmann, much celebrated as a public philosopher with a strong realist bent, struck the same notes sounded by Sorensen, Schlesinger, and others who sang songs of Kennedy's life. Appraising the Kennedy "legend," what I have called the Kennedy brand, Lippmann gave the president high marks for engineering a revolution in fiscal policy. His foreign policy triumphs outweighed his failures, Lippmann added, and his domestic policies went as far as Congress would permit. Most important, however, was the spirit of the man, by which Lippmann, much like Schlesinger, Sorensen, and others, meant

Kennedy's ability to inspire a whole generation of Americans to imagine a better future for themselves and for the world around them.[39]

Reading these comments reveals how easily even some hardheaded journalists could be seduced by Kennedy's personal appeal. He presented what most of them wanted to see; indeed, what most Americans saw as a set of attributes that supposedly inhered in the nation as a whole. He was, in this sense, the ideal American. Their assessments, moreover, dovetailed with the presidential brand that Kennedy had polished in the White House and that his wife tried to imprint on the nation's memory beginning with the president's funeral. In fact, the press and the Kennedys were partners in this effort, even though some of the former questioned the cost of their fealty. The *Washington Post, Times Herald*, to cite one example, wondered if the "hope and promise" of the Kennedy administration might one day be remembered more than its achievements.[40] Marquis Childs, writing in a similar vein, worried that Kennedy's "legend" might so far outstrip reality that future historians would "underestimate" his contributions.[41] It had only been a year since his death, wrote Karl E. Meyer on the first anniversary of the assassination, yet Kennedy had already "become the stuff of legend," so much so that myth was "swallowing the man."[42]

There were critics, of course, particularly among certain segments of the population. Protestants, Republicans, older Americans, white southerners, conservative journals and newspapers, and even some mainstream magazines, such as *US News & World Report*, had always been less enamored of the president than liberals and the liberal press, Democrats, minority voters, young people, Catholics, Jews, and voters in the northeastern states. Most of the former cluster, particularly in the South, slowly reverted to their traditional views over the course of the 1960s, even as Kennedy remained enormously appealing to the population as a whole.[43]

Just before the president's death, moreover, conservative writer Victor Lasky had published an unflinchingly critical book on Kennedy. As suggested by his title, *JFK: The Man and the Myth*, Lasky struck directly at the heroic image of the president, attacking him as just another politician, cold and calculating, ruthless, unethical, and insincere. These themes, particularly Lasky's notion that Kennedy was all style and no substance, foreshadowed the critical reframing of the president's reputation by liberal and left-wing revisionists a decade later. But there is little evidence that it did much damage to Kennedy's popular appeal at the time, in part because it was published in September 1963, and then quickly withdrawn after the president's assassination, when it came to be seen as tasteless and disrespectful to the memory of the martyred hero. Then, too, liberal and mainstream commentators who had done so much to construct the president's heroic image in the first place were particularly anxious to guard against its deconstruction by conservative critics. Writing in the *Atlantic*, for example, William Barrett accused Lasky of "approaching his subject with the resolute tread of a man clubbing a rabbit," while James MacGregor Burns, himself a Kennedy biographer, told readers of the *New Republic* that he deserved a "Good Conduct Medal" for slogging his way through an overwritten narrative drawn from old and unreliable reports published largely in conservative newspapers.[44]

A year later, Richard J. Whalen's biography of Joseph P. Kennedy offered some blistering criticism of the president's father but said little about the president himself, who, if anything, took from his upbringing a competitive spirit and a deep sense of family loyalty. Beyond that, Whalen, a conservative writer, framed the story of John F. Kennedy in a narrative that could only remind readers of his success in escaping the often myopic and biased views of his father.[45] There were other critics as well, particularly the British writer Henry Fairlie, who viewed Kennedy as little more than an immature and inexperienced politician with few clear principles and little understanding of the major issues of the day. Fairlie's essay presaged his subsequent, full-blown assault on Kennedy's reputation in a book that helped to launch a wave of revisionist publications in the 1970s.[46] Like Lasky's book, however, Fairlie's article barely cleaved a page from the literary monument that others were erecting to the memory of the late president.

IV

As this suggests, the idealized picture of the former president faced few sustained challenges in the decade after his death. There were few counter memories or alternative narratives in the major biographies, memoirs, and journalistic accounts of the era, nor, for that matter, in the memory that most Americans had of him. On the contrary, judging by the sheer flood of Kennedy books and articles published, the nation remained deeply fascinated by the late president, his family, and his administration. The foremost author, of course, was Kennedy himself. One of the most prolific of all presidents, he had published dozens of articles and essays in serious magazines and journals, written several books, and won a Pulitzer Prize. This explains why so many people considered him a real intellectual. But there was more to his literary standing than that.

As James Crown noted several years ago, Kennedy was one of the top twenty-five best-selling authors in all of American history, a group that included writers of both fiction and nonfiction. The posthumous sales of his collected work only added to his status. Harper & Row brought out a memorial edition of *Profiles in Courage*, with proceeds going to establish a John F. Kennedy Memorial Book Award for works showing a deep understanding of national or international affairs. The memorial edition made *Profiles* the best-selling general book in the country – for the second time in its literary history. By the end of the 1960s, it had sold over four million paperback copies in the United States and been translated for publication in at least ten other countries.[47] If consumers did not want to read Kennedy's words, moreover, they could hear them in one or more of the memorial albums available within six months of his death.[48]

Books about Kennedy were very popular as well. By 1968, Crown, focusing only on selected major works, counted approximately forty books on Kennedy, with more than half of them published after his assassination.[49] A more comprehensive survey, published nine years later, put the number of such books at more than five hundred, with about half of them published after the assassination.[50] What is more, the list did not include the ever-expanding literature on the assassination and its investigation, including many books on Lee Harvey Oswald, his family, and his killer. According to Joan I. Newcomb, by 1977, the Kennedy literature published both before and after the assassination had reached a total of nearly seven hundred books, a number rivaling the accumulated literature on Abraham Lincoln and Franklin Roosevelt that had been piling up for many years. In addition to countless memoirs and insider accounts, not to mention new collections or editions of his addresses and essays, the list included books on Kennedy's Catholicism, his use of biblical citations, and his religious views; his thoughts on Israel, Vietnam, Africa, Poland, Germany, England, France, and other countries; his policies toward Latin America, Europe, Asia, and Africa, including the Alliance for Progress and the Peace Corps; and his many initiatives, from the space program to the Test Ban Treaty, from the General Agreement on Trade and Tariffs to his work in such areas as education, the economy, civil rights, and media management. Although much of the Kennedy literature, as this sample suggests, focused on serious issues of public policy and was not without its criticism of the Kennedy administration – particularly when it came to civil rights, counterinsurgency, and Vietnam – it was still more likely than not to fit within the thematic framework first set out by Schlesinger and Sorensen.[51]

Put differently, even as some cracks began to appear in the paper monument to the dead president, and even as these grew wider in the 1970s, the narrative of Kennedy's life approved by the former first lady remained largely intact for most of the decade following his assassination. This was particularly evident in the many photographic collections of the president and his family, often very expensive coffee table books that nonetheless flew off the shelves at bookstores everywhere. In her efforts to control how people remembered her husband, Jacqueline Kennedy, as mentioned earlier, had helped Joan Meyers to assemble her book, *John Fitzgerald Kennedy: As We Remember Him.* She also played a direct or indirect role in the Kennedy memorial editions issued by *Look, Life,* and United Press International, which included photographs taken under her supervision during Kennedy's White House years. Jacques Lowe, Mark Shaw, and Cecil Stoughton, all photographers who had served the White House, also brought out popular photographic biographies. So did Tazewell Shepard, the president's naval aide, who used his photographs to capture Kennedy's love of sailing and the sea, as well as Anne H. Lincoln, who worked with the Kennedys on many of the famous White House parties and state dinners. Doris E. Saunders even published a photographic account of Kennedy's work in civil rights. All of these publications generally reinforced the brand that Kennedy had constructed as president, though it was now covered with the holy cloth of a murdered martyr. In the picture books, in particular, we see again his handsome face and bright smile, his lovely wife and beautiful children, his athleticism and derring-do on the high seas, his wartime heroism, his often thoughtful countenance, his commitment to social justice, his assassination and funeral, and all the other flashbulb memories of his life and death.[52]

Neither photographic remembrances nor the serious literature written by scholars, journalists, and former colleagues tell the whole story of Kennedy's claim on American memory. In the aftermath of his assassination, the president inspired more poetry than any of his predecessors with the possible exception of Abraham Lincoln. Kennedy had honored American poets, and the arts in general, when he invited a crowd of literary luminaries to his inauguration, especially Robert Frost, who read a poem. Other White House tributes to the arts followed, including notable performances by literary stars and famous musicians on the White House stage, Kennedy's support for a new performing arts center in the nation's capital, and his memorable eulogy for Robert Frost, offered only weeks before his own assassination. "A nation reveals itself not only by the men it produces," the president said of Frost, as others would say of him, "but also by the men it honors, the men it remembers." Poets reciprocated these salutes by paying homage to the president in verse, not only during his brief term in office but even more substantially after his assassination. Much of this literature was the spontaneous outpouring of unsung poets published in journals and newspapers at the time of the funeral or shortly thereafter. But established poets also joined the procession of mourners who grieved at his death and who remembered the life of a man whose presidency "seemed like a renaissance." The list included a range of different poets, often with very different styles, among them Gwendolyn Brooks, Gregory Corso, Richard Eberhart, Allen Ginsberg, Paul Goodman, and Donald Hall. Included as well was W. H. Auden, whose "Elegy for J. F. K." would be set to music by Igor Stravinsky and performed in honor of the president's memory in Los Angeles's Fiesta Hall in April 1964. Their poems were suffused with the same flashbulb memories that quickly became part of the collective memory of the nation – the murder in the motorcade, the military funeral, the first lady's strength and dignity, the eternal flame. Poets, like others, recounted the president's youth and cautious idealism, his energy and grace, his intelligence and humor, and his ability to be not only the idealist but also the realist, not only a politician but also "a credible and attractive human being."[53]

Similar themes emerged in the blues and gospel songs written by black artists in the wake of Kennedy's death and for some time thereafter. Black Americans had been supportive of the president from his election, although their approval was mixed with criticism of his reluctance to act decisively on civil rights and welfare policies, or too aggressively on the draft and national security issues. Muddy Waters captured this ambivalence in his blues song "Tough Times." By 1963, however, equivocation had given way to adulation as Kennedy increasingly threw his weight behind the civil rights struggle, aid to education, and support for the ill, the elderly, and the poor. To be sure, some black leaders remained skeptical of the president's record even after his assassination, but for most, November 22, 1963, was "The Day the World Stood Still," to borrow a phrase from the "Sensational Six," a blues group from Birmingham, Alabama. A wave of tears washed over the black community as blues and gospel artists joined journalists and poets to canonize the slain president. They compared him to Abraham Lincoln and Franklin Roosevelt. "Big" Joe Williams, a blues guitarist who had earlier recorded a piece in honor of Roosevelt, issued a revised version, "A Man Amongst Men," in memory of Kennedy, whom Williams now considered "the best president we ever had." Kennedy was the "light that shines," as another artist put it, and was to be compared not only to Roosevelt – nor even to Lincoln – but to Jesus Christ, who had also been crucified for his convictions. It would not be long before artists, notably Mahalia Jackson, were linking the slain president to other martyred heroes. Jackson had been a Kennedy fan from the start. She had campaigned for him in 1960 and sang at his inauguration. Shortly after the assassination, moreover, Jackson recorded "In the Summer of His Years," accompanied only by a muffled drumbeat reminiscent of the muffled drums at the president's funeral.[54]

Taken together with the poetic remembrances of the late president, the flood of memoirs, and the serious scholarship cast in the Schlesinger mode, the blues and gospel songs written and performed by black artists helped to fix in public memory the portrait of Kennedy as a man of democratic conviction, a champion of equality, and a liberal reformer who gave his life for the downtrodden. Added to this, moreover, was the homage to Kennedy by American artists, whose narratives in stone or on canvas became part of the Kennedy script. Their works began to appear more or less spontaneously in the year or so after Kennedy's death, and were then exhibited in galleries around the country. They included paintings and prints as well as sculptures, cast in different styles and created by artists of different generations who had one thing in common: the need to pay tribute to a president who had clearly been their hero.[55]

Popular literature, one wing of an expansive heritage industry, also found an almost inexhaustible market in Kennedy's remembrance. Several publishers offered books on what Kennedy had to say to and about young people. Others published letters that children had written to him or books that aimed to inspire youth with stories drawn from his life or the life of his family, with special emphasis, not surprisingly, on his idealism, love of country, courage, heroism, and devotion to family.[56] All of these were familiar attributes of the image that Kennedy had cultivated while alive, that his wife was trying to imprint on American memory, and that commercial publishers now reinforced. Much the same could be said of his great rhetorical skills. In addition to his speeches, publishers never tired of printing whole books of excerpted quotations showing his views on particular topics or his fondness for quotes from the classics and other literary sources.[57] In addition, James J. Dobbins brought out a collection of newspaper cartoons featuring the former president, while others gathered examples of his wit and good humor. Eugene Wortsman edited *The New Frontier Joke Book*, a collection of jokes about the administration, and Bill Adler published several books on Kennedy's humor, including *The Kennedy Wit, More Kennedy Wit, The Complete Kennedy Wit,* and *Presidential Wit.*[58]

Virtually no aspect of Kennedy's life and work escaped attention. Some authors wrote of his fondness for the sea and sailing. His rigged sloop *Victura* and the presidential yacht *Manitou* would also be featured in several photo displays of the president, his wife, friends, and colleagues. The president's sailing skills were considerable, but the photographs were even more valuable as romantic reminders of Kennedy's youth, athleticism, and loving family. Part of the image that Jacqueline Kennedy wanted to keep alive long after her husband was dead, many of these photos, and those of the young hero on board PT 109, were republished time and again in the years after the assassination.[59]

Something similar can be said of Clare Barnes's lovely book on Kennedy's scrimshaw collection. Barnes wove a history of the whaling industry and the folk art of scrimshaw around the president's scrimshaw collection in a way that highlighted attributes of character central to the Kennedy brand. The president, he made clear, not only collected the carved teeth of great whales that had been hunted and slain in the nineteenth century. The carvings he collected, many of them displayed in his White House Oval Office, also told the story of his own values and of the qualities that had come to be associated with him. Besides images of great whales and sailing ships, his collection included carvings of patriotic symbols such as Bunker Hill, Independence Hall, the White House, and the American flag; famous fighting vessels, such as the USS *Constitution* and PT 109; historic statesmen, such as Alexander Hamilton, George Washington, John Adams, and Abraham Lincoln; heroic military figures such as General Grant, Commodore Stephen Decatur, and Commodore John Barry, the father of the American navy; and epic battles between the great ocean leviathans and the brave sailors who harpooned them.[60] Read as text, Kennedy's collection spoke of more than his love of country or the sea. It said something about his own life and purpose, the romantic ideals and manly values he admired, his sense of history and of his own place in the sweep of time.

Several writers compared Kennedy to other great men: G. Darrell Russell outlined parallels in the lives of Kennedy and Lincoln; Tom Wicker discussed the influence of personality on the politics of Kennedy and Johnson; Pauline Bloncourt compared Kennedy to Winston Churchill.[61] Still others discussed Kennedy's Irish ancestry and travels in Ireland, notably the famous trip to his ancestral home shortly before his death.[62] It seemed as if anyone who knew Kennedy, or something about him, wanted to publish a book on some aspect of his life, no matter how insignificant. One author told *The Story of JFK in Montana* while another, the author of *Pa and Ma and Mister Kennedy*, recounted Kennedy's life and policies in the dialect of a West Virginia mountaineer.[63] Charles Hamilton, apparently serving as his own publisher, contributed a book on Kennedy's use of an automatic signature machine, which raised in his mind the question of whether a law was truly a law if the president had not actually signed it.[64]

The publication of so many books on Kennedy is a good measure of the deep interest that readers had in the president and his administration, not to mention the commercial possibilities for publishers who pandered to an audience that was obviously enamored of the Kennedy image. It was an interest more immediate and more intense than for any other president, including Lincoln and Roosevelt, two presidents with whom Kennedy was often compared. Taking all subjects into consideration, Andy Logan estimated the Kennedy literature at nearly two hundred books by 1968. Looking at all entries – books, articles, edited collections and more – from 1963 to 1969, Vincent Toscano counted four thousand Kennedy-related publications in such reference guides as the *Reader's Guide to Periodical Literature*, the *Biography Index*, and the *Social Science and Humanities Index*.[65]

In fact, the Kennedy literature grew so substantial that it soon required a literature of its own in the form of bibliographical surveys intended to help casual readers as well as scholars and collectors keep track of the books, articles, collections, and editions that flooded the market. Within a year of the assassination, the Jenkins Company of Austin, Texas, issued its "catalogue number three," claiming to list the "largest collection of material relating to John F. Kennedy ever offered for sale." It listed nearly five hundred items by and about the late president, "from the choicest of all Kennedy books ... to the insipid and vulgar movie magazine tripe." The variety of material, as the Jenkins Company rightly claimed, was "indicative of the large number of institutions and private collectors interested in gathering material on Kennedy." It was for that reason only that "some tasteless and worthless items have been offered here."[66] The Jenkins Company catalog was followed by the annotated and selective bibliography assembled by James Tracy Crown in 1968, which in turn gave way to the more comprehensive survey published by Joan I. Newcomb in 1977. The years in between saw the publication of *A Catalogue of Old, Used,*

Rare and Out-of-Print Books on John F. Kennedy, and approximately a dozen other bibliographies and source guides, including publications by the National Archives and the Kennedy Library.[67]

V

In these vehicles of memory, whatever their subject, Kennedy remained more or less fixed in time, forever the handsome family man, the charming wit, the pragmatic idealist, the peacemaker at home and abroad, and the progressive champion who had given his life, much like Lincoln and FDR, in the cause of democratic reform and world peace. This was the substance of the paper monument, of the books and articles contributed by so many authors, some of whom were guided directly by the hand of Jacqueline Kennedy, the most important memory maker of them all. As we will see in the following pages, moreover, the paper monument to Kennedy was only one of the vehicles of memory that commemorated the fallen leader. Others, from the smallest coin to a mountaintop, drove home the same image of the martyred president as the mythical hero, the larger-than-life legend whose attributes and values reminded Americans of who they were or could become.

Some authors challenged this image, beginning in the 1960s and peaking over the next two decades, when a changing political environment brought on by the Vietnam War and the Watergate scandal produced a wave of revisionist literature that echoed, in many ways, the earlier views of Lasky and other skeptics. As we will see, these accounts encountered round after round of rebuttals by Kennedy loyalists, leading finally to something of a standoff and what might be termed a balanced view in the historiography of the Kennedy administration. Much to the chagrin of historians, however, the historiographical battles, so fiercely fought in professional meetings and graduate seminars, floated above the general public like hot air balloons above the ground. Judging by the polls, or by the many visitors who paid their respects at the president's gravesite, most Americans seemed largely indifferent to what the experts had to say and far more interested in the new monuments and many mementos being cast in his honor. In the collective memory of the nation, to put it differently, the Kennedy image would remain intact, creating a gap between memory and history, myth and the real man. This would remain the case over the next forty years, in part because of ongoing efforts by the Kennedys to nourish and protect the sacred image of the late president, and in part, no doubt, because so many Americans wanted to believe that memory was a better guide than history to who they once were and could be again. In this sense, as Gerald Johnson had put it, Kennedy, "once touched by romance," had become an epic figure largely immune to the criticism of historians, journalists, and others. He had written the songs of the nation, if not always its laws, and page after page of historical criticism could not overwrite his legend.

6

In Death There Is Life

Monuments of Glass, Steel, and Stone

Monuments of paper and pen were not the only vehicles of memory through which Jacqueline Kennedy and her family and friends would shape the image of John Fitzgerald Kennedy in the years following his death. There were other monuments as well, the most important being sites of memory where the president could be recalled in rituals of remembrance often approved by his widow. Through these sites, as through the many books she influenced, the former first lady would inscribe on the past her own vision of how the president should be remembered: as a man of strength and courage, a war hero and peacemaker, a daring explorer of new frontiers at home and in space, a champion of excellence in all venues, a man of faith and family, and a progressive reformer who had shed his blood – as Lincoln had before him – in service to his country and to all it represented. Her goal was to make John F. Kennedy a symbol of the nation, of what it meant to be an American, or at least of the ideals to which all Americans should aspire. With this goal in mind, she acted quickly to design her husband's memorial grave, launch a campaign to fund the Kennedy Presidential Library, and importune the new president to place his predecessor's name on both the National Culture Center in Washington, DC, and the space center in Cape Canaveral, Florida.

Much of this memorializing went on while the world remained in deep mourning for the president. It was expressed not only in state-sanctioned commemorations but also in private efforts to remember John Fitzgerald Kennedy, if only through the smallest gesture, the least expensive token. Such acts of commemoration, much like the president's funeral, further assuaged a nation still in the throes of an acute cultural trauma. They relieved the guilt and anxiety that many Americans felt, leaving in their place new symbols of national pride and confidence in the future. They also furthered the process by which the president was transformed into an American icon, very much the larger-than-life figure that Jacqueline Kennedy had in mind. His death would be framed in a narrative of national greatness; his identity linked to that of the nation itself; his life invested with meaning and purpose that would survive the grave. In death, John F. Kennedy would find renewed life in monuments of glass, steel, and stone that commemorated his achievements, the values he supposedly embodied, and the ultimate sacrifice he had made trying to bring a fractured nation together in a new and better union.

II

While the most impressive monuments to Kennedy's memory had the family's blessing and were, for the most part, sanctioned by the American government, not all monuments were monumental; nor was the urge to memorialize confined to the United States. The Navy Department commissioned a new aircraft carrier in Kennedy's name and the postal service brought out a Kennedy memorial stamp that sold over five million copies on the first day it was available in Boston. Sales were brisk in other markets as well, forcing the postal service to double its original print order of 250 million stamps. The Treasury Department, for its part, issued a memorial coin. Not long after Kennedy's assassination, President Johnson proposed, and Congress passed, a bill replacing the Franklin half dollar with the Kennedy half dollar. The new coin, with design features selected by Jacqueline Kennedy herself, became a collector's favorite in its first year of issue. The Treasury Department struck almost four hundred million units of the new coin in 1964, but it did not go into general circulation until later, mainly because so many Americans, having acquired one, refused to part with what they saw as a personal keepsake, its value as a memento exceeding its worth as a coin. Local and state governments also joined the memorial parade, honoring the late president by naming or renaming literally hundreds of schools, streets, highways, bridges, parks, playgrounds, government buildings, and airports in his honor, including John F. Kennedy International Airport in New York, formerly known as Idlewild.[1]

A similar phenomenon swept across the world. Altogether, more than sixty countries honored the late president by placing his image on hundreds of postage stamps, as compared to thirty-four countries that so memorialized Franklin Roosevelt after his death in 1945. On these stamps, Kennedy was remembered as a family man, an athlete, a sportsman with a particular love of sailing, a man of strong faith, a heroic war veteran, and the courageous captain of PT 109. Other stamps highlighted his commitment to civil rights, sometimes featuring images of Kennedy with Lincoln or Martin Luther King Jr. Still others celebrated his efforts on behalf of the space program; his call to voluntary service, including the Peace Corps; his commitment to social reform and to the development of Third World nations; his funeral, gravesite, and the eternal flame.[2] To a great degree, in other words, they memorialized Kennedy in images that recalled the brand that he and his wife had presented in their White House productions.

Besides issuing four postage stamps commemorating Kennedy, Argentina named several streets and schools in his honor and dedicated a thirteen-story marble-and-granite monument to his memory. In Peru, remembrance took the form of a massive Kennedy Park, complete with a large bronze bust of the president; in Israel, the John F. Kennedy Peace Forest came with a sculptured bust; in Melbourne, Australia, an island in the middle of an ornamental lake in one of the city's major parks commemorated the young president, together with a bronze base relief of his head atop a seven-foot-high granite boulder. Dozens of governments, both national and local, named bridges, streets, and roadways after the late president. In Paris, for example, Kennedy joined Washington, Lincoln, Wilson, and Franklin Roosevelt as the only American presidents to have major avenues named in their honor. Not surprisingly, Catholic parishes everywhere dedicated new or old spaces to the late president, including a parish near Parma, Italy, where the cornerstone of a church erected in Kennedy's honor and dedicated to St. Patrick included earth taken from the president's grave in Arlington, Virginia and St. Patrick's Hill in Ireland. Many countries named public works such as youth hostels, hospitals, and housing projects after the president, sometimes with the help of funds made available by the Alliance for Progress. In other places, cultural centers, schools, libraries, student scholarships, new academic facilities, and university professorships were branded with the president's name.[3]

Aubrey Mayhew, in a study of Kennedy's commemoration in medallic art, once speculated that more such items of tribute were issued for the late president in a shorter period of time than for any other person or subject. In his estimation, most of the two thousand jewelry stores in New York City issued at least one Kennedy medal. He predicted as early as 1966 that the Kennedy series of medallic mementos would surpass

the Columbus, Washington, and Lincoln series that were then the ranking collections. By that time, one hundred thousand people had already
collected some Kennedy item and twenty-five thousand serious collectors were willing to buy almost anything issued on the late president,
including key chains, tie tacks, and cufflinks. The business in these items
became so brisk, so fast, that one manufacturer, the Canada Centennial
Numismatic Company in Sudbury, Ontario, erected its own tribute to
the fallen president – a giant Kennedy monument standing thirty-five feet
high and including at its center a replica of the Kennedy half dollar, itself
twenty feet in diameter.[4]

Governments and private dealers in more than a dozen countries
issued commemorative medallions of one sort or another. Business was
especially brisk in Europe, where the high gold content of some medallions made collecting them a rich man's hobby. Less affluent customers,
both abroad and in the United States, settled for a Kennedy half dollar or chose from the millions of Kennedy trinkets produced to meet
a popular demand that was almost insatiable, if often deplorable. In
Maryland, a local dentist set up shop in his laboratory, where he used
his dental equipment to fashion a Kennedy ring and a Kennedy bust for
the local market. In Germany, one large producer issued a death medal,
more or less an exemplar of bad taste, that featured, on one side, the
moment when Oswald's bullet struck the president, and on the other, an
image of Oswald himself being murdered. Other producers offered everything from cigarette lighters, to medals inscribed with quotations from
Kennedy's most famous speeches, to lapel pins cast as the eternal flame,
to key chains and bracelets with rocking chair charms.[5]

Indeed, the commercialization of Kennedy commemoratives may be
one of the best examples of the modern heritage industry at work. Unlike
the complicated business of writing a history of Kennedy and his administration, heritage productions, including many of the commercial publications mentioned earlier, presented a simple, heroic picture of the late
president, replete with redemptive expressions, uplifting messages, and
an optimistic and patriotic narrative. Like the former first lady, moreover, they often forgot as much as they remembered about the president.[6]
Needless to say, they prompted their share of criticism. Writing tongue-
in-cheek for the *Saturday Evening Post*, for example, Anne Chamberlin
claimed that it was "now possible to eat an entire meal off President
and Mrs. Kennedy plates," including one dinner plate with a drawing
of Kennedy's grave "about where the lamb chops would land." To go
with the dinnerware, manufacturers also offered Kennedy beer mugs and

highball glasses, coffee cups, salt and pepper shakers, silverware, frying pans, water pitchers, and other items, many of them complete with an image of the late president stamped on the surface. In addition to collecting recordings of the president's speeches or new editions of his books, those in search of mementos could walk into any drugstore, gift shop, or five-and-dime, such as Woolworth's, and find his-and-her ashtrays featuring a likeness of the late president and his wife, as well as plaster busts, rocking chairs, fountain pens, and more. There was even the "Vig'ah" candy bar, sold by the Vig'ah Corporation of Springfield, Massachusetts, and the "Eternal Flame of Light to Remember," an electric nightlight complete with a portrait of the late president.[7]

However tawdry or ridiculous these small and inexpensive mementos might seem, they amounted nonetheless to a spontaneous expression of personal grief so deeply felt, so widespread, that it spawned a multimillion-dollar business almost overnight. According to *Newsweek*, it was the largest heritage boom in history. Even Chamberlin, her undisguised sarcasm notwithstanding, understood that "most of the people who buy these things are sincerely groping for a way to commemorate" the slain president. They could not afford a meaningful gift to the Kennedy Center or the Kennedy Library; and they might never visit these distant sites of memory in any event. But they still wanted a remembrance of the late president – something of their own – even if it was a simple lapel pin, tie tack, or key chain. "We wanted something permanent," said Yale Meyer of Manhattan, "something we can keep, something that can't be taken away, like they took him." Those who made and sold these items understood what drove the market for their goods. People had an urgent need for some "association" with President Kennedy, as one merchant explained, and shopkeepers everywhere took a kind of patriotic pride in making little mementos available at a price anyone could afford.[8] The same sentiment explains why so many visitors to Arlington Cemetery would leave flowers, even expensive bouquets, at the president's grave, and why soldiers, sailors, and airmen would toss their caps onto the mound of pinecones that covered this most important site of memory.

Such rituals of remembrance further codified themes and images already associated with the former president. Here was the eternal flame to remind Americans of his enduring contributions, the PT 109 pins and plastic models to commemorate his courage and wartime heroism, the rocking chairs that told of his perseverance and willingness to sacrifice, and the dinner plates, embossed with quotes from his speeches, that recalled his oratorical skills, his patriotism, and the principles by which

he steered. Much the same was true of the medallic art commissioned
in his honor, not to mention the many memorials that took his name –
the public works projects, culture centers, parks and athletic facilities,
schools and university buildings, libraries, youth hostels, and even the
navy warship, which spoke of his wartime heroism, his love of the sea,
and his commitment to the nation's security. All of these memorials, and
others like them, honored the president by associating his name and likeness with projects that supposedly reflected his deepest values.

Taken together, they served to elaborate the Kennedy image as performed by the president on the White House stage and as cultivated by
his wife, not only in her White House productions or in her husband's
funeral but also in so much of the Kennedy literature she helped to shape.
Here again was the champion of peace through security, of détente and
arms control, and here too was the great explorer of new frontiers at
home and new worlds in space. Here again was the compassionate man
of character who called for national service and sacrifice, for civil rights
and social justice on a global scale. And here again was the courageous
war hero, the father and family man – in short, the ideal American who
reminded his countrymen of who they were at their best and whose many
deeds and sacrifices made him worthy of remembrance. This is how
Americans wanted to see themselves; this was the brand they wanted to
believe in, which explains, at least in part, the great demand for the many
mementos produced in Kennedy's honor.

III

Two international memorials deserve special attention: Mt. Kennedy
in Canada and the Kennedy memorial at Runnymede in England. Both
spoke to values often associated with Kennedy and to the larger-than-
life dimensions of a man who was quickly becoming the stuff of legend.
Located in the Yukon Territory, Mt. Kennedy had been discovered in
1935 and was, at nearly fourteen thousand feet, Canada's tallest unscaled
and unmapped mountain. Prime Minister Lester B. Pearson announced
in January 1965 that Canada would name the mountain in honor of
the former president, whereupon the Canadian government, the National
Geographic Society, and the Boston Museum of Science made plans for
an expedition that would map the mountain and surrounding area. The
expedition was to proceed in several phases, but the final climb to the
summit would be led by Robert Kennedy, followed by a group of nine

other Americans and Canadians, including James W. Whittaker, the first American to scale Mt. Everest, and Barry W. Pratker, another American member of the famed Everest expedition. In July 1963, only months before his death, President Kennedy had actually met Whittaker at a White House ceremony honoring the mountaineer's triumphant climb to the summit.[9] That ceremony, like those recognizing American astronauts, revealed Kennedy's fascination with the heroic virtues of these new frontiersmen.

Both Robert Kennedy and Whittaker wrote about the three-day expedition, with Kennedy freely confessing the fears and hardships he had to overcome. Although he came from a family of athletes and loved sports of almost any kind, he had never climbed a mountain and admitted to being afraid of heights. The climb was physically demanding as well, including high winds, biting cold, blizzard conditions, and narrow pathways thousands of feet up the mountain. At one point, Kennedy slipped through a snow bridge, fell into a crevasse up to his shoulders, and struggled to pull himself free. The final part of the climb was particularly difficult. The air was thin and cold, Kennedy suffered from continuous headaches, and every inch of progress required a strenuous effort just to put one foot in front of the other. He made it to the summit, however, the first person ever to do so. And once there, he stood in icy silence, saying a prayer for the soul of his older brother before making the sign of the cross and planting the family flag, the American flag, and two Canadian flags in the frozen snow. He also carried to the mountaintop a copy of his brother's inaugural address, a medallion commemorating his inauguration, and several PT 109 tie clasps.[10]

President Kennedy did not climb the mountain, of course, but his brother's self-deprecating description of his own travail and the courage he had to muster seemed calculated to remind readers of the late president, or at least of how the senator wanted his brother (and himself) remembered. So did Kennedy's description of his climbing partners and the mementos he brought to the summit. While Whittaker, Pratker, and the others thought politics "far more dangerous than climbing," Kennedy marveled at their strength and courage, their dedication and "tenacity of purpose," their intelligence and good humor, and their willingness to endure excruciating pain to achieve their goals.[11] These were men who walked mountains and faced death at every turn. What made them do it, he asked, before answering his own question with a quote from James Ramsey Ullman, who had chronicled the American expedition to the top of Mt. Everest. "Challenge is the core and mainspring of all human activity," Kennedy quoted. "If there's an ocean, we cross it; if there's a disease, we cure it; if there's a wrong, we right it; if there's a record, we break it; and if there's a mountain, we climb it."[12]

The quotation could have been a Kennedy family anthem in those days. Not only did it express the virtues that Robert Kennedy saw in his climbing companions; it also expressed the virtues that he saw in his brother and that he and the former first lady wanted inscribed forever on the nation's memory of the former president. Courage was the virtue his brother admired most, he wrote in his description of the climb. He had been an athlete, too; he loved the outdoors, welcomed adventure, and was fearless in the face of battle, including battle against the elements. Robert Kennedy did not mention his brother's support for space exploration and the Peace Corps; nor did he write about his love of family or his service as captain of PT 109. But these, too, must have been on his mind as he scaled the heights of a mountain dedicated in remembrance of the late president. Certainly his brother had shared the climbers' tenacity of purpose, their intelligence and good humor, their strength and courage, and their willingness to take risks – even face death – to achieve their goals. The PT 109 tie clasps, the inaugural address and medal, the family flag and the American flag, were all signs of what it meant to be John Fitzgerald Kennedy, at least as he was idealized by family and friends. As Whittaker put it, just as he and Robert Kennedy struggled to the summit: "This climb and mountain ... have some meaning now for President Kennedy."[13]

A similar interpretation can be read into the Kennedy memorial at Runnymede in England. Kennedy was more at home in England than in any country outside the United States. His father had been the US ambassador there prior to the Second World War; his older brother, Joe, had died fighting for the British; and his younger sister, Kathleen, had married into British aristocracy and was buried in England following her untimely death in an airplane crash. Kennedy himself had traveled to England on several occasions and had written his first book on Britain's failure to prepare for the Second World War. During his presidency, moreover, Kennedy had formed an especially close relationship with British Prime Minister Harold Macmillan, not to mention the even deeper relationship he and his wife enjoyed with Lord David Harlech, another aristocrat who served as British ambassador to the United States. Given these associations, as well as the special relationship, both political and cultural, that Great Britain and the United States had shared over many years, it's not surprising that the government in London wanted to commemorate Kennedy's memory with a very special monument.

Almost immediately after the president's death, the House of Commons decided, and the queen agreed, to dedicate a memorial to Kennedy at Runnymede, a grassy meadow and woodland close by the River Thames where King John had signed the Magna Carta 750 years earlier. The memorial consisted of an acre of land gifted in perpetuity to the United States. Visitors crossed from the meadow through the woodland to the memorial along a path of stone steps carved from the same Portland quarry that had produced the stone for St. Paul's Cathedral – a testimony, perhaps, to the importance the British attached to their relationship with the United States and their memory of John Fitzgerald Kennedy. A seven-ton block of the same Portland stone formed the centerpiece of the memorial. It was inscribed with words designating the site as a gift to the United States in memory of the late president and included words drawn from his famous inaugural address.[14]

Queen Elizabeth II dedicated the Kennedy memorial on May 14, 1965. Lord Harlech presided over the ceremonies, which included remarks by the queen, Prime Minister Harold Wilson, and former prime minister Harold Macmillan. The queen clearly saw the American constitution as heir to the rights and privileges gained in the Magna Carta, just as the United States was heir to Great Britain's role as defender of those rights in the Cold War struggle with the Soviet Union. After all, the quotation inscribed on the memorial spoke of America's resolve to "pay any price, bear any burden, meet any hardship, support any friend or oppose any foe in order to assure the survival and success of liberty."

All three speakers noted the great affection they had for President Kennedy and their personal bereavement upon learning of his death. The queen recalled how her people "wept" on hearing the news. "Every home, every family in Britain," added Macmillan, "seemed in mourning as though a member of the family had been snatched away." They clearly embraced Kennedy as one of their own. Although no one mentioned the president's father, whose tenure as US ambassador in London had not been a happy experience for either side, they had fond memories of his son's sojourns in England, both as aide to his father and on many other occasions. The queen spoke of his book on England's failure to prepare for the Second World War, as well as his lifelong interest in British history and literature, his brother's death fighting for England's survival, and his sister who was buried in an English churchyard. She also spoke of his many accomplishments and personal attributes, which she identified as those so often recalled in American tributes to the slain president. Although "valiant in war," she said, Kennedy was a champion of peace who also envisioned a "just and valiant society" and would always be remembered for his "courage," his "dedication to public service," his "distinction of heart and mind," and his "wit and style." [15]

Jacqueline Kennedy, who attended the brief ceremony with her children and members of the late president's family, later expressed her appreciation in remarks that touched upon the same themes as her British hosts. She associated her husband with the British people, with what they "represent around the world," and with Runnymede itself as a symbol of everything her husband held dear. "For free men everywhere," she said, Runnymede was "sacred soil." It was "the birthplace of our ideals of human freedom and individual dignity in which my husband passionately believed." She also spoke, as she often did, of her husband's love of British literature and admiration for the great men of British history, both of "which shaped him as did no other part of his education." It was in this sense, she concluded, that "he returns today to the tradition from which he sprang." [16]

It is difficult to imagine a parcel of land more precious to the British and more important to British history than Runnymede and its environs. In their minds, it was the birthplace of constitutional government, if not democracy itself, so that no higher honor could be conferred than to be memorialized in that sacred space. By honoring the president in this way, the British, much like the former first lady, were identifying Kennedy not only with America but with democracy as well, almost as if he and Runnymede were synonymous in their symbolism. Nor did the British stop there. Among other things, they dedicated a youth hostel known as Kennedy House to the president's memory, and they raised funds, as part of the Runnymede memorial, to endow Kennedy scholarships to support young British students who wanted to spend a postgraduate year attending Harvard, MIT, or Radcliffe. In both initiatives, as in Runnymede, the British chose to remember Kennedy in memorials that celebrated the values they associated with him, namely, his commitment to education, social justice, and democracy.

Runnymede also highlights another theme in so many of the Kennedy memorials – the importance of nature in rites of remembrance. Earth, as in "dust to dust," has long been a metaphor in burial rituals, reminding everyone that life springs from the earth and to earth it shall return. Much like the flame at Kennedy's gravesite, however, earth could also be a symbol of eternal life, of death and rebirth, of Christ risen from the grave to a life beyond. This was the metaphor attached to many Kennedy memorials. The president might be gone, they seemed to say, but as long as his memory endured, the lessons of his life would live on. This was the meaning of Runnymede, a beautiful meadow and woodland memorial that linked Kennedy to more than five hundred years of British history, from the birth of constitutional government to the New Frontier.

A similar meaning could be read into the Kennedy Memorial Peace Forest in Israel, which associated Kennedy with the cause of world peace, and into the many parks, playgrounds, and lakes that were dedicated to his memory in Peru, Australia, and other countries around the world.[17] The idea also had some resonance in the United States, judging from an editorial in *American Forests*, a journal sponsored by the American Forestry Association. Impressed by the Kennedy Forest in Israel, the editors urged their readers to do something similar in the US. They praised a decision by the Dr. Thomas Dooley Council of the Knights of Columbus in Oakdale, California to plant a grove of oak trees in the president's memory. Similar plans were taking shape in other communities, reported the editors, who reminded readers that trees were a characteristic feature of cemeteries, including Arlington Cemetery, where the president was buried. Trees had grace and vitality, much like Kennedy, they said, and much like the eternal flame, they carried the seeds of their own renewal and the promise of "even greater things to come."[18]

IV

As Mt. Kennedy made clear, some monuments were truly monumental, including several in the United States. These sites of memory also enshrined an idealized image of the president, and examining their creation reveals again the important role often played by the former first lady. This was the case with the Kennedy Center for the Performing Arts in the nation's capital, the Kennedy Space Center in Florida, and especially the Kennedy Library outside Boston and the president's memorial gravesite in Arlington, Virginia. Jacqueline Kennedy personally requested President Johnson to commemorate her husband's memory by putting his name on the launching center that NASA operated in Florida. Ever anxious to court the former first lady, Johnson agreed to her request and actually went further, naming not only the space center after his predecessor but also the whole of Cape Canaveral, where the center was located. He took the last step without consulting the Kennedys or, for that matter, the residents who lived on what suddenly became Cape Kennedy. His overreach resulted in complaints from residents who lobbied Congress to restore the original name, which it did in 1973, just as the nation was commemorating the tenth anniversary of the president's assassination. Nevertheless, John F. Kennedy's name remained on the space center, as Jacqueline Kennedy had wanted, making it a living memorial to the late president and the important role he had played in launching the nation's space program, including the famed mission to the moon.[19]

Jacqueline Kennedy also secured Johnson's promise to push forward with her husband's plans to "make Washington a world-class capital," which included, among other things, plans for what became the John F. Kennedy Center for the Performing Arts.[20] President Kennedy had done a good deal to support the arts during his administration. Though his personal taste ran more to Hollywood movies and spy novels than to serious literature, he did have a fondness for works of history and a keen appreciation for architecture. His wife's appreciation ran even deeper, and each understood the importance of cultivating the arts, both as proof that great art could only emerge in a free society and as evidence that America's global leadership was both deserved and enlightened. By all accounts, moreover, Kennedy had an unconcealed admiration for those who truly excelled at worthy endeavors, including notable artists and musicians whose talents far exceeded his own. With this thinking as his guide, and with his wife as spur, Kennedy put his energy behind numerous efforts to recognize the arts, beginning with his decision to invite Robert Frost and other artists to his inaugural and including numerous White House events to which writers and artists of all kinds were invited, and not always as the entertainment. He also breathed new life into the President's Medal of Freedom recognizing success in the arts. He saved from the wrecking ball the old homes that lent elegance and charm to Lafayette Square, laid plans to rehabilitate Pennsylvania Avenue, and did what he could to support what was called the National Culture Center, chartered by Congress in 1958 but not yet constructed or fully funded.[21]

The proposed center was important to Kennedy and his wife. Both were embarrassed that Washington, DC, was the only capital of a great power without a major venue for the performing arts. Both had championed the project, raised funds for its construction, and agreed that Jacqueline Kennedy should serve as honorary chairman of its board. Under the circumstances, it was not surprising that Kennedy's death sparked support for renaming the center in honor of the late president and all he had done on behalf of the arts. Popular sentiment, together with his promise to Jacqueline Kennedy, help to explain Johnson's decision to endorse what she and others envisioned as a central piece in Kennedy's plan to make Washington, DC, a world-class capital. Johnson quickly requested legislation, which Congress passed and he signed in January 1964, renaming the center after Kennedy and providing $15.5 million in federal funds for its construction. These funds were matched by private contributions, the bulk of which came from large foundations, private corporations, and foreign governments. Ten thousand individuals also made donations, however, and their gifts, too, helped organizers to exceed their goal in only eighteen months.[22]

It would take more than money, however, to bring the Kennedy Center to fruition. The former first lady also wanted assurances that it would be in good hands, which included her hands, and would meet her standards of performance. If "I do not think it is what I wish for him," she wrote Roger L. Stevens, chairman of the center's board of trustees, "I will ask Congress to change its name – which they will do." What would it take to ransom her support? To begin with, she said, the artistic director "must be respected in Washington, … must be willing to live there, … cannot have any other job, … [and] must be acceptable to me." In addition, a member of the Kennedy family "should always be on the board" and she, too, should always have a personal representative, even if it meant sacrificing one of the current board members (although not one she liked). "I cannot go on this way unless I have my representative," she told Stevens. From there, she evaluated three board members who were due for reappointment, declared two of them unacceptable and insisted, without any sense of irony, that new appointments "never be allowed to fall into the realm of political patronage."[23]

Apparently assured on these counts, Jacqueline Kennedy and members of the Kennedy family gathered in Washington on December 2, 1964, when President Johnson officially broke ground for the John F. Kennedy Center for the Performing Arts. Located on the banks of the Potomac and designed by architect Edward Durell Stone, the gleaming white marble edifice was surrounded by columns finished in bronze and gold, and enveloped, under one roof, enough performance space for symphonic and theatrical productions, opera, ballet, musical theater, festivals, exhibits, band concerts, and restaurants.[24] It opened in September 1971 to mixed reviews from architectural, music, and drama critics. For some, Leonard Bernstein's "Mass," a mixed composition of chorale, song, and dance written especially for the occasion, was little more than kitsch and totally inappropriate for a federal cultural center. For others, it was the building that failed. A rectangular structure the size of three football fields, the design had been approved by the Kennedy's prior to the president' assassination. Nevertheless, critics considered it poorly situated and fatally simplistic in its exterior appearance, with an interior, moreover, that was too cavernous and luxurious for a facility constructed in part with public funds. One critic called it a "public works project for the rich," with an excess of opulence and ticket prices far beyond what ordinary Americans could afford.[25]

There were admirers, of course, who considered Bernstein's composition daringly original and Stone's building delightfully modern. No amount of criticism, moreover, could obscure the symbolic significance of this imposing site of memory, which, at that point, was to serve as the nation's only official memorial to the late president. In the dedication and groundbreaking ceremonies, actor Jason Robards, one of many performers present, read an excerpt from the speech that Present Kennedy had delivered at Amherst College just weeks before his assassination. Kennedy, he quoted, envisioned an "America which will reward achievement in the arts as we reward achievement in business or statecraft." Both President Johnson and Robert Kennedy spoke of the new center as a living memorial. It was intended to present the best in the performing arts, discover and nurture new talent, and promote art, art education, and artistic expression in communities across the country, all in remembrance of President Kennedy, who had done so much to foster the arts during his presidency. As both made clear, moreover, Kennedy understood that other countries would judge the United States on its success in the arts, in part because artistic endeavor symbolized the quality of American civilization, in part because it inspired confidence in American leadership. He was also a man who admired excellence in the arts, and who shared with artists "the courage to confront the world as it is" and to search within himself "for the truth." These were familiar attributes of the Kennedy brand that he and his wife had cultivated in their White House years. They supposedly inspired the president, as they had the best of his predecessors, whose names were often associated with his own. It was no accident that Johnson used the same spade at the December 1964 groundbreaking that had earlier been used to break ground for the Lincoln Memorial, which stood nearby. The symbolism could not have escaped the Kennedys; nor could the symbolism evident in the center's location, which lay within eyesight of the president's grave just across the Potomac in Arlington National Cemetery.[26]

There is no more successful site of memory, or one more popular, than President Kennedy's grave in Arlington Cemetery. Within hours of the president's death, as we have seen, Jacqueline Kennedy had decided to bury her husband there on a site aligned with the Lincoln Memorial. This was one in a series of decisions that invited the American people to share in her grief and to recall her husband as she wanted him remembered. She made it possible for people everywhere to participate in the president's funeral – if not in person, then on television. In a remarkable gesture, she also opened the White House to public visitation each day during the thirty-day period of official mourning. On the first day alone, roughly nine thousand people visited the East Room to see the catafalque on which the president's casket had rested and the chandeliers and windows still draped in black crepe.[27] As she must have known, even the gravesite became a place of public mourning and remembrance, the likes of which had never been seen before. Here more than anywhere else, people were invited to share in the sorrow of a wife who had lost her husband, a family that had lost its father, a nation that had lost its leader. In this sense, the gravesite came to resemble nothing less than a shrine in remembrance to the late president, maybe not as he was, but as his wife and family wanted him remembered.

"If it can be said that any grave is beautiful, the President's is," wrote reporters for the *Washington Post, Times Herald* days after John F. Kennedy had been interred. A simple plot at that point, surrounded by a white picket fence, it had already become the "nation's newest and saddest shrine." A line of mourners, up to a quarter-mile long, climbed the hill and crossed before the grave at a rate estimated at about a quarter of a million per week, a total equal to 10 percent of the population in the area around Washington, DC. They were the largest crowds ever to visit the cemetery – so large, in fact, that the *Washington Post, Times Herald* published tips for visitors to the gravesite. They should be patient, the paper advised. They should have plenty of fuel in their vehicles and comfortable shoes on their feet because they might have to park as far away as the Lincoln Memorial and stand in line for two hours, maybe more, before reaching the gravesite. By the end of May 1964, just six months after the president's death, three million people had visited his grave. Members of the Kennedy family and the president's staff, along with dignitaries representing other governments, paid their respects on a regular basis, especially during the period of official mourning. But most were ordinary men and women of all ages and colors, from all parts of the country and all parts of the world. They reenacted time-honored rituals of mourning and remembrance as they moved slowly up the line and past the grave. Heads bowed, they were somber and respectful, some praying quietly as they walked, some saying the rosary, some in tears, some carrying flowers that were carefully deposited inside the little picket fence that enclosed the site. The president's grave, as army officials concluded, had "become in a very real sense the 'family plot' of the nation."[28]

In the year following Kennedy's death, approximately seven-and-a-half-million people made a pilgrimage to his gravesite, more than visited the Washington Monument and the Lincoln Memorial combined and nearly three times the number of visitors to the cemetery in previous years. By April 1966, the number of visiting mourners had climbed above twelve million, an astonishing figure. The large crowds also drove attendance to record-breaking numbers at other sites in the cemetery. The Tomb of the Unknowns had more visitors than ever before, and paid attendance at the Custis-Lee Mansion, just above the Kennedy gravesite, doubled in the six months after the president's burial.[29] Even today, more than fifty years after his death, the president's gravesite remains a destination for tourists visiting the capital, for children on school tours, and for those wanting to commemorate his life and memory. Of the four million people who visit Arlington National Cemetery each year, the overwhelming majority still pay their respects to the late president, many of them stopping at his grave before going anywhere else.[30]

Nor were the living the only ones coming to Arlington in larger numbers; the dead increased as well. In the year following Kennedy's burial, interments grew from nineteen to twenty-five veterans per day in a cemetery that already held the graves of 125,000 members of the armed forces.[31] This was part of the genius behind Jacqueline Kennedy's decision to inter her husband in Arlington Cemetery, and part of her larger strategy for shaping how the president would be remembered. As a veteran, of course, and as commander in chief of the armed forces, Kennedy was entitled to be buried there, though only one other president, William Howard Taft, had made that choice before. For the former first lady, however, there was no choice at all. Her husband had been president of all the people, as she once explained, and his memory belonged to them, not just to the citizens of Massachusetts. What is more, Arlington National Cemetery was hallowed ground, the final resting place of many veterans, some of whom had died in battle. Kennedy's burial in this sacred space reminded Americans that he, too, had been a veteran, a decorated war hero who had risked his life in service to the nation.

As we have seen, by aligning Kennedy's grave with the Lincoln Memorial, the president's widow also established a symbolic bridge between two presidents widely viewed as struggling to extend the rights of citizenship to those deprived of its advantages. The same symbolism operated at another level as well. Arlington National Cemetery and the

Custis-Lee Mansion, situated at one end of the capital's memorial axis and just across the Potomac from the Lincoln Memorial, had long stood as symbols of national reconciliation and reunion after the Civil War, much as Kennedy was viewed, at least in his idealized image, as giving his own life to unify a country increasingly rent by economic, racial, and regional divisions. In case even this symbolism was too abstract to be easily understood, an ecumenical group of religious leaders brought it into clear view with a candlelight ceremony marking the end of the official thirty-day period of mourning. Held at the Lincoln Memorial, the ceremony began at dusk on Sunday afternoon, December 19, 1963. The high point came when President Johnson, who presided over the ceremony, lit a candle with fire carried from the eternal flame at his predecessor's grave in Arlington Cemetery. Others in the large crowd lit candles of their own, or one of the twenty-five thousand candles donated by Giant Food Stores. Invoking the familiar theme of death and rebirth, not to mention what some must have recognized as a symbolic connection between Kennedy, Lincoln, and Christ, the memorial service ended with a march to the Ellipse for the ceremonial lighting of the nation's Christmas tree.[32]

Less than four years after his assassination, the president's remains were moved to a permanent gravesite about two dozen steps from his original resting place. The new site, which reverberated with themes already evident in the temporary location, is particularly important as one of only two major memorials – the other being the Kennedy Presidential Library near Boston – where the lead designers worked under the direct supervision of Jacqueline Kennedy. This had not been the case with the Kennedy Space Center or the Kennedy Center for the Performing Arts; they had been renamed in Kennedy's honor, but were already commissioned or in use at the time of his death. Because of her personal involvement, moreover, both the gravesite and the Kennedy Library became works of art as well as sites of memory, and both say as much about Jacqueline Kennedy as her husband's principal memory maker as they do about the president himself.

The Army Department, which administered Arlington National Cemetery, set three acres aside for the president's final resting place. It was a large amount of space in a cemetery where the burial plots of deceased veterans averaged only 10 x 5½ feet. There were only two other exceptions to this rule: the Unknown Soldiers occupied eight-tenths of an acre, and General John J. Pershing, commander of the American Expeditionary Force in World War I, was buried in a plot of slightly more than seven-tenths of an acre. The size of Kennedy's plot prompted some criticism when it was announced in December 1963. Given the circumstances, however, complaints were muted and quickly gave way to army justifications. The steep contour of the three-acre site, according to the Army Department, made it unsuitable for a large number of graves. In addition, Kennedy's wife and deceased children, as well as his two brothers, both veterans, and their spouses and minor children, could also be buried in the same location. What is more, all three acres would remain the property of the federal government, and the Kennedy family would cover the cost of the grave itself, if not the entire three acres, which the Army Department would manage as a memorial to the slain president. By the time the whole project was finished, the total cost added up to approximately $2 million, with the Kennedys contributing roughly $300,000 for the gravesite itself and the balance covered by the federal government, including funds for the architectural design of the entire three-acre space.[33]

John Carl Warnecke became the principal architect for the new memorial gravesite. He and Kennedy had become friends in the years prior to the president's assassination. A tall, handsome, broad-shouldered man, he was just two years younger than the president and a graduate of Stanford; he had played tackle on the university's football team, which enjoyed an undefeated season in his senior year and a Rose Bowl victory in 1941. After graduation, Warnecke went to Harvard, as Kennedy had before him. He took an advanced degree from the School of Architecture there, worked for a short time in his father's successful Bay Area architectural firm, and then started his own business. By the time Kennedy met him, he had a record of considerable achievement as the architect on large projects for a number of California schools, including Stanford University and the University of California. He had been commissioned to design both the US embassy in Thailand and a new Hawaiian state capitol, and to draft master plans for the US Naval Academy and the California state capitol. Kennedy, who had a fondness for nicknames, called him "Rose Bowl," worked with him to redesign Lafayette Square, appointed him to the US Commission on the Fine Arts, and sought his advice on a design for his proposed presidential library on the campus of Harvard University.[34]

Jacqueline Kennedy shared her husband's fondness for Warnecke and admired his plan for Lafayette Square. That plan carefully blended past and present, old and new, in an architectural design that suited its setting and appealed to Kennedy's aesthetic sensibilities. Under the circumstances, it came as no surprise that she selected him to design the president's memorial gravesite in Arlington National Cemetery. Nor was it a surprise when Warnecke announced, after he and Jacqueline Kennedy visited the president's grave in late November 1963, that he would work under the "very close direction" of the former first lady, emulate the historic simplicity of what he had done in Lafayette Square, and include the eternal flame as the essential element in the final monument.[35]

Warnecke faced a daunting task. He had never designed a memorial gravesite. His first effort would face intense scrutiny from professional architects and art critics, and would be supervised by a demanding widow who had a clear vision of how she wanted her husband remembered. Nor did memorial architecture enjoy a particularly good reputation at the time, as evident in the controversy then engulfing plans for an FDR memorial in the nation's capital. Those plans, which included an architectural competition with five hundred contestants, exploded when the judges selected a design featuring five large slabs of irregular size, each inscribed with lines from one of Roosevelt's many speeches. The design was wildly unpopular and ultimately rejected by the Fine Arts Commission, which had oversight of such memorials in the District of Columbia.[36]

As William Walton pointed out, moreover, few modern monuments were truly inspiring. Most failed "in their tribute to the dead," in part because the very idea of a monument to the memory of a great man seemed outdated in the modern era, and in part because modern monuments were more likely to express the sensibilities of the artist than the life and spirit of the subject being remembered. The result in many cases, which Walton cited, was a strange disconnect between the monument and the man it memorialized. An artist himself, as well as Kennedy friend and member of the Fine Arts Commission, Walton had strong convictions about the elements he considered essential to a successful monument. He told readers for the *New York Times* that monuments had to be scaled to their setting and simple in concept and detail. They had to be evocative and therefore "symbolic rather than literal." Only these elements would add "spiritual quality" to a monument, and only such a quality would "stir men's minds and emotions." The Lincoln Memorial had this character, he said, as did the famous statue of "Grief" that Henry Adams had commissioned for his wife's grave in Rock Creek Cemetery.[37] Walton had every reason to expect the same of Kennedy's gravesite, particularly since its principal features were already evident in Warnecke's work, notably the idea that architecture should be scaled to its setting, simple in concept, and symbolic.

Similar advice came from other experts, most of whom were delighted with the plans that Warnecke finally developed. For the most part, he relied on advice from his colleagues on the Fine Arts Commission, including Walton, and from the Kennedy family, especially Jacqueline Kennedy, who vetted every step in the process of design and construction. She met several times with Warnecke's design review committee, which held nearly fifty meetings between December 1963 and August 1965. The committee also interviewed the former president's brothers and sisters, colleagues and friends, as well as specialists in church liturgy, officials from the US Park Service and the Department of the Army, prominent architects, landscape designers, and notable art and architecture experts. The experts included Wolf Von Eckardt, William Walton, and the other members of the Fine Arts Commission, which formally approved the final design. There was some criticism, of course, especially from architects whose ideas Warnecke had rejected, and from Eunice Kennedy Shriver and her husband, Sargent Shriver, who wanted a greater emphasis on Kennedy's Catholic faith at the gravesite, particularly symbols, such as winged angels, that conveyed the notion of resurrection and eternal life. For others, however, a small etched cross on the grave marker and the eternal flame, itself a symbol of eternal life, went as far as they thought appropriate for the grave of a man who had led a nation of many faiths.[38]

Warnecke grounded his work in a comprehensive review of topics ranging from Western burial traditions, the burial sites of other presidents, the history of Arlington National Cemetery, and the relationship of the Kennedy grave to the city of Washington. He studied monumental architecture from ancient times forward, and concluded that ancient symbols and old rituals of remembrance lost their meaning unless linked to the feelings and ideas of the present, much as he had tried to do with Lafayette Square. The same conclusion emerged when he surveyed the graves of past presidents. Only the simplest designs seemed to stand the test of time, from George Washington's modest crypt at Mount Vernon to Franklin Roosevelt's simple headstone at Hyde Park. To his way of thinking, this approach seemed particularly appropriate to the gravesite at Arlington Cemetery, which was "not a place of mourning or sorrow" but of "national pride" and fallen heroes.

What is more, Kennedy's grave would rest at the southern terminus of the capital's great axial spine, which stretched from the Lincoln Memorial across Memorial Bridge to Arlington Cemetery. With the Capitol Dome, the Washington Monument, and the Jefferson Memorial, not to mention the Kennedy Center, spread around and behind the Lincoln Memorial, the president's burial site would become an integral part of the city's great monumental architecture and, indeed, occupy "the most significant location of

any presidential grave." As a result, "there was no need for overt monumentality," as Warnecke told Wolf Von Eckardt, because "the location of
the grave is itself monumental." The goal instead was to strengthen the
monumental aspects of the location, to make sure that the hillside below
the Custis-Lee Mansion, with its remarkable view of the capital city, was
"more beautiful than before." "This particular hillside," this "flame, this
man and this point in history must be synthesized in one statement,"
Warnecke concluded in words that might have been uttered by the former
first lady, who had worked in so many ways to idealize her late husband, to
identify him with the nation itself, and to synthesize his virtues into a single
statement about what it meant to be an American.[39]

Von Eckardt was among the many critics who heaped praise on the
architect when Warnecke displayed a model of his design at the National
Gallery of Art a year after the president's death. He called it "a master-
work of dignified restraint," neither modern nor traditional, and "in perfect harmony with its place in nature and history." He and others noted
the absence of even a vertical tombstone, let alone a formal sarcopha-
gus, statue, or building. The site began with a circular granite walkway,
embracing near its center a magnificent old oak tree and leading up the
hillside to an elliptical overlook. On one side, the overlook afforded a
spectacular view of the Lincoln Memorial and the capital city, while the
other stepped up to a marble-framed terrace where the president and his
two deceased children were to be buried in a grassy, rectangular plot.
The three graves would be identified with simple slate markers with the
eternal flame just behind the president's marker and in front of a marble
retaining wall incised with the presidential seal and quotations from the
president's speeches. At seven and a half feet, the retaining wall would be
the highest structure at the site. It would afford some protection for the
eternal flame, which could be seen at night from the Lincoln Memorial,
1.3 miles away, and which Warnecke still considered the "primary symbol at the grave, stronger than any sculpture or any structure that might
be added to it." In his mind, the total design was simple, "and out of its
simplicity and dignity will come its beauty."[40]

"Simplicity, openness and respect for the landscape," said Walton,
was "what makes this design succeed." Joseph Watterson, editor of the
Journal of the American Institute of Architects, considered the gravesite
a work of landscape sculpture, as did *Time* magazine, which thought
the design "more an appreciation of a natural site than a monument
of masonry." The "whole concept," said *Architectural Record*, "was
conceived as sculpture – the hillside contours, the walks, the terraces,

the walls, all leading to the central theme" and symbol of the eternal flame. Dr. S. Dillon Ripley, a prominent art historian and secretary of the Smithsonian, was struck by the "strong, mystical overtones" of the design, and Carter Brown, assistant director of the National Gallery of Art, thought it actually captured Kennedy's personality, particularly his "marvelous understatement."[41]

In a flurry of media commentary on Warnecke's design, only one commentator raised concerns. Ada Louise Huxtable, a distinguished architectural critic writing in the *New York Times*, reminded readers of the historic and artistic value of the green slope in which Kennedy's remains would rest. It had long been considered a prominent visual feature of the city and one of its best vistas. She cited a report issued in 1902 by city planners who wanted to reestablish L'Enfant's original vision for the capital. They considered the site inviolable and warned "against the invasion of monuments" that could "utterly annihilate" its "beauty and repose." If left up to Huxtable, Kennedy's grave would have been located elsewhere, although in the end, even she conceded that Warnecke had done everything he could to exercise "good judgment and taste." He had aimed for understatement, rather than monumentality, for maximum meaning in minimal terms, for an inoffensive design where almost anything would offend. He had achieved "fitness, simplicity, and dignity" in a work of landscape architecture made more difficult by the need for "symbolism, ceremony and a specific emotional ambiance."[42]

Huxtable's concerns may help to explain why Warnecke and Jacqueline Kennedy modified their original thinking in the last phase of the design work. The changes took some critics by surprise, particularly Wolf Von Eckardt, who was not entirely happy with the results. The former first lady had commissioned her old friend, the self-taught horticulturalist Bunny Mellon, to soften the stony aspects of the memorial grave with magnolia, cherry, and hawthorn trees, as well as other plantings. The additions enhanced the natural beauty of the site, relaxed its otherwise formal appearance, and created something more akin to a park-like atmosphere. The change delighted Von Eckardt, as it did others, but he was less enamored of a decision to replace the grass covering on the burial plot with New England fieldstones that had been quarried at Cape Cod more than one hundred and fifty years earlier. This was Jacqueline Kennedy's decision and it gave the burial plot the appearance of a cobblestone terrace stitched together by patches of grass and wildflowers that grew between the stones.

For the former first lady, the fieldstones were clearly intended to remind visitors of her husband's New England origins; for Von Eckardt, however, they took Mellon's parklike theme too far. They created a rustic appearance that detracted from the dignity of the site and was grossly incompatible with the marble platform on which the burial plot rested. He was even more disturbed by a decision to eliminate the seven-foot-high marble retaining wall at the back of the gravesite. No doubt removed because its height obscured the Custis-Lee Mansion above it, Von Eckardt thought its absence took the otherwise laudable simplicity of the overall design too far. The quotes from Kennedy's inaugural address now appeared on the smaller wall along the northeastern side of the elliptical overlook. To Von Eckardt, the change left no clearly visible backdrop to mark the presence of the president's grave, now barely elevated above the ground. Even the eternal flame, once a clear marker, simply shot from a hole in a large granite fieldstone that grew so blackened with soot that Von Eckardt demanded an immediate improvement. All of these changes must have pleased Huxtable, but not Von Eckardt, though in the end, he still considered the completed gravesite "the most cherished monument of modern American history."[43]

Von Eckardt did have his way when it came to the hats. On the day of Kennedy's burial, the Honor Guard, whose members represented each of the services, had left their hats on his grave. This tribute to their slain commander in chief was a particularly important gesture for the Green Berets. Kennedy had established this Special Forces unit and had approved of their distinctive berets in spite of opposition from their army superiors. In the months following the burial, members of the armed forces who visited the grave, especially the Green Berets, would fling their caps over the white picket fence onto the gravesite. Von Eckardt considered it a heartfelt gesture but completely inappropriate at the new gravesite, in part because the hats and other emblems lent a military cast to the gravesite, and in part because they deprived the site of its dignity, simplicity, and beauty. His complaint drew support from other sources, including the editorial board of the *Washington Post, Times Herald*. In its view, too, the accumulating headgear detracted from the simple dignity of the gravesite and the symbolism it held for all Americans, not just those in uniform. The Army Department agreed. It praised the original gesture as spontaneous and well-intentioned, but ordered the hats removed once and for all.[44]

Even before this little controversy unfolded, President Kennedy's remains and those of his two deceased children were moved from their burial site behind the white picket fence to what Von Eckardt had called "the most cherished monument." The reburial occurred in the dark of night with only the workmen and a few family witnesses on hand. Early the next morning – March 15, 1967 – Cardinal Cushing formally consecrated the new gravesite. President Johnson joined Jacqueline Kennedy, the late president's two brothers, and other members of the Kennedy family for the brief ceremony. Held in the chilling rain of a gray dawn, the ceremony featured Cushing's dedication and some of the same music played at the president's funeral, including "The Star-Spangled Banner," the "Navy Hymn," and that old Irish tune, "The Boys of Wexford." At the end, Jacqueline Kennedy stepped forward to place a handful of lilies on the slate tablet that identified her husband's grave.[45]

As she gazed from the elliptical overlook back across the Potomac to the Lincoln Memorial, the Washington Monument, and the Capitol Dome, the former first lady must have been proud of what she and Warnecke had accomplished. *Architectural Record* called it "the noble Kennedy grave site at Arlington National Cemetery." Its "symbolic value" was enhanced by the very space it occupied and by Warnecke's "inspired use of every dramatic, expressive and evocative potential" the setting had to offer. The grave was centered on the cemetery's main gate, as well as Memorial Bridge and the Lincoln Memorial, and was linked "obliquely" to the Washington Monument and the Capitol Dome along the second major axis in the capital's "great axial fabric." Its location alone conferred on the modest but dignified tomb "a civic consequence comparable to that possessed by the Washington and Jefferson as well as the Lincoln memorials." This is what Jacqueline Kennedy and the Kennedy family must have wanted, concluded *Architectural Record*, "and Warnecke did not fail them."[46]

The national anthem, "Navy Hymn," and "The Boys of Wexford" were all symbolic reminders of the president's life prominent in both his funeral and in his burials. What is more, the gravesite itself was written in a language of representation, thick with symbols of the Kennedy brand that would remind visitors of how Jacqueline Kennedy wanted the late president to be remembered. Its location in the sacred soil of Arlington Cemetery recalled his devotion to service, his heroism in the Second World War, and his willingness to sacrifice everything for the greater good. Positioned as it was on the capital's "great axial fabric" within view of the Washington Monument, not to mention the Lincoln and Jefferson Memorials, the gravesite told visitors that Kennedy was among the greatest presidents in American history, comparable in particular to

Abraham Lincoln, who had also given his life in the cause of freedom. The simplicity of the site reflected the president's dignity and lack of pretention, not to mention the dignity of his office. The magnificent oak tree, standing tall and strong on a grassy mound inside the rounded walkway, recalled his fortitude and strength of character. Other symbols reminded visitors that a man, not just a president, was buried there. The cobbled fieldstones recalled his boyhood in New England. The graves of his two children told the nation that he had been a loving father and family man. The small crosses etched into their slate markers gave the site a spiritual significance and were intended, as Warnecke made clear, to recognize the president's religious belief and faith in God.[47]

The eternal flame, a familiar religious symbol of resurrection and the promise of life everlasting, suggested that death need not conquer John Fitzgerald Kennedy if Americans followed the bright light of his example, cherished his legacy, and emulated the values that made him a true American, synonymous with the nation itself. All of the gravesite's many symbols were calculated to remind visitors what it meant to be an American, though perhaps none more so than the words from the president's inaugural address that had been incised on the memorial wall along the elliptical overlook. "Ask not what your country can do for you but what you can do for your country," read one of the excerpts selected by Jacqueline Kennedy, a clear reference to the president's commitment to public service and sacrifice. "With a good conscience our only sure reward, with history the final judge of our deeds, let us go forth," read another excerpt, in full confidence that the "energy, the faith, the devotion which we bring to this endeavor will light our country and all who serve it – and the glow from that fire can truly light the world." However simple and dignified the site might be, however abstract its language of mourning and remembrance, these words in this piece of landscape architecture defined monumental in a new way. Although cast in minimalist terms, the memorial grave had a grandeur that defied its simplicity. It became a solemn space, at one with nature and the divine. It sacralized the man who was buried there, made him more symbolic than human, and put him above reproach.

V

Or did it? As we have seen, the Kennedy Space Center, the Center for the Performing Arts, the president's gravesite, Mt. Kennedy, Runnymede, and a thousand other monuments and mementos, all commemorated Kennedy as an American icon whose identity was that of the nation and whose virtues were those to which all Americans should aspire. But only a few years after Kennedy's remains were moved to the permanent gravesite, historians began in earnest to contest this representation and revise the way they assessed the former president. They did so, moreover, just as the Kennedy Library and Museum was opening its doors to visiting tourists and scholars alike. Another monument designed by a famous architect working under the close supervision of the former first lady, the library, like the gravesite, would thus become not only a celebrated work of art but also a vehicle of memory in what amounted to an emerging war over Kennedy's reputation. It would add luster to the idealized image of the former president and try at the same time to protect the sacred symbol against the counter narratives of revisionist scholars.

The Kennedys began their work on behalf of the library on what would have been the president's forty-seventh birthday, May 29, 1964. It was a busy day. Jacqueline Kennedy and her children made a sorrowful visit to the president's temporary gravesite. They passed through the gate of the white picket fence, knelt before the grave, and prayed silently, heads bowed, as the eternal flame flickered in front of them. At about the same time, in anticipation of Memorial Day, former Kennedy staffers and top officials in his administration held a tearful commemoration of their own, with President Johnson recalling the tragedy of Dallas and urging all on hand to rededicate themselves to his predecessor's vision. Meanwhile, and more to our point, thousands of New Yorkers stood for hours to process, as if in solemn ceremony, through a traveling exhibit of Kennedy memorabilia, assembled by Jacqueline Kennedy, her family and staff, for eventual deposit in the John F. Kennedy Presidential Library and Museum. The crowd walked slowly, sometimes three abreast, usually in silence, often for an hour or more before reaching the entrance. "Well-dressed women with department-store shopping bags," as *Newsweek* described the crowd, "men with attaché cases, gum-chewing teen-agers," all kinds of people came, seven or eight thousand every day, to see mementos of the president's life.[48]

The exhibit would travel across the country from New York to almost two-dozen cities before stopping at San Francisco in mid-October.[49] Although the goal was to raise funds for the Kennedy Library by showing who the president "really was," as Jacqueline Kennedy told *Life* magazine, what the exhibits actually revealed was her husband as she wanted him remembered. There were photographs of the president in formal settings, as well as official documents, including a letter from Nikita Khrushchev written at the height of the Cuban Missile Crisis. But the collection also included the president's White House rocking chair and the coconut on which he had scratched his famous rescue message after his PT boat had been sunk. These items were enough to call up the image of the president as a navy veteran and war hero, a man of strength and fortitude who suffered silently, a resolute leader, fearless in the face of great peril and ultimately triumphant. These were the images, already well known, that Jacqueline Kennedy wanted Americans to hold in their memory.

Many of the exhibits evoked Kennedy's personal side, although these, too, elaborated familiar themes long part of the Kennedy brand. The photographs, for example, often captured a relaxed man in family settings, laughing and playing with his children or enjoying the company of his wife, brothers, sisters, and friends. The exhibit also displayed sheets of yellow, legal-pad paper on which he doodled or scribbled during meetings, as well as a Riviera scene he had painted while recovering from a difficult back surgery in 1955. It displayed the president's scrimshaw collection, too, along with some of his favorite books and the famous "Resolute" desk with the false front from which his son would burst forth, much to the president's amusement. Included, also, were some of the president's ship models, notably one presented as a gift from Khrushchev; a set of wood-carved shore birds his wife had given him; the bust of an ancient Roman he had given her; and a handwritten letter to his father, composed when he was a boy at prep school, requesting a raise to his allowance. All of these items tended to personalize and humanize the president, but in ways that stressed how his most important attributes had remained the same throughout his life, whether in private or in public. Here again, Kennedy was revealed as a man of character, a loving husband, father and son, an athletic man who enjoyed nature and the sea and who had an active and curious mind – an intellectual of sorts with a serious interest in art, literature, and history. In Jacqueline Kennedy's exhibit, as in the books she shaped and the gravesite she designed, the personal and official sides came together in a portrait of the great man, the ideal American, who was one of us, to repeat the words of Arthur Neal, but also the best of us.[50]

The traveling exhibit was a great success. In the first nine cities alone, approximately half a million people toured its displays and made donations.[51] At that point, certain items were selected for showing at the New York World's Fair, while the remainder traveled to Europe for an eight-city tour that continued into early 1965.[52] By promoting the Kennedy brand, the exhibit previewed the work of the Kennedy Library and Museum and raised a good deal of money the Kennedys did not want squandered elsewhere. The gravesite and the library were their priorities, which may help to explain why they often discouraged other memorials, particularly the many schools, parks, streets, and playgrounds dedicated to the president's memory. These gestures, not to mention the tie clasps, bracelets, glassware, nightlights, and other trinkets, could make memorializing the late president a trivial affair and cheapen his image, as they had constructed it. But they might also divert resources from the Kennedy Library at a time when it could play a useful role in defending Kennedy's reputation against a growing number of revisionist scholars, who seemed to sprout like mushrooms from the dank soil of American politics in the years after Kennedy's death.[53]

The same issue of *Newsweek* that described the touring exhibit of Kennedy memorabilia also described rising racial violence in Mississippi and elsewhere in the South, including the bombing of black churches and more Klan attacks on Freedom Riders arriving from the North. Still another story, summarizing the work of the Warren Commission, gave an early preview of the controversy that would engulf its final report, as critics began to ask if the president's murder had been the work of more than one assassin, perhaps even a conspiracy.[54] These stories, not to mention those describing the country's growing involvement in the Vietnam struggle, captured a political and social climate that was increasingly unstable, not to mention a new generation of critics who were cynical about political leadership and inimical to the notion of idealizing any president. In this environment, it would become increasingly difficult to defend the approved narrative of the president's life against the assault of revisionists who were anxious to expose flaws in his personality and attack what they saw as his hawkish foreign policy, tardy response to the civil rights crisis, halfhearted commitment to social justice, and essentially conservative economic views. Under these circumstances, as we will see, the Kennedy Library became important, not only as another example of memorial art but also as a battleground in the historiographical war over how the president would be remembered.

7

The Memory Wars

Contesting Kennedy

Neither Jacqueline Kennedy nor Carl Warneke had thought of Arlington National Cemetery as an appropriate setting for a traditional work of monumental architecture. The site was naturally monumental in itself, and plans quickly formed behind the National Cultural Center as the federal government's major memorial to the president. Besides, the former first lady had monumental plans for another location, which the president himself had selected, if not necessarily for this purpose. Kennedy had decided to deposit his papers in a presidential library to be built on the campus of Harvard University. He and Warneke, another Harvard graduate, had actually searched the campus for an appropriate location shortly before the president was assassinated. After that, final decisions rested with the Kennedy family, especially Jacqueline Kennedy, who was determined to honor her husband's wishes, though in a fashion that joined his plans to her own dreamy vision of the man she wanted everyone to remember.[1]

Several of Kennedy's predecessors had established presidential libraries, starting with Franklin Roosevelt, who donated his Hyde Park home for that purpose. Truman, Eisenhower, and Hoover followed with modest ventures that included an archive for the benefit of scholars and a museum of presidential artifacts, mostly for the benefit of tourists. Thanks to Jacqueline Kennedy, however, the Kennedy Library and Museum became something more – an impressive work of art in its own right and a grand monument to her husband's memory. Although her vision came to fruition after President Johnson had opened his own, Texas-sized structure on the campus of the University of Texas at Austin, planning for the Kennedy Library had begun much earlier and clearly inspired

Johnson and subsequent presidents, many of whom tried to outdo the others with expensive monuments to themselves and their administrations. Another example of the heritage boom, these American "pyramids," as one critic has called them, often presented their subjects as heroic figures in American history, occasionally at the expense of history itself. They did so not only in the museums they sponsored but also in the records they archived and sometimes hid from public view.[2] In both regards, the Kennedy Library and Museum set the standard for much of what followed.

As a site of memory, the Kennedy Library and Museum revealed in its architecture the same themes that Jacqueline Kennedy had captured so successfully in her design for the president's gravesite. This was especially true of the museum and its exhibits. They recalled her restoration of the White House as a stage for the performance of her husband's presidency, her careful attention to the symbolic value of costumes and other props, the spectacular state dinners she produced and directed, and the dramatic presentation of her husband's funeral, with its powerfully emotive rituals and theatrical flourish. As in these cases, she tried to manage impressions by going beyond a literal reading of the past to a staged reproduction that left some parts in but others out. In the museum's final design, as in her White House restoration, the past would be a seductive blend of history and aesthetics, as much about feeling as fact, as much about the imagined as the real. It would represent the president as his wife wanted him remembered and as the two had played their parts at center stage, not backstage, in the White House.

By managing the library and museum with this goal in mind, Jacqueline Kennedy and her family became active participants in the long struggle over who owned the president's historical identity. This struggle reveals again one of the major themes that runs throughout this narrative: the tension between history and memory, between what is recalled and what is forgotten, between the historical profession and the heritage industry – in this case the Kennedy Museum.

The battle commenced when a new generation of revisionist historians challenged the received orthodoxy of Schlesinger, Sorensen, and others in the first generation of Kennedy scholars. Journalists, too, got into the fray, offering their own views, taking sides in the historiographical wars, and setting the stage for a third, post-revisionist wave of scholarship. After a twenty-year struggle, the post-revisionist group seemed to be gaining the upper hand, though you wouldn't know it by looking at opinion polls or the many public representations of the president's image.

Nor was it evident in the work of the Kennedy Library and Museum. On the contrary, both remained wedded to an idealized memory of the former president and tried at every turn to conceal, or erase altogether, alternative narratives and counter memories.

II

Libraries seemed to be a particularly appropriate reflection of John F. Kennedy. After all, he was an avid reader with a strong penchant for works of history. He had published several books, won a Pulitzer Prize, and talked about spending his post-presidential years writing his memoirs, lecturing in campus classrooms, or serving as a college president – perhaps even president of Harvard University. How better to honor his memory than with libraries dedicated in his name, and not just at Harvard. Sargent Shriver, the brother-in-law that Kennedy had asked to head the Peace Corps, launched a book drive for the benefit of Kennedy libraries to be founded in countries where Peace Corps volunteers were serving. The campaign joined in symbolic union many of the qualities for which the former president was known, including his call to service, support for education, commitment to the betterment of underdeveloped nations, and love of learning. Within six months of the assassination, publishing houses and other donors had contributed more than four thousand books to the Peace Corps libraries, which developed alongside the many libraries in the United States and around the world that would bear his name.[3]

Nor did the Kennedys waste time in launching the John F. Kennedy Presidential Library and Museum in Boston. In doing so, they were building on efforts that began in the first year of the Kennedy administration, when Kennedy and Nathan Pusey, president of Harvard University, negotiated an agreement to house all of Kennedy's papers at a presidential library on that campus. Each agreed to designate representatives to work out the necessary details. Arthur Schlesinger, who had been involved in the negotiations from the start, led this effort on the president's behalf. He and others returned to the campus in search of a suitable location, drafted appropriate acquisition policies, and framed a set of guidelines that would help cabinet officers, agency heads, and other members of the Kennedy administration to determine which of their personal papers might be contributed to the library's holdings.[4]

The work accelerated sharply after the president's assassination. In early December, the Kennedys established the John F. Kennedy Memorial

Library Corporation, with Robert Kennedy as president, to work with Harvard on the library project.[5] Also in December, Robert Kennedy and Arthur Schlesinger hosted a dinner meeting to discuss what the library might do besides archiving the president's papers. Out of this gathering came a series of position papers by, among others, Professors John Kenneth Galbraith and Samuel H. Beer, both of Harvard University, Don K. Price, dean of Harvard's School of Public Affairs, Professor Richard E. Neustadt of Columbia University, and assistant US archivist for presidential libraries, Herman Kahn.[6] At the same time, the group established a committee to coordinate the work ahead. They made a checklist of issues that had preoccupied the president, began microfilming records related to those issues, and started contacting cabinet members, agency heads, White House staff, key legislators, and members of the family, all of whom were asked to donate their papers to the Kennedy Library.[7]

Look magazine reported that technicians and photographers employed by the National Archives were scurrying through government offices, like bewildered rabbits through a maze, filming entire drawers of documents dealing with the Kennedy administration. By mid-June, more than two million documents had been microfilmed in a multitude of government agencies. Archivists had also collected twenty personal file cabinets from the president's White House office, as well as his office furniture for display in the presidential museum. In addition, the Kennedys wanted to supplement these records with miles of recorded oral histories contributed by almost anyone who had served in the administration. By March 1964, 150 people had agreed to contribute their oral histories, a number that grew to 350 just eighteen months later. The Carnegie Corporation provided a major grant to defer the cost of the project, which, by that time, had been turned over to Charles T. Morrissey, a National Archives historian who had achieved success organizing the oral history collection at the Harry S. Truman Presidential Library in Independence, Missouri. The project was "unprecedented in American history," said Robert Kennedy, in a bit of Kennedy hyperbole, and would make the new library far more expansive than any of its predecessors.[8]

Besides assembling an archive, the Kennedys, through the Library Corporation, immediately established a fundraising arm led by James V. Lavin, who reported to Stephen Smith, a Kennedy brother-in-law and treasurer of the corporation.[9] Under federal law, the cost of constructing a presidential library had to be paid with funds raised privately. Once built, the library would be turned over to the federal government and operated by the National Archives at taxpayer expense. The corporation set the initial fundraising goal at $10 million. Most of the total would be earmarked for the library and the remainder for a policy institute to be connected academically to Harvard University through its Graduate School of Public Administration. The institute was to be a living memorial to the former president. In theory, at least, it would bring government officials and academic experts together in a common forum, much as Kennedy and his "action intellectuals" had collaborated in the White House. There, in the cloistered environment of the ivory tower, they would analyze public problems and produce innovative solutions shaped as much by nonpartisan experts as by partisan politicians.[10] Although the proposed institute went beyond what other presidential libraries had done to that point, it quickly set the standard for those that followed.

Fundraising was an immediate success. Smith reported in March 1964 that nearly half of the total cost of the library had been collected, including $1 million from the Joseph P. Kennedy Foundation. The AFL-CIO levied a fifty-cent tax on its members for the library fund; William Manchester, as we have seen, pledged a large chunk of the royalties from the sale of his book on Kennedy's assassination; the Boston Red Sox donated the proceeds from a benefit game; and individual donors contributed several million dollars, sometimes in pennies, nickels, and dimes. In fact, gifts of $10 or less poured into the library fund by the thousands. Other revenue came from contributions generated by the traveling exhibit of presidential mementos that Jacqueline Kennedy had organized and from a television appeal she made when thanking those who had sent condolences following the death of her husband.

Smith and his colleagues also established fund-raising committees in more than forty states, recruited state governors or other prominent citizens to chair the committees, and assigned fund-raising goals to each of them. They asked Eugene Black, former head of the World Bank, to chair the Kennedy Library Corporation, in which capacity he petitioned foreign embassies for gifts that would aid the project. Another committee, led by Black, IBM chairman Thomas Watson, and former secretary of defense Robert Lovett, solicited major gifts – usually of $100,000 or more – from corporate and financial institutions. The Kennedys even held fund-raising rallies featuring members of the family as well as prominent political friends and allies. Rose Kennedy and Senator Edward Kennedy, for example, appeared at a rally in North Carolina with Governor Terry Sanford and evangelist Billy Graham. Ted Kennedy went from there to Europe, where he solicited contributions from governments in France, Italy, Germany, and Brussels. Stephen Smith met with donors in

New York, as did Robert Kennedy, and in Washington, DC, the Kennedys worked through the many agency heads appointed by the late president to solicit federal employees for gifts in his honor.[11] President Johnson spearheaded this effort, which also had the bipartisan support of leaders in both houses of Congress. Organizers asked every employee of the federal government to contribute and kept track of who donated and how much.[12] By the end of 1964, all of these efforts had helped the Library Corporation go well beyond its original goal of $10 million.[13]

At the same time, the Kennedys organized an expert board of distinguished architects, chaired by William Walton of the Fine Arts Commission, to advise on the selection of an architect who would design the library. If Robert Kennedy served as president of the Library Corporation, and Stephen Smith handled fundraising, no one doubted that Jacqueline Kennedy would commission the architect and oversee that part of the project, as she had the design for Kennedy's gravesite in Arlington National Cemetery. For this reason, she dispensed with an open international competition for the commission, as that would "surrender to the judges," in Walton's words, control she reserved to herself. Instead, she asked the advisory board to nominate a handful of candidates from its own ranks, whereupon Walton burned the nominations to avoid hard feelings. "It was a bit like electing a pope," he said. Jacqueline Kennedy, together with Walton and another member of the Kennedy family, then interviewed the finalists. They offered insights into the president's life and noted his preference for contemporary structures in harmony with their environments – which, of course, squared with what Jacqueline Kennedy preferred as well. In March 1964, they awarded the commission to Ieoh Ming Pei, who was, as Gerry Nadel put it in an essay for *Esquire*, "the personal choice of Jacqueline Kennedy."[14]

It was a daring choice. I. M. Pei was a Chinese-born American citizen, only forty-seven years old, who had established his own architectural firm just seven years earlier. He was "not unknown," as one critic put it, "but not famous either," in part because, as Pei himself acknowledged, "the big commissions of the monumental sort" had not "usually come my way." He was not a traditionalist, Ada Louise Huxtable noted, but a modernist. He tried to avoid the purely decorative in favor of straight lines and an open, honest design that was sensitive to its setting and took advantage of new construction technologies, including reinforced concrete exteriors with little more than glass as a complement. Sometimes called the "people's architect," Pei's work had focused to a great extent on urban renewal projects in Cleveland, Philadelphia, and Boston, where his designs had rejected the traditional gridiron patterns and conventional interiors that gave most urban spaces a dreary similarity. Not only did he adapt his exterior designs to their surroundings; his interiors, including plumbing pipes, heating ducts, and support beams, were usually left unadorned or exposed altogether. "We've tried to free ourselves from the servitude of conventional building technology," as one of his partners explained, and achieve "a structural integrity in which the building itself, not the furnishings, is the most important part of the interior." Pei's bold new style appealed to the Kennedys, as did his youth and reputation as the people's architect, all of which seemed to cast him in the family mold. His work captured "the spirit and style" the family wanted, Robert Kennedy explained. Others might be better known, Jacqueline Kennedy said, "But Pei! He loves things to be beautiful." Critics generally applauded Pei's selection as well, and the architect himself enthused about the prospect of finishing his work by the end of the decade.[15]

That prospect turned out to be a pipe dream, in part because Jacqueline Kennedy and other planners had decided to include two large amphitheaters in their proposed design. The policy institute would be included as well. It would be named in honor of the late president and attached to Harvard's Graduate School of Public Administration, which would thereafter be called the John F. Kennedy School of Government. The original site for the Kennedy Library and Museum could not accommodate these additions, which meant that another site had to be found. After several months, and a personal plea from the late president's mother, the state of Massachusetts donated twelve acres of land to the enlarged project. Near Harvard Square in Cambridge, the land was home to trolley barns and other storage facilities used by the metropolitan transit authority. Legal wrangling would delay the project for years, but at the time, both Jacqueline Kennedy and the Kennedy family were thrilled with the new location. So were many community and university leaders, who saw the project as an aid to local growth and a vast improvement over the trolley barns. It had been the president's first choice, they also said, and was large enough to fit the complex of buildings and functions they had in mind, including coffee shops, bookstores, green gardens, and perhaps even a replica of the White House Rose Garden, where students and others could gather.

But if the Kennedys were happy, the same could not be said of local residents who had been watching as millions of people flocked to the Kennedy gravesite in Arlington Cemetery. They worried that a Kennedy museum would draw similar hordes to Cambridge, not to mention the fast-food restaurants, souvenir shops, and cheap motels that catered to the needs of out-of-town tourists, whose gum wrappers and sandwich bags would litter the landscape. They also warned of insufficient parking and overcrowding in the little town, higher taxes to support additional public services, and rising property values that would drive low- and middle-income homeowners from their neighborhoods.[16]

These complaints came to a head for the first time in June 1973, when Pei unveiled his design before local and state officials as well as members of the Kennedy family, including Jacqueline Kennedy, who had gathered in Boston for the occasion. The design featured an eighty-five-foot pyramid of glass flattened at the top and framed on three sides by a crescent-like structure where the Kennedy School of Government and the Institute of Politics would have their homes. Although Walton had once said that elements of monumentality would be part of the final design, Pei thought his use of glass actually made the structure "less monumental" and less likely to overwhelm the smaller structures around Harvard Square.[17] Others thought differently. Cambridge residents, who had organized their own task force to study Pei's plan, were stunned at the size and "aloofness" of the structure, which they called a "cross between Camelot and Disneyland." They said it would be a "people magnet" and warned again of overcrowding, higher taxes, and urban blight. They also accused the Kennedys of ignoring their concerns and threatened to throw themselves before the bulldozers if that's what it took to delay construction until a federally commissioned environmental impact study could validate their charges. And when the study dismissed much of what they had to say, the group accused Cambridge officials, university leaders, and the Kennedys of using their political influence to fix the outcome, rejected the study's findings, and promised to challenge its authority in court.[18]

Adding insult to injury, architectural critics joined community organizers in damning the design. One critic dubbed the glass pyramid an "Instant Giza" without a peak, a symbolism so obvious as to be unworthy of I. M. Pei. Wolf Von Eckardt agreed, calling the flat-topped pyramid a "banal" symbol of the "pyramidical power of John Kennedy's achievement tragically truncated by fate." Ada Louise Huxtable complained as well and so did Carter Brown, chairman of the Federal Commission on the Fine Arts, who compared Pei's design to Kennedy's plan for the Bay of Pigs and begged him to reconsider. Jane Holtz Kay, a well-known architectural critic of decidedly liberal views, delivered the most stunning rebuke in an essay for the *Nation*. She accused Pei of presenting a "monolith with all the finality of a Pharaoh presenting a *fait accompli* to generations yet unborn." His "super-scale monument," she wrote, an "arrogant and ponderous shrine to JFK," glorified the former president but ignored the community. An "isolated tomb of glass" surrounded by windowless concrete walls, it was "visually as well as socially" inconsistent with the "human pattern and more intimate if motley pedestrian architecture of Harvard Square." Pei, she said in words that combined her thoughts with those of another critic, was "the last of the great 17th Century architects" whose "imperial scale" was anti-environment and would "ruin the neighborhood."[19]

The dispute dragged on for months and months. Pei and the Kennedys offered several adjustments to make the proposed complex more palatable to community critics. They reduced the scale of the project by a third, mostly by eliminating the two theaters and shrinking the size of the library and archives. They redesigned the architecture to fit more neatly with its surroundings in Harvard Square and with the Georgian style of campus buildings. They also scrapped the glass pyramid that many considered "supercilious," "grandiose," "overbearing," and "pretentious," although Pei would have his revenge years later when he resurrected the idea in his famous design for the Louvre in Paris.[20]

None of this satisfied the critics, however. Their major concern was the museum portion of the design and all the tourists, traffic, eateries, and junk shops it would draw to their neighborhood. Nor did the Kennedys help their case when they scaled back the library and archives, leaving millions of documents in storage at the federal depository in Waltham in order to preserve as much space as possible for the museum. "This opened our eyes," said a leader of the Harvard Square Development Task Force. "The Kennedys want people, droves of people, to come to a new kind of Disneyland" while "scholars can go to Waltham." This made "a mockery" of the university's academic mission and of the president's dream, which envisioned – as the critics saw it – a library, not a museum, on the Harvard campus.[21]

The unthinkable had happened. Ten years after the assassination, a tide had turned against the Kennedys. The long period of mourning had ended. The president's reputation was under attack by revisionist scholars, as we will see, and the citizens of Cambridge were no longer willing to put his memory above their convenience. New social and political forces had emerged since 1963, including a newfound concern for an urban environment overburdened with excessive development, not to mention a profound skepticism of presidential leadership brought on by Lyndon Johnson's deceitful management of the Vietnam War, the Watergate scandal of the Nixon administration, and recent revelations regarding President Kennedy's personal life. Jaded by these developments, the Cambridge critics, denounced by the Library Corporation as "a snobby few," had little tolerance for "grandiose" monuments erected to honor a former president whose administration, many now believed, had started the country on the road to ruin.[22]

Desperate for a workable compromise, university leaders were ready to divide the complex. In deference to community protesters, and increasingly convinced that their concerns were justified, Derek Bok, the new president of Harvard, wanted to leave the library, the Kennedy Institute, and the Kennedy School of Government in the proposed location but move the museum to a more distant site.[23] Jacqueline Kennedy and the Kennedy family rejected the suggestion. With legal action promising to stall progress indefinitely and inflation driving up the cost, they decided in December 1975 to move the project, minus the Kennedy Institute and the Kennedy School of Government, to another location. There was no end of bidders eager to accommodate them; proposals came flooding in from Amherst, Hyannis Port, Newport, and elsewhere. In the end, however, the Kennedys chose a bloc of land offered by the University of Massachusetts on its new Boston campus at Columbia Point. On the site of a former landfill and at the edge of a seedy public housing project, it had the advantage of overlooking Boston Harbor and being large enough to accommodate what the Kennedys had in mind, which was something close to the monumental structure that Pei had originally proposed.[24]

Disappointed and exhausted by the long battle, Pei nonetheless unveiled a third, and triumphant, design for the library in 1976. Intended to evoke Kennedy's love of sailing and the sea, the new design put the library and museum at the end of Columbia Point peninsula, where it would stand like a "whitewashed, baroque lighthouse" overseeing the entrance to Boston Harbor. It would look outward in one direction to the Atlantic, and in the other to "the city upon a hill," as Pei called Boston, where Kennedy had begun his political career.[25] Comprised of linked geometric forms of smoked glass and polished white concrete, the dazzling complex had an almost playful appearance, like a children's park of unrelated shapes and sizes, including long, angular walls leading down to the waterfront, a tall, triangular structure to house the archives and research rooms, a cylinder-shaped construction where the museum and two theaters would be located, and a boxlike pavilion of tinted glass climbing one hundred feet off the ground. Marked only by a hanging American flag of enormous proportions and a wall inscription from Kennedy's much quoted inaugural address, the pavilion was a vaguely similar substitute for the glass pyramid at the center of Pei's original design.[26]

Because visitors entered the pavilion from the museum and theater, where they viewed a film and surveyed mementos of the president's life and achievements, Pei clearly intended the space, with its windowed view of the vast horizon, to prompt a quiet contemplation of Kennedy's life and how to honor his memory. Much the same can be said of the words etched into the wall. Kennedy had told his inaugural audience that his ambitious agenda, the agenda of the New Frontier, could not be achieved in his first hundred days in office, "nor even in the life of this Administration, nor even perhaps in our lifetime on this planet. But let us begin," he concluded, in words that gave the glass pavilion its symbolic meaning. Here, visitors could reflect on the great man and his unfulfilled agenda, but also remind themselves of the boundless space beyond the celestial sphere where Kennedy's spirit could live on, if only the American people were inspired by his example to complete the work of democracy.[27] Arthur Schlesinger captured this sentiment in a talk to high school students in connection with the library's dedication. The Kennedy administration, he said, amounted to an "exhilarating" departure in American politics, not only because of its substantive achievements but also because the president had forced his countrymen to confront the wide gaps between their performance and their ideals. They could do better, the message seemed to be, if they followed the agenda he had set for them.[28]

A similar message resided not only in the pavilion but also in the structure taken as a whole. It brought to mind, as noted earlier, a lighthouse that shone the way, like the eternal flame, to the safe shores of Camelot. The linked set of geometric forms might appear to have neither front nor back nor sides, but its changing shapes and vantage points led ultimately from a progressive past, enshrined in the museum, library, and archives, to the gleaming glass pavilion, standing like a crystal cathedral, where visitors could contemplate the president's vision as they gazed outward to the endless ocean expanse.[29] The setting called to mind the last scene in a film recounting the death of a tragic hero, when the camera, panning upward to the sky, reminds viewers of the hero's sainthood. Kennedy had not died, it seemed to say; he had ascended to a higher place where the light of his example would illuminate a path to the new frontier he had envisioned.

These were the views of most, if not all, architectural critics, including Wolf Von Eckardt, who praised the third version of Pei's design as an "exuberant sculpture" and great work of "abstract art."[30] Even Jane Holtz Kay pulled her punches – though not by much. She didn't care for the glass pavilion, which reminded her of the atrium at a Hyatt hotel. She called the whole complex a "Sermon-on-the-Mount structure," a fair characterization, it seems to me, where people came, as they would to a "shrine," to hear hymns of praise to the Kennedy family. She complained again that the Kennedy Library and Museum would draw more tourists and cars than the environment could tolerate and foreclose forever the possibility of a "graceful, suburban enclave" at Columbia Point. It was a "mall encased by cars," her critique concluded. It was "a windswept energy consumer wrapped in a pseudoscientific shell whose structure is dictated only by personal aesthetics."

Yet even Kay had to concede the effectiveness of Pei's work, and that of Charles Guggenheim, who produced the Kennedy biopic that played repeatedly in two theaters, not to mention Chermayeff & Geismar, the design firm that Jacqueline Kennedy had commissioned to stage the museum exhibits. Here again were the treasured artifacts, including Kennedy's iconic rocking chair, his books and scrimshaw collection, a replica of his Resolute Desk with false front panel, the coconut on which he had carved his famous rescue message, and most of all, the many pictures of the immensely photogenic president at work and play. Even his sloop, the *Ventura*, had a place of pride by the sea outside the museum. Here again, visitors were witness to the president's triumphs in standing up to the communists but also his love of peace and vision of a future without nuclear war. Here again, they could see him as the champion of new frontiers on earth and in the heavens, of sacrifice and public service, of social justice at home and abroad. In this dense forest of images and symbols, visitors could discover once more the values that supposedly made Kennedy the ideal American, including his courage, heroism, and resolve, his capacity for self-sacrifice, and his intellect and humanity. More than ever before, they could see Kennedy as a family man, with adoring wife and loving children, to be sure, but also as a man whose strength of character came from his family and their remarkable journey through American life. The museum devoted space to the first lady, of course, and to the life and memory of the president's brother, who had been assassinated in 1968, but also to both sides of the president's family, the Fitzgeralds as well as the Kennedys, who were revealed as self-made Americans struggling for success over the generations. In this sense, and despite his wealth, Kennedy himself could be remembered as self-made, although his log cabin story had less to do with the triumph of will over poverty than with the religious and ethnic biases he had overcome on his march to the highest office in the land.

Drafts of the exhibit at the Kennedy Library reveal what the designers intended to convey, as does the long oral history later recorded by four top officials of the Kennedy Library. These included Dan Fenn, a former White House aide to President Kennedy and the first director of the Kennedy Library, and John Stewart, who served variously as head of the oral history program, acting director, chief archivist, and director of educational programs. They talked, sometimes guardedly, about setting up the first permanent exhibits at the museum and drafting the script that went with them. Although much of the initial work was done by library staff in collaboration with Chermayeff & Geismar, the designers ran "every bit of text past Arthur," said Fenn, referring to Arthur Schlesinger. Schlesinger was "the final editor," as Stewart called him, and was always anxious to present a favorable view of the president he once served in the White House, particularly when it came to "Kennedy and Vietnam." Schlesinger also stressed how important it was to go beyond displays of what the president actually accomplished. Like the former first lady, he wanted to capture what Kennedy represented, what he "stood for," which included "reason; candor; excellence; public service and concern; citizen responsibility; … the young; the minorities; the poor; the future; idealism without illusions;" and the conviction that individuals could make a difference.[31]

Besides Schlesinger, the designers worked very closely with Jacqueline Kennedy, by that time Jacqueline Kennedy Onassis, especially on exhibits dealing with entertainment in the White House, and with Patricia Kennedy Lawford, who served as a liaison between the exhibit planners and the Kennedy family. Dave Powers and Lemoyne Billings, both close personal friends of the former president, got involved as well. Powers participated in the most important meetings that library officials had with Chermayeff & Geismar, and Billings, at one point, vetoed a proposed exhibit featuring gifts presented to the Kennedys by foreign dignitaries. Much the same can be said of Ted Sorensen, who was an active participant in planning the museum and who, at one point, nixed an exhibit dealing with Kennedy's policies toward the developing world. And then there was Milton S. Gwirtzman, a Kennedy friend and lawyer, who also served as a "representative of the family" in everything having to do with the museum and its exhibits. Given the involvement of so many friends and relatives of the former president, it's hardly surprising that Fenn, Stewart, and others worried about offending the Kennedy family. Nor is it surprising that the final narrative revealed in the exhibits more or less mirrored what Schlesinger and Sorensen had written in their heroic histories of Kennedy and his administration. The museum, as one scholar explained after viewing the exhibits, "left no room for dispute, no room for doubt."[32]

Indeed, it was Sorensen who provided the main theme around which the exhibits would be organized – the theme of "courage, compassion, and innovation."[33] As noted in the first draft of an exhibit covering the presidential years, these were the "three essential qualities JFK brought to the presidency." The president's courage could be captured in his performance during the Cuban Missile Crisis, the steel crisis, and the Berlin crisis. His space program, Test Ban Treaty, and planned tax cut could illustrate his innovative thinking, while his compassion could be seen in his civil rights proposal, commitment to international aid initiatives, and support for progressive social programs such as Medicare. A second draft, dated April 28, 1977, noted how the emphasis throughout should be on decisions and actions taken personally by the president. It should leave visitors with the clear impression that he "responded well to ... domestic and international challenges and crises"; that his administration "marked a period of new departures and new initiatives in many policy and program areas"; and that he "brought an unusually high level of style, grace, and morality to American political and governmental affairs."[34] It was a "capsule Camelot," as Kay called the museum, "a visual ensemble" with powerful emotional chords. Whatever misgivings visitors might have about the president – or his library and museum – it was "impossible not to be touched" by the evocative power of the exhibits.[35]

If the museum often presented a saccharine sweetened version of the past, so typical of the modern heritage industry, it was exactly what the Kennedys wanted, particularly Jacqueline Kennedy, who had once told Theodore White that she was not interested in "bitter histories" written by "bitter old men." She was interested in memory. Her husband's life "had more to do with myth, magic, legend, saga, and story than with political theory or political science," and she wanted him remembered in these romantic terms. Seen in this light, the museum amounted to a work of performance art, staged as a remembrance of her husband's presidency as she had staged so many events in her renovated White House. Replete with the familiar props and elaborate scenery associated with his administration, it called to mind the iconic image of the president as he had played his part in American politics – the same image that Jacqueline Kennedy had cultivated in the symbolic pageantry of his funeral, itself a work of performance art, and in the many literary and physical monuments to his memory.

Pei's soaring design also captured her vision perfectly. Its playful ensemble of geometric shapes, pointed triangle thrusting upward to the sky, boxed glass pavilion, vast ocean vista, and "soaring modernity," as Schlesinger put it, "was a triumphant evocation of the spirit of the Kennedy years."[36] "In its elegant sweep," noted another commentator, "the building perfectly symbolizes the career of the man it honors."[37] If the age of heroes had died in the wake of Vietnam and Watergate, and if heroic architecture had died with it, commented Jane Holtz Kay, you would never know it by the large crowds that toured the museum and were moved, like Kay, by the remarkably evocative power of its exhibits. Whatever historians might be saying, "deification" still had "mass appeal" when it came to John Fitzgerald Kennedy.[38]

III

If memory is as much about forgetting as remembering, the museum forgot a lot. It overlooked the administration's plots to overthrow Fidel Castro and slighted Kennedy's early contributions to the global arms race and his escalation of Eisenhower's commitment to Vietnam. It also concealed his health problems, the drugs he was taking, and the romantic liaisons he conducted in the White House. For Jacqueline Kennedy, these stains could not be allowed to soil the sacred image of the slain president, as framed not only in the museum but in the institute and library as well. When it came to the institute, she and her allies wanted to control the purpose to which his memory and their money would be put; and when it came to the library, they wanted to safeguard the president's reputation by managing his records, even if it sparked, as it did, concerns about censorship and a long battle with scholars who wanted to write their own histories of the president and his administration.

Although the main struggle centered on the library at Columbia Point, the battle line stretched from there to the campus of Harvard University, where Robert and Jacqueline Kennedy, as we have seen, wanted the Kennedy School of Government and Institute of Politics to serve as living memorials to the dead president. To achieve this goal, they agreed to use some of the funds raised for the Kennedy Library to establish a $12.5 million endowment for the new school and the institute that went with it. Under the terms of the endowment, moreover, the institute enjoyed its own advisory board, or visiting committee, that had to include at least one member of the Kennedy family. Jacqueline Kennedy was the first family member to serve in that capacity, although other members of the board and some of the school's faculty affiliates were Kennedy friends or former colleagues. These and other details, including the charge that Jacqueline Kennedy could veto the selection of the first three directors of the new institute, caused something of a stir when they first became known to the press. British journalist and Kennedy critic Henry Fairlie accused the Kennedys of penetrating the ivory walls of Harvard. They had carved out a portion of the university for their own purposes, he said, which included not only a living memorial to the dead president but also a talent pool of academic experts to support the next Kennedy administration.[39]

Although Fairlie went too far, it is true that Jacqueline Kennedy and her family enjoyed considerable influence, if not full control, over the institute's mission and governance structure. In some of the original planning, Schlesinger and others had wanted the institute to be "administratively independent from Harvard." But nothing in what the Kennedys finally proposed suggested that the institute, once established, would operate wholly outside of Harvard's normal system of governance. That said, the Kennedys did insist on naming the institute's first director; and thereafter, as Fairlie noted, Jacqueline Kennedy could reject up to "three candidates successively proposed" for the directorship by the officers of Harvard University. That provision was "intended to provide a specific safeguard against an appointment which in her judgment would be offensive to President Kennedy's memory." As noted earlier, moreover, they insisted that Jacqueline Kennedy or one of the president's brothers should have a seat on the institute's advisory board or visiting committee, and that the committee also include a member of the Kennedy Library board – a provision that would give them still more influence over the institute itself. "The family's always been involved in the visiting committee," as Derek Bok explained later. "They've always had a lot to do with who's on that visiting committee," and there has "always been a kind of special place for them" in the Kennedy School and Institute.[40] That "special place," moreover, would always be used to influence how the late president would be remembered.

This would be the case as well in their management of the president's papers and other collections at the Kennedy Library, including those of his wife, his brother Robert, and the many friends and colleagues who contributed their papers and oral histories to the library. To be sure, laws restricting the release of classified information pertaining to national security affairs applied to all presidential libraries. Before these records could be opened to the public, they had to be reviewed and declassified by the national security agencies involved. But the problems that researchers encountered at the Kennedy Library went much further. They included the slow processing of the president's papers, the library's original mismanagement of its oral history collection, and deed-of-gift restrictions imposed by the Kennedy family and others who donated their records. These restrictions allowed the Kennedys to seal items related to the "personal, family, and business affairs" of the former president, including his medical history and private correspondence, as well as any documents that might be used to "injure, embarrass, or harass" them or any other person. These records could be opened only with the prior approval of a three-person review committee representing Senator Edward M. Kennedy and Jacqueline Kennedy Onassis. Burke Marshall, a Kennedy friend and former colleague, headed the review committee, which also included, at least in its early days, both Ted Sorensen and Harvard political science professor Samuel Beer.[41] Restrictions of this sort, which applied to other collections as well, gave the Kennedys substantial control over what parts of the president's life would be recalled and what parts would be slighted or ignored altogether. Not surprisingly, researchers often found the collections disappointing and sometimes accused the library and the Kennedy family of sealing material that might damage the president's place in American history and memory.

In 1987, Mary Ann Watson explained in an essay for *Prologue*, the magazine of the National Archives, that only "bits of information" about Jacqueline Kennedy were available to researchers at the Kennedy Library. This had been the case from the start. In 1977, for example, Burke Marshall and the review committee had decided to close her papers "indefinitely" because they overlapped "into the First Lady's private affairs or her private relationships with people (including public figures)." Nine years later, Dave Powers was still fighting any effort to open Jacqueline Kennedy's White House Social Office files, specifically a request by the author C. David Heymann, who was then writing a biography of the former first lady. At that point, the Social Office files held 1,227 boxes of records, including 1,014 stuffed with correspondence arranged alphabetically by name and subject. A year later, when Watson wrote her article, only 114 of these boxes had been made available and the process of opening the remainder was extremely slow. In the meantime, historians had to plow through other collections, such as oral histories or the papers of Pierre Salinger, to track the activities of the former first lady.[42] Even now, more than two decades after her death and more than fifty years after the death of her first husband, a large portion of Jacqueline Kennedy's papers remains sealed to historians.

Robert Kennedy's papers were slow to be opened as well, or even deeded to the National Archives. This branch of the Kennedy clan felt slighted by the library. To their way of thinking, it had not afforded Robert's records or his memory the space and attention accorded to his younger brother or even his brother-in-law Stephen Smith, who worked tirelessly on the library's behalf over many years. The library eventually paid tribute to Smith with a new meeting facility dedicated in his name, and honored Edward Kennedy with an elaborate institute for the study of the US Senate. But over the years, there had been "nothing out there for Robert Kennedy," complained his son, Joseph P. Kennedy III. When the library promised to dedicate a small wing in Robert Kennedy's honor, taking his papers in exchange, the younger Kennedy ridiculed the space as nothing but a "hallway." For a while, he and other members of the family considered selling some or all of Robert Kennedy's papers at public auction. They even went so far as to ask Sotheby's to appraise their value. At one point, they also negotiated to deed the papers to George Washington University, which was willing to include them with its other library holdings and provide some rooms for appropriate staff. But the negotiations collapsed when the university's offer did not go far enough to please members of Robert Kennedy's family, who really wanted a "special place" where they could build a grand "R.F.K. Memorial."[43]

Meanwhile, the Robert Kennedy collection, like the Jacqueline Kennedy collection, remained more or less closed to scholars. It was 2011 before the library finally announced plans to open just sixty-three boxes of his papers to the public. This was less than 20 percent of the total collection and contained, as the library director had to admit, virtually nothing beyond what scholars already knew from different sources. Most of his papers as attorney general, so essential to any history of his brother's administration, including records relating to the civil rights struggle, the wiretapping of Martin Luther King, Jr., the Cuban Missile Crisis, assassination plots against Castro, and other major events, remained closed to the public in a presidential library maintained and operated at public expense.

Only those researchers favored by the family, such as Arthur Schlesinger and Evan Thomas, were permitted access in connection with the largely positive assessments they were writing about the president or his brother. This policy recalled Jacqueline Kennedy's earlier efforts to grant special access to "court" historians like Schlesinger and Sorensen, not to mention the part she and her brother-in-law played in the Manchester affair in hopes of shaping how history would remember the president. It was a policy hardly calculated to please the many journalists and historians who were shut out, not that the Kennedys seemed to care. Designated by his mother to oversee his father's papers, Maxwell Taylor Kennedy freely admitted to granting selective access to favored historians while denying those who came with what he considered to be "poorly-conceived projects." His job was to "grant use responsibly," he said, in words that echoed what Jacqueline Kennedy had told Jim Bishop and William Manchester. Historians and journalists had to "explain their projects" in a satisfactory fashion. They had to "do their homework and observe the correct procedures for seeking permission to consult the papers."[44]

A similar attitude governed access to President Kennedy's papers, much to the chagrin of scholars and reporters who were anxious to consult them. In a memorandum of October 1969, the National Archives announced plans to house Kennedy's papers, pending completion of the Kennedy Library, at the Federal Records Center in Waltham, Massachusetts. The announcement deflated expectations by noting that only a small percentage of the material, mostly of little research value, would be available for some time, partly because of deed-of-gift restrictions imposed by the donors.[45] Not much had changed by August 1971, when the National Archives and the Kennedy Library opened 3.3 million pages of documents at the records center in Waltham. Chalmers Roberts, a contributing editor for *Newsweek* magazine, went to peruse the material and was frustrated by what he found. Compared to the Pentagon Papers, he wrote, in reference to a cache of secret government documents leaked to the *New York Times* by Daniel Ellsberg, the newly released Kennedy papers "make rather tame reading." Because of national security restrictions, they did not include a single document stamped "top secret" or "confidential." There were documents relevant to Kennedy's appointment of Dean Rusk as secretary of state, but virtually nothing about his policy toward Vietnam or other matters of substance. There were only tidbits, Roberts wrote, about the president's grades in school or gifts purchased by his wife and sisters abroad, and even these tidbits were "riddled" with deletions, a result, no doubt, of deed-of-gift restrictions that permitted the Kennedys to seal records that might be used to "injure, embarrass, or harass any person," including any member of the Kennedy family. Under the circumstances, as Burke Marshall told Roberts, most of the papers released were "trivial" in nature.[46]

In 1997, Seymour Hersh claimed in his book, *The Dark Side of Camelot*, that Kennedy's papers had been carefully culled before being deeded by the family to the federal government. In his telling, at least one Kennedy aide, George Dalton, had destroyed or edited portions of the collection that might embarrass the president or his family, including recordings of his telephone conversations with Judith Exner and Marilyn Monroe.[47] Although Hersh marshaled few facts to support his charge, there is good reason to have at least some regard for his suspicions. Between July and September 1962, as we now know, Kennedy had installed a recording system in several rooms of the White House, including the Oval Office and the Cabinet Room, and on telephones in various locations. According to a summary report prepared in 1977 by the Kennedy Library and revised by Kennedy's secretary, Evelyn Lincoln, the system operated until the president's death, at which point it was dismantled and Robert Kennedy ordered Lincoln to take the recordings home until new office space could be found. About a week later, Lincoln moved into the Old Executive Office Building, where the recordings (and other presidential records) were locked away while George Dalton, under instructions from Robert Kennedy, began to review and transcribe them. Dalton continued his work when Lincoln and the recordings moved to offices in the National Archives, which received the last of Kennedy's White House records in June 1965. By that time, the archives had prepared preliminary shelf lists for the records, "except those in the charge of Mrs. Evelyn Lincoln," which were the subject instead of a brief inventory prepared by Kennedy friend, Burke Marshall. In a cover letter to Kennedy, Marshall made a special but oblique reference to "the tapes," noting that they "obviously present a special problem which we should talk about." Six months later, with Robert Kennedy's permission, journalist Theodore White also explored the papers, and found them completely disorganized and with large sections missing or misfiled. The papers included those assembled by Evelyn Lincoln, about sixty-six file drawers of material packed into 330 archival boxes. But eight additional file drawers, according to White, still "remain with Mrs. Lincoln, presumably tape recordings that are to be transcribed."[48]

At that point, the fate of the tapes became confusing, including the dictabelts that recorded the president's phone conversations. Evelyn Lincoln later recalled that in 1966, about a year before she resigned her employment with the Kennedys, the dictabelts had somehow been separated from the other records in her office, relocated to a different part of the archives building for reasons that are still unclear, and could not be found when Robert Kennedy and Burke Marshall came to see them. Lincoln and Herman Kahn of the National Archives subsequently searched again, found the missing tapes, and handed them over to Robert Kennedy's secretary, Angela Novello, who continued the work of transcribing the tapes begun by George Dalton. In 1973, the dictabelts, tape recordings, and transcripts were removed to the Federal Records Center in Waltham, where archive officials remembered seeing Dalton, under instruction from the Kennedys, still taking "out some of those tapes and typed transcripts" and doing other things that did not always comport with archival policy – at least until August 1975, when the Kennedys finally turned formal control of them over to the Kennedy Library.[49]

During the whole period between the president's death in November 1963 and August 1975, access to this collection had been strictly limited to the Kennedys, Evelyn Lincoln, Burke Marshall, George Dalton, and Angela Novello, with Dalton and Novello charged with reviewing and transcribing these important sources. According to the summary report, when the Kennedy Library took control of the collection, it included 125 reels of audiotape and 27 dictabelts, along with some rough transcripts and summaries of both. About two-thirds of the recordings dealt with national security issues and would remain closed pending formal review by the government agencies involved; another 5 percent would remain closed because of deed-of-gift restrictions imposed by the donor, namely the Kennedys. The collection included six transcripts for which there were no tapes; one audiotape for which there was no transcript; and five items listed in the inventory for which there was neither a tape nor a transcript. Of the 178 dictabelts donated, only 8 had to be reviewed for national security reasons, and another 30 because of donor restrictions. According to the summary report, one dictabelt and one transcript of a dictabelt had apparently been removed before the items were given to the library.[50]

Despite these findings, the library claimed that it had found no evidence of tampering with the tapes. At the same time, however, library officials clearly had doubts about Evelyn Lincoln, as evinced by some of the remarks they appended to the summary report she had revised. The remarks speculated that Lincoln had withheld some of her own records, as well as some of the tape recordings and dictabelts. They wondered if she was "covering herself" and if she had "some records tucked away," which turned out to be the case when it was discovered years later that she had withheld materials once entrusted to her and gave or sold them to a Kennedy collector she had befriended.[51] Under the circumstances, it's easy to understand why Hersh was suspicious, particularly when the Kennedy Library, the review committee, and the National Archives seemed determined to keep the recordings it had under wraps for as long as possible. They did not publish even so much as a list of the recordings until 1981, and then deleted from the list telephone conversations deemed private and personal, including calls between the president, his family, or close personal friends. Other material, although listed, dealt with national security matters and could only be released after review and declassification by the national security agencies involved.[52]

No wonder many historians were frustrated, including James N. Giglio, author of a major biography of the president, who complained in 1992 about his own experience with the Kennedy Library. "Crucial manuscript material" remained closed, perhaps 30 to 40 percent of the entire collection, he said, citing the library's chief archivist as his source. Giglio blamed the dismal situation in part on the slow process of declassifying national security documents and the lack of sufficient staff to manage the collections. But he found most disconcerting the "deed-of-gift restrictions" that sealed items relating to the "personal, family, and business affairs" of the former president, his medical history and private correspondence, or that might be used to "injure, embarrass, or harass" the Kennedy family or any other person. This included audiovisual materials. When it came to these materials, the staff was instructed "to place in a 'non-available' category all items of a certain sort, including those that reveal "aspects of a person's character which in some way contradict the image of that person held by the general public"; those "intended to be humorous but apt to be taken seriously by the general public"; and those of people who "would consider it embarrassing to be seen in a particular location or setting." Members of the screening committee, according to these instructions, should review "the work of the staff on audiovisual materials in the same way as they review the work on papers." Provisions of this sort made the library "more overly protective of its donors than other presidential libraries," Giglio said, giving, as one example, some three hundred oral histories that were not open to researchers because of deed-of-gift restrictions, including, at that point, the oral histories of Jacqueline Kennedy, McGeorge Bundy, and Robert McNamara.[53]

The oral history project, much touted by the Kennedys when it was launched, came in for special criticism, and not only because so many of the histories remained closed or otherwise restricted. Almost all of the histories recorded in the early days of the project were executed badly, with no professional training for those who conducted the interviews and no attention to conflicts of interest. They had "everybody interviewing everybody," recalled Charles T. Morrissey, the archivist who tried, but failed, to professionalize the project in its early stages. One member of the Kennedy administration would interview another; sometimes a subordinate would interview the boss. The idea at the time was to capture memories while they were still fresh in the minds of Kennedy's associates. But the resulting histories, which were highly subjective and almost always favorable to the administration, mostly reaffirmed the idealized image of the president found in works by Schlesinger, Sorensen, and other members of the Kennedy faithful. In addition, Morrissey reported to another archivist, Herman Kahn, who censored his work and denied him access to records he needed to conduct his interviews. He was not "free to pursue subjects with the independence and the scholarship" that his work required, Morrissey concluded, and was falling instead "into the trap of becoming a house historian." In the spring of 1966, he told Kahn that he could no longer live with the "inhibitions" placed on his work, and resigned.[54]

As Giglio has noted, the situation barely improved in the years ahead, and then only because scholars like himself used the Freedom of Information Act to pry open previously restricted material. Because of their efforts, historians would begin to learn more about Kennedy's medical problems, his relationship with a shady dispenser of homeopathic drug concoctions, and his White House visits with Marilyn Monroe, Mary Meyer, and other women. By 1992, however, nearly thirty years after the assassination, most of Robert Kennedy's papers remained sealed, as did Jacqueline Kennedy's and a large portion of the former president's. The library was still processing Kennedy's personal correspondence as well as papers dealing with the Bay of Pigs, the Cuban Missile Crisis, and other historic events. The work was still moving at a snail's pace and more scholars were joining the chorus of those complaining bitterly about censorship at the Kennedy Library.[55] Favored historians were granted special access, others were denied, and many were coming to see the Kennedy Library and Museum as a battleground in a war over the president's memory.[56] As historians pressed on, moreover, the Kennedy family, as well as the Kennedy Library, found it increasingly difficult to defend the president's heroic image – although they still had allies in the world of public opinion, where the old orthodoxy, as we will see, held steady against the weight of professional opinion.

IV

For nearly a decade after the assassination, there had been few challenges to the glowing assessments of the late president offered by Sorensen, Schlesinger, and other contributors to the Kennedy orthodoxy. By the early 1970s, however, the spirit of Camelot, which had once suffused the nation with brimming self-confidence, optimism, and hope for the future, had begun to dissipate. The Vietnam War and the angry protests it sparked, the deceitful management of the conflict by Presidents Johnson and Nixon, the violent turn of the civil rights movement, the reversal of liberal fortunes that began with Nixon's cynical southern strategy, the Watergate scandal, economic inflation, and the energy crisis – all of this and more had created a political culture that was not particularly kind to the sacred image of the slain president. Confidence gave way to doubt, optimism to pessimism, the heroic age to the age of disillusionment. Where once Americans had faith in the redemptive power of a strong executive, now they feared what Arthur Schlesinger called the "imperial presidency."[57] The new mood of the nation, evident in popular resistance to the proposed Kennedy Library in Cambridge, also revealed itself in a new generation of revisionist writers who were as anxious to overturn the literary monuments erected in Kennedy's honor as the president's wife and friends had been to construct them.

Although revisionists might concede that Kennedy was a charming and attractive man of great personal magnetism, they were not enamored of him. On the contrary, they argued that charisma was no substitute for achievement and that Kennedy had achieved very little, in part because he was reluctant to challenge the conservatives who dominated Congress. Kennedy needed less profile and more courage, they said, paraphrasing Eleanor Roosevelt's famous quip. His domestic policy was timid on the major issues of the day, including civil rights, where he acted only when forced to act by Martin Luther King, Jr. and other civil rights leaders; his major initiatives in education and health care also languished in Congress; his tax policy – part of the famed Keynesian revolution – did more for corporate interests than for any other group; and the same was true of his trade policy. Kennedy, they said, was far too conservative and far too cautious. First and foremost a politician, he was paralyzed by his narrow margin of victory in the 1960 election and was more concerned with his prospects for reelection than with the immediate needs of the nation. This line of argument, similar in some ways to Lasky's conservative critique, now surfaced in books written by scholars and journalists, including, among others, political scientist Bruce Miroff, journalist Henry Fairlie, and historians Allen Matusow, Garry Wills, and William O'Neill.[58]

If anything, the revisionists were even more damning of Kennedy's foreign policy. Aided by the publication in 1971 of the Pentagon Papers, they castigated Kennedy for adding significantly to the number of American military advisors in Vietnam and taking other steps, including the overthrow of President Ngo Dinh Diem's government in Saigon, that hardened the American commitment to Vietnam and set the stage for the ruinous war that followed. To their way of thinking, Kennedy charted the path that Johnson traveled and that Kennedy himself would have taken had he lived to be reelected. To be sure, some of Kennedy's initiatives were well intentioned – the Peace Corps, for example, and the Alliance for Progress – but the former was essentially inconsequential and the latter rested on the naive assumption that repressive regimes could somehow be persuaded to adopt progressive reforms. They also criticized Kennedy for escalating the nuclear arms race, which his Test Ban Treaty did little to abate; denounced his incompetent handling of the Bay of Pigs disaster; and accused him of risking nuclear war with the Soviet Union over Berlin and Cuba. By their lights, Kennedy's macho mentality, especially his determination to reverse his setback at the Bay of Pigs, inspired a lust for confrontation in the Missile Crisis that nearly blew up the world.[59]

Although earlier scholars, such as Schlesinger, had claimed that Kennedy learned from his mistakes, matured in office, and became more inclined toward a pragmatic détente with the Soviets as well as the Cubans, revisionists claimed just the opposite. They did not see the Missile Crisis as Kennedy's finest hour or as proof of his growing restraint. They accused him of provoking the crisis in the first place and then humiliating Khrushchev with a settlement that only perpetuated the arms race. Kennedy's rhetoric remained hawkish until the day he died, they said. He was never serious about arms control and never abandoned plans to rid the Western Hemisphere of Castro and other anti-American influences. On the contrary, revelations coming out of a US Senate investigation in 1975 seemed to implicate Kennedy, or at least his administration, in plots, sometimes involving the American mafia, to overthrow the communist government in Cuba and assassinate Castro. Clearly, Richard Walton concluded in 1983, Kennedy was the most dangerous world leader of the postwar era. Five years later, Thomas G. Paterson, a distinguished historian of US foreign policy, came to a similar conclusion in an edited collection of essays that featured several leading revisionists.[60]

Even the vaunted Kennedy style, critics now argued, was as hollow as a drum. He was not a great rhetorician but a president, like many others, who relied on speechwriters such as Sorensen for the clever turn of phrase. He was not a highbrow intellectual but a lightweight whose reading habits ran more to spy novels than serious history, and who received a Pulitzer Prize, thanks to his father's influence, for a book he didn't write. If this charge made the president out to be a liar, so did revelations regarding his sexual exploits that began to emerge in the Senate investigation mentioned above. Then came the publication in 1977 of Judith Exner's tell-all account of her affairs with the president and mob boss Sam Giancana, one of the mafia leaders that Kennedy supposedly encouraged to assassinate Fidel Castro. Revelations about other women followed. Even the president's kennel keeper cashed in with a lurid account of orgies in the White House swimming pool, among other things.

Some began to wonder how Kennedy had time or energy for his official duties. The answer apparently was that he and his wife were hooked on amphetamines and other substances supplied by Max Jacobson, otherwise known as "Dr. Feel Good," the sleazy medical man who provided similar drugs to many of Kennedy's friends in high society and the film industry. In theory, his prescriptions were to help Kennedy deal with a wide variety of ailments, from a bad back to Addison's disease, all of which, like his extramarital affairs and drug use, he concealed from public view in order to protect his electoral prospects. Kennedy, the critics claimed, even experimented with recreational drugs, including marijuana and LSD, which he tried with another of his many lovers, the socialite and artist Mary Meyer. No wonder one critic, Thomas C. Reeves, titled his Kennedy book *A Question of Character*, although the most trenchant critique of the whole Kennedy image, as the president and his wife had constructed it, came from historian and public intellectual Garry Wills. Sounding like the prosecutor at a Jesuit inquisition, Wills delivered a punishing indictment of John F. Kennedy as a macho, self-absorbed, and self-aggrandizing manipulator who used his charm and style as weapons in a ruthless pursuit of power over others, not only in politics and diplomacy, but in all areas of his life, including his love life.[61]

By 1990, revisionist writers had nearly shattered the idealized image of the president that earlier scholars had worked so hard to construct, replacing it with the image of a debilitated and drug-addicted womanizer without an ounce of moral fiber. Put beside the idealized image, the revisionist representation looked like a different person altogether – not a mirror image but a Jekyll-and-Hyde contrast. Some of the president's most ardent early fans turned against him, as evident in a collection of remarks assembled by Sidney H. Nertzberg and published in the *Washington Post, Times Herald* in November 1973. Shortly after the assassination, as noted earlier, Nertzberg had used his editorship of the journal *Current* to publish assessments of the Kennedy administration by leading American intellectuals, mostly historians, whose opinions were almost uniformly positive. Ten years later, however, he found that many of the same scholars, including Arthur Link and William Leuchtenburg, were ready to dismiss Kennedy as a soiled and mediocre president of little consequence.[62] As evidence against the president piled higher and higher, even Schlesinger had to build a new defense for his wounded hero. He claimed now that Kennedy's sexual misadventures were exaggerated and did not, in any event, influence the performance of his official duties. He and others mounted the same defense when it came to the president's physical disabilities and use of narcotics. There was no evidence, they said, that Kennedy's personal health and medical treatments had a debilitating effect on his professional life. What they revealed, said Schlesinger, making a virtue of necessity, was the president's enormous personal courage and capacity for sacrifice in the face of crippling pain.[63]

V

The negative turn in Kennedy scholarship signified, if nothing else, the country's ongoing fascination with the former president, how he was to be remembered, and who would define his legacy. In a fashion seldom seen with other presidents, the historiographical battle became a popular topic in much of the mainstream media, particularly during major anniversaries of the president's death. Editorial writers and columnists not only reported the scholarly controversies; they offered their own assessments, too, and in the process, helped to create a third or post-revisionist trend in the historical literature.

Robert Reinhold, writing in the *Cleveland Plain Dealer* on November 22, 1973, provided a concise summary of the revisionist critique, which he largely accepted. Borrowing, no doubt, from Nertzberg's findings, he noted that many historians who had once marked Kennedy for greatness now considered him little more than average, including William Leuchtenburg of Columbia University and Richard Neustadt of Harvard, who agreed, in Leuchtenburg's phrase, that Kennedy would "be swallowed up in history." To be sure, Kennedy was an attractive and inspirational figure, but he turned ordinary problems into major crises, mostly to enhance his own authority. He promised more than he could deliver, created a cult of personality, and exaggerated his ability to get things done. The latter attributes, part of the liberal ideology of the day, with its emphasis on strong executive leadership, set the stage for popular disillusionment in subsequent years and for the imperial presidency that revealed itself in the Vietnam War and the Watergate scandal.[64]

Reinhold's summation of the revisionist critics reflected the views of other journalists who addressed Kennedy's record on the tenth, twentieth, and twenty-fifth anniversaries of his assassination. Clifton Daniel, writing in the *New York Times*, went even further. He claimed that Nixon had a far better legislative record than Kennedy and had actually wound down the war in Vietnam that Kennedy escalated. He did not endorse Nixon's secret bombing of Cambodia nor Johnson's use of the Tonkin Gulf incident to justify air attacks against North Vietnam, but they were no worse, he insisted, than Kennedy's invasion of Cuba at the Bay of Pigs. The only difference was that Kennedy got away with it. Whereas Johnson had been driven from office and Nixon faced impeachment, Kennedy enjoyed a nearly 60 percent approval rating at the time of his death.[65]

Richard Cohen, writing in the *Washington Post*, castigated Kennedy's character. Not only was he a laggard on civil rights who approved the FBI's surveillance of Martin Luther King Jr.; he also took credit for a book he didn't write, lied about his health, and was a flagrant womanizer.[66] This was Cohen's thinking on the twentieth anniversary of Kennedy's death, and he had not changed his mind by the twenty-fifth, when he claimed that Kennedy represented a "self-intoxicated America," drunk with its success in the Second World War and unable to see that Kennedy's grandiose visions would lead to disaster in Vietnam, street riots in the United States, and disillusioned youth.[67] Then there was Andrew Kopkind, a so-called New Left critic, who thought Kennedy's real legacy was basically conservative. He opposed the Cuban revolution, risked nuclear war, championed the welfare state rather than a more radical program of reform, and sacrificed the Alliance for Progress and the Peace Corps to a worldwide program of counterinsurgency.[68]

However typical of conservative and left-wing commentators, criticism of this sort did not fully capture the mainstream media, which struck its own position in the struggle to define Kennedy. Columnists and editorialists in this camp were more likely to balance the revisionist critique against the old orthodoxy in a way that still privileged Kennedy. Some attacked central points in the revisionist argument. David S. Broder, for example, dismissed the notion that Kennedy had created an imperial presidency. He did not deny that Kennedy believed in the kind of strong executive that was increasingly out of step with contemporary opinion, but he did so openly, Broder said. He made presidential power a topic of public discussion, just as he did with other controversial issues, including church-state relations, civil rights, and strategies for economic growth. He did not enter a war by stealth, as Johnson did, or run a covert campaign to subvert his political opposition, as Nixon did.[69] The difference was important to Broder, as it was to Joseph Kraft, who went on to fault revisionist writers for generally ignoring the constraints that operated on Kennedy, particularly his narrow margin of victory in the 1960 election and the conservative coalition he confronted in Congress. To Kraft, Kennedy deserved credit for moving steadily forward despite the obstacles he faced, particularly when it came to civil rights, tax policy, and détente with the Soviet Union.[70]

Even some voices on the left complained about the revisionist critique. Michael Harrington recalled his conviction in 1960 that Kennedy and Nixon were "peas in a pod," as well as his subsequent criticism of Kennedy's hesitation on civil rights and his escalation of the war in Vietnam. By 1963, however, and in the years thereafter, Harrington had come to see Kennedy as successful in the context of his times, given the deadlock in Congress and the mood of public opinion, particularly on civil rights. On issues like civil rights, Kennedy did not go as far as Harrington wanted, but "much further than one could have expected." He was hardly a socialist on economic policy, either, but he was "our first Keynesian" in the White House and "began the economic re-education of Americans on issues of budget and economy." His Alliance for Progress was flawed but well intentioned. He admitted his mistakes at the Bay of Pigs and learned from them, and what he learned, according to Harrington, would have kept the United States from a ground war in Vietnam. Even his management of the Cuban Missile Crisis, which Harrington had criticized at the time, now looked restrained in hindsight and prelude to his American University speech, the Test Ban Treaty, and subsequent hopes for détente with the Soviet Union.[71]

Like other writers in this vein, Harrington faulted the revisionists for not analyzing Kennedy in historical context, a perspective that made his presidency look better than revisionists were willing to admit. Joseph Kraft and Irving Howe made the same point, as did Richard Boeth in a column for *Newsweek* magazine. Boeth did not dispute that Kennedy's reputation had been overblown in the wake of his assassination, but "the current fashion," he said, in a reference to revisionism, was to blame Kennedy for everything that went wrong in the years after his death. Revisionists wanted "to take everything away from him but his so-called style," and then "say that he used that style to promote foreign adventurism and an impossibly high level of expectation at home." If viewed in the context of his own time, he argued, Kennedy was "an authentic hero" in a country where heroes mattered. Boeth reminded readers of the "dour remoteness of the Eisenhower years," when government seemed to be losing its "human dimensions," and said that Kennedy's greatest gift was to make people feel "confident of their ability to take responsibility for their own lives." Seen in this light, many of the good things coming out of the 1960s, including the civil rights revolution and early soundings of the feminist and environmental movements, appeared to spring from Kennedy's conviction that vigorous people could make a difference.[72]

Much of what Boeth had to say squared with the last lines of Harrington's commentary. "We were a happier nation then," Harrington told his readers. Problems seemed solvable and the American people "had a president they loved."[73] This line of argument, which again stressed the importance of context, was a major step toward a postrevisionist balance in the debate over how Kennedy should be remembered. What is more, it made an asset of Kennedy's style, which revisionists deplored, and brought Harrington, Boeth, and others back to a point that orthodox historians had stressed earlier. That point had less to do with Kennedy's legislative record or foreign policy than with the political culture his style expressed and how it changed in the years after his death. Because of Vietnam, Watergate, and civil unrest, Boeth argued, "the nation had slowly been purged of much of its vitality, much of its confidence and practically all of its gaiety," attributes once associated with Kennedy and his times. These had been replaced by the pessimism and cynicism increasingly obvious in American political culture after the mid-1960s and reflected in the revisionist literature, with its skeptical view of presidential leadership and the ability of the United States to direct positive change at home or abroad.[74]

Similar expressions came from the editorial boards of the *Cleveland Plain Dealer*, the *Los Angeles Times*, and the *New York Times*, among others. In the 1960s, said the *Plain Dealer*, Kennedy's style reflected the mood of a people who were confident, strong, and purposeful. He "represented many of those qualities we think of as especially American," agreed the *Los Angeles Times*, and "stirred in us all that fundamentally American sense of the possibilities of life, of the great things this country can yet achieve." In this sense, Kennedy's death marked "the end of an

era filled with the ebullient optimism and confidence identified throughout the world with the spirit of America." Now a "sadder" and "more
realistic people," concluded the *New York Times*, had come "to question
whether the world will ever again be this, or any nation's oyster," or
whether it could ever conform, as Kennedy believed possible, "to man's
noblest ideals and aspirations."[75]

Themes struck on the tenth anniversary appeared consistently over
the next two decades, as many in the mainstream media recalled their
own memories of the late president and his times. The *Los Angeles Times*
marked the twentieth anniversary of Kennedy's death by repeating the
very positive assessment it had published ten years earlier.[76] David Broder
did much the same thing, as did the *Cleveland Plain Dealer*.[77] Revisionist
scholars, the *Washington Post* editorialized on November 22, 1983,
had spent more than a decade trying to change Kennedy's "gold" into
"brass" but had not succeeded.[78] If his legend had been "scratched" by
their criticism, or by reports of his "affair with a gangster's mistress,"
wrote Robert Donovan, Kennedy still had the "heroic aura" of an idealist
who always "strove for loftier goals than he could achieve."[79] He was
the "quintessential American," Ted Sorensen wrote on the twenty-fifth
anniversary of Kennedy's death, and "still stands," despite the revisionist
assault against him.[80]

If revisionist writers traced all the world's problems back to the
Kennedy years and the president's style, many editorial commentators
blamed the policies and personalities of his successors. Kennedy had
made Americans feel good about themselves; Johnson and Nixon had
turned their joy to despair. What the country had been mourning since
Kennedy's death, William Attwood wrote in the *Virginia Quarterly
Review* in 1983, was "the progressive erosion of grace and integrity and
courage in our succeeding presidents," including Johnson, Nixon, Ford,
Carter, and Reagan, all of whom lacked the attributes of personality
and character that Kennedy displayed.[81] The *Plain Dealer* made a similar point. In hindsight, it said, Kennedy and his administration looked
so good because everything after the assassination looked so bad; confidence in government had been shattered as the nation struggled with
war, oil crises, ghetto riots, recessions, Watergate, runaway inflation, and
the Iranian hostage crisis.[82] In short, where revisionists remembered the
Kennedy years as the beginning of an imperial presidency, their media
critics recalled the same period as an era of good feelings.

Even readers of the *Chicago Tribune*, a particularly conservative newspaper, got a dose of this viewpoint. Writing in the *Tribune*, Jon Margolis

found it hard to take the revisionists seriously, not only because historians were constantly revising their earlier assessments, but also because he disliked the cynicism so evident in their work, their suspicion of authority, the anti-heroic tone of their narrative, and their tendency to disparage not just Kennedy but all the other icons of American history, including Washington, Jefferson, Lincoln, and Roosevelt. Whatever his faults, Margolis said, Kennedy made people feel better about themselves and never appealed to their basest instincts, as did Johnson, Nixon, and Reagan. Besides, it was a mistake, in his view, as in Jackie Kennedy's, to rank presidents only on the basis of their legislative tallies, especially Kennedy, whose legacy "has less to do with what he accomplished than with what he represented."[83] Like others, Margolis thought that Kennedy embodied much of what was best in the American people and should be remembered that way.

As this suggests, the revisionist critique had not entirely erased the heroic narrative of the former president that his wife and others had so carefully scripted. On the contrary, at stake in the popular press – as in the scholarly literature – was a battle over how Kennedy should be remembered. Was he the ideal American portrayed in the old orthodoxy or the ugly American drawn by revisionists? Or was he something in between? The revisionist critique was so harsh that it sparked a small defense of the old orthodoxy, evident in some of the media commentary noted earlier and in Ralph Martin's *A Hero for Our Time*, the 1983 best seller that continued to describe Kennedy in heroic terms, as if new revelations about his personal life and medical history didn't matter at all.[84] More typical, however, was the largely balanced assessment that we see emerging in much of the mainstream media after the tenth anniversary of the assassination and continuing through the anniversary assessments of 1983 and 1993. By failing to put Kennedy in the context of his times, and by faulting him for disasters that came after his death, revisionist writers, according to these commentaries, had done Kennedy's memory a great disservice.[85] Their goal was to correct the imbalance in the revisionist literature, not by exaggerating the president's legislative success or ignoring the misadventures in his personal life, as the old orthodoxy had done, but by giving him credit for making progress against the odds, setting the stage for further triumphs down the road, and inspiring Americans, especially young Americans, to believe they could make a positive difference in the world.

What is more, historians themselves began turning increasingly toward this interpretation, with more balanced accounts starting to surface just as the revisionist wave was cresting. Although the major scholars in this group – including Herbert S. Parmet, James N. Giglio, Irving Bernstein, Nigel Hamilton, and Richard Reeves – differed in their views and coverage, with Giglio and Bernstein, for example, more positive in their assessments than Parmet and Reeves, all struck a posture similar to that apparent in much of the mainstream media. Published between the twentieth and thirtieth anniversaries of Kennedy's death, their works did not ignore Kennedy's health, medical treatments, and romantic life. In some cases, particularly Hamilton's readable account, they added new details and insights into Kennedy's childhood, family life, and sexual habits. Nor were they sparing in their criticism of his public policies. Kennedy came to office as a traditional Cold Warrior and an economic conservative, they agreed, and was cautious when it came to domestic reforms, including civil rights, education, and health care. At the same time, however, they were more inclined to complicate their analyses by placing Kennedy in the context of his time, looking at all the challenging issues he faced concurrently, and reminding readers that even the most skillful leader would have found it difficult to escape the legislative constraints that operated on the president.[86]

At the risk of simplifying or slighting their accounts, these post-revisionist authors saw Kennedy as a Cold Warrior, much like other major political figures of the day, but one whose views became less aggressive and more reasonable after the Bay of Pigs and the Berlin crises, both of which aroused in him a fear of nuclear war and a growing distrust of officials in the Pentagon and the CIA. The results were evident in the Cuban Missile Crisis, where his approach was more restrained than that of his colleagues; in the Test Ban Treaty; and in the spirit of rapprochement that marked his famous speech at American University. Although Hamilton's book did not cover Kennedy's White House years, the others acknowledged that foreign policy preoccupied Kennedy, as well it might, given the state of the world he inherited and the many crises he encountered. On the other hand, they gave him high grades for paying more attention to civil rights than any president since Lincoln, and for finally making a dramatic commitment to legislation that became the Civil Rights Act of 1964. They generally considered his economic policies a success, launching not only a Keynesian revolution in fiscal policy but contributing to a remarkable period of economic growth and high employment. Finally, they credited Kennedy for many of the social programs, including Medicare, aid to education, and the war on poverty, that Congress enacted in the years immediately after his assassination.

He may not have had the legislative mastery that Johnson demonstrated, they conceded, but the real barrier to progress was a powerful coalition of Republican and Democratic Party conservatives that stalled action on every front. They were inclined to believe that a Kennedy victory in the 1964 election would have broken the deadlock and given him the credit for legislative successes that Johnson later claimed for himself. As it was, these successes came after his death in large part because of a universal desire to commemorate his memory in law.[87]

VI

While revisionists and postrevisionists battled over Kennedy's legacy and how to remember him, public opinion appeared largely indifferent to what either side had to say and more inclined, if anything, toward the original orthodoxy. Although many historians dismissed Kennedy as the most overrated public figure in American history, history textbooks tended to be more positive.[88] Public opinion polls continued to give the president high ratings as well. A 1973 Harris poll rated him the most popular of all presidents. According to a *Wall Street Journal*-NBC News poll taken in 1988, Americans considered Kennedy a more effective leader than any other president since the Second World War. A 1990 Gallup poll revealed that 84 percent of Americans approved of his administration, and a similar poll taken three years later showed his popularity remaining strong, even among a generation of younger Americans who had not been born at the time of his assassination.[89] As late as 2000, when a Gallup poll asked people to name the greatest American president, Kennedy topped the list with 22 percent of those who responded.[90]

The number of visitors to Kennedy's grave provides another mark of his lingering appeal. Seven thousand people visited the gravesite in November 1983, 3.5 million over the course of that year. Five years later, on the twenty-fifth anniversary, hundreds gathered in Washington for a memorial Mass with the Kennedy family, or stood in silent vigil in the Capitol, as did five hundred former Peace Corps volunteers. Once again, thousands streamed past the president's grave, including a group of fifty Green Berets and an unidentified civilian who stopped to play "Taps." In 1993, on the thirtieth anniversary, twenty-five thousand people visited the gravesite, many of them with no personal memory of the slain president. Each year, the visitors repeated the now familiar rituals. They walked quietly, respectfully up the hill to the shrine, some praying as if they were in church, others crying, still others leaving flowers, poems, and other grave gifts upon the silent tomb of the slain president.[91]

If anything, interest in Kennedy and his family, unflagging since the assassination, reached new heights on the twentieth anniversary of his death and in the years that followed. Two national television networks aired prime-time specials, one on NBC and the other on ABC. The NBC special offered a seven-hour miniseries starring Martin Sheen as President Kennedy, John Shea as his brother Robert, and Blair Brown as his wife Jacqueline. The series, which aired in 1983, ran over three nights before airing again in twenty-seven other countries on four continents. By that time Sheen had become a friend of the Kennedy family, having starred in a 1974 TV miniseries, *The Missiles of October*, based on Robert Kennedy's book *Thirteen Days*. Both series followed themes similar to those established by Schlesinger, Sorensen, and other first generation Kennedy scholars and by the Kennedy Library and Museum. They generally ignored or downplayed the darker side of Kennedy's life, including his reckless womanizing, ill-health, and dependence on drugs. Nor did they pay much attention to his early escalation of the arms race, his commitment of additional forces in Vietnam, or his efforts to overthrow Castro's government in Cuba. All this was more or less erased from historical memory. Instead, both series presented Kennedy as a progressive reformer who supported civil rights and expanded social programs at home, as well as new foreign aid initiatives abroad, the control of nuclear weapons, and détente with the Russians. In their view, not only did Kennedy push these initiatives over the determined opposition of many of his advisors in the military and intelligence communities, not to mention conservative politicians and right wing extremists, he did so at the risk of his own life.[92]

Also in 1983, Martin's *A Hero for Our Time* hit the best seller list even before it was available in print. Senator Edward Kennedy published a rare "reminiscence" of his brother in *Parade* magazine, *Life* served up a cover story on the murdered president, and other newspapers and magazines did something similar. These were just a few of the Kennedy anniversary highlights summarized by Clarke Taylor in a long story for the *Los Angeles Times* in November 1983. A one-man show starring actor Mike Farrell as Kennedy also started touring college campuses that year. National Public Radio aired a twenty-minute special on the former president, and many local television and radio stations did the same. In November alone, a half-dozen TV specials appeared on public television and independent stations, including, in the Boston market, "Being John F. Kennedy," with Nancy Dickerson as the narrator, and "John Fitzgerald

Kennedy," a one-hour biography narrated by Cliff Robertson, who had earlier starred as Kennedy in the movie *PT 109*.[93] It was a regular Kennedy "festival," wrote Leanita McClain of the 1983 tributes, perhaps more "garish" and "maudlin" than in previous years, but all adding up to Kennedy's further "canonization" in the popular mind.[94]

Most of these productions, if not good history, said a lot about what many Americans would accept as part their national heritage. As Taylor noted, Kennedy had never looked more appealing or more glamorous than in these TV specials, all of which confirmed his well-deserved reputation as the country's first and best television president. There was even a special featuring his famous press conferences, which had been so popular with the American people. All of the specials, not just the network series, reaffirmed the heroic image of Kennedy that his wife wanted inscribed in American memory. He was forever young and attractive, full of energy and good humor. He was the loving son, husband, and father. He was brave, optimistic, hopeful, and intelligent. He was progressive and self-sacrificing. He was, in short, the ideal American, champion of the downtrodden and defender of the national interest. Only ABC's "JFK," which affected a more scholarly pose, deviated noticeably from this portrait. Summarizing the views of dozens of scholars and former colleagues of the late president, it presented something more like the "balanced" assessment evident in portions of the press and in the post-revisionist books by Parmet, Reeves, and others.[95]

The "festival" continued in 1988, when the country commemorated the twenty-fifth anniversary of the president's assassination. New books and articles about Kennedy and his family went flying off the shelves at bookstores across the country, including Doris Kearns Goodwin's best seller, *The Fitzgeralds and the Kennedys*.[96] Once again, dozens of film crews descended on Washington, DC, to record the religious services, public readings, speeches, and other ceremonies commemorating Kennedy's assassination; and once again, hours of additional news reports and television specials hit the airwaves, including a rebroadcast of NBC's 1983 miniseries *Kennedy*, starring Martin Sheen.[97] Kennedy's aura seemed to resist the chill of history, as one commentator put it. By 1993, in fact, the Kennedys had been featured in more than a dozen TV specials running for a total of forty-eight hours. The fortieth anniversary brought more of the same, with the History Channel broadcasting a three-hour special on *JFK: A Presidency Revealed*, and PBS airing a documentary on Jacqueline Kennedy.[98]

As Paul Henggeler noted in his masterful study of the Kennedy style in American politics, these specials catered to the high esteem in which the general public still held Kennedy and his family. To be sure, they made an occasional bow to the balanced view of the late president now increasingly favored by post-revisionist scholars. This was the case, for example, with the History Channel's *JFK: A Presidency Revealed*. But like the series produced in 1983, they were far more likely to slight the underside of his life, follow the lead of the former first lady, and further burnish the heroic image that Arthur Schlesinger, Ted Sorensen, and the first generation of Kennedy scholars had constructed in their literary monuments to the dead president.[99]

Kennedy was also portrayed in the same favorable light when it came to the movies. In a 2000 television film drawn from the documentary record of an executive committee that had advised Kennedy during the Cuban Missile Crisis, the president looked as close to heroic as he had in the 1974 TV production based on Robert Kennedy's book *Thirteen Days*. In an odd way, he even looked good in two of the most important films dealing with his assassination, neither of which offered substantive criticism of the president's policies or personal failures. In *Executive Action*, a 1973 film starring Burt Lancaster, and in Oliver Stone's 1991 classic *JFK*, starring Kevin Costner, Kennedy is pictured as a progressive politician and peacemaker who is basically the victim of right-wing groups that resented his push for civil rights and social reforms at home, for the withdrawal of American troops from Vietnam, and for arms control with the Soviet Union. These same themes, moreover, also run as undercurrents through some of the most important literary fiction of the day, in this case, Don DeLillo's *Libra*, published in 1991, and Norman Mailer's *Oswald's Tale: An American Mystery*, published in 1995. Both focus on Oswald, not Kennedy, but both see the assassin's murderous act as the consequence of a Cold War that Kennedy was trying to end.[100]

Kennedy had clearly become a profitable commodity, a commercialized brand and boon to the heritage industry. But the flood of documentaries, Hollywood movies, and television specials, not to mention the many books, both fiction and nonfiction, testified to more than the public's enduring fascination with the former president. They also contributed to the way that most Americans would remember him. In effect, they mediated between history and memory, particularly for those too young to have experienced the early 1960s or remember the former president in real life. For them, modern media productions, indeed the heritage industry as a whole, were more likely to construct the past, not as authentic experience, but as media-made memories that squared in most ways with the idealized image that Kennedy had constructed of himself on the White House stage – and that his wife and family had inscribed on the many literary and physical monuments to his memory. He was the mythical, larger-than-life figure, the ideal to which all Americans should aspire, the defender of democracy, and the victim of those who opposed it.

Yet another token of Kennedy's lingering appeal played out in the world of politics. Despite a conservative resurgence that would over-whelm his liberal politics, Kennedy remained an actor in American pol-itics long after his death, his memory invoked repeatedly by presidents and presidential hopefuls in both parties. Republicans praised his Cold War rhetoric, his resolve to stand up to the Soviets, and his call for large defense budgets and tax cuts. Democrats remembered his support for education, Medicare, and civil rights, for the Keynesian revolution in public finance, for the Test Ban Treaty, the Alliance for Progress, and the Peace Corps, and for voluntarism and public service.

Not only did both sides try to capture Kennedy's memory for them-selves; they invariably tried to project the Kennedy style that had been so appealing to American voters. Although they resented Kennedy's lin-gering popularity, both Johnson and Nixon invoked his name and tried to copy his rhetorical style and personal appearance. Johnson went so far as to don a two-button suit for the cover of *Gentlemen's Quarterly*, much as Kennedy had done earlier. Nixon let himself be posed walking thoughtfully along the California coastline, trying to look like a contem-plative Kennedy strolling along his Hyannis Port beachfront. Both efforts failed because neither captured the spirit of the real man behind the pose. During his beach walk, for example, Nixon wore a dark suit, tie, and wingtips, much to the amusement of photographers who remembered Kennedy strolling barefoot in an open-collared shirt and slacks rolled almost to the knees. Jimmy Carter, for his part, cultivated the notion that he looked and sounded like a young John Kennedy with a southern accent. He also claimed that as a moderate Democrat, he was a more legitimate heir to Kennedy's legacy than liberal Democrats, including Edward Kennedy, the president's brother and Carter's potential rival for the party's nomination. Reagan was the only Republican to cultivate the Kennedy connection with some success. He helped raise funds for the Kennedy Library, attended, with members of the Kennedy family, reli-gious ceremonies marking the twentieth anniversary of the assassination, awarded the Medal of Freedom to Eunice Kennedy Shriver for her work with the mentally retarded, invited Rose Kennedy to the White House,

and quoted Kennedy more than any of his predecessors – all this to mobilize working-class voters who had once cast their ballots for the former
president.[101]

In the 1988 campaign, Republicans and Democrats vied with each
other for control of Kennedy's memory and what it meant, or should
mean, to the American people. Republican contenders, from Congressman
Jack Kemp to Senator Dan Quayle, tried to project the youth and vigor
of the former president. Governor Michael Dukakis, a Democratic Party
contender, reminded voters that he shared Kennedy's intellectual rigor,
campaign vigor, and pragmatic liberalism, not to mention his Bay State
birthplace. Much the same was true of Dukakis's rivals for the party
nomination. These included Tennessee Senator Al Gore Jr., Missouri
Congressman Richard Gephardt, Delaware Senator Joseph Biden, and
especially Indiana Senator Gary Hart, whose mimicry of Kennedy ultimately contributed to his own undoing. Dukakis eventually prevailed
and when he selected Senator Lloyd Bentsen of Texas as his running
mate, neither the party nor the press could resist talk of reviving the
Boston-Austin axis that had led the Democrats to victory in the 1960
campaign. The struggle for Kennedy's memory peaked when Dan Quayle
tried to invoke the dead president's name during a vice presidential
debate, whereupon Bentsen mocked his pretentions by bragging that he,
not Quayle, had actually known the slain hero and that young Quayle
was "no Jack Kennedy." Kennedy, as Parmet noted, still set "the standard
for the Presidency in the television age."[102]

By 1988, Kennedy had become so sanctified in the popular mind that
everyone wanted to claim him. He was the everyman of American politics: "the Democrat quoted by Republicans, the liberal invoked by conservatives," the "white man revered by blacks," the wealthy man loved by
working-class voters, the former president, gone twenty-five years, who
was nonetheless the favorite of people too young to remember him in
life.[103] Four years later, in 1992, Bill Clinton worked hard to appear as
Kennedy-esque as possible. He projected the same image of youth and
energy and the same wit, self-deprecating humor, and quick intelligence
as the former president. He also endorsed programs of support for the
downtrodden, the ill, and the aged, as Kennedy had, and touted the benefits of voluntarism and public service. To solidify his connection to the former president, Clinton and his aides publicized a photograph of Kennedy
shaking hands with a young Bill Clinton at a Rose Garden ceremony
honoring Boys Nation. Like Reagan, moreover, he was careful to cultivate the Kennedys on every occasion. He invited them to the nominating

convention where the former president and his brother were honored. He visited Kennedy's grave the day before his inauguration, and brought the famous Resolute Desk back to the Oval Office. He also appointed Jean Kennedy Smith to be the US ambassador to Ireland; enjoyed a yachting lunch with Jacqueline Kennedy Onassis; and joined the family again for the rededication of the Kennedy Presidential Library in 1993, thirty years after the assassination.[104]

VII

By 1993, it was clear that the Kennedys had not completely staunched the wave of revisionism that washed across the historical profession after the mid-1960s, try as they might to deny critics fair and equal access to the historical record so carefully guarded at the Kennedy Library. But revisionist writers had not prevailed either, and not just because the Kennedys punished and censored their critics. Millions of Americans now learned their history from television specials and documentaries, from popular films and books, and from other productions of a heritage industry whose commercialized version of the president reinforced the sacred image on display in the Kennedy Museum or at the gravesite in Arlington Cemetery. What is more, despite the truth in much of what they had to say, revisionist historians went too far to be wholly credible. They took Kennedy out of context, blamed him for the sins of his successors, and ignored or slighted what he gave to the American people – not only in Cold War triumphs and legislative victories but also in confidence, inspiration, and faith in the future.

Perhaps because of these shortcomings, the revisionist critique had little appeal in the public realm. Revelations regarding the president's personal life and political setbacks notwithstanding, Kennedy remained a box office success in Hollywood films and television documentaries. His standing in public opinion polls stayed astonishingly high for decades after his death. His lingering appeal to voters required politicians in both parties to emulate his style and copy his image. Even professional journalists and scholars found it difficult to resist the old orthodoxy if the only alternative was the revisionist critique. By the end of the century, however, both revisionism and the old orthodoxy had begun to succumb to a more balanced, postrevisionist view of Kennedy and his administration. This view did not deny the president's political failures or the flaws in his private life, but it did give him credit for making progress against a conservative bloc in Congress, not to mention the country's conservative political culture, and for inspiring people to believe they could still do better. As we will see in the next and final chapter, this postrevisionist view, perhaps even more benignly stated, would reach its apogee with the fiftieth anniversary of Kennedy's death, even though it would not completely replace the old orthodoxy in the popular mind.

8

Gone but Not Forgotten

History, Memory, and Nostalgia

The rededication of the Kennedy Presidential Library and Museum in 1993, one year before Jacqueline Kennedy's death, marked the culmination of her efforts to freeze in public memory the romantic image of her husband as the ideal American. The rededication followed a major renovation of the Columbia Point complex. Just as the Kennedys had once performed the presidency on the White House stage, the former first lady would now use the renovated museum, much like a theater, to reproduce her husband's life – not in all aspects, to be sure, but as she wanted others to see him. As before, the goal was to control the president's identity, define his legacy, and make him worthy of remembrance. With that goal in mind, a familiar narrative unfolded inside the museum, set amidst the usual props, precious artifacts, costumes, and symbols of the Kennedy presidency, but with little room left over for counternarratives or alternative memories. In its own way, the library half of the complex pursued the same goal. Family and friends still protected the president's memory, as they defined it, by limiting access to his records, favoring some scholars over others, and punishing those who would tarnish the sanctified image of the fallen hero. Not surprisingly, all of this led to yet another round of controversy between the library and the community of scholars who wanted to tell their own story of Kennedy's life and administration.

As this suggests, the library's purpose and that of the museum had not changed much, if at all, over the years. Nor, for that matter, had the ongoing debates, in both media commentary and historical scholarship, over how to define Kennedy and his place in American history. In the twenty years following the rededication of the Columbia Point complex, the old orthodoxy, once so aggressively championed by Jacqueline Kennedy, had only a little to add to what Schlesinger and Sorensen had said in the 1960s. Much the same was true of left-wing revisionism, which had its heyday in the 1970s and 1980s but faded thereafter. Some conservative critics, in their own version of revisionism, still denounced Kennedy as a weak and ineffective liberal while others made a tortuous effort to redefine the president as a virtuous conservative and precursor of Ronald Reagan. Through it all, postrevisionism held sway over other points of view, except when it came to public opinion, which remained largely indifferent to what scholars and pundits had to say.

Most Americans continued to form their own opinions of Kennedy, as evident in opinion polls and other forums, and their thinking still had more in common with Schlesinger, Sorensen, and Jacqueline Kennedy than it did with revisionists or post-revisionist scholars. Why did Kennedy, now fifty years gone, remain incredibly popular in the public mind, so much so that high public regard for the dead president may have dragged at least some post-revisionist scholars to a more benign view of his life and administration? Many have puzzled over this question, and we'll take it up as well in the concluding pages of this chapter.

II

The renovated museum was spectacular, even to those who could see through its artful manipulation. Scripts were redrafted, videos reproduced, exhibits recast to become more interactive, more up to date with technology, and more appealing to generations of people who had no living memory of the former president and who relied increasingly on film and technology to mediate their knowledge of the past. Despite the changes, however, the goal was still an approved version of Kennedy's biography, which meant focusing on some aspects of his life while obscuring others. Curators and designers chose to scrap the Charles Guggenheim film that had originally introduced visitors to the museum exhibits. That film had ended with Kennedy's death and was followed by another film on Robert Kennedy's assassination. The combined effect had saddened and depressed viewers, where the goal now was to leave them uplifted by the person and spirit of the former president.

This goal set the Kennedy museum apart from the Sixth Floor Museum in the former Texas School Book Depository building in Dallas. That museum opened on President's Day 1989 with an exhibit that focused almost entirely on events surrounding Kennedy's assassination. The exhibit featured the sniper's perch from which Lee Harvey

Oswald fired the fatal bullets that killed the president, as well as panels dealing with the president's trip to Dallas, his motorcade through the city, and the aftermath of his assassination, including his funeral, the global response to his death, and the Warren Commission and its critics. It included, at the start of the exhibit, only a brief description of the president's life and family, the 1960 presidential campaign, the Kennedy White House, and the president's domestic and foreign policies; and it closed with an equally truncated discussion of his legacy, featuring, among other things, limited coverage of the space program, the Peace Corps, civil rights, and the Vietnam war. Unlike the Kennedy museum in Boston, it avoided any historical verdict on the man and his administration.

This explains why the Kennedys did little to recognize or assist those who put the Sixth Floor Museum together. In May 1988, Charles Daly, then director of the Kennedy Library in Boston, described the museum as "morbid or disgusting or both," and the Kennedy family declined to disavow his remark. On the contrary, Senator Edward Kennedy admitted to being "disturbed" by the exhibit and Daly himself remained a critic, particularly of the museums lack of background on Kennedy, his family, and his policies, not to mention its brief and noncommittal discussion of the president's legacy. Their criticism may account in part for why the museum's organizers never secured federal support for their venture and why the museum, by itself, was never added to the National Register of Historic Places.[1]

Unlike the Sixth Floor Museum, the Kennedy Museum in Boston paid little attention to the president's assassination. Its exhibits, which focused instead on the president's life and legacy, presented Kennedy as a living memory, as if, in fact, he had not died at all but lived on, not only in what he accomplished but in what he represented, what he inspired and was yet to be achieved. Indeed, for designers involved in the 1993 renovation the challenge was to protect this illusion while at the same time acknowledging the assassination. With this in mind, they commissioned a new film that ended with the president's triumph in the 1960 election, rather than his brutal murder in 1963. Designers addressed the assassination only in a darkened hall with television sets on either side broadcasting the news from Dallas and scenes from the president's magnificent state funeral – but nothing more. This was as far as they would go, no doubt because it left intact the impression, at the heart of the sacred image, that somehow Kennedy would continue to live so long as the American people honored the legacy he had bequeathed to them. Indeed, as they departed the darkened hallway, visitors entered another exhibit dealing with the president's "legacy."[2]

The film that now introduced the exhibit was impressive, to say the least. It covered Kennedy from childhood through the 1960 campaign, leaving the rest of his life to be traced in the museum exhibits that followed. What made the film so successful was what appeared to be its intimate informality, an appearance that imitated Kennedy's persona in real life. It had no swelling soundtrack, no titles or credits, no deep-throated, third-person narrator. It gave the impression of a well-done home movie and seemed at once more realistic and more autobiographical than the original film. This was especially so because Kennedy himself narrated the history of his life as it unfolded before viewers in photos, films, and newsreels – all of which were used to mediate between history and memory and even, at times, to overwrite history with a memory more constructed than real. In these ways, the film humanized the president by employing his own strengths on his behalf, namely the so-called Kennedy style that revisionist historians had always deplored, including his youth and good looks, beautiful family, sense of humor, rhetorical flourish, and all the other attributes that were central features of the iconic brand that viewers found so appealing.[3]

As often as possible, the exhibits following the film also told Kennedy's story in his own voice and in the context of his own time, with photos and video clips spread throughout. They opened with a reproduction of the famous Kennedy-Nixon television debates, the president's campaign speeches, and the nail-biting election returns, occasionally interspersed with contemporary TV programming that lent the presentation an air of authenticity. They captured these and other highlights in black-and-white film projected on television sets stationed, together with other appliances and artifacts of the time, in storefront windows along what appeared to be a small-town Main Street in 1960. It was as if visitors were watching Kennedy's campaign pass before them until they came to a full-screen viewing, in color, of the president's famous inaugural address.

With White House images now in the foreground, the folksy, small-town scenes gave way to the grandeur and glory of the Kennedy presidency. Here, exhibits on either side of a long, chandeliered hallway, all heavy with videos and photographs, offered a narrative of the Kennedy administration. As was true of the original museum, some exhibits made clear that visitors were seeing not only the journey of John F. Kennedy to the White House but also the rags-to-riches story of the Kennedy family as a whole – from its humble Irish origins to the pinnacle of American success. Again, Jacqueline Kennedy had her own exhibit, as did Robert Kennedy. Some exhibits captured the glitz and glamor of social life in the White House, while others featured Kennedy's commitment to civil rights, the Peace Corps, foreign aid, and support for the poor, the aged, and the ill. Still other exhibits focused on his foreign policy triumphs, in the Cuban Missile Crisis, for example. These histories were usually recounted in the president's own words and usually complemented a recurring emphasis throughout the museum on his strength, courage, and heroism, including his wartime experience on PT 109.[4]

Every aspect celebrated the already well-established image of the president as the ideal American. As with the first generation of histories by Schlesinger, Sorensen, and others, Kennedy was revealed as a great president who grew in office, instilled in Americans a new sense of hope and confidence, and inspired them with his call to voluntarism and self-sacrifice on behalf of a better world. "Triumphalism" was the main theme, Stephen Ambrose once remarked, in what was still a "shrine to JFK as his family and associates want him remembered." Their goal was "legacy burnishing," with no narrators, no interpreters, and no critics given space to deconstruct the ideal image or offer counter narratives of their own. The Bay of Pigs was not omitted, but was mostly a sideshow and warm-up to the president's great triumph in the Cuban Missile Crisis, which curators presented so far as possible in the president's own words and without much reference to the many plots against Fidel Castro. They used the same strategy to capture Kennedy's commitment to civil rights, showing a TV clip of his famous speech to the American people but saying little about his hesitant and cautious posture before that point. There were pictures of Kennedy sailing and playing touch football, but barely a mention of his chronically poor health, just as the photos and films of a devoted husband and family man concealed much of the president's romantic life behind the scenes.[5] This was a museum, not a textbook, and its mission, apparently, was to mediate between history and memory in a way that illuminated some parts of the president's life while leaving others in the shadow.

As noted earlier, designers also wanted to go beyond the story of Kennedy's life to his legacy. Visitors were thus reminded of all the Kennedys who had served their country. A piece of the Berlin Wall also tied Kennedy's defense of Berlin to the ultimate collapse of the Soviet Union. Photographs of President Johnson signing the Civil Rights Act in 1964 and of the moon landing in 1969, keyed viewers to the important role that Kennedy had played in some of the great events that came after his death. A film of President Bill Clinton's visit to the museum reminded tourists of the legacy that Kennedy had bequeathed to the Democratic Party, particularly since Clinton's remarks at the time recalled his predecessor as the Kennedys wanted him remembered. Visitors then took all of these images with them into a "space of unlimited expectations," as Andrew Rotter described the towering glass pavilion with its expansive view of the sea beyond.[6] Inspired by Kennedy's example, as Pei intended, they could reflect on his legacy, as if he were still alive, and remind themselves of work yet to be done.[7]

The renovated museum was a great success for the Kennedys. Dedicated in 1993, the refurbished space became a new stage for the reproduction of Kennedy's presidency, not as historians might record it, but as the Kennedys told it. The exhibits presented a past with some parts revealed, others concealed; they emphasized aesthetics as much as history, as Jacqueline Kennedy had done in her restoration of the White House; and they did all of this in an effort to manipulate the emotions and manage the impressions that visitors took away. As in the original, the exhibits amounted to a collection of performance art displayed on stage for the benefit of an audience whose members invariably loved what they saw, just as they did when Kennedy was alive. Indeed, the designers reminded visitors why the president was worth remembering by using his own style – his real words and images – to advance their claims and defeat their critics. To the extent that criticism was acknowledged at all, it was obscured by an offsetting narrative, often told in Kennedy's own voice and intended to reinforce his idealized image. His civil rights policy, for example, was not hesitant and insincere, as critics charged, but thoughtful and judicious; his confrontations with the Soviets in Berlin and Cuba were not reckless and impetuous, but bold, calculated, and decisive. In these and other ways, as Rotter has explained, the exhibits were "so artfully done" and "so persuasive and clever" that it was "easy to give oneself over" to what the designers and the Kennedys had in mind. This was especially true if the visitors were not historians or if their view of the past had been mediated by new technologies, rather than lived experience, and by popular literature, movies, documentaries and other products of the modern heritage industry.[8]

What the Kennedys had in mind was consistent with their efforts to present John F. Kennedy in history and memory as he had played the president on the White House stage. This was the orthodoxy that Jacqueline Kennedy had promoted not only in the monuments of glass, steel, and stone erected in the president's honor, including the Kennedy Library and Museum, but also in the literary monuments to her husband's memory. As we have seen, she did what she could to assist Schlesinger, Sorensen, and other writers who scripted the original, heroic narrative of her husband's life. She discouraged writers, like Jim Bishop, whom she did not trust; punished old friends like Ben Bradlee and Red Fay, who allowed even a hint of criticism to creep into their narratives; and worked with her brother-in-law to censor William Manchester, whose history of the assassination she had actually commissioned. By managing access to records at the Kennedy Library, moreover, she and the Kennedy family had tried over the years to bring history itself into line with the story they told in the museum, as opposed to the counter narratives offered by revisionist or post-revisionist historians. Under the circumstances, it is not surprising that historians viewed the library with a jaundiced eye. What they often saw was a sanctuary for the sacred image of the slain president, an institution that was more interested in tourism than historical scholarship.[9]

III

There was a good deal of truth in the last observation. As we saw in I. M. Pei's second design for the Columbia Point complex, the Kennedys had been willing to sacrifice archival and research space in order to preserve the room they wanted for the museum. In the third and final design, it was the Kennedy School and Institute that lost out to the library and museum. A similar preference also defined priorities even after the complex opened, as we learn from David Powers. The first and longest-serving curator at the Kennedy Library and Museum, Powers had been Kennedy's presidential aide and devoted friend of many years. There was no doubting his love for Kennedy or his devotion to the sacred image of the slain president that he and others had created in the first place. Nor could anyone question his loyalty to the Kennedy family, which may help to explain his appointment as curator, a job for which he was otherwise completely unqualified. Powers had no tolerance for historians who wanted to recount the dark side of Camelot. He called them "bounty hunters" who were only interested in making money on their books.[10] He also valued the museum portion of the library complex more than the library itself, perhaps because he had more control over Kennedy's representation in the museum than he had over what historians wrote about him. At one point, he wondered if the word "library" actually discouraged tourists from visiting the museum. He thought it might help to detach that word from the president's name and bury it at the end of a new title, such as: "The John F. Kennedy Museum and Presidential Library."[11] What is more, while Powers and others claimed that insufficient funds slowed the opening of Kennedy's papers, they had little trouble getting all the funding, including federal funding, they needed when it came time to renovate and reopen the museum in 1993.

In their 2004 oral history for the Kennedy Library, Dan Fenn, the library's first director, and longtime library executives John Stewart, William Moss, and Larry Hackman gave further weight to whatever suspicions historians might have had. They noted that archivists at the Kennedy Library, not just historians, complained frequently about restrictions on their access to the records housed there. These restrictions hampered their work, or so they said, repeating a charge that Charles Morrissey had leveled in the early days of the oral history program. Sometimes it was the Kennedys who limited what the archivists might see; sometimes it was one of the president's former colleagues. They were particularly suspicious of Powers, who came to the library with no professional credentials, did not get along with the archivist to whom he reported, and sometimes meddled with the release of records, all of which led some library officials to wonder if he was actually a spy for the Kennedy family. They were nervous about the screening committee, too, not because they saw much evidence of its direct intervention – although they saw some – but because it granted preferential access to a few scholars while denying access to others. What is more, its oversight authority intimidated the staff, as well as the National Archives, and encouraged both to act conservatively when it came to releasing records. This was a particularly serious problem because any mistake by an archivist could anger donors and discourage others from contributing their records to the Kennedy Library.

Still worse, at least for the archivists, the library's leadership clearly favored outreach and education programs over the processing and declassification of records, which meant that when scholars complained about the slow pace of this work, it was the archivists who invariably took the blame. There always seemed to be enough money for the museum and for education and outreach, but never enough for the important work of opening the historical record to scholars. Fenn, who was not a historian and had no formal archival or library training, more or less confessed to the charge leveled against him.[12] Recommended by Arthur Schlesinger, he had this to say when the head of the National Archives asked if he would take the job: "Well, I'll tell you," Fenn answered. "If your view of the Kennedy Library is that it is an exciting outreach, popular, people-oriented place, education and politics and government and so forth, and so on, yes, I think I'd like to." But he did not want a job that was "backward looking and sort of keeping papers and stuff," which is to say he did not care much for the work that historians and archivists did. He wanted the library to be "a source of exciting programs and projects which would nurture interest in politics and government," not history, and carry forward the "passion" for public service and the other values that Kennedy and his family had supposedly inspired in the American people. Fenn's emphasis on museum work and outreach programs rather than archival work and historical scholarship became one of the hallmarks of his years at the Kennedy Library. In effect, as his oral history makes clear, he used the outreach and education programs to propagate the Kennedy brand. That brand was increasingly disconnected from the work being done by historians, except the favored few who had access to records denied to others and who became, consciously or not, active collaborators in promoting the family's view of how the president should be remembered. "There was a fair amount of resistance within the Library staff," Fenn admitted, in discussing his outreach and education initiatives. He "remembered some people ... talking about it being PR. Which it was," he confessed.[13]

Not surprisingly, historians voiced complaints similar to those of the archivists, thereby opening another front in the war to determine who owned Kennedy's identity and how he should be remembered. Nigel Hamilton is a case in point. Just as the architects and designers were putting the finishing touches on the renovated museum, Hamilton accused the library and the Kennedy family of blocking access to records he needed for the second volume of his proposed three-volume biography of John F. Kennedy – a charge to which Fenn later confessed. The family, in particular, objected to what Hamilton had said in his first volume about Kennedy's sex life as an adolescent and young man, and about his upbringing in what the author described as a dysfunctional family. He pictured the president's mother, Rose Kennedy, as emotionally constrained, unable to display affection toward her husband or children, and obsessed with religion, expensive clothing, world travel, and her children's personal grooming. Joe Kennedy was not an engaged parent either, at least in Hamilton's telling. He, too, was emotionally shallow, as cold and unloving as his wife, and seldom available to his children. A rabid womanizer and anti-Semite, he was obsessed with wealth and power and was ruthless in the expectations he set for his children, often pitting them against each other in competition for his respect and approval. All of this, in Hamilton's mind, contributed to John Kennedy's own emotional detachment, his inability to give or receive physical affection, and his habit of jumping from one shallow affair to another rather than building a strong and stable relationship with his wife.[14]

Hamilton's account clearly revealed his admiration, even affection, for Kennedy, in part because he had made a success of himself despite the dysfunctional family he had to overcome. What is more, elements of his analysis had appeared in earlier works and would be taken up in subsequent studies as well. Nevertheless, the remaining children of Rose and Joseph Kennedy went after the author with a vengeance remarkably similar to that evident in the attacks launched earlier against Jim Bishop and William Manchester. As soon as they got wind of his project, at least according to Hamilton, they sent a lawyer to discourage the author from his interpretation of the president's parents, much as Jacqueline Kennedy had tried to discourage Jim Bishop from his book on her husband's assassination. When this effort at censorship failed and the book was published, they denounced the author in an opinion piece for the *New York Times*. In Hamilton's telling, they also used their influence to have him barred from an international conference of Kennedy scholars; discussed his work with staff at the Kennedy Library, which had a chilling effect on his research there; discouraged colleagues, relatives, and friends of the family from cooperating in his ongoing work, much as Jacqueline Kennedy had treated Jim Bishop; and mobilized their literary friends, notably Arthur Schlesinger and Doris Kearns Goodwin, to savage Hamilton's book in major forums. This was the same tactic they had used against Manchester, with Schlesinger reprising the role he had played in that earlier battle and Goodwin stepping into a part similar to the one her husband, Richard, had played in the same controversy.[15]

Despite all the hoopla surrounding the Hamilton affair, the author's trouble with the Kennedys and their library was more typical than exceptional. As we have seen, many library collections remained closed or otherwise restricted, including a substantial number of oral histories. Scholars had been fighting for years to gain access to the papers of Robert and Jacqueline Kennedy, for example, not to mention the president's own collection, a large portion of which remained closed as well. A flood of protests, similar to Hamilton's, had come from other historians, who also complained about restricted access and preferential treatment for some scholars as opposed to others. Besides Hamilton and James Giglio, whose complaints were noted earlier, the list included Ronald Kessler, Stephen Ambrose, John H. Davis, Richard Reeves, and Joan Hoff Wilson, as well as Benjamin Hufbauer, author of a substantial book on presidential libraries, which he called *Presidential Temples*, and Richard J. Cox, who compared the presidential libraries to the pyramids erected in memory of the ancient pharaohs.[16]

Well into the new century, critics continued to point to censorship at the hands of the Kennedy family and its allies, including the pressure they mounted to prevent the History Channel from airing a miniseries that featured, among other things, the family's apparent addiction to drugs, alcohol, and sex. Most complaints came directly from individual historians, however. They still objected to a presidential library system that was spinning out of control and cited the Kennedy Library as the best example. It was "the library scholars denounce most, hands down," as one critic put it.[17] It was not there "to serve history," said Richard Reeves, one of the premier Kennedy biographers, but to "serve the Kennedys." Its staff might be "paid by the U.S. government but they acted as if" the public "had no right to see this stuff." What is more, they still moved at such a slow pace that it would take another twenty years to clear the backlog of documents waiting to be released. As usual, the library's management blamed its problems on insufficient staff and the need to declassify so many documents, while archivists, as we have seen, saw the problem as one of balance between investment in the library's archival function and its museum, outreach, and educational programs. For their part, historians pointed a reproachful finger at the three-person review committee headed by Kennedy friends or relatives who still exercised a tight grip on access to the papers, and at the Kennedy Library Foundation, which raised funds for the library but invested most heavily in education and outreach programs that would take an unstained image of the former president to the world beyond the archives.[18]

The library and the Kennedy family, notably Caroline Kennedy, the president's daughter, tried to counter criticism by releasing a small sample, about twenty thousand pages, of Jacqueline Kennedy's papers as well as selected portions of the secret White House tapes that had been sealed for years. Some of the recordings had been released as early as 1983, and others were opened periodically thereafter, including tapes dealing with civil rights issues and the Cuban Missile Crisis. It was not until 2012, however, that the Kennedy Library made available the previously unreleased balance of approximately 265 hours of taped conversations between the president and others. Following the deed-of-gift restrictions, moreover, each release had come only after a national security review by appropriate government agencies and only after the Kennedy family or its representative had redacted anything that might injure or embarrass the family or reveal the "personal, family, and business affairs" of the former president.

In addition, the Kennedy Library had earlier announced plans to digitize the president's papers and make them available to researchers online. But the digital archive was not launched until 2011, at which point it included only two hundred thousand of the more than eight million pages in the president's personal and official papers. In the same year, Caroline Kennedy released the seven oral history interviews her mother had recorded with Arthur Schlesinger after her husband's funeral. An instant best seller, the recordings featured Jacqueline Kennedy's whispery voice recounting her life – though mostly her husband's life – in the White House. She gave her candid, sometimes spiteful, impressions of various American and world leaders and in the process revealed herself to have had more influence on her husband than she acknowledged in public. No doubt she understood that a woman, in her day, was not supposed to be her husband's intellectual equal, but at the same time, she clearly believed that her White House restoration, not to mention her linguistic, social, and cultural skills, were enormous aids to the president's success. Mostly she spoke adoringly of her husband, praising his courage in dealing with the constant physical pain he had to endure, his love of life and good humor, his tolerance of people, even his enemies, whom she despised, and how much he cherished his friends and family. Not surprisingly, she said nothing about the dark side of his life or their marriage. Even under the stress of the moment, just months after the assassination, she remained remarkably composed and wholly devoted to the image of the president as she wanted him remembered.[19]

The release of additional records, publication of the Schlesinger interviews, and digitization of the library's holdings, however late in coming, were at least hopeful signs of a better future. But they were shrouded in a cloud of suspicion that hung over the library, like Banquo's ghost over the feast, when it came to its relationship with historians and other critics. For researchers, digitizing some records was less important than opening them all on fair and equal terms. They felt the same way about the museum, not to mention the outreach and education programs, which to their way of thinking could not substitute for a fully transparent presentation of the president's life and accomplishments – warts and all.[20]

As we have seen, library initiatives left little room for debate on the subject of Kennedy and his presidency, even though historians were still struggling to define the man and his administration. This was evident in the constant clamor for greater access to his records and in the vast out-pouring of Kennedy-related books in the years leading up to the fiftieth anniversary of the president's death. By that time, according to some esti-mates, more than forty thousand books had been published on Kennedy, his family, and his assassination. Not all of these are worth reflection; nor is it possible to survey all of the media assessments that marked the years around the fiftieth anniversary. But even a brief summary of the leading publications and popular press reveals that scholars and commentators had not yet reached consensus on the president. If anything, their reflec-tions had settled into something of a rut, with the exception of a new conservative twist on Kennedy's presidency and a more benign tone in some post-revisionist scholarship.

The original orthodoxy of the first generation of Kennedy scholars enjoyed a modest second life in the early years of the new century, resus-citated, in fact, by some of the same scholars who had fashioned the first literary monuments to the dead president. In 2007, Penguin Press published Arthur Schlesinger Jr.'s *Journals*, which included entries for the years he worked with Kennedy. Six years later, Andrew and Stephen Schlesinger also brought out an edited collection of their father's letters. As Stephen F. Knott has pointed out, these volumes offered ample evi-dence of Schlesinger's almost maniacal efforts to defend Kennedy's legacy, and his own scholarship, against attacks by conservative and revisionist writers alike. Something similar can be said of Ted Sorensen's memoirs, published in 2008. As we have seen, moreover, even the president made a contribution when the Kennedy Library published selected portions of his secret White House tape recordings, when it went online with the president's digital archive, and when Martin Sandler published a collec-tion of Kennedy's correspondence – although nothing that would tarnish the sacred image of the former president.[21]

If the works by Schlesinger and Sorensen represented the last hurrah of the old orthodoxy, the same years also saw occasional eruptions of an unrelenting left-wing revisionism, as noted by Knott, himself a spokes-man for that group. Far more typical, however, was a brand of revision evident in leading conservative journals. Although these writers never tired of reminding everyone that it was a self-styled communist, not a Dallas right-winger, who killed Kennedy, they spent most of their energy attacking the former president as a weak liberal who failed the country.[22]

While left-wing revisionists portrayed Kennedy as cautious when it came to social programs, civil rights, and taxes, yet recklessly aggressive in the context of the Cold War, traditional conservatives saw him as a tax-and-spend Democrat at home and a hopeless appeaser abroad – a man who cowered in the face of Khrushchev's bully-boy tactics at the Vienna conference; stood silently by as communists erected the Berlin Wall; abandoned the Cuban freedom fighters at the Bay of Pigs; gave up more than he got in the Cuban Missile Crisis; neutralized Laos rather than fight for its freedom; and betrayed Diem in Vietnam. In all of these ways, Kennedy revealed himself to these writers as a true liberal, indeed, a "proto-liberal," as one conservative explained in a post to *American Spectator*. Kennedy attacked the legitimate role that religion must play in the political life of the nation and opened the floodgates "to the economic and social facets of socialism." With Kennedy, it was "less religion, less respect for private property, more collectivism, and much, much more government control," which liberals "worship above all."²³

Pat Buchanan, among others, took this line of attack, to which he added a vigorous denunciation of Kennedy as a flagrant womanizer who was weak on civil rights and indifferent to the social legislation favored by most liberals. If anything, Buchanan argued, Nixon was a better choice for liberals in 1960 and proved as much after 1968. While Kennedy talked about détente and nuclear arms control with the Soviet Union, it was Nixon who negotiated the Strategic Arms Limitation Treaties and Anti-Ballistic Missile accord. While Kennedy started the American war in Vietnam, it was Nixon, according to Buchanan, who brought American troops home. It was also Nixon, not Kennedy, who was the real family man and who had much more success than his old rival when it came to social policy. It was Nixon, after all, who desegregated the great majority of public schools in the South and who established the Environmental Protection Agency, National Cancer Institute, and Occupational Health and Safety Administration.²⁴

Another wing of conservative thinking took a very different tack, best illustrated in Ira Stoll's provocative and much discussed book, *JFK, Conservative*. As the title suggests, writers and pundits in this category wanted Kennedy remembered as a real conservative, not a liberal – a closet Republican, not a Democrat – who set the agenda that Ronald Reagan would adopt two decades later. Stoll's best seller, published in time for the fiftieth anniversary, cited every Kennedy quote he could find to highlight the president's conservative credentials, as well as every liberal complaint ever leveled against him. More than that, Stoll filed his own brief for the president as a conservative. Kennedy, he argued, was not a spendthrift liberal, but something of a penny-pincher who tried to restrain government spending at almost every turn, including a tight-fisted management of budgets for the executive branch and White House staff. If not a big-spending liberal, neither was Kennedy a fan of higher taxes. On the contrary, Stoll argued, he favored a substantial reduction of individual and corporate tax rates, which he saw as the best way to create private sector jobs, spur economic growth, and generate the revenues needed to achieve the goal dearest to his heart – a balanced budget. He felt the same way about free trade, to which he was committed, even though many liberal and labor groups were opposed. Moreover, and despite his remarks during the 1960 campaign, Kennedy never separated his religious convictions and Christian faith from his public policies, as some conservatives claimed. On the contrary, he remained deeply religious to the end of his days, peppered his speeches with references to God and to his own religious convictions, and accepted America's God-given mission to safeguard freedom everywhere in the world. Guided by the last conviction, Kennedy was a hawk on defense spending and an aggressive Cold Warrior who stood up to the communists in Europe, Asia, and Latin America.[25]

As it turned out, this supposedly novel interpretation was not novel at all. According to Robert Mason, key Republican conservatives, including Ronald Reagan, had been making a similar argument since the Nixon administration.[26] And while hardly calculated to please conservatives like Pat Buchanan, whose hellfire-and-brimstone critique of the Kennedy administration had more in common with the revisionist assaults of the 1970s and 1980s, Stoll's updated version of an old argument did find support among conservatives who wanted to recapture the magic connection that Reagan had forged with white working class voters, in part by invoking Kennedy's memory more often than that of any other president. George Will, Ronald Radosh, L. Gordon Crovitz, Jeff Jacoby, and many others raced to praise Stoll's analysis and embrace what they saw as Kennedy's conservative legacy. Stoll's Kennedy, announced Radosh, was not Schlesinger's, for whom the late president epitomized the kind of liberalism that had paved the way for Lyndon Johnson's Great Society. On the contrary, the real Kennedy resembled Ronald Reagan more than anyone else. In 1960, Crovitz claimed, Kennedy was the most conservative candidate in the race, much to the right of Nixon on foreign policy and even on domestic policy, where the Republican candidate was actually the one touting new government programs and higher wages for public employees. Today's Democrats, said Jacoby, would "not give the time of day to a candidate like JFK," who was "anything but a big-spending, welfare-state liberal." On the contrary, explained Will and others, Kennedy was a fiscal conservative who promoted tax cuts that liberals hated, then and now, and whose hardline foreign policy, buttressed by substantial defense spending, had nothing in common with the pusillanimous and defeatist strategies pursued by President Barack Obama and his allies in the modern Democratic Party. All of this had to be emphasized, said Crovitz, because doing so would crown "conservatism with the halo of Camelot."[27]

Even senators as geographically diverse as Rob Portman of Ohio and Ted Cruz of Texas joined the Republican chorus singing Kennedy's praise. For Portman, Kennedy was a bold leader who urged Americans to face the challenges of their time. He stressed, as an example, Kennedy's leadership of the space program, no doubt because it gave him an opportunity to celebrate the prominent role played by Ohio astronauts John Glenn and Neil Armstrong. For Portman, however, the space race was merely a metaphor for the kind of challenges that Americans faced in the new century, foremost among them being the country's mounting debt, a weak economy, high unemployment, a broken health care system, and the pending bankruptcy of Medicare and Social Security, all of which required bold leadership of the sort that Kennedy had demonstrated and, by implication, modern Democrats had not. Cruz was even more explicit in linking Kennedy to Republican causes. Writing in the *National Review*, he said that Kennedy had "embraced the American spirit." He wanted nothing more than to fight for his country, becoming a war hero in the process. He won a Pulitzer Prize for a book that celebrated heroic senators – including Texas Senator Sam Houston –who stood up for their beliefs regardless of the consequences. He was also a champion of economic growth, which he achieved through "aggressive tax cuts," and a strong Cold Warrior who "refused to accommodate the Soviets" or shortchange the defense budget. Winning the Cold War might "have been Ronald Reagan's crowning achievement," according to Cruz, but it was John Kennedy who laid the foundation for that victory.[28]

On the opposite side, Stoll's work infuriated liberals. They went apoplectic whenever Kennedy's political identity was conflated with conservative causes, and wasted no time firing back. He "put the weight of his presidency behind a liberal program," wrote David Greenberg, echoing an argument that historian Sean Wilentz had made a decade earlier. Writing in the *New Republic*, Greenberg had no doubt that Kennedy was a genuine liberal who did not deserve the criticism heaped upon him by revisionists and conservatives of any stripe. Yes, he admitted, Kennedy wanted to reduce taxes; but he supported a demand-side rather than a supply-side reduction that would benefit average Americans more than big corporations and the wealthy. He also envisioned what became the War on Poverty, pushed for Medicare, expanded Social Security and unemployment benefits, and gave federal workers the right to bargain collectively. He may have started cautiously on civil rights, Greenberg conceded, but he ultimately put his full weight, and that of the federal government, behind the integration of black students into southern universities, not to mention the most important piece of civil rights legislation since the Civil War. What is more, as Greenberg and others pointed out, Kennedy supported progressive immigration reform, implemented the first affirmative action program for government employees, and helped frame the political agenda of modern feminism when he established the President's Commission on the Status of Women, which went on to endorse workplace equality, child care facilities for working women, paid maternity leave, and equal pay for comparable work.

Kennedy may have campaigned to the right of Richard Nixon when it came to foreign policy, Greenberg admitted, but in practice he was cautious and prudent, particularly after his setback at the Bay of Pigs. He stopped short of full-scale war in the Cuban Missile Crisis, would not get involved militarily in Laos, was hesitant in Vietnam, and negotiated the first Nuclear Test Ban Treaty. Just as important, he "organized and inspired a generation ready for something new," according to Richard Reeves, author of one of the most popular Kennedy biographies. His idealism, his soaring rhetoric, his call to public service, and his faith that Americans could meet the challenges of the day inspired not only the Peace Corps, VISTA, the space program, and the Alliance for Progress; they also infused American politics with a generous spirit, full of hopefulness, confidence, and optimism, that has not been seen since his tragic death. No wonder, wrote E. J. Dionne in the *Washington Post*, that both parties, both sides of the ideological divide, wanted to claim him.[29]

Although Kennedy's identity was still contested by voices on both the left and the right, all of whom wanted to claim his memory for their own purposes, it's nonetheless clear that revisionist writers had taken a toll on the president's reputation. Most historians could not go back to the old orthodoxy expounded by Schlesinger, Sorensen, and others in the first generation of Kennedy scholars. They were all postrevisionists now, prepared to admit Kennedy's shortcomings, including his modest success in

Congress, his cautious approach to civil rights, his philandering, medical problems, and drug addiction, all of which he had concealed from public view. At the same time, however, they were becoming, if anything, more benign in their judgments, perhaps because the bitter partisanship in contemporary politics and the legislative deadlock in Washington made it easier for them to sympathize with the situation that confronted Kennedy during his years in the White House. Although the odds were stacked against him, they were inclined to agree that he had accomplished more on the home front than conservatives and revisionists would admit and more successes would have followed had he lived to be reelected. He made mistakes, to be sure, with the Bay of Pigs being the obvious example, but post-revisionists were also more inclined than before to say that Kennedy learned from his mistakes and matured in office. While concern about the prospects for his legislative agenda, as well as his own reelection, made him cautious on civil rights, he finally accepted his responsibilities and acted aggressively when the only other choice was a cowardly betrayal of democratic principles. In addition, what Kennedy wanted to do, what he represented politically, was important in its own right and should not be dismissed because it fell short of enactment in his lifetime. And then there was the famous Kennedy style, which revisionists and conservatives often mocked but which postrevisionists were coming to see as an asset. It inspired Americans to believe in themselves, accept the challenge of involvement, and know that problems caused by man, as Kennedy once said, could be solved by man.[30]

These are the themes that surfaced in many of the major publications that appeared in the years leading up to the fiftieth anniversary of Kennedy's death. They evince the continued salience of postrevisionism, which, if anything, actually became more dominant as it became more benign in its treatment of the late president. To be sure, historians like Alan Brinkley, in his pithy little book on the former president, offered a somewhat conservative synthesis of post-revisionist themes, which is to say that he often seemed more inclined to emphasize Kennedy's shortcomings, both personal and political, than his strengths and accomplishments. More typical was Robert Dallek's magisterial work, *An Unfinished Life*, and Michael O'Brien's large and impressive biography, *John F. Kennedy*. Both tilted the balance in a more positive direction, and both set the stage for a small flood of largely sympathetic books about Kennedy and the Kennedy family published around the fiftieth anniversary of the assassination. Dallek himself brought out two new books, one, a severely condensed version of his great monograph, the other, *Camelot's Court*, a study of the men who advised Kennedy and who, for the most part, fell substantially short of the president's ability. Larry Sabato, a well-known political scientist and pollster, also published an impressive monograph, *The Kennedy Half Century*. Cast, like Dallek's, as a major work of post-revisionist scholarship, Sabato's giant book, which spans Kennedy's presidency, assassination, and legacy, also offered a largely positive assessment of the late president. Even more sympathetic accounts came from Thurston Clarke, whose book on *JFK's Last Hundred Days* focused on the liberal leader's growing maturation and the promise of a brilliant future cut short by the assassination; and Jeffrey D. Sachs, whose book, *To Move the World*, offered the most positive account yet of how Kennedy's enormous rhetorical and negotiating skills set the stage for his greatest triumph, the Nuclear Test Ban Treaty. For the most part, these authors did not ignore the president's shortcomings, from the Bay of Pigs disaster to his slow-motion approach to civil rights, his health problems, and his addictions to sex and unorthodox medical prescriptions. Indeed, Dallek was among the first to prod the Kennedy Library into releasing records relating to the president's health and medical treatment. Still, it is difficult to find in earlier works, certainly not revisionist works, anything like the relatively benign view evident in their books. In fact, Clarke and Sachs often lean more to the older orthodoxy of Schlesinger and Sorensen than to any of the revisionist or postrevisionist writers who came later.[31]

Much the same can be said of new works about the president's family. Sara Bradford and Donald Spoto opened the new century with popular biographies of Jacqueline Kennedy as *America's Queen*, in Bradford's words. Sally Bedell Smith came next with *Grace and Power*, a best seller about the Kennedys in the White House. Following Smith was Barbara Leaming, who had already written a biography of the president and who now gave her readers the "untold story" of Jacqueline Bouvier Kennedy Onassis. Collaborating with Lisa McCubbin, Clint Hill offered his own loving remembrance of Jacqueline Kennedy – and her husband – in a book about his time as head of the first lady's Secret Service detail. Barbara Perry followed her earlier biography of Jacqueline Kennedy with a largely sympathetic portrait of the president's mother, Rose, who was also remembered in a new book of her family photographs, introduced by granddaughter Caroline Kennedy. On the more scholarly side, besides Perry's book on Rose Kennedy, David Nasaw published a thoroughly researched and judicious assessment of Joseph P. Kennedy and his spectacular career in business, politics, and diplomacy. Although *The Patriarch* takes a critical look at the elder Kennedy's opportunism, anti-Semitism, and wartime reputation as an appeaser of Nazi Germany, Nasaw also covered the bright spots, including Kennedy's relatively progressive leadership of the Security and Exchange Commission and the deep interest he had in the well-being of his children.[32]

Added to all this was new scholarship on Kennedy's pre-presidential career, especially his service in the Senate; works examining his foreign and domestic policies; and yet another round of books reprinting some of the condolence letters sent to Jacqueline Kennedy or recalling where people were and what they were doing when they learned of the assassination.[33] Included as well was Mimi Alford's poignant account of her affair with the president and works by celebrity journalists like Chris Matthews, whose affectionate biography of the late president aimed to discover what Kennedy was really like; Jeff Greenfield, who tried to imagine what the world would be like if Kennedy had not been killed; and Bill O'Reilly, whose pot-boiler rendition of Kennedy's assassination was one of more than a dozen books on that subject published in the run-up to the fiftieth anniversary. What they all revealed was the nation's enduring fascination with the thirty-fifth president, including even the smallest detail of his life and times, such as a full volume, *Hatless Jack*, on the myth that Kennedy's aversion to head gear killed the hatting industry, and another volume that tells the Kennedy family story through the prism of its love for the sea, for sailing, and for one of the family's favorite boats, the *Victura*.[34]

Nor was it all about books. As James Carroll noted, the president and his family also "dominated the magazine racks" prior to the fiftieth anniversary of the assassination. The *Saturday Evening Post* simply reprinted its December 14, 1963 edition with Norman Rockwell's iconic portrait of Kennedy on the cover. *Time* had the Kennedys on its cover as well, in this case, a photo of them as seen through what appears to be the telescope of a rifle as they rode through Dallas in the backseat of their black limousine convertible. The photo was captioned, not surprisingly, "The Moment That Changed America." *Life* brought out "The Day Kennedy Died," in both magazine and book format; the first version included the famous photo sequence of Kennedy's assassination that *Life* had purchased from Abraham Zapruder and published in the original edition of the magazine fifty years before. *People* devoted its regular issue to Jacqueline Kennedy and the "private agony" she endured after her husband's brutal murder, as well as a special edition, "Remembering Camelot," which was mainly an ensemble of attractive photographs of the world's most famous couple. *TV Guide* celebrated

Kennedy's relationship with the new medium in a special issue of its own. *American Spectator*, a magazine for conservatives, featured a selection by Ira Stoll on Kennedy as a conservative, with a cover drawing of the late president enjoying a cozy conversation with Ronald Reagan. *Cigar and Spirits*, not surprisingly, recalled Kennedy's love of cigars, as well as the deleterious effects of the Cuban trade embargo on the American market for that product. Three magazines devoted to historical subjects, *History Magazine*, *American History*, and *All about History*, also featured covers of the handsome young president, as well as inside stories of his triumphs and tragedies, his death, and the way Americans have remembered him. *Atlantic* and *Vanity Fair* had special issues of their own, as did other publishers, many of which focused specifically on the president's assassination.[35]

All of this frenzy had been typical of earlier anniversaries, but the fiftieth anniversary seemed to be celebrated as if there would never be another, at least for those who were adults at the time of the assassination. Besides the flurry of books and newsmagazines, the run-up to 2013 saw the promotion of new novels, films, documentaries, and exhibits. These included Stephen King's 2011 novel, *11.22.63*, which, much like Oliver Stone's 1991 classic, sees Kennedy's assassination leading inevitably to the Vietnam War and the deaths of thousands of American soldiers.[36] They included as well a TV miniseries on the Kennedys that was televised in 2011, at about the same time that Diane Sawyer interviewed Caroline Kennedy about her mother's just-published conversations with Arthur Schlesinger. Sawyer's TV special, it's worth noting, drew an audience of eight million viewers, the largest audience for any ABC program, not counting a sports event, in five years. Two years later saw a Tom Hanks production of *Parkland*, a movie about events surrounding the Dallas hospital where Kennedy died, a Fox News adaptation of O'Reilly's *Killing Kennedy* starring Rob Lowe as Kennedy, and a TLC documentary about the thousands of condolence letters that Jacqueline Kennedy received following the death of her husband. PBS aired a four-hour documentary on the former president as well, and Dallas itself held its first full-blown memorial to the slain president in Dealey Plaza, with tickets distributed by lottery to an audience of five thousand people. The Newseum in Washington presented an exhibit on the president's assassination, displaying artifacts from that day in Dallas, a documentary film, and the usual photographs of the handsome former president. The exhibit drew hundreds of thousands of visitors to the museum of American news. Other museums followed suit, ranging from the Yale University

Art Gallery in New Haven, to the International Center of Photography in New York, to the Amon Carter Museum in Fort Worth.[37]

The Kennedy Library also marked the anniversary with a special, though still modest, display featuring the American flag that draped the president's casket and the saddle, sword, and boots that rested atop Black Jack, the riderless horse that marched in the president's funeral procession. Displayed as well was film footage of the president's funeral, one of the hats left by a Green Beret at Kennedy's gravesite, and a photograph of the former president and first lady – happy, smiling, handsome – taken in Texas the day before the assassination. All of these artifacts were exhibited in a dimly lit room that also featured cartoonist Bill Mauldin's famous drawing of Abraham Lincoln weeping in his memorial on hearing of Kennedy's death, and a quote from a *New York Times* article by James Reston. "What was killed in Dallas," Reston had written, "was not only the president but the promise." It was "the death of youth and the hope of youth, of the beauty and grace and the touch of magic." Clearly, the Kennedy Library and Museum had not lost its touch when it came to manipulating the symbolism of the president's death to frame how viewers should remember him. The Mauldin cartoon made the familiar connection between Kennedy, Lincoln, and the expansion of democratic liberties, while the documentary film footage included the famous scene of Jacqueline Kennedy lighting the eternal flame, with all its symbolic significance. Added to this was the library's public ceremony marking the assassination, which included a poet, an astronaut, and Deval Patrick, the black governor of Massachusetts, to remind those watching of Kennedy's love of the arts, his role in launching the modern space program, and his support for civil rights.[38]

Judging by the public opinion polls, moreover, most Americans were still more inclined to share the museum's view of the late president than the professional assessments offered by historians. As far as these assessments were concerned, Adam Clymer, in a 2013 review of college textbooks, found that Kennedy's reputation had lost some of its shine. The president's record was seen as not much better than average, in part because his tenure in office had been so short and his legislative achievements so few. The textbooks still spoke highly of the Peace Corps, the space program, and the president's inspiring rhetoric and sense of style, but they also noted his tardiness when it came to civil rights and the fiasco at the Bay of Pigs. Nor were they sure that Kennedy had not made the Cold War worse in the Cuban Missile Crisis and with his policy toward Vietnam. These textbook assessments coincided, by and large, with what historians had to say in a variety of surveys taken in the first decade of the new century. One still had Kennedy ranked in the top ten; another, involving conservative lawyers and historians, ranked him about average; a third pronounced him eleventh best of all presidents; and yet another put him in sixth place. Although still ranked comparatively high, usually as average or above average, Kennedy's standing was less than it had been in the first decade or so after his death – a reflection, no doubt, of the influence that revisionist and postrevisionist scholarship had on the thinking of historians, including those writing textbooks after the mid-1970s.[39]

Nevertheless, there was still a significant gap between these professional judgments and the views evident in public opinion polls generally. A 2010 Gallup poll gave Kennedy an 85 percent approval rating among those who responded, higher than any of the presidents who succeeded him. Another Gallup poll, this one in November 2013, found that respondents ranked him higher than any president from Eisenhower to Obama. Nearly three-fourths of those responding thought he would go down in history as either an outstanding or above-average president. These polls confirmed the results that Gallup had tracked consistently since 1990. A survey by the Center for Politics at the University of Virginia found the same results. Revelations about Kennedy's philandering habits and ill health made a difference, but not enough to sink his overall reputation as perhaps the greatest president since Franklin Roosevelt. Whatever the textbooks might say, moreover, according to a Gallup Poll of November 2013, the Americans who most admired Kennedy were those between eighteen and twenty-nine years of age.[40]

There are also indications that public fascination with Kennedy remained relatively high outside of the United States. As we have seen, movies and documentaries about the president and his family, though made for an American audience, also ran on TV networks abroad, just as best selling books on the same subjects circulated in a global market. Indeed, it's likely that Kennedy is still remembered more fondly abroad than any of his successors, none of whom, as Andreas Daum points out in his book on Berlin, has been able to recreate the almost hysterical reception that Kennedy enjoyed when he traveled to the divided city in 1963.[41] Indeed, several countries are still holding memorials to the slain president.

In 2013, for example, Britain commemorated the fiftieth anniversary of the president's assassination with a wreath laying at Runnymede, which continued to draw more than a thousand visitors each year. The

US ambassador attended the ceremony, together with other British and American representatives, including Tatiana Schlossberg, Kennedy's granddaughter and one of Caroline Kennedy's three children.[42] For their part, the French commemorated the anniversary by mounting a JFK exhibition at the Gallerie Joseph in Paris. Billed as one of the "essential cultural events" of the year, it recalled the great moments in Kennedy's life "through original photographs, letters, and period films," and invited visitors to immerse themselves "in a journey into the world of the most beloved president in the history of the United States."[43]

Germany, especially Berlin, marked the year by celebrating Kennedy's "I am a Berliner" speech of June 26, 1963. They replayed old television footage of the president's visit, including his famous speech, and mounted a major exhibit, titled "The Kennedys," in a section of what was formerly East Berlin. The exhibit included historical artifacts, memorabilia, and hundreds of photographs taken of the president on his visit, not only to Berlin but to other German cities as well. In addition, Kennedy was featured in exhibits at the Berlin Wall Memorial and the Allied Museum in Clayallee. During the course of the year, moreover, Berlin was flooded with films, lectures, and conferences focusing on Kennedy, not to mention bus tours retracing every leg of his German trip, especially his visit to the Brandenburg Gate, where he had peered over the newly built Wall. "For us, Kennedy is still very much alive," said Alina Heinze, the director of "The Kennedys."[44]

Even the Japanese marked the occasion, although the most sentimental remembrance occurred in Ireland, where the US Embassy invited citizens to reflect on what Kennedy meant to them and to the world. Taoiseach Enda Kenny hosted a major event at the Kennedy homestead in Dunganstown, while New Ross saw the opening of an impressive Kennedy Visitors Center, which featured a replica of the vessel that had carried Patrick Kennedy from Ireland to Liverpool and ultimately to the United States in 1840. After that came a parade and a VIP visit to the Kennedy Arboretum for a ceremonial tree planting. Caroline Kennedy, her husband and three children, her cousin, Sydney Lawford, and her aunt Jean Kennedy Smith, former US ambassador to Ireland, headed the guest list. The highlight of the day came with the arrival of a flame, lit from the eternal flame at Kennedy's gravesite in Arlington National Cemetery and presented to a group of Irish Special Olympians who used it to light Ireland's own eternal flame at the visitor's center in New Ross. The ceremonies closed with an uplifting performance of "Amazing Grace," sung by Judy Collins.[45]

IV

What explains the long afterlife of John Fitzgerald Kennedy? Why does he remain today, more than fifty years after his death, nearly as popular as he was during his presidency – even with Americans too young to have known him in life? And why is he still regarded as a successful president by most of those responding to opinion surveys? Even serious scholarship seems to be moving in his direction. To be sure, Kennedy took a beating at the hands of revisionist historians in the 1970s and 1980s, so much so that he never fully recaptured the high esteem he had once enjoyed among orthodox historians, such as Schlesinger, Sorensen, and others in the first generation of Kennedy scholars. Nevertheless, post-revisionist historians such as Robert Dallek and Larry Sabato emerged from the historiographical wars over Kennedy's memory with a balanced view that restored much of what the president had lost at the hands of revisionists. Even some conservative writers, notably Ira Stoll, as well as conservative politicians like Ted Cruz have tried to claim Kennedy as one of their own. Like Schlesinger and other liberals before them, these conservatives wanted to appropriate Kennedy's memory and link his image to their version of the nation's basic identity. According to the last round of polls measuring professional opinion, moreover, most scholars still ranked Kennedy in the top third among all presidents, and near the top among presidents serving since the end of the Second World War. In short, even among professional historians, Kennedy is highly ranked, especially for a president who had few legislative triumphs to his credit and whose personal life was less than ideal. Why?

To begin with, the president and his wife had painted a very popular portrait of themselves during their tenure in the White House. I have described them as actors playing the roles of president and first lady on the White House stage, which Jacqueline Kennedy had carefully restored for the performance of her husband's presidency. That stage and the productions it hosted, including their celebrated state dinners with their elaborate costumes and orchestrated entertainment, were important pieces of the mosaic that Kennedy and his wife crafted of themselves. So was their youth, charm, and apparent vitality, as well as the president's optimism, self-confidence, and inspirational rhetoric, which supposedly drew people into public service and gave everyone hope that all problems could be solved, all obstacles overcome. Taken together, these attributes constituted the famous "Kennedy style" – or Kennedy brand – that had such strong appeal to most Americans at the time, particularly when added to his supposed virtues, including his heroism, compassion, devotion to duty, and loyalty to family and nation, all of which supposedly inspired his commitment to world peace and social justice. All of these characteristics made Kennedy and his wife appear to be ideal Americans, even though appearance was often an illusion that concealed as much as it revealed. With the aid of a largely supportive media, which the Kennedys carefully managed, they filtered out any aspect of personality at odds with the idealized image they had constructed. Americans knew little about the first lady's nicotine habit or her lavish spending, not to mention her use of amphetamines; nor did they know of the president's dependence on the same drug, his use of other drugs, his serious medical problems, and his frequent trysts with other women. The president and first lady presented themselves to the world only as they wanted to be seen, and so carefully that in the public eye hardly a difference could be found between the real Kennedys and the parts they played on the White House stage. In this light, as James Reston once described him, Kennedy came to look like a "story-book president" who was not only young, athletic, and handsome, but also "graceful, almost elegant, with poetry on his tongue and a radiant young woman at his side."[46]

The attributes summarized above are not only those that Kennedy and his wife presented in their White House productions; they were the ones that came to mind for most Americans when they learned of the president's brutal murder. As we have seen, that event triggered a major cultural trauma in the United States, one feature of which was a general tendency to further burnish Kennedy's constructed image. Kennedy was compared to Lincoln and Roosevelt, each of whom had given his life so that others might enjoy the blessings of liberty. His image became a sacred symbol of all that was good in America, his virtues those of the nation itself. In this sense, the manner of Kennedy's death was an important source of his enduring fame in American memory. It transformed the constructed image of the president, now glossed in the glory of a fallen hero, into a flashbulb memory that most Americans carried with them into the future.

Jacqueline Kennedy took nothing for granted, however. She told Theodore White that she wanted her husband remembered in romantic terms, as the stuff of legend rather than history or political science, as a mythical figure whose influence on American life would transcend his death and the limited achievements of his time in office. She wanted him remembered for what he represented, not alone for what he did, and she set out to accomplish that goal from the moment of his death.

She covered his shattered head in Dallas, took his body to be autopsied at the naval hospital in Bethesda, and decided on a closed casket for his funeral – all so that people would remember him as the handsome and animated man he was in life. Similar concerns inspired her careful staging of the president's funeral. Working under the burden of enormous grief, she nevertheless transformed the funeral into a dramatic reproduction of his life and presidency, as she wanted them remembered. She missed no opportunity to recall his Irish ancestry, his love of family, his heroic wartime service, his sacrifice on behalf of the nation – all in an effort to humanize her husband and recount the values that had supposedly guided his life.

Nor did she miss a chance to link her husband symbolically to at least two of the most important reform presidents in American history, using for this purpose the caisson that carried Roosevelt's remains to the Capitol and the catafalque upon which Lincoln's lifeless body rested when lying in state in the Rotunda. The burial plot in Arlington National Cemetery had its own symbolism as well. Not only did it remind everyone of the president's blood sacrifice on behalf of the nation but also of his wartime heroism and the experience he shared with the other fallen heroes who were buried in the same sacred ground. What is more, Jacqueline Kennedy chose a gravesite at one end of the capital's great axial fabric, which meant that her husband's Arlington memorial shared space with the great monuments erected in honor of Washington, Jefferson, and especially Lincoln. Located below the Custis-Lee Mansion and above the Lincoln Memorial, it recalled his commitment to civil rights, his wartime heroism, and his belief in public service and sacrifice, as well as his role as a peacemaker who gave his life trying to reconcile factions and calm a nation racked by racial and regional strife. All of this added symbolic and emotional content to the funeral, not to mention the eternal flame, which called to mind Kennedy's devotion to liberty and the hope that he might live beyond death itself, if only the American people honored his memory and completed the unfinished work of his presidency.

In all these ways, or so Jacqueline Kennedy hoped, her husband would serve as a timeless example, both inspirational and aspirational, to the American people. In an effort to calm and unify a nation in the midst of a profound trauma, political leaders and editorial writers repeated the same themes, thereby further reinforcing the sanctified image of the president that his wife wanted inscribed on the collective memory of the nation. In the process, moreover, they also transformed the former first lady into a symbol, like her husband, of strength and courage, of grace and dignity, of devotion to family and nation, of what it meant to be an American.

This was the beginning of the memory work that would occupy Jacqueline Kennedy for the rest of her life and that also explains, in part, why the heroic image of the dead president, self-constructed in his lifetime, burnished by his tragic death, and enshrined in his funeral, would survive in public memory over the next fifty years. Indeed, the former first lady became an active participant, even judge and jury, when it came to the many literary monuments erected in the president's honor. She converted first-generation scholars like Schlesinger and Sorensen into scriptwriters for her own narrative of the president's life; she discouraged counter memories and alternative narratives; and through the Kennedy Library in Boston, she managed the president's records, as well as her own, with the same goal in mind. Because memory is as much about forgetting as remembering, she and her family gave privileged access to those who would write the president's biography as they wanted it recorded; denied similar access to those who might cast a more critical eye on his life and legacy; and reproduced his presidency in a skillfully contrived museum that revealed some aspects of his life while slighting others or erasing them altogether.

In these and other ways, the Kennedys asserted their ownership of the president's identity, controlled his legacy, and kept his image, as they defined it, alive in the minds of the American people, for many of whom it became an intimate public memory. Along the way, moreover, they had a lot of help from friends and allies, not only in the mainstream press but also in television films and documentaries, which typically mediated the difference between history and memory in ways that presented Kennedy in the same self-constructed role he had played on the White House stage. The same was true of leaders in both political parties who wanted the benefits of associating themselves with the ever-popular president, claiming his policies as their own and mimicking his celebrated style. Even as late as the presidential campaign of 2008, and then into his administration, Barack Obama spelled out the similarities between himself and the former president: both had battled prejudice to win nomination and election, both were inspiring speakers, both were liberal reformers, both were moderate in their foreign policies. The Kennedy family responded by endorsing Obama's candidacy over that of Hillary Clinton, after which the new president appointed Caroline Kennedy as the US Ambassador to Japan. All of these gestures brought Kennedy to mind for a new generation of Americans. So did Jacqueline Kennedy's death in 1994; the tragic death of

John F. Kennedy Jr. in a plane crash off Martha's Vineyard five years later; and the repeated celebration of various milestones in the life of the former president. This included the fiftieth anniversary of his election, which the New York Mint commemorated with a special coin featuring the stamped image of the former president. Only one year later, moreover, the Kennedy Center in Washington celebrated the fiftieth anniversary of the president's inauguration with a special composition performed by the National Sympathy Orchestra. Paul Simon, Yo-Yo Ma, and other stars also performed for the large audience on hand, which included more than one hundred members of the Kennedy clan, led by Caroline Kennedy. As had always been the case, these celebrations and commemorations, including the fiftieth anniversary of the president's assassination, recalled Kennedy as his wife and family wanted him remembered, with slight attention, if any, to aspects of his life that might support a different narrative of the president's life and policies.[47]

Something similar can be said of the monuments of glass, steel, and stone erected in honor of the former president. Kennedy was remembered in hundreds, even thousands of individual mementos in the United States and abroad. These memory markers, often the production of a vast and profitable heritage industry, nonetheless revealed the enormous affection and respect that Kennedy commanded among ordinary people everywhere and their profound commitment to his remembrance. They contributed to his enduring popularity as well, or at least, to the enduring popularity of the Kennedy brand. Whether a spontaneous and private memento or a grand government monument, whether a tiny trinket or a mountaintop, whether a peace forest or the fields of Runnymede, whether a public housing project or a space center, these mementos and memorials invariably represented Kennedy's life as people wanted to remember him. They spoke of his commitment to voluntarism and public service, to space exploration and peace, to education, racial equality, and aid to the sick, the poor, and the aged. This was the same image that Kennedy and his wife had presented in their White House productions and that Jacqueline Kennedy tried to capture in her husband's funeral and in the literary monuments to his memory. It was also the image she wanted to imprint on the physical monuments named in his honor, including the Kennedy Space Center in Florida, the Kennedy Center for the Performing Arts in Washington, DC, and especially his gravesite in Arlington National Cemetery and the Kennedy Library and Museum in Boston.

The Kennedy Center, as we have seen, recalled Kennedy's commitment to the arts as a noble endeavor in its own right, but also as a token of free expression in a democratic society and proof of the nation's legitimate claim to leadership of the civilized world. The space center memorialized his commitment to the space program, to be sure, but also his sense of adventure, his faith in the future, and his confidence that no dream was too small, no goal beyond reach. The library brought to mind his life as a man of letters, his love of learning, his sense of history, and his appreciation of all that might be gleaned from the study of politics and the past. As was the case with the memorial grave, moreover, the very architecture of the library spoke to the president's soaring spirit and to the conviction that he would live in the memory of the American people as long as they followed the shining light of his example and finished the unfinished work of democracy.

Through all of these efforts, originating with the brand that Kennedy and his wife had constructed for themselves as president and first lady, through the dramatic performance of the president's funeral, to the many monuments and memorials in his honor, Jacqueline Kennedy embedded her husband's identity, as she defined it, so deeply in the collective memory of the American people that even the most aggressive revisionist could not fully dislodge it. On the contrary, Kennedy remains today, five decades after his assassination, one of the presidents that Americans like and admire most, particularly among presidents of the postwar era.

Journalist Gerald W. Johnson, among others, anticipated this phenomenon in his tribute to the late president, and in the process offered still another reason for Kennedy's long afterlife in American memory. Johnson was sure that Kennedy's reputation would stand the test of time, if only because he had been "touched by romance," a phrase that invoked Jacqueline Kennedy's reference to Camelot in her interview with Theodore White shortly after her husband's death. Whereas Dr. Dryasdust, as Johnson called historians, might care who wrote the nation's laws, others cared more who sang its songs. To him, this meant that Kennedy could only be judged against "the legendary," not against the normal standards of historical scholarship. What mattered most was his style, not his substance, what he represented, not what he did, and how he made Americans feel about themselves.[48]

As this suggests, Kennedy's image would be sustained in American memory not only by the diligent efforts of his family and friends, but also by history itself. Almost immediately after his death, Americans began to debate Kennedy's place in history and what it meant. Was he a man of the 1950s, a short-lived but attractive appendage to the Eisenhower years, or did his election mark the start of the 1960s? Some thought the 1960s actually began with his death, which was followed by race riots, urban violence, the Vietnam War, the Watergate scandal, and other national traumas of a dark and dismal decade. Most associated him with the brighter aspects of the 1960s, even claiming that his call to public service, faith in the future, and confidence that all problems could be solved inspired many of the positive developments that followed his death, including the women's movement and environmentalist movement. Still others saw the Kennedy years as a shining interlude between the lethargy of the Eisenhower era and the imperial presidency that came later.[49]

Each of these perspectives carried ideological implications, as we have seen. Commentators on the center-left of American politics divided into two camps. Some, the so-called revisionists, saw Kennedy as a deeply flawed and unaccomplished president whose arrogance led inevitably to disasters at home and abroad. Others, mostly mainstream media commentators and post-revisionist scholars, came to admit Kennedy's shortcomings but still pictured him as an inspiring leader whose progressive agenda pointed to Johnson's Great Society and even to the reforms later engineered by Barack Obama. Conservatives divided into two camps as well. Some wanted to decouple Kennedy from the happy days of the Eisenhower administration and link him instead to the Vietnam War, the Watergate scandal, and the other failures of the late 1960s and after. Others, such as Ira Stoll, saw Kennedy as a generational bridge that might have linked the solid Republicanism of the Eisenhower period to the Reagan revolution of the 1980s. If only Kennedy had lived, as one pointed out, he might have crowned the modern conservative movement with the halo of Camelot.

Whether Kennedy inspired a new progressive movement or a conservative revolution, most could agree that history after his assassination was more nightmare than fairy tale. To be sure, any interpretation of the post assassination period as one of national decline should be viewed with skepticism. Nevertheless, it may help to explain why so many Americans searched their memories for an inspiring leader and for an era that seemingly evoked their better selves. It was this sense of nostalgia, as much as anything else, that deepened Kennedy's significance as a symbol of all that was good in American life and that sustained his memory over time, despite the revisionist assaults against him, the revelations regarding his personal life, and the loss of his most important memory maker when Jacqueline Kennedy Onassis passed away in 1994.

Although originally diagnosed as a medical disease or mental illness, nostalgia would later be viewed as a psychological or sociological phenomenon. Once considered synonymous with homesickness, it was first associated with a period of prolonged absence from home and a deep-seated longing for the cherished experience of a bygone time and place. Today, however, nostalgia is generally viewed as a common feature of modernity brought on by the rapid pace of change in the modern world and its tendency to obliterate the local, replace the homestead with life on the move, and destroy old ways and traditional identities. It is often marked by feelings of loneliness and meaninglessness, a profound distaste for some aspects of the present, fear of the future, and longing for a past filtered of any disappointing or unpleasant experience. Nostalgia is thus linked to both identity and memory, though often memory as mediated by television, the movies, and even by museums and monuments – a memory more idealized than real, particularly in the minds of those too young to have actually experienced the past being recalled. Nostalgic memories are usually happy memories, captured and promoted by a heritage industry that is more interested in commercializing the past than in history itself. In Kennedy's case, these were memories of a leader whose self-constructed identity squared perfectly with an idealized image that was made and remade in Hollywood films and television specials in the years following the president's death.[50]

As Fred Davis noted in his classic work on the sociology of nostalgia, the 1970s and 1980s saw a stunning wave of nostalgia wash across the United States under just the kind of conditions noted above. In addition to the shattering experiences that shook the nation to its core after Kennedy's assassination, including subsequent assassinations, the Vietnam War, and Watergate, the country also experienced a rapid and sustained attack on traditional values. This was evident in the feminist movement, the sexual revolution, the decline of marriage rates, the rise of a drug culture, and the campaign to legalize abortion and protect gay rights. Taken together, this assault on tradition led to a collective identity crisis that included, among other things, a retreat into nostalgia as a way to salvage traditional identities and values, such as those Kennedy supposedly embodied.[51]

What was happening in the social and cultural sphere was happening as well in the political world, which was marked by a growing distaste for contemporary politics and politicians, loss of confidence in the future, and distrust of government. Already by the 1970s, and lasting much longer, the American people had become increasingly cynical about government and skeptical of its ability to solve the complex problems facing the nation, let alone lead the world into a new era of peace, security, and progress. It was in this context that Americans looked back nostalgically on the early 1960s in general and on Kennedy's leadership in particular. Their nostalgic gaze, their tendency to see Kennedy through the rearview mirror of the modern world, did as much as anything else to sustain his image in American memory, although the image recalled was little more than another remodeling of the brand that Kennedy had constructed for himself when he played the part of president in his own White House productions.

In this connection, it's worth repeating some of the commentary mentioned earlier. "We were a happier nation then," Michael Harrington recalled of the Kennedy years. The American people "had a president they loved," and who inspired them with hope in the future and the conviction that all things were possible.[52] Since then, according to Richard Boeth, "the nation had slowly been purged of much of its vitality, ... much of its confidence and practically all of its gaiety" – attributes once associated with Kennedy, who had "stirred in us," according to the *Los Angeles Times*, "that fundamentally American sense of the possibilities of life, of the great things this country can yet achieve." That optimism had since given way to a dim view of presidential leadership and the ability of Americans to play a positive role in world affairs. In this sense, Kennedy's death marked the end of an era filled with "the ebullient optimism and confidence identified throughout the world with the spirit of America."[53] In its place, according to the *New York Times*, was a new order where people doubted if the world could ever again be the "nation's oyster," or if it could ever conform "to man's noblest ideals," as they had believed when Kennedy was in the White House.[54]

In other words, from the perspective of the 1970s and later, Kennedy looked increasingly good because the years following his death looked increasingly bad by comparison. "Kennedy is remembered as a success," Robert Dallek said on the fiftieth anniversary of the assassination, "mainly because of what came after: Johnson and Vietnam, Nixon and Watergate."[55] In this context, Kennedy became, to nostalgic Americans, a much more polished version of the image he had presented in his popular news conferences, campaign speeches, television specials, and ubiquitous photographs, the same image that his wife, family, and friends reproduced in the monuments to his memory and in the museum that constantly restaged his life as they wanted him remembered. He was one of us, to cite Arthur Neal once again, but also the best of us.[56] He was the ideal American, and with his death, and all that followed, his countrymen wanted to preserve that memory of him, however constructed, and perhaps of themselves and their country when he was in office. As a man, Kennedy may have perished, but his symbolic identity lived on in the popular devotion to his memory and to a time when many Americans were more hopeful than they were later, when they had a sense of shared purpose, optimism about the future, faith in leadership, and confidence in government. In their minds, it was what Kennedy represented, not what he did, that was important – and that made him a president worthy of remembrance.

Notes

1 The Afterlife of John Fitzgerald Kennedy: An Introduction

1 Jacqueline Kennedy quoted in Kenneth P. O'Donnell and David F. Powers, with Joe McCarthy, *"Johnny, We Hardly Knew Ye": Memories of John Fitzgerald Kennedy* (Boston: Little, Brown, 1972), 24.

2 For a brief summary of the Texas trip and Texas politics, see ibid., 3–26; Arthur M. Schlesinger Jr., *A Thousand Days: John F. Kennedy in the White House* (Boston: Houghton Mifflin, 2002), 752, 1020–24; Thurston Clarke, *JFK's Last Hundred Days: The Transformation of a Man and the Emergence of a Great President* (New York: Penguin, 2013), 329–44; and Robert Dallek, *An Unfinished Life: John F. Kennedy, 1917–1963* (New York: Back Bay Books, 2004), 433, 691–93. Lady Bird Johnson later recounted how the Dallas mob assaulted her and her husband when they campaigned there. "It was a sea of mad slogans," she said of the angry crowd, with nearly everyone waving a placard on a stick. It was "very obvious they didn't like Johnson, couldn't stand Kennedy." See Claudia "Lady Bird" Johnson, Oral History Interview XLIII by Harry Middleton, November 23, 1996, 13–16, Internet copy, LBJ Library.

3 See sources cited in the previous note. Dealey is quoted in Dallek, *Unfinished Life*, 433. For a recent discussion of the politics and political culture of Dallas at the time, see Bill Minutaglio and Steven L. Davis, *Dallas 1963: The Road to the Kennedy Assassination* (London: John Murray, 2013), esp. 9–19. For contemporary reports on the Dallas political scene, see Christine Camp, interview by Ann M. Campbell, November 24, 1969, 48, OHC; and Thomas P. Costin, interview by William J. Hartigan, April 5, 1976, 34–36, OHC. Costin was a U.S. Postal Service official who had spent time in Texas just prior to the assassination and was shocked by the local hostility toward President Kennedy, including threats against his life. Camp was Assistant White House Press Secretary and, during the course of her oral history, discusses the *Dallas Morning News*, its attack on Kennedy, and its publisher, E. M. Dealey.

4   Kennedy quoted in O'Donnell and Powers, *"Johnny, We Hardly Knew Ye,"* 25.

5   Mrs. Connelly and Kennedy quoted in Clarke, *JFK's Last Hundred Days,* 346. See also ibid., 342–45.

6   According to Jill Abramson, approximately forty thousand Kennedy-related books had been published by 2013, when the nation commemorated the fiftieth anniversary of the president's assassination. See Abramson, "Kennedy, the Elusive President," *New York Times,* October 22, 2013, www.nytimes .com/2013/10/27/books/review/the-elusive-president.html?_r=0.

7   Readers may wish to explore what some see as a subtle but important difference between "memory" and "remembrance," and between "collective" and "collected" memory. I use the term "collective memory" throughout and only occasionally use "memory" and "remembrance" interchangeably. See on these subjects James E. Young, *The Texture of Memory: Holocaust Memorials and Meaning* (New Haven: Yale University Press, 1993), especially xi–xii; and Jay Winter, *Remembering War: The Great War Between Memory and History in the Twentieth Century* (New Haven: Yale University Press, 2006), especially 1–10. On the distinction between "history" and "heritage," see note 9 of this chapter.

8   Although historians are very familiar with the terms "revisionism" and "postrevisionism," a brief explanation might be helpful for the general reader, if only to distinguish my use of the term "revisionism" from the negative connotations attached to that word in Holocaust studies, where it is often associated with those who deny the Holocaust altogether. In my case, a revisionist scholar is one whose work "revises" the original historical interpretation of a particular event, era, or personality. "Postrevisionism," by contrast, describes a third wave of scholarship that usually balances and often blends arguments and conclusions drawn from both the original scholarship on a topic and the scholarship of subsequent revisionists.

9   Here I make the same distinction that Michael Kammen draws between "history" and "heritage" in his book, *In the Past Lane: Historical Perspectives on American Culture* (New York: Oxford University Press, 1997), 213–25. Heritage, he points out, can often be "an antonym for history" or a "sugarcoated" version of the past. Inspired by an impulse to remember what is attractive, and to ignore the rest, heritage can also lead to a vulgar commercialization of the past by heritage industries looking to make a profit.

10 On the 1960 campaign, the two classic insider accounts, both very favorable to Kennedy, are Theodore H. White, *The Making of the President, 1960* (New York: Atheneum, 1961); and Schlesinger Jr., *A Thousand Days,* 62–76. For a recent and revisionist account of the 1960 campaign, see W. J. Rorabaugh, *The Real Making of the President: Kennedy, Nixon, and the 1960 Election* (Lawrence: University Press of Kansas, 2009). Rorabaugh presents an excellent nuts-and-bolts account with an emphasis on the importance of charm and style to Kennedy's success, as well as his strong campaign organization, the financial resources available to him, and his readiness to resort to bare-knuckle tactics when they seemed necessary.

11 Dallek, *Unfinished Life,* 325–26, 338–42, 346–48, 350.

12 Herbert S. Parmet, *JFK: The Presidency of John F. Kennedy* (New York: Penguin, 1983), 157–79; Schlesinger, *Thousand Days*, 232–66; Dallek, *Unfinished Life*, 357–70. There is an enormous amount of literature on Kennedy's Cuban policy, including the Bay of Pigs invasion and the Cuban Missile Crisis. For a brief overview, see Mark J. White, "The Cuban Imbroglio: From the Bay of Pigs to the Missile Crisis and Beyond," in *Kennedy: The New Frontier Revisited*, ed. Mark J. White (New York: New York University Press, 1998), 63–90. For a review of the literature, see Alan McPherson, "Cuba," in *A Companion to John F. Kennedy*, ed. Marc J. Selverstone (Chichester,UK: John Wiley & Sons, 2014), 228–47.

13 For an excellent summary of the Vienna Conference and the Berlin crisis, see Alan Brinkley, *John F. Kennedy* (New York: Times Books / Henry Holt, 2012), 77–82. See also Georg Schild, "The Berlin Crisis," in White, *Kennedy: The New Frontier Revisited*, 91–131. For a thorough review of the literature, see Andreas W. Daum, "Berlin," in Selverstone, *Companion to John F. Kennedy*, 209–27.

14 Parmet, *JFK*, 131–55; Richard Reeves, *President Kennedy: Profile of Power* (New York: Simon & Schuster, 1994), 115; Dallek, *Unfinished Life*, 350–53, 523–25; Brinkley, *John F. Kennedy*, 86–88, 132–46; and Larry J. Sabato, *The Kennedy Half Century: The Presidency, Assassination, and Lasting Legacy of John F. Kennedy* (New York: Bloomsbury, 2013), 122–26. As these sources and many others make clear, we will never know for sure what Kennedy would have done about Vietnam had he lived. Historians are divided in their opinions. For arguments on both sides, and for his own view, see the excellent essay by Fredrik Logevall, "Vietnam and the Question of What Might Have Been," in White, *Kennedy: The New Frontier Revisited*, 19–62. See also the interesting and provocative work by James G. Blight, Janet M. Lang, and David A. Welch, *Vietnam If Kennedy Had Lived: Virtual JFK* (Lanham, MD: Rowman & Littlefield, 2009).

15 There is an enormous literature on the Cuban Missile Crisis, but among the many Kennedy biographers, the best treatment is in Dallek, *Unfinished Life*, 535–74. See also McPherson, "Cuba."

16 Brinkley, *John F. Kennedy*, 126–133; and Robert Dallek, *John F. Kennedy* (New York: Oxford University Press, 2011), 48–55. For an excellent and original treatment of Kennedy's trip to Germany in the summer of 1963, see Andreas W. Daum, *Kennedy in Berlin*, trans. Dona Geyer (New York: Cambridge University Press, 2008), especially 125–63.

17 Lawrence F. O'Brien, *No Final Victories: A Life in Politics from John F. Kennedy to Watergate* (New York: Ballantine Books, 1975), 106–38; Brinkley, *John F. Kennedy*, 63–65, 75, 89–91; Dallek, *John F. Kennedy*, 28–29, 31; and Lawrence F. O'Brien, Oral History Interview II by Michael L. Gillette, October 29, 1985, 27–29, Internet copy, LBJ Library. For a brief but excellent overview of Kennedy and the arts, see Schlesinger, *Thousand Days*, 729–38; and Donna M. Binkiewicsz, "Culture from Camelot: The Origins and Goals of Arts Policy in the Kennedy Administration," *UCLA Historical Journal* 16 (1966): 103–30. See also John Carl Warnecke, "John F. Kennedy on Architecture: A Legacy and a Challenge," a twenty-nine-page

manuscript in David F. Powers Personal Papers (hereafter cited as DFPPP), 018-010; and August Heckscher, interview by Wolf Von Eckhardt, New York, December 10, 1965, JFK Library, Oral History Collection (hereafter cited as OHC).

18 For overviews of Kennedy's approach to civil rights, see Douglas Field, "JFK and the Civil Rights Movement," in *The Cambridge Companion to John F. Kennedy*, ed. Andrew Hoberek (New York: Cambridge University Press, 2015), 75–88; Brinkley, *John F. Kennedy*, 94–112, 147–48; Dallek, *John F. Kennedy*, 29–30, 55–61; and W. J. Rorabaugh, *Kennedy and the Promise of the Sixties* (New York: Cambridge University Press, 2002), 67–125. For a review of the literature, see also Derek C. Catsam, "Civil Rights," in Selverstone, *Companion to John F. Kennedy*, 540–57.

19 For a somewhat dramatic but detailed account of the political culture and climate in Dallas during the year leading up to the assassination, see Minutaglio and Davis, *Dallas 1963*.

2 All the World's a Stage: Constructing Kennedy

1 For readers who might be interested, the interpretive framework outlined in the paragraphs above derives from the classic work of the famous sociologist Erving Goffman, especially his book, *The Presentation of Self in Everyday Life* (London: Penguin, 1990). Much of what Goffman had to say later inspired scholars working in the fields of performance and theater studies. For an introduction to that work, see Richard Schechner, *Performance Studies*, 2nd ed. (New York: Routledge, 2006); Henry Bial, ed., *The Performance Studies Reader*, 2nd ed. (New York: Routledge, 2007); and Erika Fischer-Lichte, *The Semiotics of Theater*, trans. Jeremy Gaines and Doris L. Jones (Bloomington: Indiana University Press, 1992). For a recent effort to apply this framework to the study of American history, see Daum's excellent book, *Kennedy in Berlin*, and Jessica C. E. Gienow-Hecht, "'The World is Ready to Listen': Symphony Orchestras and the Global Performance of America," *Diplomatic History* 36, no. 1 (January 2012): 17–28. See also her helpful essay, "Nation Branding," in *Explaining the History of American Foreign Relations*, 3rd ed., ed. Frank Costigliola and Michael J. Hogan (New York: Cambridge University Press, 2016), 232–44.

2 Jackie as quoted in John H. Davis, *Jacqueline Bouvier: An Intimate Memoir* (New York: John Wiley & Sons, 1996), 151. Davis was Jacqueline Kennedy's first cousin.

3 The paragraphs dealing with Jackie's background and character draw on a wide variety of sources, beginning with the firsthand accounts of Davis, including *Jacqueline Bouvier*, 1–155; and *The Bouviers: Portrait of an American Family* (New York: Farrar, Straus & Giroux, 1969), esp. 337–451. See also C. David Heymann, *A Woman Named Jackie: An Intimate Biography of Jacqueline Bouvier Kennedy Onassis* (New York: Penguin, 1989), 1–83; Donald Spoto, *Jacqueline Bouvier Kennedy Onassis: A Life* (New York: St. Martin's Press, 2000), 3–75; and Sarah Bradford, *America's Queen: The Life of Jacqueline Kennedy Onassis* (New York: Penguin, 2001), 1–50.

4   On Jackie's French connection, see, in addition to the sources cited in the previous note, Alice Kaplan, *Dreaming in French: The Paris Years of Jacqueline Bouvier Kennedy, Susan Sontag, and Angela Davis* (Chicago: University of Chicago Press, 2012), 7–80. Kaplan's chapters provide a particularly elegant and sensitive treatment of the young Jacqueline Bouvier.

5   For Jackie's remarks, see Carl Sferrazza Anthony, *As We Remember Her: Jacqueline Kennedy Onassis in the Words of Her Family and Friends* (New York: HarperCollins, 2003), 129; Oleg Cassini, *In My Own Fashion: An Autobiography* (New York: Simon & Schuster, 1987), 327; and Heymann, *Woman Named Jackie*, 254. For the president's complaints and the dinner party plans, see Bradford, *America's Queen*, 169–71; and Mary Van Rensselaer Thayer, *Jacqueline Kennedy: The White House Years* (New York: Little, Brown, 1971), 102–5. For White House renovations prior to 1961, see James A. Abbott and Elaine M. Rice, *Designing Camelot: The Kennedy White House Restoration* (New York: Van Nostrand Reinhold, 1998), 15–17; and Barbara A. Perry, *Jacqueline Kennedy: First Lady of the New Frontier* (Lawrence: University Press of Kansas, 2004), 95–101.

6   See Hugh Sidey, "The First Lady Brings History and Beauty to the White House," *Life*, September 6, 1961, 54–65. Sidey was one of the Kennedys' closest friends in the press and his article was the result of an interview and close collaboration with the first lady. See also Perry, *Jacqueline Kennedy*, 96–97, 102–3; Bradford, *America's Queen*, 174–75; and Barbara Leaming, *Mrs. Kennedy: The Missing History of the Kennedy Years* (New York: Touchstone, 2002), 47–49.

7   For good examples of how closely the first lady monitored and directed the restoration work, see her exchanges with Lorraine Waxman Pearce, the White House curator, regarding furniture, art works, and other materials for the restoration, in Jacqueline Bouvier Kennedy Onassis Personal Papers (hereafter cited as JBKOPP), SF006-014. For a firsthand account of the whirlwind redecoration of the family quarters and the first lady's attention to detail, see the reminiscences of J. B. West, chief usher of the White House, in his *Upstairs at the White House: My Life with the First Ladies*, with Mary Lynn Kotz (New York: Coward, McCann & Geoghegan, 1973), 197–200. See also his interview by Nancy Tuckerman and Pamela Turnure, 1967, 3–5, OHC. A similar portrait emerges in Nancy Tuckerman and Pamela Turnure, interview by Mrs. Wayne Fredericks, 1964, 38–39, OHC; and in the reminiscences of Letitia Baldrige, the first lady's social secretary, in her *Of Diamonds and Diplomats: An Autobiography of a Happy Life* (New York: Houghton Mifflin/Ballantine Books, 1969), 135–50. Finally, see again Abbott and Rice, *Designing Camelot*, 52; and Perry, *Jacqueline Kennedy*, 103–4, 109, 111.

8   Sister Parish tells much of her own story, with the help of her daughter and granddaughter, in Apple Parish Bartlett and Susan Bartlett Crater, *Sister: The Life of Legendary American Interior Decorator, Mrs. Henry Parish II* (New York: St. Martin's Press, 2000), 87–113.

9   For the expert advice she received, see, for example, the memorandum by L. H. Butterfield and Julian P. Boyd, April 24, 1961, JBKOPP-SF035-012. The White House, according to Butterfield and Boyd, was not only the

president's home and the headquarters of the executive branch but also "a museum" and "cultural monument" that should reflect "the struggles and aspirations of the American people." As such, its interior design should not be static but should reflect the whole history of the United States, at least through the 1920s.

10 White House, press release, February 23, 1961, JBKOPP-SF017-005. See also the sources cited in the following note.

11 The Fine Arts Committee was advised by a separate committee of experts composed mainly of historians and museum curators and directors. White House, press release, April 18, 1961, JBKOPP-SF017-005. See also Bradford, *America's Queen*, 175–77; Bartlett and Crater, *Sister*, 100–102; Abbott and Rice, *Designing Camelot*, 22–23, 29; Pierre Salinger, *With Kennedy* (Garden City, NY: Doubleday, 1966), 306–8; and Schlesinger, *Thousand Days*, 670.

12 See Abbott and Rice, *Designing Camelot*, 25; and Perry, *Jacqueline Kennedy*, 108–9.

13 For the committee members, including Du Pont, see the list attached to White House, press release, February 23, 1963, JBKOPP-SF017-005.

14 Ibid. See also Bradford, *America's Queen*, 175–78; and Abbott and Rice, *Designing Camelot*, 9, 18–22, 49.

15 See Bradford, *America's Queen*, 175–78; Abbott and Rice, *Designing Camelot*, 34, 47–49, 52–53; and Bartlett and Crater, *Sister*, 105.

16 Abbott and Rice, *Designing Camelot*, 47–53.

17 Jackie quoted in Sally Bedell Smith, *Grace and Power: The Private World of the Kennedy White House* (New York: Random House, 2005), 206–7. See also Perry, *Jacqueline Kennedy*, 102, 110; and Leaming, *Mrs. Kennedy*, 121.

18 Jackie is quoted in Anthony, *As We Remember Her*, 141. See also Abbott and Rice, *Designing Camelot*, 23–24, 38–39.

19 The White House announced the opening of each room when it was restored. The announcements always included a detailed description of the room and its furnishings. For the Blue Room, see the press release issued by the Office of the Press Secretary to Mrs. Kennedy, January 21, 1963, JBKOPP-SF017-005. The announcement also gave the White House's explanation for the choices made regarding color selections for the wall coverings and accessories. See also the unsigned memorandum for Pierre Salinger regarding the third article in Cheshire's series, September 4, 1962, JBKOPP-SF025-010. The president and first lady tried to preempt the negative criticism in Cheshire's series, asking Clark Clifford to get the necessary assurances from the paper's editor. See the untitled, unsigned note, probably written by Evelyn Lincoln, "Clark Clifford called – dictated the following," in Papers of John F. Kennedy, Presidential Papers, President's Office Files (hereafter cited as JFKPOF), Subjects, White House Restoration, 110-021. For the Blue Room controversy, see West interview, 10–11, OHC.

20 Jackie quoted in Perry, *Jacqueline Kennedy*, 111; and Abbott and Rice, *Designing Camelot*, 101–4.

21 Office of the Assistant Social Secretary, press release, January 17, 1962, JBKOPP-SF017-005. See also Abbott and Rice, *Designing Camelot*, 77–87.

22 Office of the Assistant Social Secretary, press release, December 4, 1961, JBKOPP-SF017-005; and Abbott and Rice, *Designing Camelot*, 55–63, 89–99, 163–64.

23 For the inaugural address, see John F. Kennedy, *Public Papers of the Presidents of the United States: John F. Kennedy, 1961* (Washington, DC: Government Printing Office, 1962), 2–3.

24 Anthony, *As We Remember Her*, 140.

25 Perry Wolff, *A Tour of the White House with Mrs. John F. Kennedy* (New York: Dell Publishing, 1963). This history of the White House includes a script of Mrs. Kennedy's tour as well as photographs and commentary. For the president's remarks, see ibid., 232.

26 Cheshire's articles appeared as "Circa 1962: Jacqueline Kennedy's White House," in consecutive editions of the *Washington Post* between September 5 and 12, 1962. See also Bradford, *America's Queen*, 179; Smith, *Grace and Power*, 300–1; and Salinger, *With Kennedy*, 308.

27 Abbott and Rice, *Designing Camelot*, 34–36, 38–39. J. B. West understood the differences between Du Pont and Boudin and saw how the first lady handled them. See his *Upstairs at the White House*, 242–43.

28 Elder quoted in Abbott and Rice, *Designing Camelot*, 42. See also ibid., 27; for Elder's very guarded assessment of Boudin's work and the first lady's taste, see William Voss Elder III, interview by Ronald J. Grele, December 15, 1965, 14–16, OHC. See also West, *Upstairs at the White House*, 248–51. West was a keen observer of politics and personal struggles in the East Wing and had little sympathy for Lorraine Pearce. He thought she "acted rather grandly" toward the first lady's social staff and violated "the unspoken White House rule: One does not provoke the First Lady." The quote is from ibid., 250.

29 The White House kept a close count on the number of tourists visiting the restored mansion, noting increases year over year. See, for example, the undated, unsigned report, "Approximate Statistics for White House Tours – 1961," JBKOPP-SF025-016; John M. McNally Jr. to Andrew Hatcher, July 31, 1961, JBKOPP-SF025-016; and McNally, memorandum for Kenneth O'Donnell, January 1, 1963, JBKOPP-SF025-016. For a sample of the fan mail sent to the first lady after her TV tour, see the letters and telegrams in JBKOPP-SF025-016 and JBKOPP-SF002, -005 and -006. See also Perry, *Jacqueline Kennedy*, 113–24; West, *Upstairs at the White House*, 248–49; Gil Troy, "Jacqueline Kennedy's White House Renovations," *White House Studies* 1, no. 3 (2001): 395–402; and Salinger, *With Kennedy*, 308–9.

30 On the guidebook, see, in addition to the sources in the previous note, John Waggaman to Pamela Turnure, March 12, 1962; Nash Castro, White House Historical Association, to Waggaman, June 11, 1962; Castro to Turnure, March 7, 1963; Conrad L. Wirth, Director, National Park Service, to the Executive Secretaries, Cooperating Associations of the National Park Service, March 11, 1963; White House Historical Association, "Text for Article in Museum News," July 16, 1963; White House Historical Association, news releases, August 23 and November 6, 1963; and unsigned letter to David E. Finley, Chairman, Board of Directors, White House Historical

Association, November 1, 1963, all in JBKOPP-SF0034-002. See also the news releases of August 4, 1962, November 25, 1962, and January 23, 1963, JBKOPP-SF035-004.

31 For an excellent essay on the role that the president and his wife played in saving and restoring Lafayette Square, see Kurt Helfrich, "Modernism for Washington? The Kennedys and the Redesign of Lafayette Square," *Washington History* 8, no. 1 (Spring/Summer 1996): 16–37. Helfrich also notes the important role they played in plans for the restoration of Blair House and the long-term revival of Pennsylvania Avenue. So does Bernard L. Boutin, administrator of the General Services Administration in the Kennedy Administration, in his interview by Dan H. Fenn, Jr., June 3, 1964, 23–28, OHC. See also Abbott and Rice, *Designing Camelot*, 9–13; Schlesinger, *Thousand Days*, 671; and Anthony, *As We Remember Her*, 144–48, 166.

32 Abbott and Rice, *Designing Camelot*, 9–13.

33 The first lady quoted in Perry, *Jacqueline Kennedy*, 111.

34 Gienow-Hecht, "Nation Branding," 233–37.

35 West, *Upstairs at the White House*, 195. West could not recall the first lady "ever wearing a dress in the White House unless she had company." See ibid., 203.

36 On the significance of costuming, see Alison Lurie, *The Language of Clothes* (New York: Henry Holt, 2000); Diana Crane, *Fashion and Its Social Agendas: Class, Gender, and Identity in Clothing* (Chicago: University of Chicago Press, 2000); and Annette Lynch and Mitchell D. Strauss, eds., *Changing Fashion: A Critical Introduction to Trend Analysis and Cultural Meaning* (New York: Berg, 2007).

37 Oleg Cassini, *A Thousand Days of Magic: Dressing Jacqueline Kennedy for the White House* (New York: Rizzoli International Publications, 1995), 38. See also the photographs in ibid., 36, 39, 40; Perry, *Jacqueline Kennedy*, 65–66; and Smith, *Grace and Power*, 58.

38 Smith, *Grace and Power*, 23; Perry, *Jacqueline Kennedy*, 58, 64–65; Bradford, *America's Queen*, 144–47; and Cassini, *Thousand Days of Magic*, 12–17, 49.

39 This account draws directly on Cassini's two memoirs, *Thousand Days of Magic*, 15, 18–23, 29; and *In My Own Fashion*, 316–37. The quotes are from *In My Own Fashion*, 325–27, 330–31, and 337. See also Smith, *Grace and Power*, 23–25; and Perry, *Jacqueline Kennedy*, 64–65.

40 Cassini, *In My Own Fashion*, 327, 342; and Cassini, *Thousand Days of Magic*, 57.

41 Cassini, *Thousand Days of Magic*, 61, 69; Thayer, *Jacqueline Kennedy*, 25; Perry, *Jacqueline Kennedy*, 85–86; Bradford, *America's Queen*, 194–97; Anthony, *As We Remember Her*, 149–50; and Smith, *Grace and Power*, 207. See also the interesting essay, "The U.S. Through the Lens of Style," *USA Today Magazine*, March 2005, 26–31; and Hamish Bowles, Arthur Schlesinger Jr., and Rachel Lambert Mellon, *Jacqueline Kennedy: The White House Years; Selections from the John F. Kennedy Library and Museum* (New York: Bulfinch Press / Little, Brown, 2001). The last book is basically a narrative, with photographs, of an exhibit mounted by the Kennedy Library

and Museum and featuring key pieces of Jacqueline Kennedy's wardrobe as first lady.

42 Schlesinger, *Thousand Days*, 352.

43 Bowles quoted in Perry, *Jacqueline Kennedy*, 83. See also ibid., 88–91; Cassini, *Thousand Days of Magic*, 118–41; Cassini, *In My Own Fashion*, 147; Bradford, *America's Queen*, 216–19; and "U.S. through the Lens of Style," *USA Today Magazine*. For a good, firsthand account of the empress of Iran's gown compared to that of the first lady, see Baldrige, *Of Diamonds and Diplomats*, 190–91. See also, Bowles, Schlesinger, and Mellon, *Jacqueline Kennedy*.

44 Perry, *Jacqueline Kennedy*, 81.

45 Kennedy is quoted in Perry, *Jacqueline Kennedy*, 182. The best source for information on official White House entertainment is Letitia Baldrige. See *Of Diamonds and Diplomats*, 159–63, 171, 185; and Letitia Baldrige Hollensteiner, interview by Mrs. Wayne Fredericks, April 24, 1964, 20–34, OHC. See also West, *Upstairs at the White House*, 254–56; Marie Smith, *Entertaining in the White House* (Washington, DC: Acropolis Books, 1967), 246–66; Thayer, *Jacqueline Kennedy*, 123–24, 147, 149, 151–53, 183–90; Anthony, *As We Remember Her*, 130; and Bradford, *America's Queen*, 172–73.

46 See Baldrige, *Of Diamonds and Diplomats*, 187–88, 190, 195 for these and other examples of how the Kennedys entertained. For more detail on the meticulous planning that went into White House dinners, see Thayer, *Jacqueline Kennedy*, 168–81, 208–9.

47 Thayer, *Jacqueline Kennedy*, 194–96; Baldrige, *Of Diamonds and Diplomats*, 192–94; and Leaming, *Mrs. Kennedy*, 196.

48 Leaming, *Mrs. Kennedy*, 146–47.

49 Kennedy's quotation is from ibid., 138. See also ibid., 136–37; and O'Donnell and Powers, "*Johnny, We Hardly Knew Ye*," 269–70.

50 Cassini, *Thousand Days of Magic*, 78–79; Thayer, *Jacqueline Kennedy*, 205–6; Letitia Baldrige, *In the Kennedy Style: Magical Evenings in the Kennedy White House* (New York: Doubleday, 1998), 48–65; Smith, *Entertaining in the White House*, 261; and Anne H. Lincoln, *The Kennedy White House Parties* (New York: Viking Press, 1967), 28–35. Lincoln served as assistant social secretary in the Kennedy White House. See also West interview, 8–9, OHC.

51 Kennedy quoted in Thayer, *Jacqueline Kennedy*, 184. For a firsthand account of the Nobel dinner, see Baldrige, *In the Kennedy Style*, 87–101. On the Medal of Honor reception, see Baldrige, *Of Diamonds and Diplomats*, 198–200.

52 Smith, *Grace and Power*, 268–69.

53 Cassini, *In My Own Fashion*, 344–45. Schlesinger was not convinced that Jackie's café society friends brought out the best in her. When he recorded this reflection in his journal, he may have been referring to Cassini and the group that partied in the family quarters after a dinner for the Indian ambassador. See his *Journals: 1952–2000*, ed. Andrew Schlesinger and Stephen Schlesinger (New York: Penguin, 2007), 155. This is not to say that

Schlesinger did not enjoy a good, even rowdy party, and took pains to record them in his journal at the time. See *Journals: 1952–2000*, 110, 122, and 157–98.

54 Smith, *Grace and Power*, 238–40, 263–65; Ben Bradlee, *A Good Life: Newspapering and Other Adventures* (New York: Simon & Schuster, 1996), 229, 232–33; and Benjamin C. Bradlee, *Conversations with Kennedy* (New York: W. W. Norton, 1984), 49, 196–98.

55 National Geographic Society, *The Kennedy Mystique: Creating Camelot* (Washington, DC: National Geographic Society, 2004), 9–11, 15–18, 28. Originally produced in film form for the National Geographic Channel, this volume contains brief essays and commentaries by Jon Goodman, Hugh Sidey, Letitia Baldrige, Robert Dallek, and Barbara Baker Burrows. Subsequent notes will cite the volume as a whole, with appropriate page numbers, rather than individual authors. See also Hellmann, *The Kennedy Obsession: The American Myth of JFK* (New York: Columbia University Press, 1997), 37–86; and White, *Kennedy: A Cultural History of an American Icon* (New York: Bloomsbury, 2013), especially 3–30.

56 Hellmann, *Kennedy Obsession*, 10, 19, 30, 34, 37, 41, 43, 48; and Salinger, *With Kennedy*, 145–60, 285–99. Ben Bradlee, then a *Newsweek* reporter, covered the 1960 campaign and noted especially the differences between Kennedy's management of the press and that of his rival, Richard M. Nixon. See Bradlee, *Conversations with Kennedy*, 18–20. As *The New Yorker* noted in a story published in 2016, the modern documentary was born when Kennedy cooperated with Robert Drew, a *Life* magazine editor, to produce a TV documentary called "Primary," on the 1960 Democratic Party primary campaign. In the process Kennedy had no trouble making himself the star of the show. See, Richard Brody, "Star Power: John F. Kennedy Welcomed Documentary Cameras, which Loved Him Back," *The New Yorker*, May 9, 2016, 6.

57 James E. Pollard, *The Presidents and the Press: Truman to Johnson* (Washington, DC: Public Affairs Press, 1964), 95–110. As Bradlee points out, Kennedy liked and admired some reporters, distrusted others, and kept close track of all. Favorites included Charles Bartlett, Joseph Alsop, Hugh Sidey, and Bradlee himself. Those who got the cold shoulder included James Reston, Walter Lippmann, and especially Arthur Krock. See Bradlee, *Good Life*, 236–39. See also Bradlee, *Conversations with Kennedy*, 102–3, 153–55, 157, 163–64; National Geographic, *Kennedy Mystique*, 189; and Salinger, *With Kennedy*, 99, 145–60, 249–302.

58 Smith, *Grace and Power*, 213–14, 289–92, 396–98; Bradlee, *Conversations with Kennedy*, 218–19.

59 National Geographic, *Kennedy Mystique*, 66.

60 Ibid., 94–95, 125–27, 129; Bradlee, *Conversations with Kennedy*, 12–13, 43–49, 114–18; Bradlee, *Good Life*, 236–39; "The Kennedy Image: How It's Built," *US News & World Report*, April 4, 1962, 56–59; John H. Kessel, "Mr. Kennedy and the Manufacture of News," *Parliamentary Affairs* 16, no. 3 (March 1963): 293–301; James E. Pollard, "The Kennedy Administration and the Press," *Journalism Quarterly* 41, no. 1 (March 1964): 3–14; and Gregg

Herken, *The Georgetown Set: Friends and Rivals in Cold War Washington* (New York: Vintage Books, 2015), 281–84. See also Carol Ann Berthold, "The Image and Character of President John F. Kennedy: A Rhetorical and Critical Approach" (PhD diss., Northwestern University, 1975), 53–57. For an insider's view of Kennedy and the media, see Pierre E. G. Salinger, interview by Theodore H. White, August 10, 1965, OHC; and Salinger, *With Kennedy*.

61 The first lady quoted in Thayer, *Jacqueline Kennedy*, 34. See also Smith, *Grace and Power*, 26–27, 251–52; Leaming, *Mrs. Kennedy*, 21; Perry, *Jacqueline Kennedy*, 1–19, 80–81; National Geographic, *Kennedy Mystique*, 94–95, 104–5; Salinger, *With Kennedy*, 14–15; and Hellmann, *Kennedy Obsession*, 132–33. An interesting note from the first lady to Pierre Salinger is a good example of her carrot-and-stick approach to managing the news, or at least media photographers. Angry with Stanley Tretick after *Look* published, without her permission, some photographs he had taken of her daughter Caroline, the first lady asked Salinger to approach the president about getting Tretick replaced by Mark Shaw for an upcoming photo shoot of the president and his son. See "J." memo for Pierre Salinger, August 6, 1963, JBKOPP-SF093-003. This turned out to be one of the last of the president's photo shoots, and included the iconic picture of young John Kennedy Jr. bursting through the false front of his father's desk in the Oval Office. That and other photos were part of a story on the president and his son that appeared just four days before the assassination. As it turned out, Jacqueline Kennedy loved the pictures and thought it an act of God that they were taken. The whole story is recounted in Stanley Tretick, interview by Diana Michaelis, September 15, 1964, 31–50, OHC. This is an excellent oral history. It says a lot about the president's careful management of the news media and why media people were so fond of him.

62 West, *Upstairs at the White House*, 214–15, 248–51, 264; Bradford, *America's Queen*, 186; Smith, *Grace and Power*, 213, 220–21, 257, 262, 340–41.

63 Jackie quoted in Thayer, *Jacqueline Kennedy*, 33–34. Laura Bergquist Knebel, a longtime journalist for *Look* magazine, referred to the first lady as "the remote fairy queen ... who didn't want to have much truck with us journalist types" and who, like her husband, played favorites among the reporters. See Laura Bergquist Knebel, interview by Nelson Aldrich, December 8, 1965, 23, OHC.

64 Jackie quoted in Cassini, *In My Own Fashion*, 331.

65 On Jackie's smoking, see Anthony, *As We Remember Her*, 134–35; and Smith, *Grace and Power*, 110–11. On the three hundred Cassini dresses, see Cassini, *In My Own Fashion*, 333. On the first lady's expenditures and her constant, generally unsuccessful efforts to economize, see the firsthand account by her personal secretary, Mary Barelli Gallagher, *My Life with Jacqueline Kennedy* (New York: Paperback Library, 1970), 155–56, 207–8, 217–18, 220–27, 259–60; Bradlee, *Conversations with Kennedy*, 118–19, 186–87; and Bradlee, *Good Life*, 255. Kennedy's health problems and womanizing are treated throughout Dallek's *Unfinished Life*, esp. 470–80. See

also Seymour M. Hersh, *The Dark Side of Camelot* (New York: Little, Brown / Back Bay Books, 1998), 5, 14–15, 102–6, 230–42, 298–325, 389–90, 404–5; Nigel Hamilton, *American Caesars: Lives of the Presidents from Franklin D. Roosevelt to George W. Bush* (New Haven: Yale University Press, 2010), 157–70; Mimi Alford's poignant account of her affair with Kennedy in *Once upon a Secret: My Affair with President John F. Kennedy and Its Aftermath* (New York: Random House, 2013); and Barbara Gamarekian, interview by Diane T. Michaelis, June 10, 1964, 15–31, OHC. See also for an excellent cultural take on the Kennedys in the White House, White, *Kennedy*, 31–58.

3 From History to Memory: Assassination and the Making of a Sacred Symbol

1 Paul B. Sheatsley and Jacob J. Feldman, "A National Survey on Public Reactions and Behavior," in *The Kennedy Assassination and the American Public: Social Communication in Crisis*, ed. Bradley S. Greenberg and Edwin B. Parker (Stanford, CA: Stanford University Press, 1965), 149–77. See also Bruce Henderson and Sam Summerlin, *1:33* (New York: Cowles, 1968), 23, 32–33.

2 Sabato, *Kennedy Half Century*, 16. On collective cultural trauma, see Jeffrey C. Alexander, "Toward a Theory of Cultural Trauma," in *Cultural Trauma and Collective Identity*, Jeffrey C. Alexander, Ron Eyerman, Bernhard Giesen, Neil J. Smelser, and Piotr Sztompka (Berkeley: University of California Press, 2004), 1–30. In the same volume, see Smelser, "Psychological Trauma and Cultural Trauma," 31–59, and Smelser, "Epilogue: September 11, 2001, as Cultural Trauma," 264–82. See also Arthur G. Neal, *National Trauma and Collective Memory: Extraordinary Events in the American Experience*, 2nd ed. (Armonk, NY: M. E. Sharpe, 2005); and Alice L. George, *The Assassination of John F. Kennedy: Political Trauma and American Memory* (New York: Routledge, 2013).

3 Much of what follows is drawn from the accounts of ordinary and extraordinary people around the world, as well as newspaper editorials and religious sermons. Hundreds and hundreds of these reflections were collected by a number of enterprising scholars to whom I am indebted. In addition to Henderson and Summerlin, noted above, they include Ellen Fitzpatrick, William M. Fine, Dan B. Fleming Jr., Chuck Fries and Irv Wilson, Jodie Elliott Hansen and Laura Hansen, John B. Jovich, Charles J. Stewart and Bruce Kendall, Abigail Van Buren, Pierre Salinger and Sander Vanocur, M. Bernadette Schmidt, and Jay Mulvaney and Paul De Angelis. Full citations to their works appear in the notes that follow. The authors of most of the individual reflections noted in the following narrative are not identified by name. Instead, the citation is to the work or works from which their accounts are drawn, with appropriate page numbers. It is worth noting the remarkable similarity between reactions recorded in the immediate aftermath of the assassination and those recalled years later, suggesting that initial reactions, so powerfully felt, were etched permanently in the memories

of those who experienced the tragedy first hand. They were not significantly influenced by intervening events, and may have become even more compelling, as was the case with the Kennedy brand, as the years passed by.

4 According to polling data, about 47 percent of respondents worried about national stability, 44 percent about the nation's security. See Sheatsley and Feldman, "National Survey," 157.

5 Ibid., 155, 164; Ted Sorensen, *Counselor: A Life at the Edge of History* (New York: HarperCollins, 2008), 374–75, 380; Dallek, *Unfinished Life*, 698–99; Lady Bird Johnson, *A White House Diary* (Austin: University of Texas Press, 2007), 4–5; O'Donnell and Powers, *"Johnny, We Hardly Knew Ye,"* 31–32; Jim Bishop, *The Day Kennedy Was Shot* (New York: Funk & Wagnalls, 1968), 154, 185–86, 190–91; Bradford, *America's Queen*, 293; Leaming, *Mrs. Kennedy*, 345; and Sabato, *Kennedy Half Century*, 22–25. For the reaction of US soldiers abroad, as well as others, see also Abigail Van Buren, *Where Were You When President Kennedy Was Shot? Memories and Tributes to a Slain President as Told to "Dear Abby"* (Kansas City: Andrews & McMeel, 1993), 32, 35–37, 39, 82–83.

6 See Henderson and Summerlin, 1:33, 24, 204–5; and Sheatsley and Feldman, "National Survey," 157.

7 Schlesinger, *Journals: 1952–2000*, 204.

8 Robert B. Semple Jr., ed., *Four Days in November: The Original Coverage of the John F. Kennedy Assassination by the Staff of the New York Times* (New York: St. Martin's Press, 2003), 90, 92–93. As its title suggests, this last volume is a compendium of stories and articles originally published in the *New York Times* at the time of Kennedy's assassination. Subsequent citations will normally cite this source with appropriate page numbers rather than a particular article and its author.

9 Ibid., 84. Similar expressions were widespread. See, for example, Robert M. Sigman to NBC news anchor Chet Huntley, November 22, 1963, Chet Huntley Personal Papers (hereafter cited as CHPP), correspondence, 1963, November 21–23, 001-001; John Hanf and Paul Plafean to Huntley, November 22, 1963, CHPP-001-001; and Eleanor Wagner to Huntley, November 23, 1963, CHPP-001-001. These are just a few of the approving letters sent to Huntley after he delivered an on-air commentary denouncing the "pockets of hate" around the country that, in his view, had poisoned the environment and set the stage for Kennedy's assassination. See also Ellen Fitzpatrick, *Letters to Jackie: Condolences from a Grieving Nation* (New York: HarperCollins, 2010), 123–24, 132, 140; M. Bernadette Schmidt, comp., *The Trumpet Summons Us … John F. Kennedy* (New York: Vantage Press, 1964), 33–34, 43, 132; and William M. Fine, ed., *That Day with God* (New York: McGraw-Hill, 1965), 11–12, 16, 27, 75, 119. This reaction appeared to be strongest among certain groups, such as religious leaders, African Americans, and political liberals. For polling data, see Sheatsley and Feldman, "National Survey," 163. In addition, see Melissa Matthes, "Assassination Sermons: Mourning JFK and Restoring Church Authority," *Journal of Church and State* 55, no. 2 (November 2012): 221–44, esp. 224–25, 230–31, 233.

10 See Reston, "Why America Weeps: Kennedy Victim of Violent Streak He Sought to Curb in Nation," in Semple, *Four Days*, 177–81. See also Matthes, "Assassination Sermons," 224, 236.

11 Semple, *Four Days*, 445–47.

12 Warren's remarks came in his eulogy to President Kennedy in the nation's capital on November 23, 1963; it is reprinted in ibid., 397–98.

13 Sayre quoted in ibid., 443–44; DeLomel to Huntley, November 24, 1963, CHPP-001-002. See also the sermons published in Charles J. Stewart and Bruce Kendall, eds., *A Man Named John F. Kennedy: Sermons on His Assassination* (Glen Rock, NJ: Paulist Press, 1964), esp. excerpts on 34–39, 40–43, 52–60, 66–69, 72–73, 88–93, 115, 140–43, 156–59, and 170–81; Pierre Salinger and Sander Vanocur, eds., *A Tribute to John F. Kennedy* (Chicago: Encyclopedia Britannica, 1964), 57–65; Schmidt, *Trumpet Summons Us*, 44–45, 66–67, 82; Fine, *That Day With God*, 64–65, 110; and the excellent analysis in Matthes, "Assassination Sermons," esp. 226, 237–38.

14 Petus to Huntley, November 29, 1963, CHPP-001-004.

15 See Roger Brown and James Kulik, "Flashbulb Memories," in Ulric Neisser, ed., *Memory Observed: Remembering in Natural Contexts* (San Francisco: W. H. Freeman, 1982), 23–40.

16 Van Buren, *Where Were You*, ix–x, 17–26, 76–90, 128–138. See also "Ten Years Later: Where Were You?," *Esquire*, November 1973, 136–37.

17 Van Buren, *Where Were You*, 5. See also ibid., 8–10, 110, 115–16.

18 Ibid., 129, 10. See also ibid., 8, 12, 112–13, 119–26.

19 Ibid., 20–21. According to one opinion poll, a solid majority of Americans felt this way. See James D. Barber, "Peer Group Discussion and Recovery from the Kennedy Assassination," in Greenberg and Parker, *Kennedy Assassination*, 114–15. See also Henderson and Summerlin, 1:33, 204.

20 Dan B. Fleming Jr., ... *Ask What You Can Do for Your Country: The Memory and Legacy of John F. Kennedy* (Clearwater, FL: Vandamere Press, 2002), 181, 104.

21 John B. Jovich, ed., *Reflections on JFK's Assassination: 250 Famous Americans Remember November 22, 1963* (Bethesda, MD: Woodbine House, 1988), 97, 48. See also ibid., 51, 150, 207, 298; Henderson and Summerlin, 1:33, 60, 63, 85, 204; Fitzpatrick, *Letters to Jackie*, 78; Jodie Elliott Hansen and Laura Hansen, *November 22, 1963: Ordinary and Extraordinary People Recall Their Reactions When They Heard the News* (New York: Thomas Dunne Books / St. Martin's Press, 2013), 158, 183; and Clarke, *JFK's Last Hundred Days*, 350.

22 Van Buren, *Where Were You*, 119. See also ibid., 15, 61, 103, 124, 137.

23 Henderson and Summerlin, 1:33, 204, 53–54. "Women wept, and men wept," reported George Barrett for the *New York Times*. See Semple, *Four Days*, 5. As Clarke notes, Walter Cronkite was not the only person of influence who shed a tear; nor was all the weeping limited to the United States. See Clarke, *JFK's Last Hundred Days*, 347–49.

24 Van Buren, *Where Were You*, 117; Henderson and Summerlin, 1:33, 207; Semple, *Four Days*, 75. See also Fitzpatrick, *Letters to Jackie*, 36–37.

25 Henderson and Summerlin, 1:33, 53–55; Semple, *Four Days*, 75.

26 Van Buren, *Where Were You*, 5, 111, 144. See also Fleming, *Ask*, 82, 124, 131, 142, 174, 186.

27 The quotations in the order cited are from Mr. and Mrs. Thomas W. Fryer to Huntley, November 25, 1963, CHPP-001-002; Herman G. Bryant, Jr. to Huntley, November 26, 1963, CHPP-001-003; Mrs. Margaret Loveland to Huntley, November 26, 1963, CHPP-001-003; Miss Kathleen Heckmann to Huntley, November 27, 1963, CHPP-001-003; and Miss Mary Kay Kraft to Huntley, November 29, 1963, CHPP-001-004. See also Mrs. William W. Fetner to Huntley, Brinkley Report, November 29, 1963, CHPP-001-004; and Miss Roberta E. Lytle to Huntley, November 30, 1963, CHPP-001-004.

28 Mr. and Mrs. R. J. Skalka to Huntley, November 25, 1963, CHPP-001-002; and Charles Watkins to Huntley, November 25, 1963, CHPP-001-002.

29 Hansen and Hansen, *November 22, 1963*, 17; Van Buren, *Where Were You*, 146; Fleming, *Ask*, 144, 84.

30 Van Buren, *Where Were You*, 112. See also Paul L. Montgomery's report for the *New York Times* in Semple, *Four Days*, 84.

31 Sheatsley and Feldman, "National Survey," 162. See also Henderson and Summerlin, 1:33, 205–6.

32 Van Buren, *Where Were You*, 96, 103.

33 Ibid., viii, 28–34. See also ibid., 98–99, 103.

34 Fleming, *Ask*, 180–81, 105, 184–85. See also the comments of an American teacher in Tanzania in Hansen and Hansen, *November 22, 1963*, 213–15.

35 Van Buren, *Where Were You*, 72, 117, 134–35, 109. See also Robert C. Doty's report for the *New York Times* in Semple, *Four Days*, 73–75; for similar reports from Chicago and Los Angeles, see Hansen and Hansen, *November 22, 1963*, 27, 45.

36 Fleming, *Ask*, 111, 113, 126; Henderson and Summerlin, 1:33, 54.

37 Fleming, *Ask*, 144, 79.

38 Van Buren, *Where Were You*, 117.

39 Fleming, *Ask*, 97, 134, 162, 114. See also ibid., 79, 180–81; Van Buren, *Where Were You*, 35, 117; Chuck Fries and Irv Wilson, *"We'll Never Be Young Again": Remembering the Last Days of John F. Kennedy*, with Spencer Green (Beverly Hills, CA: Tallfellow Press, 2003), 89; and Hansen and Hansen, *November 22, 1963*, 37, 77, 126, 143.

40 Henderson and Summerlin, 1:33, 203.

41 See Conrad Cherry, ed. *God's New Israel: Religious Interpretations of American Destiny*, revised and updated edition (Chapel Hill: University of North Carolina Press, 1998), 1–8.

42 Frank C. Costigliola, "'Like Children in the Darkness': European Reaction to the Assassination of John F. Kennedy," *Journal of Popular Culture* 20, no. 3 (Winter 1986): 115–24.

43 De Gaulle cited in Clarke, *JFK's Last Hundred Days*, 349. Clarke provides a brief summary of reaction around the world, as does Schlesinger in *Thousand Days*, 1028–29. See also Henderson and Summerlin, 1:33, 127–28.

44 Radio commentator quoted in Semple, *Four Days*, 224.

45 Fitzgerald quoted in Schlesinger, *Thousand Days*, 1028.

46   Ibid., 126–27; Van Buren, *Where Were You*, 29; Semple, *Four Days*, 416–17.

47   Semple, *Four Days*, 418; Fleming, *Ask*, 228; and especially Daum, *Kennedy in Berlin*, 187–97.

48   Semple, *Four Days*, 108–10, 149, 419–20; Henderson and Summerlin, 1:33, 112, 115, 146–48, 152, 155, 166. See also Van Buren, *Where Were You*, 134; and the international reaction as noted in Fleming, *Ask*, 198–236.

49   Henderson and Summerlin, 1:33, 140–41, 163; Hansen and Hansen, *November 22, 1963*, 184, 267–68; and Semple, *Four Days*, 419–29.

50   Castro quoted in Henderson and Summerlin, 1:33, 117–18. Of course, Castro's comment may also have reflected his fear that Cuba would be blamed for the assassination.

51   Van Buren, *Where Were You*, 93–94, 96–97, 99.

52   Ibid., 100. See also ibid., 93–94, 101.

53   Ibid., 96, 98–99, 101–102; Fleming, *Ask*, 228, 230, 233; Hansen and Hansen, *November 22, 1963*, 39, 42, 118, 124–25; Van Buren, *Where Were You*, 34; and Semple, *Four Days*, 419.

54   Van Buren, *Where Were You*, 104.

55   Ibid.

56   Ibid., 95.

57   Ibid., 4. See also ibid., 105; and Hansen and Hansen, *November 22, 1963*, 213–15.

58   Henderson and Summerlin, 1:33, 146–49, 419.

59   Van Buren, *Where Were You*, 93.

60   Ibid., 103. See also Hansen and Hansen, *November 22, 1963*, 121.

61   Schlesinger, *Thousand Days*, 1028; Sabato, *Kennedy Half Century*, 238–39, 255; William Manchester, *The Death of a President: November 20 – November 25, 1963* (New York: Galahad Books, 1967), 249–51.

62   Dallek, *Unfinished Life*, 686.

63   The quotation is from F. J. Brode to Chet Huntley, November 24, 1963, CHPP-001-002. See also Fine, *That Day With God*, 49–51, 82–89; Fleming, *Ask*, 100, 102, 104, 115, 133, 144, 150; Fitzpatrick, *Letters to Jackie*, 54, 101, 267–68; Jay Mulvaney and Paul De Angelis, *Dear Mrs. Kennedy: The World Shares Its Grief; Letters, November 1963* (New York: St. Martin's Press, 2010), 25–26, 91; Salinger and Vanocur, *Tribute to John F. Kennedy*, 37–38, 55–56; and Schmidt, *Trumpet Summons Us*, 33, 47–48, 51, 55, 102–3, 116. See also Sabato, *Kennedy Half Century*, 408–9, for a discussion of how these views of Kennedy's personal traits endured over time. For other accounts focusing on some but not all of the traits noted above, see Sheatsley and Feldman, "National Survey," 166; and Barber, "Peer Group Discussion," 118.

64   Van Buren, *Where Were You*, 26, 7. On the appeal of Kennedy's war record, see Fleming, *Ask*, 114.

65   Henderson and Summerlin, 1:33, 64, 60; Fleming, *Ask*, 102; and the cover of *Look* magazine, special edition, December 3, 1963.

66   Van Buren, *Where Were You*, 141, 102; Fitzpatrick, *Letters to Jackie*, 35; Barber, "Peer Group Discussion," 114–15.

67   Van Buren, *Where Were You*, 30, 158, 28.

68 Fleming, *Ask*, 104. See also ibid., 123, 126, 144; and Fries and Wilson, *"We'll Never Be Young Again,"* 121–22.

69 For a sampling of these views, see Fleming, *Ask*, 100, 144–47, 151–54, 160–63; and Van Buren, *Where Were You*, 82.

70 Fleming, *Ask*, 80–81.

71 Van Buren, *Where Were You*, 89, 137, 90.

72 Ibid., 11, 26. See also ibid., 16, 55, 142, 144; and Fleming, *Ask*, 19.

73 Van Buren, *Where Were You*, 87; Fleming, *Ask*, 81.

74 Fleming, *Ask*, 160, 166; Van Buren, *Where Were You*, 57, 144; Semple, *Four Days*, 78.

75 Fleming, *Ask*, 82. See also ibid., 112, 133.

76 Van Buren, *Where Were You*, 60, 143. James Farmer would be amazed years later to see Kennedy's photograph still hanging on the walls of many African homes. See Fleming, *Ask*, 162. In Africa, too, as this suggests, many people also saw Kennedy as "the reincarnation of President Lincoln." See Henderson and Summerlin, 1:33, 149.

77 Mrs. Dorothy DeLomel to Huntley, November 24, 1963, CHPP-001-002. See also Semple, *Four Days*, 84; Fitzpatrick, *Letters to Jackie*, 99; and Schlesinger, *Thousand Days*, 1027. For references to Christ and Moses, see Fitzpatrick, *Letters to Jackie*, 53, 83. For additional references to Lincoln in connection with Kennedy and his assassination, see the sermons in Stewart and Kendall, *Man Named John F. Kennedy*, 53–63, 89–93, 111, 115, 171–83. See also the letters in Mulvaney and De Angelis, *Dear Mrs. Kennedy*, 92–93, 214–15, 218–19.

78 Fleming, *Ask*, 151–53, 154–60. See also ibid., 165–66.

79 Ibid., 160–63.

80 Stewart and Kendall, *Man Named John F. Kennedy*, 110; Fitzpatrick, *Letters to Jackie*, 100, 105. See also the letters written to Jacqueline Kennedy after her husband's death in Fitzpatrick, *Letters to Jackie*, 102–8, 139–41, 154–55.

81 Fitzpatrick, *Letters to Jackie*, 53; Fleming, *Ask*, 83–84, 112, 114–15. See also Stewart and Kendall, *Man Named John F. Kennedy*, 171–73; Fitzpatrick, *Letters to Jackie*, 54–55, 160–61, 166, 168–69; and Dorothy DeLomel to Huntley, November 24, 1963, CHPP-001-002.

82 Van Buren, *Where Were You*, 141.

83 See Henggeler's excellent book, *The Kennedy Persuasion: The Politics of Style since JFK* (Chicago: Ivan R. Dee, 1995).

4 Ritual and Remembrance: Cultural Trauma, Collective Memory, and the Funeral of John Fitzgerald Kennedy

1 On collective cultural trauma, see Alexander, "Theory of Cultural Trauma"; Smelser, "Psychological Trauma"; Smelser, "Epilogue: September 11, 2001"; Neal, *National Trauma*; and George, *Assassination*.

2 For the classic work, see Durkheim, *The Elementary Forms of Religious Life*, trans. K. E. Fields (New York: Free Press, 1995). A number of works in the tradition of this classic have been helpful to me. See Michael C. Kearl, *Endings: A Sociology of Death and Dying* (New York: Oxford University

Press, 1989); Douglas J. Davies, *Death, Ritual, and Belief: The Rhetoric of Funerary Rites*, 2nd ed. (New York: Continuum, 2002); William G. Hoy, *Do Funerals Matter? The Purposes and Practices of Death Rituals in Global Perspective* (New York: Routledge, 2013); and Johanna Sumiala, *Media and Ritual: Death, Community, and Everyday Life* (New York: Routledge, 2013). For two excellent examples of how historians have used the insights of Durkheim and his followers, see the important book by John Wolffe, *Great Deaths: Grieving, Religion, and Nationhood in Victorian and Edwardian Britain* (New York: Oxford University Press, 2000); and the equally important essay by Barry Schwartz, "Mourning and the Making of a Sacred Symbol: Durkheim and the Lincoln Assassination," *Social Forces* 70, no. 2 (December 1991): 343–64.

3 On the importance of ritual, symbolism, and theater in state funerals, see the works by Kearl, Sumiala, Hoy, and Schwartz cited in the previous note; and Harry Garlick, *The Final Curtain: State Funerals and the Theatre of Power* (Amsterdam: Rodopi B.V., 1999). On America's civic religion and how it is expressed in state funerals and memorial celebrations, see Cherry, *God's New Israel*, 1–10, as well as the classic essay by Robert N. Bellah, "Civil Religion in America" in Bellah, *Beyond Belief: Essays on Religion in a Post-Traditionalist World* (Berkeley: University of California Press, 1991), 168–89.

4 Schwartz, "Mourning," esp. 358–60; and William A. Mindak and Gerald D. Hursh, "Television's Functions on the Assassination Weekend," in Greenberg and Parker, *Kennedy Assassination*, 130–41.

5 Robert Dallek, *Flawed Giant: Lyndon Johnson and His Times, 1961–1973* (New York: Oxford University Press, 1998), 49–50, 55–57; and Randall B. Woods, *LBJ: Architect of American Ambition* (Cambridge, MA: Harvard University Press, 2007), 419–27. For LBJ's interpretation of these events, see Lyndon Baines Johnson, *The Vantage Point: Perspectives of the Presidency, 1963–1969* (New York: Holt, Rinehart & Winston, 1971), 9–20.

6 For two excellent overviews dealing with party politics and political leadership in the 1960s, see Jeff Shesol, *Mutual Contempt: Lyndon Johnson, Robert Kennedy, and the Feud That Defined a Decade* (New York: W. W. Norton, 1998); and Sean J. Savage, *JFK, LBJ, and the Democratic Party* (Albany: State University of New York Press, 2004). Shesol is particularly good at focusing his discussion of the issues around the deep, personal animosity between Robert Kennedy and Lyndon Johnson, a theme also evident in the books cited in the next three notes.

7 See Jeff Shesol's wonderful comparison of the two men in *Mutual Contempt*, 3–8. See also Arthur M. Schlesinger Jr., *Robert Kennedy and His Times* (New York: Houghton Mifflin, 2002), 623.

8 Shesol, *Mutual Contempt*, 35–56; Schlesinger, *Robert Kennedy*, 204–10; Evan Thomas, *Robert Kennedy: His Life* (New York: Simon & Schuster, 2002), 96–99; and Robert A. Caro, *The Passage of Power: The Years of Lyndon Johnson* (New York: Alfred A. Knopf, 2012), 96–138.

9 Schlesinger, *Robert Kennedy*, 624–25; Dallek, *Flawed Giant*, 32–44; Woods, *LBJ*, 375–82, 400–401, 412–14; Shesol, *Mutual Contempt*, 61–112; and Caro, *Passage of Power*, 264–66, 294–95.

10 O'Brien, *No Final Victories*, 166; Shesol, *Mutual Contempt*, 114–24; Schlesinger, *Robert Kennedy*, 626–28; Woods, *LBJ*, 419–26; Dallek, *Flawed Giant*, 49–50; Historical Studies Division, Historical Office, Bureau of Public Affairs, Department of State, *The Funeral of President Kennedy and United States Government Actions, November 22–25, 1963*, Research Project No. 662, March 1967, DOS Record Number 1191001710094, Record Series Lot 71D411, S/S Files, National Archives II, College Park, MD (hereafter cited as *FPK* with appropriate exhibit information), exhibit 9, memorandum of conversation (memcon), Harold D. Langley, Historical Office, Department of State, and Brigadier General Godfrey T. McHugh, former air force aide to President Kennedy, June 1, 1964. The State Department's Historical Office wrote this narrative history of JFK's funeral and appended numerous exhibits, including this and other memoranda of conversations with people who played a role in planning and executing the funeral.

11 Martin S. Nowak, *The White House in Mourning: Deaths and Funerals of Presidents in Office* (Jefferson, NC: McFarland, 2010), 4–10, 29–30; and Dallek, *Flawed Giant*, 49–50.

12 *FPK*, exhibit 4, memcon, Langley and Colonel Paul C. Miller, Major Eugene J. Christian, and Captain Gary L. Patton of the Military District of Washington, March 9, 1964; and Jim Leeke, *Long Shadows: The Farewell to JFK* (Alexandria, VA: Attic Window Publishing, 2008), 7–9. The rules and regulations governing state funerals are conveniently printed in Nowak, *White House in Mourning*, 217–27.

13 *FPK*, exhibit 8, memcon, Wehle and Harold D. Langley, April 15, 1964. See also O'Donnell and Powers, *"Johnny, We Hardly Knew Ye,"* 33–34; Clint Hill, *Five Days in November*, with Lisa McCubbin (New York: Gallery Books, 2013), 116; Leeke, *Long Shadows*, 11–24; and Billy C. Mossman and M. W. Stark, *The Last Salute: Civil and Military Funerals, 1921–1969* (Washington, DC: Department of the Army, 1971), 188. O'Donnell, Powers, and Hill give somewhat comical firsthand descriptions of their struggle with Texas authorities to remove the president's body for autopsy in Washington. See also *FPK*, exhibit 9, memcon, Langley and General McHugh, June 1, 1964; and Godfrey McHugh, interview by Sheldon Stern, May 19, 1998, 44–45, OHC.

14 Mossman and Stark, *Last Salute*, 188.

15 Kennedy quoted in O'Donnell and Powers, *"Johnny, We Hardly Knew Ye,"* 7.

16 Ibid., 38–39; O'Brien, *No Final Victories*, 162; and Manchester, *Death of a President*, 347–49.

17 O'Donnell and Powers, *"Johnny, We Hardly Knew Ye,"* 38–40.

18 Ibid., 36.

19 *FPK*, exhibit 9, memcon, Langley and General McHugh, June 1, 1964; Manchester, *Death of a President*, 348; Leaming, *Mrs. Kennedy*, 343; and Perry, *Jacqueline Kennedy*, 180.

20 Hill, *Five Days in November*, 111–12, 127; Manchester, *Death of a President*, 349–50; and *FPK*, exhibit 9, memcon, Langley and General McHugh, June 1, 1964.

21 Manchester, *Death of a President*, 350, 372. See also O'Donnell and Powers, *"Johnny, We Hardly Knew Ye,"* 39. Although O'Donnell and Powers argue that Jackie decided on Air Force One to bury her husband in Arlington, the whole record seems to suggest that her final decision came later. Bradlee recalls the subject still under discussion at Bethesda Naval Hospital. See Bradlee, *Good Life*, 260; and Bradlee, *Conversations with Kennedy*, 243. See also Manchester, *Death of a President*, 417–18.

22 Leeke, *Long Shadows*, 26–27; Perry, *Jacqueline Kennedy*, 181–82.

23 *FPK*, exhibit 3, memcon, Langley and Ralph A. Dungan, Special Assistant to the President, April 15, 1964; *FPK*, exhibit 4, memcon, Langley, Colonel Miller and others of the Military District of Washington, March 9, 1964; *FPK*, exhibit 6, memcon, Langley and Angier Biddle Duke, July 21, 1964; *FPK*, exhibit 16, memcon, Langley and Richard N. Goodwin, June 15, 1964; and *FPK*, exhibit 10, memcon, Langley and Arthur M. Schlesinger Jr., March 3, 1964. See also Schlesinger, *Journals: 1952–2000*, 203; Baldrige, *Of Diamonds and Diplomats*, 261; Goodwin, *Remembering America: A Voice from the Sixties* (New York: Harper & Row, 1989), 227; Manchester, *Death of a President*, 380, 420–23; and Leeke, *Long Shadows*, 26–27. See also Pam Turnure's remark in Anthony, *As We Remember Her*, 202.

24 In addition to the Langley memoranda of conversations cited in the previous note, see West, *Upstairs at the White House*, 276–77; Goodwin, *Remembering America*, 228–29; Leeke, *Long Shadows*, 27; Manchester, *Death of a President*, 420–21, 435–39; and Joe English's recollections in Gus Russo and Harry Moses, eds., *Where Were You? America Remembers the JFK Assassination* (Guilford, CT: Lyons Press, 2013), 104–113.

25 Manchester, *Death of a President*, 438.

26 *FPK*, exhibit 10, memcon, Langley and Schlesinger, March 3, 1964; Schlesinger, *Journals: 1952–2000*, 204–5; Charles Spaulding, interview by Larry J. Hackman, March 22, 1969, Robert F. Kennedy, 56, OHC; and Goodwin, *Remembering America*, 230. See also Manchester, *Death of a President*, 435, 442–43. The Walton, Schlesinger, Spaulding, and Jacqueline Kennedy quotations are on page 443 of Manchester's account.

27 Bradlee, *Conversations with Kennedy*, 244; Manchester, *Death of a President*, 506–7, 555. See also Bradford, *America's Queen*, 279; and Smith, *Grace and Power*, 449, 452. Smith reports a third wake in the evening following the president's burial at Arlington Cemetery. It, too, was full of reminiscing and singing, as well as drinking. See Smith, *Grace and Power*, 456.

28 Hill, *Five Days in November*, 158–60; Manchester, *Death of a President*, 510, 515–16; Bradford, *America's Queen*, 277; Perry, *Jacqueline Kennedy*, 183; Smith, *Grace and Power*, 444–45; and Nowak, *White House in Mourning*, 202.

29 Penny Coleman, *Corpses, Coffins, and Crypts: A History of Burial* (New York: Henry Holt, 1997), 123–24; and Hoy, *Do Funerals Matter*, 9, 28–29, 36–39.

30 Hoy, *Do Funerals Matter*, 10–12, 35; and Mary Ryan, "The American Parade: Representations of the Nineteenth-Century Social Order," in *The*

New Cultural History, ed. Lynn Hunt (Berkeley: University of California Press, 1989), 131–53.

31 Leeke, *Long Shadows*, 35–36; Nowak, *White House in Mourning*, 200. Members of the executive branch, in this case, included former presidents Truman and Eisenhower.

32 Several close observers remarked on the first lady's remarkable attention to every aspect of her husband's funeral. Much like her management of the White House renovation, or her wardrobe and state dinners, no detail was too small. See, for example, Letitia Baldrige Hollensteiner interview, 99–105, OHC; and Elmer Young and James Nelson, White House florists, interview by Pamela Turnure, June 11, 1964, 8–12, OHC. Virtually every detail of the funeral, from the lying in repose to the burial at Arlington, was then scripted in a comprehensive narrative prepared under Shriver's direction. See the "Time Sequence" and attached documents in R. Sargent Shriver Personal Papers (hereafter cited as RSSPP), Series 10.3, Subject Files, 1948–1972, 291-005.

33 Hill, *Five Days in November*, 149. FPK, exhibit 8, memcon, Langley and Major General Wehle, April 13, 1964; FPK, exhibit 3, memcon, Langley and Ralph A. Dungan, April 15, 1964; and FPK, exhibit 4, memcon, Langley and Colonel Miller, March 9, 1964. See also Nowak, *White House in Mourning*, 201–2; Leeke, *Long Shadows*, 44–46; Manchester, *Death of a President*, 488–97; Bradford, *America's Queen*, 277; and Smith, *Grace and Power*, 445–46.

34 Philip Hannan, *The Archbishop Wore Combat Boots: Memoir of an Extraordinary Life*, with Nancy Collins and Peter Finney Jr. (Huntington, IN: Our Sunday Visitor, 2010), 10, 13–14. See also Smith, *Grace and Power*, 452–54; Manchester, *Death of a President*, 484, 507, 549–50; and Leeke, *Long Shadows*, 96–97.

35 FPK, exhibit 5, memcon, Langley and Ralph Dungan, April 15, 1964; FPK, exhibit 5, memcon, Langley and Reverend Monsignor John K. Cartwright of St. Matthew's Cathedral, May 27, 1964; and FPK, exhibit 6, memcon, Langley and Angier Duke, July 21, 1964. See also Leaming, *Mrs. Kennedy*, 346, 348; Manchester, *Death of a President*, 484–85; Perry, *Jacqueline Kennedy*, 183–84; and Bradford, *America's Queen*, 279.

36 Hill, *Five Days in November*, 175–76; Manchester, *Death of a President*, 580–82; Nowak, *White House in Mourning*, 203; Leeke, *Long Shadows*, 86–89, 92.

37 Bradford, *America's Queen*, 278; Leaming, *Mrs. Kennedy*, 349; and Manchester, *Death of a President*, 529–30.

38 Hill, *Five Days in November*, 172–73, 206–9; Leeke, *Long Shadows*, 98–100; Manchester, *Death of a President*, 539, 542, 578, 588–89; Bradford, *America's Queen*, 278, 280.

39 Manchester, *Death of a President*, 536–40, 562–64, 570–71, 574, 577–91; Nowak, *White House in Mourning*, 203.

40 Hoy, *Do Funerals Matter*, 38, 40; FPK, exhibit 8, memcon, Langley and Major General Wehle, April 15, 1964; FPK, exhibit 6, memcon, Langley and Angier Biddle Duke, Chief of Protocol, State Department, July 21, 1964; and

FPK, exhibit 3, memcon, Langley and Ralph Dungan, April 15, 1964. See also Smith, *Grace and Power*, 451–52; Manchester, *Death of a President*, 550–52, 600–02; Perry, *Jacqueline Kennedy*, 185–86; and Hill, *Five Days in November*, 223–25.

41 For a month-to-month summary of Kennedy's approval ratings from March 1961 through mid-November 1963, see Hazel Gaudet Erskine, "The Polls: Kennedy as President," *Public Opinion Quarterly* 28, no. 2 (Summer 1964): 334–42. As Erskine points out, Kennedy's approval ratings in his last year in office ranged from a high of 76 percent in January 1963 to a low of 57 percent in October, and then rebounded to 59 percent by mid-November. As noted in an earlier chapter, most Americans considered him unbeatable in the 1964 election, and after his assassination, far more Americans claimed to have voted for him in 1960 than had actually done so. For an excellent summary of the relevant polling data, see George, *Assassination*, 9–14.

42 Eugene Patterson, "He Saw the Hills and Fell," *Atlanta Constitution*, November 23, 1963, 4; Uncle Dudley, "Another Martyred President," *Boston Globe*, November 23, 1963, 10; Russell Reeves, "President Kennedy Gave Nation Cause for Thanks," *Cleveland Plain Dealer*, November 24, 1963, 6AA; Eugene Patterson, "John Kennedy's Legacy to America: New Purpose, New Hope, New Belief," *Atlanta Constitution*, November 26, 1963, 4; and Joseph Alsop, "Kennedy Was Supremely Fitted to Lead Nation through Perils," *Los Angeles Times*, November 27, 1963, A6. See also "Kentucky Senator John Sherman Cooper's Eulogy of John F. Kennedy," *Courier-Journal*, November 22, 2013 for a reprint of the senator's remarks delivered on December 11, 1963 at a congressional memorial for the president: www.courier-journal .com/story/news/local/2013/11/22/kentucky-sen-john-sherman-cooper's- eulogy-of-john-f-kennedy/3668641/. Virtually every member of Congress who eulogized the president cited his courage and illustrated it by reference to his wartime experience, battles with ill health, and fight against bigotry. See, for example, the addresses by Senators Mike Mansfield of Montana, Everett Dirksen of Illinois, and George A. Smathers of Florida, all dated December 11, 1963, in US Congress, *Memorial Addresses in the Congress of the United States and Tributes in Eulogy of John Fitzgerald Kennedy, Late a President of the United States* (Washington, DC: Government Printing Office, 1964), 1–3, 5–10.

43 Alsop, "Kennedy Was Supremely Fitted."

44 "John Fitzgerald Kennedy," *New York Times*, November 22, 1963, reprinted in Semple, *Four Days*, 186; "The Death of the President," *New York Times*, November 23, 1963, reprinted in Semple, *Four Days*, 302–3; James Reston, "Cruel Lessons of Fortune and Caprice," *Cleveland Plain Dealer*, November 24, 1963, 5AA; Reeves, "President Kennedy"; "Johnson's Cup of Culture is New Flavor," *Cleveland Plain Dealer*, November 24, 1963, 4A; "President Kennedy," *Wall Street Journal*, November 25, 1963, 8; Drew Pearson, "Memories of Triumph, Tragedy," *Washington Post, Times Herald*, November 25, 1963, B11; "Kennedy as Father, Husband Eulogized Sunday by Cardinal," *Boston Globe*, November 25, 1963, 10; Bill Henry, "John F. Kennedy – Man to Remember," *Los Angeles Times*, November 26,

1963, A1; Patterson, "John Kennedy's Legacy to America"; and Samuel Eliot Morison, "John Fitzgerald Kennedy, A Eulogy," *Atlantic*, February 1964, 47–49, www.theatlantic.com/magazine/archive/2013/08/john-fitzgerald-kennedy-a-eulogy/309491/. Readers may also consult the large number of eulogies, all making the same points, printed in US Congress, *Memorial Addresses*.

45 Goldzwig and Sullivan, "Post-Assassination Newspaper Editorial Eulogies: Analysis and Assessment," *Western Journal of Communication* 59, no. 2 (Spring 1995): 126–50.

46 "The Presidency Carries On," *Los Angeles Times*, November 25, 1963, A4; "The Nation Lives," *Washington Post, Times Herald*, November 26, 1963, A18; "A Time for Action," *Washington Post, Times Herald*, November 28, 1963, A20; and Uncle Dudley, "So Let's Get Moving," *Boston Globe*, November 29, 1963, 16. See also the same points made in the eulogies delivered in Congress. For a sample, see the remarks by Senators Thomas J. Dodd of Connecticut, Wayne Morse of Oregon, Frank Church of Idaho, and Philip A. Hart of Michigan, all dated December 11, 1963, in US Congress, *Memorial Addresses*, 30–32, 70–71, 73–75, 129–30.

47 "Presidency Carries On," *Los Angeles Times*. See also "President Kennedy," *Wall Street Journal*; Ralph McGill, "Prophet Isaiah and Today," *Atlanta Constitution*, November 25, 1963, 1–2; "Nation Lives," *Washington Post, Times Herald*; Erwin D. Canham, "Need for Self-Examination Confronts U.S.," *Christian Science Monitor*, November 26, 1963; Barry Goldwater, "Nation is United in Its Sorrow," *Atlanta Constitution*, November 26, 1963, 4; "A Time for Action," *Atlanta Constitution*, November 28, 1963, A20; and Uncle Dudley, "So Let's Get Moving."

48 Alsop, "Kennedy Was Supremely Fitted."

49 "Time for Action," *Washington Post, Times Herald*.

50 Patterson, "John Kennedy's Legacy to America." See also Patterson, "He Saw the Hills and Fell"; "For Us, the Living," *Cleveland Plain Dealer*, November 25, 1963, 6AA; and Max Freedman, "Kennedy Remembered as Man Who Walked to Far Horizons," *Los Angeles Times*, December 1, 1963, M2.

51 "Female Profile in Courage," *Cleveland Plain Dealer*, November 24, 1963, 6AA.

52 McGraw, "Tears Must Wait – Jackie Goes On," *Atlanta Constitution*, November 23, 1963, 1–2.

53 Thomas, "A Heroic Jackie Wins Hearts of All," *Atlanta Constitution*, November 26, 1963, 1, 10.

54 Josephine Ripley, "Mrs. Kennedy Displays Fortitude," *Christian Science Monitor*, November 26, 1963, 3; Dorothy Kilgallen, "Legacy Left by Widow," *Washington Post, Herald Tribune*, November 27, 1963, A24; and Joseph F. Dineen, Jr., "Every Detail … Her Decision," *Boston Globe*, November 28, 1963, A7.

55 Hutchinson, "Courage Shines through Agony of Mrs. Kennedy," *Chicago Tribune*, November 26, 1963, 3.

56 For the remarks by Gore, Yarborough, McCormack, Boland, and Mathias, see US Congress, *Memorial Addresses*, 129, 136, 210, 227, 300.

57 "Toward Tomorrow," *Christian Science Monitor*, November 26, 1963, 18.
58 McGrory, "He Would Have Liked It," *Boston Globe*, November 26, 1963, 1.
59 "Jacqueline Kennedy's Courage," *Los Angeles Times*, November 26, 1963, A4.
60 Ibid.
61 Coates, "Mrs. Kennedy's Great Strength is an Inspiration for All of Us," *Los Angeles Times*, November 26, 1963, A6.
62 Mary Hornaday, "Mrs. Kennedy's Poise Cited," *Christian Science Monitor*, December 3, 1963, 3.

5 In Death There Is Life: Monuments of Paper and Pen

1 Brown and Kulik, "Flashbulb Memories," 23–40.
2 Neal, *National Trauma*, 117–21.
3 Schwartz, "The Reconstruction of Abraham Lincoln," in *Collective Remembering*, ed. David Middleton and Derek Edwards (Newbury Park, CA: Sage Publications, 1990), 81–107.
4 The phrase "vehicles of memory" comes from Alan Confino, "Collective Memory and Cultural History: Problems of Method," *American Historical Review* 102, no. 5 (December 1997): 1386–403. As the previous paragraphs suggest, my treatment of the Kennedys in this and subsequent chapters draws much of its framing from theoretical literature in the field of memory studies. See, first and foremost, Maurice Halbwachs, *On Collective Memory*, ed. and trans. Lewis A. Coser (Chicago: University of Chicago Press, 1992); and Pierre Nora, *Realms of Memory: Rethinking the French Past*, ed. Lawrence D. Kritzman, trans. Arthur Goldhammer, 3 vols. (New York: Columbia University Press, 1996–98). For a compendium of different approaches to the study of memory, see Jeffrey K. Olick, Vered Vinitzky-Seroussi, and Daniel Levy, eds., *The Collective Memory Reader* (New York: Oxford University Press, 2011). In addition to the sources cited in the two previous notes, see David Lowenthal, *The Past is a Foreign Country* (New York: Cambridge University Press, 1985); Paul Connerton, *How Societies Remember* (New York: Cambridge University Press, 1989); Michael G. Kammen, *Mystic Chords of Memory: The Transformation of Tradition in American Culture* (New York: Knopf, 1991); Eric J. Hobsbawm and Terence O. Ranger, eds., *The Invention of Tradition* (New York: Cambridge University Press, 1992); Michael Schudson, *Watergate in American Memory: How We Remember, Forget, and Reconstruct the Past* (New York: Basic Books, 1993); Emily S. Rosenberg, *A Date Which Will Live: Pearl Harbor in American Memory* (Durham, NC: Duke University Press, 2003); and George, *Assassination*. As far as scholarly articles and essays are concerned, see Schwartz, "The Social Context of Commemoration: A Study in Collective Memory," *Social Forces* 61, no. 2 (December 1982): 374–402; David Thelen, "Memory and American History," *Journal of American History* 75, no. 4 (March 1989): 117–29; Barbie Zelizer, "Reading the Past against the Grain: The Shape of Memory Studies," *Critical Studies in Mass Communication* 12, no. 2 (June 1995): 214–39; and Jay Winter, "The Generation of Memory: Reflections on the 'Memory Boom'

in Contemporary Historical Studies," *Bulletin of the German Historical Institute* 27, no. 3 (Fall 2000): 69–92.

5   Jackie quoted in Bradford, *America's Queen*, 285–86. For White's notes on his November 29, 1963 interview with Jacqueline Kennedy, see Theodore H. White Personal Papers (hereafter cited as THWPP), Camelot documents, 059-009-011 and -012. For Schlesinger's views, see Paul H. Santa Cruz, *Making JFK Matter: Popular Memory and the Thirty-fifth President* (Denton: University of North Texas Press, 2015), 191. See also Heymann, *Woman Named Jackie*, 429–31; White, "For President Kennedy: An Epilogue," *Life*, December 6, 1963, 158–59; and Lee Konstantinou, "The Camelot Presidency: Kennedy and Postwar Style," in Hoberek, *The Cambridge Companion to John F. Kennedy*, 149–163.

6   Hersh, *Dark Side of Camelot*, 1–12.

7   In addition to Gallagher's book, cited earlier, see Maud Shaw, *White House Nannie: My Years with Caroline and John Kennedy, Jr.* (New York: New American Library, 1965); and Paul B. Fay Jr., *The Pleasure of His Company* (New York: Harper & Row, 1966). See also Paul B. Fay Jr., interview by James A. Oesterle, November 9, 1970, 98–119, OHC; Walter Sheridan, a campaign coordinator for Robert Kennedy, interview by Roberta W. Green, June 12, 1970, 115, OHC; and Rowland Evans Jr., newspaper columnist, interview by Roberta W. Green, July 30, 1970, 46–47, OHC. In addition, see Bradlee, *Good Life*, 399–400; Thomas Brown, *JFK: History of an Image* (Bloomington: Indiana University Press, 1988), 7; Richard Bradley, *American Political Mythology from Kennedy to Nixon* (New York: Peter Lang, 2000), 68; Garry Wills, *The Kennedy Imprisonment: A Meditation on Power* (Boston: Houghton Mifflin, 2002), 154; Thomas, *Robert Kennedy*, 330; and Gore Vidal, "The Holy Family," in Vidal, *United States: Essays 1952–1992* (New York: Random House, 1993), 812–13. For an early and sarcastic exposé of Jacqueline Kennedy's efforts to censor early accounts of her husband's life and administration, see Andy Logan, "JFK: The Stained-Glass Image," *American Heritage*, August 1967, www.americanheritage.com/content/jfk-stained-glass-image.

8   The quote is from Walter Sheridan, OHC.

9   Bishop, *Day Kennedy Was Shot*, xiii–xiv. Bishop gives no explanation for why Funk & Wagnalls rather than Random House eventually published his book, saying only that it had nothing to do with pressure from the Kennedys. See also "JFK Censored?," *Newsweek*, October 3, 1966, 65–66; and Barbara Leaming, *Jacqueline Bouvier Kennedy Onassis: The Untold Story* (New York: St. Martin's Press, 2014), 151–52, 186.

10 See Bishop, *Day Kennedy Was Shot*, xiv; and "JFK Censored?," *Newsweek*.

11 Vidal, "The Manchester Book," in Vidal, *United States*, 805–8. See also Manchester, *Controversy and Other Essays in Journalism, 1950–1975* (Boston: Little, Brown, 1976), 6–8; William V. Shannon, *The Heir Apparent: Robert Kennedy and the Struggle for Power* (New York: Macmillan, 1967), 258–59; and John Corry, *The Manchester Affair* (New York: G. P. Putnam's Sons, 1967), 21–23, 29–31.

12   Thomas quoted in Manchester, *Controversy and Other Essays*, 7–8, 20–21.
     See also Shannon, *Heir Apparent*, 259; and Corry, *Manchester Affair*, 26–27.
     For a summary of the Manchester controversy, including background on
     Evan Thomas, see "Battle of the Book," *Time*, December 23, 1966, 15–18.

13   Manchester, *Controversy and Other Essays*, 20–23. See also Wills, *Kennedy
     Imprisonment*, 154; Vidal, "Manchester Book," 804–8; Corry, *Manchester
     Affair*, 56–57, 61; Schlesinger, *Robert Kennedy and His Times*, 760–63; and
     Shannon, *Heir Apparent*, 261–62. Shannon tends to absolve Evan Thomas,
     saying that ultimately, he came to support Manchester rather than the
     Kennedys. In his account, Schlesinger tries to straddle some of the key issues.
     He agrees that Thomas went too far in censoring parts of the manuscript, but
     he calls Manchester "a highly emotional man" who misunderstood what the
     Kennedys were really concerned about, namely that they "had never given
     Johnson a fair chance." He faults Manchester for signing a contract that gave
     the Kennedys the right to approve the entire manuscript prior to publication
     and for insisting that he, rather than Jacqueline Kennedy, owned the tran-
     scripts and tapes of the oral histories he conducted with her.

14   Manchester, *Controversy and Other Essays*, 14–15, 18–23, 25, 27, 37. See
     also Corry, *Manchester Affair*, 45–47, 99–100, 129, 134, 148, 161; and
     Lawrence Van Gelder, *Why the Kennedys Lost the Book Battle: The Untold
     Story* (New York: Award Books, 1967), 32–37.

15   Carroll Kilpatrick, "Author Manchester Hospitalized, Johnson Bars
     Comment on Book," *Washington Post, Times Herald*, December 27,
     1966, A1, A6. See also Sam Kashner, "A Clash of Camelots," *Vanity Fair*,
     October 2009, 30–31; and Manchester, *Controversy and Other Essays*,
     40, 42, 48–49, 50–53, 56, 58, 61, 65, and 69. Manchester himself sought
     advice from Goodwin as well as another friend, Arthur Schlesinger, both of
     whom were also close to Robert Kennedy. Not surprisingly, perhaps, both
     claimed to like the manuscript very much but were nonetheless critical of
     the author's treatment of Johnson and the Kennedy-Johnson relationship.
     Goodwin, in particular, worried that the manuscript, when published,
     would injure Robert Kennedy's political prospects. See Shannon, *Heir
     Apparent*, 263–64.

16   Manchester, *Controversy and Other Essays*, 13. See also ibid., 35, 45–46;
     and Corry, *Manchester Affair*, 103–6. Goodwin later claimed that it was
     Manchester who raised the issue of a Kennedy speech on academic freedom.
     See Corry, *Manchester Affair*, 152.

17   Manchester, *Controversy and Other Essays*, 11, 39. See also ibid., 16, 31, 34,
     59; Shannon, *Heir Apparent*, 274; and Van Gelder, *Why the Kennedys Lost*,
     53–55. In her recent book on Jacqueline Kennedy, Barbara Leaming does
     not deny the often hysterical and high-handed behavior of the former first
     lady, but softens her criticism by claiming that she suffered from what today
     would be diagnosed as post-traumatic stress disorder. See *Jacqueline Bouvier
     Kennedy Onassis*, 171–73, 204–5.

18   Corry, *Manchester Affair*, 118–27; and Van Gelder, *Why the Kennedys
     Lost*, 51–53.

19 Manchester, *Controversy and Other Essays*, 42–53, 142–47. The quotation is from ibid., 52. See also Shannon, *Heir Apparent*, 275; Corry, *Manchester Affair*, 145–47, 154–56; and Van Gelder, *Why the Kennedys Lost*, 63–64.

20 Manchester, *Controversy and Other Essays*, 53–59. Manchester quoted in ibid., 59.

21 Edwin Guthman, *We Band of Brothers* (New York: Harper & Row, 1971), 314. In his oral history interview for the Kennedy Library, Frank Mankiewicz, who had joined Robert Kennedy's press staff, claimed that both he and Kennedy thought the lawsuit a bad idea. Both agreed that Kennedy should not join the suit as a plaintiff, and he did not. But he remained loyal to the former first lady and defended her aggressively in spite of the damage it did to his own reputation. See Mankiewicz, interview by Larry J. Hackman, October 2, 1969, 24–25, 35, 46–48, OHC.

22 Vera Glaser, "Uneasy Rests the Crown of JFK's Jackie," *Cincinnati Enquirer*, December 22, 1966. See also "JFK Censored?," *Newsweek*; Wicker, "In the Nation: William Manchester's Sponsors," *New York Times*, December 27, 1966, 34; and Manchester, *Controversy and Other Essays*, 66. For another media account generally critical of the Kennedys, see "Growing Rift of LBJ and Kennedys," *US News & World Report*, January 2, 1967, 22–27. For a media account more critical of Manchester, see "Battle of the Book," *Time*, 15–18. For Robert Kennedy's growing distaste for the whole controversy and a summary of press commentary, see also Schlesinger, *Robert Kennedy and His Times*, 762–63. "The press had a field day," is how Schlesinger put it, "riding their high horse about the sacred cause of freedom of information." He quoted the *Washington Post* as writing that the "lives of public men – the records of their careers, the thoughts of others about them – are not the property of their families, but the property of posterity." Mankiewicz offered a similar criticism, complaining in his oral history interview for the Kennedy Library that Manchester, *Look* magazine, Harper & Row, and others used freedom of the press as a stalking horse to discredit the suit against them, bolster their legal defense, and market Manchester's manuscript. See Mankiewicz, 50, OHC. For more on media criticism of Jacqueline Kennedy as a spoiled, self-indulgent woman who had become something of a "professional martyr" when it served her interest, see Leaming, *Jacqueline Bouvier Kennedy Onassis*, 217–18, 221–22. For a blistering attack on Manchester, see Theodore H. White to John Oakes, editor of the *New York Times*, December 19, 1966, Camelot documents, THWPP-059-015. White's letter to the editor was a response to *Times* columnist James Reston's criticism of Jacqueline Kennedy's handling of the Manchester affair.

23 Manchester, *Controversy and Other Essays*, 70; and Vidal, "Holy Family," 811. Regarding revisions that Manchester made as part of the final settlement, see Bradley, *American Political Mythology*, 70. The terms of the settlement gave Jacqueline Kennedy ownership of the tapes and transcripts of her interviews with Manchester. They are in the possession of the Kennedy Library and are still not available to scholars or the general public. The exact number of words or pages cut from the manuscript seems to be a matter of

dispute – in part because some give the number in pages and others in words, and in part because there had been pages excised throughout the negotiating process. Most agree, however, that the cuts made little difference, as the censored material found other ways into publication. See "Jacqueline Kennedy's 'Victory,'" *Newsweek*, January 2, 1967, 16–19; and "Publishing: Start the Presses," *Time*, January 20, 1967, 47–48.

24   "Book Battle Hurts Jacqueline Kennedy's Image," *Boston Globe*, January 31, 1967, 15; Manchester, *Controversy and Other Essays*, 72–76; Leaming, *Jacqueline Bouvier Kennedy Onassis*, 224; Van Gelder, *Why the Kennedys Lost*, 90–92; Kashner, "Clash of Camelots," 25–26, and White, *Kennedy*, 99. It didn't help relationships that Manchester and his critics in the Kennedy camp waged their feud in public throughout the controversy and for some time thereafter. See, for example, "Text of Manchester Interview Giving His Side of Book Row," *Boston Globe*, January 24, 1967, 16; John Kenneth Galbraith, "Galbraith Defends Mrs. JFK's Book Decisions," *Boston Globe*, January 29, 1967, 60; "Jacqueline Blazed Like a Bonfire, Manchester Says," *Boston Globe*, March 20, 1967, 1; Manchester, "William Manchester's Own Story," *Look*, April 4, 1967, 62–67; and the letters exchanged between Manchester and Pierre Salinger in *Look*, May 16, 1967, 8. On Robert Kennedy's falling out with Harper & Row, see "New Publisher for Kennedy," *Boston Globe*, September 4, 1967, 57. It's worth noting that the Kennedys had used Galbraith as their censor and public defender more than once. For example, he had been one of the allies and authors they used to edit "Red" Fay's memoir of his days with JFK. See "JFK Censored?," *Newsweek*, 65.

25   In addition to the works cited earlier by Shaw, Fay, Salinger, O'Donnell and Powers, and Salinger and Vanocur, see Evelyn Lincoln, *My Twelve Years with John F. Kennedy* (New York: David McKay, 1965); Joan S. Meyers, ed., *John Fitzgerald Kennedy: As We Remember Him* (New York: Atheneum, 1965); and Rose Kennedy, *Times to Remember* (Garden City, NY: Doubleday, 1974).

26   On Jacqueline Kennedy's dissatisfaction with Schlesinger's book and their subsequent reconciliation, see Manchester, *Controversy and Other Essays*, 18; Leaming, *Jacqueline Bouvier Kennedy Onassis*, 200–01; and especially the biting account by Nigel Hamilton, "The Rise and Fall of Camelot," *New England Journal of History* 52, no. 2 (Fall 1995): 91–108.

27   Schlesinger, *Thousand Days*; and Sorensen, *Kennedy* (New York: Harper & Row, 1965). Reviewers of these two books, especially those who came from the same academic circles as Schlesinger, usually echoed the same rosy assessment of Kennedy and his administration. Not surprisingly, they viewed the books themselves in equally rosy terms. See, for example, John M. Blum, "Schlesinger's Kennedy," *New Republic*, December 4, 1965, 21–24; and Hans J. Morgenthau, "Monuments to Kennedy," *New York Review of Books*, January 6, 1966, 8–9. See also Erwin D. Canham, "Report from a Friendly Insider," *Christian Science Monitor*, December 2, 1965, B6. Schlesinger, according to Canham, offered a "most loving portrait" of Kennedy with "no hint that the great man ever slipped," except in the case of the Bay of Pigs. For contemporary academic appraisals similar to Schlesinger's and Sorensen's, see James MacGregor Burns, "The Legacy of the 1,000 Days," *New York Times Magazine*, December 1, 1963, 27, 118,

120; and Richard E. Neustadt, "Kennedy in the Presidency: A Premature Appraisal," *Political Science Quarterly* 79, no. 3 (September 1964): 321–34. For a more skeptical assessment of both books, see Henry Pachter, "JFK as an Equestrian Statue: On Myth and Mythmakers," *Salmagundi* 1, no. 3 (1966): 3–26; and Logan, "JFK: The Stained-Glass Image." See also White, *Kennedy*, 92–96.

28 Morgenthau, "Monuments to Kennedy," 8; and Tugwell, "The President and His Helpers: A Review Article," *Political Science Quarterly* 82, no. 2 (June 1967): 253.

29 See the essays by Irving Howe, Dwight Macdonald, and David T. Bazelon in "The Fate of the Union: Kennedy and After," *New York Review of Books*, December 26, 1963, 3–11. See also the essays in "The Meaning of the Life and Death of John F. Kennedy," *Current*, January 1964, 6–42. Some of the essays included in this edition of *Current* had been previously published in the earlier issue of the *New York Review of Books*.

30 Leuchtenburg and Rovere quoted in "Meaning of the Life and Death," *Current*, 13, 28. For other positive assessments, see the essays by David Riesman, Rovere, Norman Mailer, and Hannah Arendt in "Fate of the Union," 3, 4, 6, 10. For a similarly favorable assessment published elsewhere, see Norman Cousins, "The Legacy of John F. Kennedy," *Saturday Review*, December 7, 1963, 21–27.

31 Leuchtenburg, Brzezinski, Hofstadter, and Link quoted in "Meaning of the Life and Death," *Current*, 28, 31, 35.

32 Carleton, Bazelon, and Johnson quoted in ibid., 6–9.

33 "JFK: Enemy of the Closed Mind," *Cleveland Plain Dealer*, November 22, 1964, 6AA; Joseph Alsop, "The Legacy of John F. Kennedy: Memories of an Uncommon Man," *Saturday Evening Post*, November 21, 1964, 15–19; and "Greatness Remembered," *Washington Post, Times Herald*, November 22, 1964, E6.

34 "JFK: Enemy of the Closed Mind," *Cleveland Plain Dealer*.

35 Saunders, "The Fleeting, Wistful Glory," *Cleveland Plain Dealer*, November 22, 1964, 6AA.

36 Kenny, "… The Wit at His Command," *Boston Globe*, November 22, 1964, 56; and Wicker, "Kennedy without Tears," *Esquire*, June 1964, 108–11, 138, 140–41. See also Wicker, *Kennedy without Tears: The Man beneath the Myth* (New York: William Morrow, 1964).

37 Alsop, "Legacy," 18.

38 Reston, "What Was Killed Was Not Only the President," *New York Times Sunday Magazine*, November 15, 1964, SM24.

39 Lippmann, "The Legend Reappraised," *New York Post*, November 22, 1967.

40 "Greatness Remembered," *Washington Post, Times Herald*.

41 Childs, "Kennedy's Legend Continues to Grow," *Washington Post, Times Herald*, November 25, 1965, A16.

42 Meyer, "The Myth Is Swallowing the Man," *Washington Post, Times Herald*, November 22, 1964, E1.

43 Vincent L. Toscano, *Since Dallas: Images of John F. Kennedy in Popular and Scholarly Literature, 1963–1973* (San Francisco: R & E Research Associates, 1978), 52–53, 82n11.

44 Lasky, *JFK: The Man and the Myth* (New York: Macmillan, 1963). See also the reviews of Lasky's book by Burns in the *New Republic*, October 26, 1963, 24–25; and Barrett in the *Atlantic*, October 1963, 157. Of course, Lasky's book tended to fare well when reviewed in conservative journals, as was the case with M. Stanton Evans's positive commentary, "'Image' Is All," *National Review*, October 8, 1963, 309–310. What is more, Lasky could give as good as he got. See, for example, his review of Sorensen's *Kennedy* in the *National Review*, November 16, 1965, 1029–30. Lasky's publisher, Macmillan, resumed sales of his book after a two-week suspension but continued to withhold active promotion. See "Macmillan Resumes Shipment of *JFK* by Lasky," *Publishers Weekly*, December 16, 1963, 22.

45 Whalen, *The Founding Father: The Story of Joseph P. Kennedy and the Family He Raised to Power* (New York: New American Library, 1964).

46 Fairlie, "He Was a Man of Only One Season," *New York Times Sunday Magazine*, November 21, 1965, SM28. See also Fairlie, *The Kennedy Promise: The Politics of Expectation* (Garden City, NY: Doubleday, 1972).

47 Crown, *The Kennedy Literature: A Bibliographical Essay on John F. Kennedy* (New York: New York University Press, 1968), 22–23, 39, 134; and "Kennedy Book to Finance Memorial Award," *Publishers Weekly*, December 30, 1963, 34–35.

48 See Herbert Kupferberg, "Kennedy Memorial Albums," *Atlantic*, July 1964, 134–37; and Carlton Brown, "The Kennedy Memorial Albums," *Redbook*, July 1, 1964, 30.

49 For a listing of all of Kennedy's publications, see Crown, *Kennedy Literature*, 51–74.

50 Newcomb, *John F. Kennedy: An Annotated Bibliography* (Metuchen, NJ: Scarecrow Press, 1977), 15–80.

51 Ibid.

52 *Look* Magazine, *Kennedy and His Family in Pictures* (New York: Cowles, 1963); *Life* Magazine, *John F. Kennedy Memorial Edition* (Chicago: Time, 1963); United Press International and Chase Studios, *John F. Kennedy from Childhood to Martyrdom* (Washington, DC: Tatler, 1963); Lowe, *Portrait: The Emergence of John F. Kennedy* (New York: McGraw-Hill, 1963); Lowe, *The Kennedy Years* (New York: Viking, 1964); Shaw, *The John F. Kennedys: A Family Album* (New York: Farrar, Straus, 1964); Doris E. Saunders, ed., *The Kennedy Years and the Negro* (Chicago: Johnson Publishing, 1964); Lincoln, *Kennedy White House Parties*; and Tazewell Shepard, *John F. Kennedy: Man of the Sea* (New York: Morrow, 1965). See also John Raymond and Paul Ballot, *The Thousand Days: John Fitzgerald Kennedy as President* (Island Park, NY: Aspen, 1964); and Diana Lurvey, ed., *The Kennedys: America's Royal Family* (New York: Ideal, 1962).

53 Erwin A. Glikes and Paul Schwaber, eds., *Of Poetry and Power: Poems Occasioned by the Presidency and by the Death of John. F. Kennedy* (New York: Basic Books, 1964), 2–3, 6. See also "When a Just Man Dies," *Newsweek*, April 20, 1964, 75–76; Paul Marten, *Kennedy Requiem* (Toronto: Weller, 1963); Aija Vilnis, *The Bearer of the Star Spangled Banner: In Memory of President John Fitzgerald Kennedy*, trans. Lilija Pavars

(New York: Robert Speller & Sons, 1964); Wendell Berry and Ben Shahn, *November Twenty Six Nineteen Hundred Sixty Three* (New York: George Braziller, 1964); John Cournos, *The Lost Leader* (New York: Twayne, 1964); Candy Geer, *Six White Horses: An Illustrated Poem about John-John* (Ann Arbor, MI: M & W Quill, 1964); and Frances Grant Nachant, *Song of Peace* (Francestown, NH: Golden Quill, 1969).

54 Guido Van Rijn, *Kennedy's Blues: African-American Blues and Gospel Songs on JFK* (Jackson: University Press of Mississippi, 2007), especially the introduction and chapter 6, which deal with the period after Kennedy's assassination; see also Brian Ward's forward, x–xii.

55 "To John F. Kennedy – Homage by Artists," *Art in America* 52, no. 5 (1964): 90–95. See also "An Image Distilled from 800 Pictures," *Life*, January 3, 1964, 29–31.

56 Bill Adler, ed., *John F. Kennedy and the Young People of America* (New York: McKay, 1965); Adler, comp., *Kids' Letters to President Kennedy* (New York: Morrow, 1962); and Nicholas A. Schneider and Nathalie S. Rockhill, comps. and eds., *John F. Kennedy Talks to Young People* (New York: Hawthorne, 1968). For a sample of the books aimed to inspire young people, see Flora Strousse, *John Fitzgerald Kennedy: Man of Courage* (New York: Harcourt, Brace & World, 1963); Lucy Post Frisbee, *John F. Kennedy: Young Statesman* (Indianapolis: Bobbs-Merrill, 1964); John C. Stewart, *Our Hero: John F. Kennedy* (Northport, AL: American Southern Publishing, 1964); Helene Hanff, *John F. Kennedy: Young Man of Destiny* (Garden City, NY: Doubleday, 1965); and Polly Curren Fedosiuk, *To Light a Torch: The Story of John F. Kennedy* (New York: Guild Press, 1966).

57 John Galloway, ed., *The Quotable Mr. Kennedy* (New York: Abelard-Schuman, 1962); Gerald C. Gardner, ed., *The Shining Moments: The Words and Moods of John F. Kennedy* (New York: Pocket Books, 1964); Alex J. Goldman, ed., *The Quotable Kennedy* (New York: Citadel, 1965); and Maxwell Meyersohn, comp., *Memorable Quotations of John F. Kennedy* (New York: Crowell, 1965). See also John F. Kennedy, *Quotations from the Scriptures* (New York: Catholic Family Library, 1964); Nicholas A. Schneider, comp., *Religious Views of President John F. Kennedy: In His Own Words* (St. Louis: B. Herder, 1965); and John F. Kennedy, Lyndon B. Johnson, Hubert H. Humphrey, and Thomas H. Kuchel, *Moral Crisis: The Case for Civil Rights* (Minneapolis: Gilbert Publishing, 1964).

58 Jim Dobbins, *Dobbins' Diary of the New Frontier* (Boston: Humphries, 1964); Gene Wortsman, ed., *The New Frontier Joke Book* (New York: MacFadden-Bartell, 1963); Adler, ed., *The Kennedy Wit* (New York: Gramercy Publishing, 1964); Adler, ed., *More Kennedy Wit* (New York: Citadel Press, 1965); Adler, ed., *The Complete Kennedy Wit* (New York: Citadel Press, 1967); and Adler, ed., *Presidential Wit* (New York: Third Press, 1966). See also Booton Herndon, *The Humor of JFK* (Greenwich, CT: Fawcett, 1964).

59 See, for example, Julius Fanta, *Sailing with President Kennedy: The White House Yachtsman* (New York: Sea Lore, 1968).

60 Barnes, *John F. Kennedy: Scrimshaw Collector* (Boston: Little, Brown, 1964).

61 Bloncourt, *An Old and a Young Leader: Winston Churchill and John Kennedy* (London: Faber, 1970); Russell, *Lincoln and Kennedy: Looked at Kindly Together* (New York: Carlton, 1973); and Wicker, *JFK and LBJ: The Influence of Personality upon Politics* (New York: Morrow, 1968).

62 See, for example, John F. Brennan, *The Evolution of Everyman: Ancestral Lineage of John F. Kennedy* (Dundalk, Ireland: Dundalgan Press, 1968); Maurice N. Hennessy, *I'll Come Back in the Springtime: John F. Kennedy and the Irish* (New York: Ives Washington, 1966); and William V. Shannon, *The American Irish* (New York: Macmillan, 1966).

63 Edmund Christopherson, *"Westward I Go Free": The Story of J. F. K. in Montana* (Missoula, MT: Earthquake Press, 1964); and Jim Comstock, *Pa and Ma and Mister Kennedy* (Richwood, WV: Appalachian Press, 1965).

64 Hamilton, *The Robot That Helped to Make a President: A Reconnaissance into the Mysteries of John F. Kennedy's Signature* (New York, 1965).

65 Logan, "JFK: The Stained-Glass Image"; and Toscano, *Since Dallas*, 1–2.

66 *John F. Kennedy: Catalogue of Books, Articles, Autographs, and Memorabilia* (Austin, TX: Jenkins, [1964–65?]). The quoted remarks are from a very brief description of the catalog published on its unnumbered first page.

67 US Library of Congress, *John Fitzgerald Kennedy 1917–1963: A Chronological List of References* (Washington, DC: Government Printing Office, 1964); Martin H. Sable, *A Bio-Bibliography of the Kennedy Family* (Metuchen, NJ: Scarecrow Books, 1969); Ralph A. Stone, ed., *John F. Kennedy, 1917–1963: Chronology-Documents-Bibliographical Aids* (Dobbs Ferry, NY: Oceana, 1971); *A Catalogue of Old, Used, Rare and Out-of-Print Books on John F. Kennedy* (Washington, DC: Q. M. Dabney, 1975); John F. Kennedy Library, *John F. Kennedy: A Reading List* (Waltham, MA: Kennedy Library, 1974); and John F. Kennedy Library, *The Kennedys: A Reading List for Young People* (Waltham, MA: Kennedy Library, 1974).

6 In Death There Is Life: Monuments of Glass, Steel, and Stone

1 Anne Chamberlin, "The Commercialization of J.F.K.," *Saturday Evening Post*, November 21, 1964, 20–21; Aubrey Mayhew, *The World's Tribute to John F. Kennedy in Medallic Art* (New York: William Morrow, 1966), 3; Edward C. Rochette, *The Medallic Portraits of John F. Kennedy* (Iola, WI: Krause Publications, 1966), 145–47. See also Laurence Stern, "I Christen Thee John F. Kennedy," *Washington Post, Times Herald*, May 28, 1967, A1; and Chris Kirk, Emma Goss, and Nicholas Duchesne, "Every John F. Kennedy Street, Park, Airport, and School in the World," *Slate*, November 22, 2013, www.slate.com/articles/news_and_politics/slate_labs/2013/11/kennedy_street_school_airport_and_more_memorials_to_john_f._kennedy_mapped.html.

2 Alex J. Goldman, *John Fitzgerald Kennedy: The World Remembers* (New York: Fleet Press, 1968), 107–115. See also Kenneth R. Wenger, ed., *John F. Kennedy Memorial Stamp Issues of the World* (Fort Lee, NJ: Wenger, 1970) for nearly two hundred pages of stamps listed with individual photographs.

3 Goldman, *World Remembers*, 17–98 passim. Jacqueline Kennedy and her staff worked constantly to acknowledge the various memorials in her husband's memory, many of which came with a request asking the former first lady to attend a dedication ceremony. The list is too long to itemize here, but the interested reader can track the memorials and other tributes in JBKOPP-SFO68-007 to -011 and JBKOPP-SFO69-001 to -003.

4 Mayhew, *World's Tribute*, ix, xi, xxiv–xxvi, 106.

5 For examples of the medallic art struck in Kennedy's memory, see ibid., 5–88. For the German death medal, see ibid., 125.

6 On the heritage industry and the difference between heritage and history, see again Kammen, *In the Past Lane*, cited earlier, and also, among many other sources, David Lowenthal, *The Heritage Crusade and the Spoils of History* (New York: Cambridge University Press, 1998).

7 Chamberlin, "Commercialization of J.F.K.," 20–21; and "Enterprise: Memorial Boom," *Newsweek*, December 30, 1963, 49–50. For recordings of Kennedy's speeches and new editions of his books, see Kupferberg, "Kennedy Memorial Albums," 134–37; and Brown, "Kennedy Memorial Albums," 30.

8 Chamberlin, "Commercialization of J.F.K.," 20–21; and "Enterprise: Memorial Boom," *Newsweek*, 49–50.

9 Goldman, *World Remembers*, 36–40; and Bradford Washburn, "Canada's Mount Kennedy, I: The Discovery," *National Geographic* 128, no. 1 (July 1965): 1–3.

10 Kennedy, "Our Climb Up Mt. Kennedy," *Life*, April 9, 1965, 22–27; Kennedy, "Mount Kennedy, II: A Peak Worthy of the President," *National Geographic* 128, no. 1 (July 1965): 5–9; and Whittaker, "Mount Kennedy, III: The First Ascent," *National Geographic* 128, no. 1 (July 1965): 11–33. See also Goldman, *World Remembers*, 36–40. After taking photographs of the Kennedy flag, medallion, PT 109 tie clasps, and inaugural address, only one tie clasp was left behind on the mountain.

11 Kennedy, "Our Climb."

12 Ullman quoted in Kennedy, "Mount Kennedy, II," 9.

13 Kennedy, "Our Climb," 27.

14 Secretary of State Dean Rusk, telegram to American embassy, London, April 27, 1963, JBKOPP-SFO75-007. See also Goldman, *World Remembers*, 52–60.

15 Goldman, *World Remembers*, 51–60; and John Whitbourn, ed., *Runnymede Memorial* (Ilford, England: Excel Press, 1965). For the text of remarks by Secretary of State Rusk and Queen Elizabeth, both dated May 14, 1965, see JBKOPP-SF075-007.

16 Whitbourn, *Runnymede Memorial*. See also Ernest Kolowrat, "Tribute to JFK at Runnymede," *Senior Scholastic*, November 18, 1966, 13. As Kolowrat notes, Runnymede became over the years not only a tourist destination for British admirers of the late president, but also for American tourists, particularly American exchange students. Although Jacqueline Kennedy attended the dedication at Runnymede, she became too overwrought to deliver her prepared remarks in person. Instead, they were later published in the British press and in Whitbourn's little pamphlet on the Runnymede memorial cited above. See also the statement by Mrs. John F. Kennedy, May 14, 1965,

JBKOPP-SF075-007; and Leaming, *Jacqueline Bouvier Kennedy Onassis*, 194–95.

17 Goldman, *World Remembers*, 68–71, 86.

18 "Say It with Trees," *American Forests* 70 (January 1964): 11. See also the undated program, "John F. Kennedy Memorial and Peace Forest," prepared for the dedication ceremony on July 4, 1966, JBKOPP-SF068-009.

19 Sabato, *Kennedy Half Century*, 260; and "Cape Canaveral Renamed for the Late President," *Science News Letter*, December 14, 1963, 375.

20 See the source cited in Sabato, *Kennedy Half Century*, 525n12.

21 Schlesinger, *Thousand Days*, 729–38; and Binkiewicsz, "Culture from Camelot." For background, see National Cultural Center, memorandum, "Accomplishments to Date," August 1961, John F. Kennedy, Presidential Papers, White House Social Files (hereafter cited as JFKWHSF), AH-028-003; Warnecke, "John F. Kennedy on Architecture," DFPPP-018-010; and Heckscher, OHC.

22 "Remarks of the President to the Advisory Committee of the National Cultural Center in the Movie Room of the East Wing," November 14, 1961, with attached remarks of the same date, JFKWHSF-AH-028-003; National Cultural Center, press release, "Closed Circuit Telecast Proposed to Raise Funds for National Cultural Center," November 14, 1961, JFKWHSF-AH-028-003; White House, press release, "Appointment of Mrs. John F. Kennedy as Honorary Chairman of the National Cultural Center," February 25, 1962, JFKWHSF-AH-028-003; Annual Report of Roger L. Stevens, Chairman, to the Board of Trustees, National Cultural Center, January 13, 1964, Arthur M. Schlesinger Jr. Personal Papers (hereafter cited as AMSPP), 04-026. See also Goldman, *World Remembers*, 137–44.

23 Jacqueline Kennedy to Roger L. Stevens, October 8, 1964, JBKOPP-SF063-009.

24 National Cultural Center, press release, September 11, 1962, JFKWHSF-TR-2008-006.

25 Goldman, *World Remembers*, 137–44; Wolf Von Eckardt, "A Center for Drive-In Culture," *New Republic*, December 22, 1962, 28–30; and Von Eckardt, "Site for Cultural Center Wrapped in Spaghetti Maze," *Washington Post*, December 16, 1962, E3. See also Kenneth Auchincloss, "Memorial on the Potomac," *Newsweek*, September 20, 1971, 22; and Hubert Saal, "A Celebration of the Spirit," *Newsweek*, September 20, 1971, 29–30. Criticism of the site and architecture went back at least to 1964. See Roger Stevens, Chairman, Kennedy Center, to Attorney General Robert Kennedy, June 5, 1964, William Walton Personal Papers (hereafter cited as WWPP), 003-015.

26 Goldman, *World Remembers*, 137–44; and Jean M. White, "President Dedicates Site of Kennedy Art Center," *Washington Post, Times Herald*, December 3, 1964, A1.

27 "Crowds Visit the White House," *New York Times*, November 30, 1963, 13.

28 For the quotes in the text, see Phil Casey and Peter S. Diggins, "Mourners Keep Vigil on Green Slope Where Kennedy Lies in Arlington," *Washington Post, Times Herald*, November 27, 1963, A1, A3; Willard Clopton and Phil Casey, "200,000 Mourners Visit Grave," *Washington Post, Times Herald*, November 29, 1963, A1-2; and "Visitors to the Kennedy Grave – An Endless

Line," *US News & World Report*, May/June 1964, 78–81. See also "Tips for Visitors to Kennedy Grave," *Washington Post, Times Herald*, December 1, 1963, B5; "Thousands Visit Kennedy's Grave as Mourning Period Ends," *Washington Post, Times Herald*, December 23, 1963, A8; Loudon Wainwright, "A Visit to the Grave," *Life*, February 14, 1964, 15; and Ernest Lotito, "Grave Visits Near 3 Million," *Washington Post, Times Herald*, May 30, 1964, B2.

29 David F. Powers, longtime Kennedy friend and curator of the Kennedy Museum, kept track of the number of people visiting the gravesite, at least through 1973, by which time the count had reached nearly thirty-eight million. See Ruby H. Braid, Department of the Army, to Powers, July 19 and 27, 1973, DFPPP-006-001. See also "Visitors to the Kennedy Grave," *US News & World Report*; Nan Robertson, "The Kennedy Tomb: Simple Design Outlined," *New York Times*, November 17, 1964, 1, 34; "Thousands Expected to Pay Respects at Grave," *New York Times*, November 22, 1964, 74; Lee Lescaze, "Tourist Boom Forces Repairs at Custis-Lee Home," *Washington Post, Times Herald*, December 31, 1964, B1; and Nan Robertson, "First Stones Placed at Permanent Site of Kennedy Grave," *New York Times*, April 12, 1966, 1, 24. In addition, see US Senate, Subcommittee on Public Works of the Committee on Appropriations, *Public Works Appropriation Hearing, Department of the Army, April 8, 1964, 88th Cong.* (Washington, DC: Government Printing Office, 1964), 1094–95.

30 This information was provided by the US Army, which has oversight of Arlington Cemetery, in an email dated March 10, 2015 (author's possession).

31 See "Visitors to the Kennedy Grave," *US News & World Report*.

32 "Words of Slain President Inspire Ceremony to End Mourning Period," *Washington Post, Times Herald*, December 19, 1963, E8.

33 Jack Raymond, "Arlington Assigns Plot of Three Acres to Kennedy Family," *New York Times*, December 6, 1963, 1, 18; "Kennedys Get 3 Acres at Arlington," *Washington Post, Times Herald*, December 6, 1963, A4; "A Burial Plot in Arlington for the Kennedys," *US News & World Report*, December 16, 1963, 8; "Congress Gets $1.77 Million Request for Permanent JFK Resting Place," *Washington Post, Times Herald*, February 9, 1965, D1; and "JFK Grave to Cost Over $2 Million," *Washington Post, Times Herald*, April 2, 1965, B2.

34 "Lafayette, He is Here," *Time*, December 13, 1963, 84; Willard Clopton, "Mrs. Kennedy to Discuss Tomb," *Washington Post, Times Herald*, November 30, 1963, D2; and Ada Louise Huxtable, "Warnecke's Capital Work," *New York Times*, November 30, 1963, 14.

35 Clopton, "Mrs. Kennedy to Discuss Tomb"; and "Mrs. Kennedy Chooses an Architect to Design Husband's Tomb," *New York Times*, November 30, 1963, 13.

36 Walton, "Monumental Failures and Successes: Why Do Most Memorials Fail in Their Tribute to the Dead? Why Are Others So Inspiring?," *New York Times Sunday Magazine*, March 15, 1964, SM32; and "An Athletic Architect: John Carl Warnecke," *New York Times*, October 7, 1964, 58.

37 Walton, "Monumental Failures and Successes."

38 See "John F. Kennedy Memorial Grave Design Development and Design Reviews," December 1963 to August 1964, JBKOPP-SF060-008. This large document contains minutes of the design team's interviews with the Kennedys and others. See also "Artists at Odds on Kennedy Tomb," *New York Times*, October 7, 1964, 58; and "Kennedy Tomb Design to Be Revealed in November," *Washington Post, Times Herald*, October 10, 1964, A8.

39 For much of the information in this paragraph, as well as the first two quotations, see "Research Report and Design Criteria for the John Fitzgerald Kennedy Memorial Grave," prepared by John Carl Warnecke and Associates, March 30, 1964, attached to Warnecke to Pamela Turnure, April 6, 1964, JBKOPP-SF060-007. The remaining quotations are from Von Eckardt, "Simplicity, Symbolism to Mark Kennedy Grave," *Los Angeles Times*, November 27, 1964, H6. See also Warnecke to Jacqueline Kennedy, April 6, 1964, JBKOPP-SF060-007.

40 Von Eckardt, "Kennedy Monument Classic in Simplicity," *Washington Post, Times Herald*, November 17, 1964, A1, A3; and Warnecke to Jacqueline Kennedy, April 6, 1964, JBKOPP-SF060-007. See also Robertson, "Kennedy Tomb"; "Model Displayed at National Gallery," *Washington Post, Times Herald*, November 17, 1964, A8; "The J.F.K. Grave," *America*, December 5, 1964, 732; and "Kennedy Grave Design is Disclosed," *Architectural Record* 137 (January 1965): 12–13.

41 For Walton's views, and those of Watterson, Ripley, and Brown, see Von Eckardt, "Kennedy Grave's Design Lauded by Architects and Art Experts," *Washington Post, Times Herald*, November 18, 1964, A17. See also "Kennedy Grave Design," *Architectural Record*; and "A Tomb for J.F.K.," *Time*, November 20, 1964, 102.

42 Huxtable, "Design Dilemma: The Kennedy Grave," *New York Times*, November 29, 1964, X30.

43 Von Eckardt, "A Critical Look at the Kennedy Grave," *Washington Post, Times Herald*, March 26, 1967, A1, A12. See also Robert B. Semple Jr., "Johnson at Grave with the Kennedys," *New York Times*, March 16, 1967, 1, 25; and "3 Changes Made in Original Design of Kennedy Grave," *New York Times*, March 17, 1967, 22.

44 Von Eckardt, "Critical Look"; "Time to Remove the Hats," *Washington Post, Times Herald*, April 12, 1967, A20; and "Military Hats Banished at JFK Grave," *Washington Post, Times Herald*, April 18, 1967, A1.

45 "At Consecration of Kennedy Gravesite," *US News & World Report*, March 27, 1967, 12, 14; and "New Kennedy Grave Consecrated," *Christian Century*, March 29, 1967, 397.

46 "The Grave of John F. Kennedy," *Architectural Record* 142 (December 1967): 128–30.

47 For Warnecke's views, see Von Eckardt, "Kennedy Monument Classic." Warnecke and his team, as well as his consultants and the Kennedys, spent a good deal of time working through the symbolism, both secular and religious, of the gravesite, including the symbolism of the eternal flame. See, for example, the minutes of the design review committee meetings in RSSPP, Series 10.3, Subject Files, 1948–1972, Boxes 291 and 292, 291-014 and -015.

48 "A JFK Legacy," *Newsweek*, June 8, 1964, 46–47. See also Thomas M. Gannon, "The Kennedy Memorabilia," *America*, September 19, 1964, 304–5.

49 Richard A. Corbett, Director, John F. Kennedy Library Tour, undated memorandum to the Kennedy Library Board, with enclosures describing the exhibit and the tour dates of cities visited, JFKWHSF-DFM-044-007.

50 Jacqueline Kennedy, "These Are the Things I Hope Will Show How He Really Was," *Life*, May 29, 1964, 32–35A. See the pamphlet describing the traveling exhibit, "The John F. Kennedy Library Exhibit," in JFKWHSF-DFM-044-001. For an inventory of items and memorabilia exhibited, see JFKWHSF-DFM-044-001 and -002. See also Richard B. Stolley, "Work, Memories, Old Friends," *Life*, May 29, 1964, 34B; "JFK Legacy," *Newsweek*; and Gannon, "Kennedy Memorabilia."

51 See the undated public attendance record in JFKWHSF-DFM-044-007. The General Services Administration (GSA) reported record-breaking attendance when the traveling exhibit opened in Washington, DC. By mid-May 1965, 601,764 people had viewed the exhibit, leading the Kennedy Library Corporation to extend the exhibit through the end of June. See GSA News Release, May 12, 1965, DFPPP-018-003. Hundreds of people who viewed the traveling exhibit sent letters and telegrams of praise to the former first lady. For a sample, see JBKOPP-SF067-007.

52 A list of the cities visited and reports on most stops can be found in the Robert F. Kennedy Papers, Senate Papers, Correspondence, Personal Files, 1964–1968 (hereafter cited as RFKPSP), Box 17, Exhibit Tour. See also Helen Keyes, "The Kennedy Library Exhibit Goes to Europe," attached to Steve Smith to Ed Guthman, April 9, 1965, in the same file.

53 The touring exhibit came with pledge cards for those who visited; see JFKWHSF-DFM-044-001 for examples. Those who pledged significant contributions were invited to a special preexhibit reception that included the viewing of a color film about the former president and his life. See E. Barrett Prettyman, Jr., "Memorandum to all those directly concerned with the tour of the Kennedy Library exhibit," March 6, 1964, JBKOPP-SF067-007. See also Chamberlin, "Commercialization of J.F.K.," 20–21.

54 See "JFK Legacy," *Newsweek*, 45–48.

7 The Memory Wars: Contesting Kennedy

1 Ben A. Franklin, "Kennedy Chose Site at Harvard for Presidential Library Oct. 19," *New York Times*, November 30, 1963, 1, 14. See also Gerry Nadel, "Johnny, When Will Ye Get Your Library?," *Esquire*, January 1975, 92–98; and Warnecke, "The President Selects His Library Site," an interview of John C. Warnecke and Robert Hart by Tom Page, December 4, 1964, RSSPP-292-002.

2 The quote is from the title of an essay by Richard J. Cox, "America's Pyramids: Presidents and Their Libraries," *Government Information Quarterly* 19 (2002): 45–75.

3 "Peace Corps Placing Kennedy Libraries Abroad," *Publishers Weekly*, December 16, 1963, 22; and "Kennedy Libraries Drive Collects over 4000 Books," *Publishers Weekly*, June 1, 1964, 57.

4 Kennedy to Pusey, September 20, 1961, AMSPP-WH13-004; Kennedy, memorandum for the Archivist of the United States, September 20, 1961, AMSPP-WH13-004; Pusey to Kennedy, September 26, 1961, AMSPP-WH13-004; Schlesinger, memorandum for Pierre Salinger, November 7, 1961, AMSPP-WH13-005; White House, press release, November 10, 1961, AMSPP-WH13-005; Schlesinger, memorandum for the president, January 22, 1962, AMSPP-WH13-006; Schlesinger, draft letter to cabinet secretaries, May 23, 1962, with attached "Acquisition Policies for the John F. Kennedy Library," AMSPP-WH12a-031; Wayne C. Grover to Arthur Schlesinger, August 22, 1962, AMSPP-WH129-032; Grover to Schlesinger, December 19, 1962, AMSPP-WH12a-032; and Boutin to Salinger, January 29, 1963, AMSPP-WH12a-032.

5 For the announcement, see the press release attached to Schlesinger, memorandum to Salinger, December 5, 1963, AMSPP-WH-13-005.

6 "Notes on meeting at 21, December 19, 1963," December 24, 1963, AMSPP-WH13-004. It was at this meeting that the idea of a Kennedy institute for the study of public affairs first began to emerge. For the position papers, see the documents attached to the interoffice memorandum from Susan to Mary Ann, both of the Attorney General's Office, March 10, [1964], in RSSPP-292-001.

7 Schlesinger, memorandum to Sorensen, January 13, 1964, AMSPP-P27-008. See also, in the same source, the undated and unsigned draft letter, no doubt written by Schlesinger, to a long list of officials and others who were being asked to contribute their papers to the Kennedy Library, and under what conditions. For a sample of the gift agreement donors signed, see "Authorization to Make Microfilm Copies of the Personal Papers of C. Mennen Williams, for Deposit in the John F. Kennedy Memorial Library," February 11, 1964, AMSPP-P27-008.

8 Robert Kennedy quoted in "JFK's Last Campaign," *Newsweek*, March 9, 1964, 25, 28. See also the "Summary of Preliminary Meeting of the Committee of Arts and Architecture for the Kennedy Library," [undated, but the meeting was undoubtedly held in December 1963] WWPP-003-016; Schlesinger, memorandum for Robert Kennedy, January 10, 1964, AMSPP-P27-08; and Florence Anderson to Wayne C. Grover, February 18, 1965, AMSPP-P27-08; Eugene Black to the John F. Kennedy Library Corporation's Trustees, re: Progress Report, December 1965, WWPP-003-013; Mary McGrory, "The Kennedy Memorial Library," *America*, March 14, 1964, 333; Jack Star, "The Kennedy Legend," *Look*, June 30, 1964, 19–21; "Voices of History," *Newsweek*, August 23, 1965, 73; and Charles T. Morrissey and Tracy E. K'Meyer, "An Interview with Charles T. Morrissey: Part I – 'Getting Started: Beginning an Oral History Career,' " *Oral History Review* 24, no. 2 (Winter 1997): 73–74.

9 See Director for the John F. Kennedy Library and Corporation, attached to the unsigned memorandum, May 18, 1965, RSSPP-292-003.

10 Eugene Black, Progress Report, December 1965, WWPP-003-013; William vanden Heuvel, memorandum to Mrs. John F. Kennedy, Attorney General

Robert F. Kennedy, Senator Edward M. Kennedy, Eugene R. Black, and Stephen S. Smith, August 4, 1964, JBKOPP-SF069-012; and Dan H. Fenn, Jr., "Launching the John F. Kennedy Library," *American Archivist* 42, no. 4 (October 1979): 429–42. Fenn was the first director of the John F. Kennedy Library. For background on both the school and institute, see John F. Kennedy School of Government, *The John F. Kennedy School of Government: The First Fifty Years* (Cambridge, MA: Ballinger, 1986). For a brief history of presidential libraries, their funding, and operations, see Nancy Kegan Smith and Gary M. Stern, "A Historical Review of Access to Records in Presidential Libraries," *Public Historian* 28, no. 3 (Summer 2006): 79–116.

11   "JFK's Last Campaign," *Newsweek*, 25, 28; "Building a Library," *Time*, May 29, 1964, 30; and Nadel, "Johnny." See also Michael Cannell, *I. M. Pei: Mandarin of Modernism* (New York: Carol Southern Books, 1995), 164–65.

12   John A. Gronouski to Committee Members and Agency Coordinators of the Federal Employees Campaign for the John Fitzgerald Kennedy Library, May 21, 1964, JFKWHSF-DFM-044-013; N. Ethelyn Thompson, memorandum for Dean Markham re: John Fitzgerald Kennedy Library Fund Campaign among Federal Employees, undated, JFKWHSF-DFM-044-013; and William vanden Heuvel to Department and Agency Coordinators for Federal Employees Campaign, April 23, 1964, JFKWHSF-DFM-044-013. For an undated White House memorandum on the number of employees making contributions and the total amount raised, see JFKWHSF-DFM-044-013. See also Joseph Young, "Drive Set among U.S. Workers to Aid the Kennedy Library Fund," *Washington Star*, May 28, 1964, copy in WWPP-003-012.

13   "Kennedy Library Drive Passes $10 Million Goal," *Washington Star*, December 15, 1964, copy in WWPP-003-012.

14   Walton quoted first in Arthur Herzog, "He Loves Things to Be Beautiful: He Loves Beautiful Things," *New York Times Magazine*, March 14, 1965, SM34, SM98, SM100; and then in Laura Bergquist, "Jacqueline Kennedy Goes Public," *Look*, March 22, 1966, 47–59. Nadel quoted in "Johnny." See also the undated "Summary of Preliminary Meeting of the Committee on Arts and Architecture for the Kennedy Library," WWPP-003-016; Walton to Lucio Costa, April 14, 1964, WWPP-003-016; notes on a meeting of the Arts and Architecture Committee at the home of Ambassador Joseph P. Kennedy, Hyannisport, Massachusetts, April 12, 1964, AMSPP-004-004; William Walton, interview by Meghan Floyd Desnoyers, March 30, 1993, 16–21, OHC; I. M. Pei, interview by Vicki Daitch, March 18, 1966, 2–4, OHC; Wolf Von Eckardt, "Stalling on the Arts," *New Republic*, March 21, 1964, 8; and "JFK Memorials Move Forward," *Architectural Forum* 120 (May 1964): 9.

15   Herzog, "He Loves Things to Be Beautiful."

16   For the previous two paragraphs, see Bergquist, "Jacqueline Kennedy Goes Public"; "Disneyland in Camelot?," *Time*, June 11, 1967, 24; "JFK's Monument," *Newsweek*, June 11, 1963, 85; Jane Holtz Kay, "Architecture," *Nation*, July 16, 1973, 61–62; "In the News: Changes in Kennedy Library," *American Libraries* 5, no. 9 (October 1974): 465–66; and Mildred F. Schmertz, "Getting Ready for the John F. Kennedy Library: Not Everyone Wants to

Make It Go Away," *Architectural Record* 156 (December 1974): 98–105. See also John F. Kennedy School of Government, *John F. Kennedy School of Government*, 48–50; Cannell, *I. M. Pei*, 175–77; and Theodore J. Musho, interview by Vicki Daitch, November 12, 2002, OHC. Musho was an architect in Pei's office and was deeply involved in the library project. He discusses the opposition to the original site at different points in his long interview.

17 For Pei's comment, see "JFK's Monument," *Newsweek*. See also Pei, 6–7, OHC.

18 John Kifner, "Kennedy Museum Blocked by Combination of Forces," *New York Times*, February 12, 1975, 40. See also the sources cited in note 16 of this chapter; and Cannell, *I. M. Pei*, 186–87.

19 See "Disneyland in Camelot?," *Time*; "JFK's Monument," *Newsweek*; Nadel, "Johnny"; and Kay, "Architecture," July 16, 1973. See also Schmertz, "Getting Ready"; and Cannell, *I. M. Pei*, 178–79.

20 See "In the News: Changes," *American Libraries*; and Nadel, "Johnny."

21 See Schmertz, "Getting Ready"; Nadel, "Johnny"; and Cannell, *I. M. Pei*, 183–84.

22 Kifner, "Kennedy Museum Blocked." I. M. Pei understood how changing political and social forces influenced the outcome of his project. Kennedy "was venerated, as you know, [in] '64, '65," he said in his oral history for the Kennedy Library. "But from '67 on, it became just the opposite," as his name became increasingly linked to the Vietnam War. See Pei, 6, OHC.

23 Bok explains the university's decision in his oral history for the Kennedy Library and notes how it left the Kennedys feeling betrayed. Derek C. Bok, interview by Vicki Daitch, November 19, 2002, 1–3, OHC.

24 Dave Powers opposed any plan to divide the library and museum complex between two sites, as did Congressman John M. McCormack, but financial considerations and the prospect of prolonged court battles seemed to determine the final decision. Powers to Senator Edward M. Kennedy, February 13, 1975, DFPPP-018-010; McCormack, press release, February 18, 1975, DFPPP-018-010; and Senator Kennedy to Powers, February 21, 1975, DFPPP-018-010. See also Pei, 7–8, OHC; Musho, OHC; Kifner, "Kennedy Museum Blocked"; "In the News: Presidential Papers: ALA Units Discuss Public Ownership; Sites of Nixon, Kennedy Libraries Uncertain," *American Libraries* 6, no. 7 (July–August 1975): 402; "U. Mass 1, Harvard 0," *Time*, December 8, 1975, 44; and Jill Rubalcaba, *I. M. Pei: Architect of Time, Place, and Purpose* (Tarrytown, NY: Marshall Cavendish, 2011), 33.

25 The first quote is from Douglas Davis, "I. M. Pei's Beacon to Camelot," *Newsweek*, October 29, 1979, 110–13. The second is from Pei, 9, OHC. See also ibid., 14.

26 "Pei Unveils New Design for Kennedy Library," *Architectural Record* 160 (July 1976): 39; "JFK Remembered," *Time*, August 6, 1979, 73; Paul Goldberger, "New Kennedy Library Plan Released," *New York Times*, August 13, 1976, 13; Doris Kinney, "JFK Undimmed," *Life*, December 1988, 64–69; "A Concrete Memorial to Camelot: After 16 Years, the John F. Kennedy Library Is to Open at Last," *Time*, October 22, 1979, 63; "Unveiling a Glittering

Tribute to John F. Kennedy," *US News & World Report*, October 22, 1979, 43–44; and "Jimmy in Camelot," *Newsweek*, October 29, 1979, 32–34.

27 Davis, "I. M. Pei's Beacon to Camelot." See also Pei, 9, OHC; and William Marlin, "Lighthouse on an Era," *Architectural Record* 167 (February 1980): 81–90.

28 Schlesinger, "Arthur Schlesinger Tells of J.F.K. Remembered on a Sunny Autumn Saturday in Boston," *People*, November 5, 1979, 36–38, 43.

29 Davis, "I. M. Pei's Beacon to Camelot."

30 Eckardt quoted in "Unveiling a Glittering Tribute," *US News & World Report*, 43–44. In his book on Pei, Michael Cannell does not seem particularly inspired by the building and quotes at least one other critic as well. See Cannell, *I. M. Pei*, 114.

31 John Stewart, Dan Fenn, William Moss, and Larry Hackman, interview by Vicki Daitch, April 16 and 17, 2004, 108, 110–11, OHC; and Schlesinger, memorandum for Stephen Smith, I. M. Pei, Theodore Sorensen, William Walton, Thomas Johnston, and Milton Gwirtzman, October 27, 1971, WWPP-003-013.

32 Stewart, Fenn, Moss, and Hackman, 108, 110–17, OHC. The quoted material is from ibid., 114 and 116.

33 Ibid., 110.

34 See the undated, unsigned ten-page draft of "The Presidential Years," and a second draft with the same title, dated April 28, 1977, in DFPPP-018-011. On the Cuban Missile Crisis, the second draft concluded that despite some critics, "most agreed it was a masterful and necessary performance by JFK and his advisors." On civil rights, notably the integration of the University of Mississippi, it concluded that "the federal-state constitutional confrontation was handled successfully and JFK/RFK had not backed down when faced with a most difficult situation." On the Bay of Pigs, it stressed that "planning for the operation was well along at the start" of the administration; that Kennedy did not obtain clear, consistent advice from those he consulted; that he nonetheless took full responsibility for the disaster; and that he subsequently restructured his staff to prevent similar mistakes and get better advice in the future. For other examples of the "impressions" that museum designers wanted visitors to leave with, see the drafts cited earlier.

35 Kay, "Architecture," *Nation*, December 15, 1979, 634–35.

36 Schlesinger, "J.F.K. Remembered."

37 Davis, "I. M. Pei's Beacon to Camelot."

38 Kay, "Architecture," December 15, 1979.

39 Fairlie, "Is Harvard's Institute of Politics a Recruiting College?," *Boston Globe*, January 15, 1964, 4. See also Betsy Beale, "The Kennedy Stories Are Only Beginning," *Boston Globe*, February 19, 1967, 70.

40 Schlesinger, memorandum on the Kennedy Library, January 6, 1964, AMSPP-P27-008; Robert Kennedy to the president and fellows of Harvard College, June 23, 1966, RFKPSP, Box 17, Meeting, Annual, 1966–67; Nathan M. Pusey, President of Harvard University, to Robert Kennedy, three letters of June 27, 1966, RFKPSP, Box 17, Meeting, Annual, 1966–67; and Bok, 12, OHC. Bok's oral history makes clear that he and the Kennedys

had their differences, particularly over whether or not the university was
doing enough to support the Kennedy School of Government and Institute
of Politics. But it also makes clear that he was ever anxious to assuage their
concerns. The exchange of letters between Pusey and Kennedy can also be
found in DFPPP-018-010. From the beginning, Harvard officials had been
anxious to reassure the Kennedys that the institute would "run with hardly
any constraints from formal Faculty procedures," in part because faculty at
Harvard were not involved with budgets and administration, in part because
the institute would not award degrees or offer courses for credit, and in
part because most of its staff would not be appointed to tenured positions.
See, for example, Dean Don K. Price, Harvard Graduate School of Public
Administration, to Robert Kennedy, July 23, 1964, and Richard Neustadt to
Edward Kennedy, January 29, 1965, both in RFKPSP, Box 17, Institute of
Politics, 7/1964-2/1965.

41 Federal law at the time gave ownership of presidential papers to the president rather than the public and allowed him, his heir, or a designee to determine which papers might be opened to researchers and which ones might be
sealed – and for how long. The law changed in 1978, so that legal ownership of presidential papers became public rather than private. But the new
law applied only to the papers of presidents who assumed office on or after
January 20, 1981. It exempted the Kennedy papers and those of other presidents who served before that date. See Smith and Stern, "Historical Review
of Access." See also National Archives, "The Availability for Research of
the Papers and Other Historical Materials in the John F. Kennedy Library
Collections," October 1969, JBKOPP-SF070-006.

42 Dave Powers to Stephen Smith, May 21, 1986, DFPPP-018-008; and Watson,
"An Enduring Fascination: The Papers of Jacqueline Kennedy," *Prologue* 19,
no. 2 (Summer 1987): 117–25.

43 Adam Clymer and Don Van Natta, Jr., "Family of Robert F. Kennedy
Rethinks His Place at Library," *New York Times*, July 12, 2011, 1. See also
the source cited in the subsequent note.

44 Kennedy quoted in Bryan Bender, "A Dark Corner of Camelot," *Boston
Globe*, January 23, 2011, A1.

45 National Archives, "Availability for Research"; and GSA, news release,
October 1, 1969, JBKOPP-SF070-006.

46 Roberts, "The Kennedy Non-Papers," *Newsweek*, August 9, 1971, 24–25.

47 Hersh, *Dark Side*, 454–55.

48 "The Kennedy Presidential Recordings – A Summary Report," as revised
by Evelyn Lincoln, DFPPP-019-002. Although the document itself was not
dated, Lincoln signed the document on condition that it not be released for
at least fifteen years from that date, or February 17, 1992. For the first quote,
see Herman Kahn, "Recent John Fitzgerald Kennedy Library Developments,"
August 19, 1965, attached to Kahn to Angela Novella, Robert Kennedy's
secretary, August 19, 1965, RFKPSP, Box 16, Correspondence, 6/17/1965-
12/27/1965; for the second quote, see Burke Marshall to Robert F. Kennedy,
May 27, 1965, RFKPSP, Correspondence, 5/27/65; and for the third quote,
see White to Robert Kennedy, December 27, 1965, RFKPSP, Correspondence,

6/17/65-12/27/65. In addition, see Evelyn N. Lincoln, interview by Larry Hackman, William Moss, Sylvie Turner, and William Johnson, July 18, 1974, 7–10, OHC.

49 Stewart, Fenn, Moss, and Hackman, 11, OHC. See also "Kennedy Presidential Recordings," DFPPP-019-002.

50 "Kennedy Presidential Recordings," DFPPP-019-002.

51 See notations attached to "Kennedy Presidential Recordings," cited above. It is not clear who made the notations. See also National Archives, press release, "National Archives Recovers Treasure Trove of Kennedy Materials," June 16, 2005, www.archives.gov/press/press-releases/2005/n/nr05-80.html; and James M. Roth, "Reclaiming Pieces of Camelot: How NARA and the JFK Library Recovered Missing Kennedy Documents and Artifacts," *Prologue* 38, no. 2 (Summer 2006), www.archives.gov/publications/prologue/2006/summer/camelot.html. These documents tell the story from the point of view of the National Archives, the Kennedy Library and the Kennedy family. For a point of view far more sympathetic to Evelyn Lincoln and the collector with whom she worked, see Robert M. Adler, "The Public Controversy over the Kennedy Memorabilia Project," in *Archives, Documentation, and Institutions of Social Memory: Essays from the Sawyer Seminar*, ed. Francis X. Flouin Jr. and William G. Rosenberg (Ann Arbor: University of Michigan Press, 2009), 225–36. A lawyer involved in the case, Adler is highly critical of the Kennedys, the Kennedy Library, and the National Archives for what he sees as the specious legal justifications and harsh tactics, including aggressive public attacks, that characterized their efforts to reclaim Kennedy memorabilia that had been entrusted to Evelyn Lincoln and that she later sold or gifted to friends.

52 William Moss, Chief Archivist, to Archives Staff, Jim Williamson, and Dave Powers, March 9, 1982, DFPPP-019-002; and Moss to historian David Levering Lewis, February 9, 1982, DFPPP-019-002. Publication of the list caused a flurry of newspaper commentary, some of it critical of Kennedy for doing what Richard Nixon did – secretly recording conversations with unsuspecting visitors. See newspaper clippings in DFPPP-019-002.

53 Giglio, "Past Frustrations and New Opportunities: Researching the Kennedy Presidency at the Kennedy Library," *Presidential Studies Quarterly* 22, no. 2 (Spring 1992): 371–79; and John F. Stewart to Burke Marshall, June 5, 1970, with enclosed "Preparation for Research Use of Audiovisual Material in the Kennedy Library," JBKOPP-SF070-007. According to Stewart's letter, the guidelines were suggested by Jacqueline Kennedy Onassis, who was concerned about "releasing photos or film which might be embarrassing."

54 Morrissey and K'Meyer, "Interview."

55 Giglio, "Past Frustrations." The White House police kept logs noting all visitors to the White House, the staff members with whom they had appointments, and the times of their arrival and departure. Originally closed for fifty years when they were given to the Kennedy Library in 1971, the restricted period was reduced to twenty years in 1978, though even then, the Secret Service had to review records and delete any information deemed private before they could be released. Giglio was one of the historians who worked

tirelessly to gain access to this information. See the following documentation in DFPPP-019-003: accession agreement signed by representatives of the Secret Service and the National Archives, November 12, 1971; Mabel Deutrich to W. Stuart Knight, January 30, 1978; William J. Bacherman to Deutrich, April 27, 1978; James E. O'Neal to Bacherman, July 5, 1978; and William Moss to Dottie Jacobson, August 22, 1981. Giglio's name is mentioned in some doodling, apparently by Powers, attached to a memorandum from Powers to William Johnson, August 13, 1990, DFPPP-019-003.

56 It's worth noting that initially, at least, the National Archives and Burke Marshall of the Screening Committee recommended against granting privileged access to the Kennedy papers to some historians. They thought the records should be opened to all, or closed to all, with nothing in between. See their discussion of the library's audiovisual collection, for example, in Stewart to Marshall, June 5, 1970, with "Preparation for Research Use," cited above; and Marshall, memorandum to Senator Edward M. Kennedy and Mrs. Aristotle Onassis, June 16, 1970, JBKOPP-SFO70-007. The Kennedy family and the library ignored this advice from the beginning and continued to do so.

57 Schlesinger, *The Imperial Presidency* (New York: Houghton Mifflin, 1973).

58 See Miroff, *Pragmatic Illusions: The Presidential Politics of John F. Kennedy* (New York: David McKay, 1976); Fairlie, *Kennedy Promise*; Matusow, *The Unraveling of America: A History of Liberalism in the 1960s* (New York: Harper & Row, 1984); Wills, *Kennedy Imprisonment*; and O'Neill, *Coming Apart: An Informal History of America in the 1960s* (Chicago: Quadrangle Books, 1971). For an excellent overview of the literature on Kennedy's domestic policy, see Giglio, "John F. Kennedy as Domestic Leader: A Perspective on the Literature," in White, *Kennedy: The New Frontier Revisited*, 222–55, esp. 226–27.

59 For good overviews of the literature on Kennedy's foreign and national security policies, see Anna Kasten Nelson, "President Kennedy's National Security Policy: A Reconsideration," *Reviews in American History* 19, no. 1 (March 1991): 1–14; Burton I. Kaufman, "John F. Kennedy as World Leader: A Perspective on the Literature," in *America in the World: The Historiography of American Foreign Relations since 1941*, ed. Michael J. Hogan (New York: Cambridge University Press, 1995), 326–57; and Mark J. White, "Introduction: A New Synthesis for the New Frontier," in White, *Kennedy: The New Frontier Revisited*, 1–17. See also the book's individual essays by Fredrik Logevall, Georg Schild, Thomas W. Zeiler, Josephine Brain, and Derek W. Elliott on different aspects of Kennedy's foreign policy.

60 In addition to the sources cited in the previous notes, see Walton, *Cold War and Counterrevolution: The Foreign Policy of John F. Kennedy* (New York: Viking Press, 1972); and Paterson, ed., *Kennedy's Quest for Victory: American Foreign Policy, 1961–1963* (New York: Oxford University Press, 1989).

61 "Jack's character," concluded Reeves, "lacked a moral center, a reference point that went beyond self-aggrandizement." See *A Question of Character: A Life of John F. Kennedy* (New York: Free Press, 1991), 415. See also Exner, *My*

Story, with Ovid Demaris (New York: Grove, 1977); Traphes Bryant, *Dog Days at the White House: The Outrageous Memoirs of the Presidential Kennel Keeper*, with Frances Spatz Leighton (New York: Macmillan, 1975), 22–25, 35–40; Wills, *Kennedy Imprisonment*; Brown, *JFK: History of an Image*, 70–75, 97–98; and Loren Glass, "The Kennedy Legacy: From Hagiography to Expose and Back Again," in Hoberek, *Cambridge Companion to John F. Kennedy*, 240–49. So far as popular studies are concerned, the attack on Kennedy's reputation, including his lack of substance, personal behavior, and moral character starts with Lasky's *JFK: the Man and the Myth* and then runs through Joan and Clay Blair's *The Search for JFK* (New York: Berkley Medallion Books, 1976) to Wills's *Kennedy Imprisonment* and Seymour Hersh's *The Dark Side of Camelot*. Almost all of these books were best sellers.

62 Nertzberg, "Kennedy and the Intellectuals," *Washington Post, Times Herald*, November 18, 1973, C3.
63 Brown, *JFK: History of an Image*, 77–78.
64 Reinhold, "Kennedy Place in History Argued," *Cleveland Plain Dealer*, November 22, 1973, I10. See also Leuchtenburg, "John F. Kennedy, Twenty Years Later," *American Heritage* 35, no. 1 (December 1983): 51–59. In his essay, Leuchtenburg gives a very good summary of the scholarly literature on Kennedy to that point.
65 Daniel, "Kennedy, Nixon: Two Faces of One Era," *New York Times*, November 22, 1973, 46.
66 Cohen, "The Letdown," *Washington Post*, November 22, 1983, B1.
67 Cohen, "Death of an Illusion: Kennedy Personified a Self-Deluded and Self-Intoxicated America," *Washington Post*, November 22, 1988, A25.
68 Kopkind, "J.F.K.'s Legacy," *Nation*, December 5, 1988, 589.
69 Broder, "The Power Concept of John Kennedy," *Boston Globe*, November 21, 1973, 19.
70 Kraft, "The Kennedy Promise," *St. Louis Post-Dispatch*, November 21, 1973, E3.
71 Harrington, "A View from the Left," *Washington Post, Times Herald*, November 18, 1973, C1.
72 Boeth, "JFK: Visions and Revisions," *Newsweek*, November 19, 1973, 76, 90, 92. See also Howe cited in Nertzberg, "Kennedy and the Intellectuals."
73 Harrington, "View from the Left."
74 Boeth, "JFK: Visions and Revisions."
75 "JFK Could Laugh at Himself," *Cleveland Plain Dealer*, November 22, 1973, 22; "… And a Man Who Stirred Them in Us," *Los Angeles Times*, November 22, 1973, D6; and "Ten Years Later," *New York Times*, November 22, 1973, 36.
76 "The Memory Lasts," *Los Angeles Times*, November 22, 1983, C6.
77 Broder, "JFK's Great Gift Was Questions," *Cleveland Plain Dealer*, November 22, 1983, A14; and Broder, "JFK – Plus 20," *Cleveland Plain Dealer*, November 22, 1983, A12.
78 "JFK: A Measure of the Man," *Washington Post*, November 22, 1983, A20.
79 Donovan, "How the Kennedy Legend Took Shape and Grew," *Los Angeles Times*, November 22, 1983, C7.

80 Sorensen, "They Underestimated J.F.K.," *New York Times*, November 22, 1988, A27.

81 Attwood, "Twenty Years after Dallas," *Virginia Quarterly Review* 59, no. 4 (Autumn 1983): 557–63. See also Philip Geyelin, "Kennedy and the Revision of History," *Washington Post*, November 29, 1988, A25.

82 "From Disillusionment to Renewal," *Cleveland Plain Dealer*, November 22, 1988, A10. See also Robert L. Turner, "A Day to Remember What We Have Lost," *Boston Globe*, November 22, 1988, 19.

83 Margolis, "John F. Kennedy," *Chicago Tribune*, November 20, 1983, D1.

84 Martin, *A Hero for Our Time: An Intimate Story of the Kennedy Years* (New York: Ballantine Books, 1983). Another example was William Manchester's popular book, *One Brief Shining Moment: Remembering Kennedy* (Boston: Little, Brown, 1983). This flattering account of the president, similar to the author's earlier biography of Kennedy, was no doubt intended in part as a Band-Aid to cover and soothe his earlier contretemps with the Kennedy family over his book on the president's assassination.

85 See, for example, Geyelin, "Kennedy and the Revision of History."

86 Parmet, *Jack: The Struggles of John F. Kennedy* (New York: Dial Press, 1980); Parmet, *JFK*; Giglio, *The Presidency of John F. Kennedy* (Lawrence: University Press of Kansas, 1991); Bernstein, *Promises Kept: John F. Kennedy's New Frontier* (New York: Oxford University Press, 1991); Hamilton, *JFK: Reckless Youth* (New York: Random House, 1992); and Reeves, *President Kennedy*. See also the excellent overview of this literature in White, "Introduction: A New Synthesis."

87 See the sources cited in the previous note. See also Giglio, "John F. Kennedy as Domestic Leader."

88 "Overrated & Underrated Americans," *American Heritage* 39, no. 5 (July/August 1988): 48–63; and John Berendt, "A Look at the Record: What the School Books Are Teaching Our Kids about J.F.K.," *Esquire*, November 1973, 140, 236–65. At worst, Berendt reported, the textbooks drained Kennedy of his personality, the very "style" that made him most appealing.

89 The polls are reported in Henggeler, *Kennedy Persuasion*, 94, 222–23, 246–74.

90 Ashley Powers, "The Mythical Man of Camelot," *Dallas Morning News*, November 16, 2003, A1. As Powers reported, however, even though Kennedy's rating remained high among poll respondents overall, it was much lower among the subset of respondents who were eighteen to twenty-nine years old. For this subset, Kennedy was mostly famous for being assassinated.

91 Charles Fishman, "Flowers, Tears and Struggle to Explain Importance of John F. Kennedy's Life," *Washington Post*, November 21, 1983, A1; David Arnold, "JFK – The Day of Remembrance," *Boston Globe*, November 23, 1988, 2–3; and Connie Cass, "Kennedy Flame Endures, New Generation Learns the Lesson," *Cleveland Plain Dealer*, November 23, 1993, 1.

92 White, *Kennedy*, 111–120.

93 Taylor, "The Media Fan the Flame of the Kennedy Legend," *Los Angeles Times*, November 6, 1983, U3.

94 McClain, "Confessions of an Authentic JFK-er," *Chicago Tribune*, November 20, 1983, D3.
95 Taylor, "Media Fan the Flame."
96 Goodwin, *The Fitzgeralds and the Kennedys: An American Saga* (New York: Simon & Schuster, 1987).
97 Peter S. Canellos, "Kennedy Mystique Revived as JFK Death Is Remembered," *Boston Globe*, November 19, 1988, 25–26. See also Peter J. Ling, *John F. Kennedy* (New York: Routledge, 2013), 251.
98 Henggeler, *Kennedy Persuasion*, 173; and Ling, *Kennedy*, 253–54.
99 Henggeler, *Kennedy Persuasion*, 173.
100 Ling, *Kennedy*, 256–59. See also Hellman, *Kennedy Obsession*, 146–61; and Santa Cruz, *Making JFK Matter*, 196–205.
101 Carl P. Leubsdorf, "JFK Imitators Usually Are Interested in Style," *Dallas Morning News*, October 13, 1988, A19; and Henggeler, *Kennedy Persuasion*, 33.
102 For Parmet's quote, see Kaufman, "J.F.K., Then and Now: After 25 Years, His Aura Resists the Chill of History," *New York Times*, November 20, 1988, E1. For Bentsen's remark, see Canellos, "Kennedy Mystique Revived." See also Leubsdorf, "JFK Imitators."
103 Sorensen, "They Underestimated J.F.K." See also Richard Higgins, "JFK and the Days of Future Passed: 25 Years after Death, a Look at Where He Might Have Led Us," *Boston Globe*, November 20, 1988, 1.
104 Henggeler, *Kennedy Persuasion*, 244–69.

8 Gone but Not Forgotten: History, Memory, and Nostalgia

1 The story of the Sixth Floor Museum is well told by Stephen Fagan in *Assassination and Commemoration: JFK, Dallas, and The Sixth Floor Museum at Dealey Plaza* (Norman: University of Oklahoma Press, 2013). See pages 109–10 of this source for the quotes by Senator Kennedy and Charles Daly.
2 See the excellent review by Carl M. Brauer, "John F. Kennedy Presidential Library and Museum," *Public Historian* 28, no. 3 (Summer 2006): 194–97; as well as Andrew J. Rotter's perceptive review, "New Museum at the John F. Kennedy Library," *Journal of American History* 83, no. 1 (June 1996): 162–66. See also Thomas Hertfelder, "With a Whiff of Royalism: Exhibiting Biographies in American Presidential Libraries," in *Institutions of Public Memory: the Legacies of German and American Politicians*, ed. Astrid M. Eckert (Washington, DC: German Historical Institute, 2007), 9–32; and Josh Getlin, "Keeper of the Legend: JFK's Closest Aide and Confidant Aims to Uphold Stellar Image of the President as Scandals and Critics Work to Tarnish It," *Los Angeles Times*, November 7, 1991, 1.
3 Lawrence Howe, "Now Playing at a Presidential Library near You: The Films of Presidential Museums," *Public Historian* 17, no. 1 (Winter 1995): 125–41. See also Brauer's review of the museum cited in the previous note.

4 See reviews of the museum by Brauer and Rotter cited in note 1; and Michelle Ulyatt, "The John F. Kennedy Presidential Library and Museum as a Cultural Representation of the Public Memory of the President," *European Journal of American Culture* 33, no. 2 (June 2014): 117–30.

5 Span, "Monumental Ambition: Presidential Libraries as History and Hagiography," *Washington Post*, February 17, 2002, W24. The quoted material is from this source. See also the essay by Ulyatt cited in the previous note.

6 Rotter, "New Museum." See also Hertfelder, "With a Whiff of Royalism," 22–23.

7 The museum celebrated "the Kennedy years as if they were still with us, and still should be," wrote Edward Rothstein several years after the rededication. "We aren't submerged in history; we may even for a moment be freed from it." Edward Rothstein, "Recalling Kennedy's Death, or Life," *New York Times*, November 21, 2013, C1.

8 Rotter, "New Museum."

9 Cox, "America's Pyramids."

10 Powers quoted in Getlin, "Keeper of the Legend."

11 Powers quoted in Eileen Keerdoja, Sylvester Monroe, and Marsha Zabarsky, "The JFK Library, A Low Turnout," *Newsweek*, December 21, 1981, 9.

12 Fenn did not meet all of the qualifications initially established for the library director, which called for the appointment of a professional historian or political scientist who hopefully had some archival, museum, or library experience. The description went on to note, however, the additional preference for a director who had some association with the Kennedy family and some experience in the federal government. See John F. Kennedy Library Corporation, Directors' Meeting, January 24, 1970, JBKOPP-SFO70-007. See also the source cited in the following note.

13 See Stewart, Fenn, Moss, and Hackman, 5–10, OHC. The quoted remarks are from pages 44–45. This is an incredibly interesting oral history, full of contradictions and self-justifications. On page 29, for example, after Hackman noted that the Kennedy Library had a reputation for being the "most protective" of all the presidential libraries, Fenn expressed concern. He claimed that pressure to restrict the records "was not coming from the family," meaning the Kennedy family, but on the same page he admitted that some decisions, like those granting Doris Kearns Goodwin privileged access to the Joseph P. Kennedy Papers while denying access to Nigel Hamilton, had "nothing to do with the Kennedy Library. The family," he said, "made those decisions."

14 Hamilton, *JFK: Reckless Youth*. For Fenn's admission, see the previous note.

15 Jean Kennedy Smith, Eunice Kennedy Shriver, Patricia Kennedy Lawford, and Edward M. Kennedy, "A Grotesque Portrait of Our Parents," *New York Times*, December 3, 1992, www.nytimes.com/1992/12/03/opinion/a-grotesque-portrait-of-our-parents.html; Doris Kearns Goodwin, "'JFK: Reckless Youth,'" *New York Times*, January 17, 1993, www.nytimes.com/1993/01/17/books/l-jfk-reckless-youth-860193.html; and Hamilton, "Why Do the Kennedys Fear History?," *Baltimore Sun*, January 27, 1993, http://articles.baltimoresun.com/1993-01-27/news/1993027221_1_kennedy-family-senator-kennedy-jfk. See also "Writer Shelves 2nd Volume of JFK

Biography, Blames Kennedy Opposition," *Chicago Tribune*, June 9, 1994, 26; and Ronald Kessler, "History Deleted," *New York Times*, April 30, 1996, www.nytimes.com/1996/04/30/opinion/history-deleted.html.

16 Kenneth Jost, "Presidential Libraries," *CQ Researcher* 17, no. 11 (March 16, 2007): 241–64; Benjamin Hufbauer, *Presidential Temples: How Memorials and Libraries Shape Public Memory* (Lawrence: University Press of Kansas, 2005); and Cox, "America's Pyramids."

17 Span, "Monumental Ambition." See also Ling, *Kennedy*, 256–57.

18 The quoted material is all from Span, "Monumental Ambition."

19 Brian R. Ballou, "Mrs. Kennedy a Savvy White House Steward," *Boston Globe*, February 14, 2012, B3; *PBS NewsHour*, "New Collection Listens In on President Kennedy's Secret White House Tapes," October 18, 2012, www.pbs.org/newshour/bb/white_house-july-dec12-kennedy_10-18/; John F. Kennedy Library Foundation, *Listening In: The Secret White House Recordings of John F. Kennedy* (New York: Hyperion, 2012); National Archives, press release, "Kennedy Presidential Library Announces Ground Breaking Initiative to Permanently Preserve the Archives of JFK," June 9, 2006, www.archives.gov/press/press-releases/2006/nr06-112 .html; National Archives, press release, "Caroline Kennedy and David S. Ferriero Unveil Groundbreaking Online Archive of the Collection of President John F. Kennedy," January 13, 2011, www.archives.gov/ press/press-releases/2011/nr11-53.html; and Onassis and Schlesinger, *Jacqueline Kennedy: Historical Conversations on Life with John F. Kennedy, Interviews with Arthur M. Schlesinger, Jr., 1964* (New York: Hyperion, 2011).

20 As of this writing, the Kennedy Library and its foundation are in the midst of another crisis that erupted in the summer of 2015, when Library Director Thomas J. Putnam, a professional archivist and employee of the National Archives, resigned in the wake of what appeared to be a power struggle with Heather Campion, a bank executive and friend of the Kennedy family who had recently taken charge of the Kennedy Library Foundation. The dust-up apparently stemmed in part from Campion's aggressive management style, which drove a large number of employees from their jobs, some of whom worked in the library but were funded by the foundation. There were other issues as well, mostly dealing with the foundation's strategic planning for the hundredth anniversary of President Kennedy's birthday in 2017. The details are sketchy at this point, but the dispute apparently centered on the foundation's desire to greatly expand the outreach and educational programs and, in the process, take charge of functions – including library admissions, reporting relationships, records management, and allocation of space – that typically belong to archivists and other library professionals. Once again, historians were up in arms. Kennedy scholars, who had grown hopeful under Putnam's leadership, now worried, as they had so often in the past, that the Kennedys were trying to usurp or "impede the independence, operations, and mission" of library professionals, with results that could only damage the "historical understanding" they seek to promote. See Jim O'Sullivan, "JFK Library Sees Exodus as New CEO, Strategy Draw

Complaints," *Boston Globe*, August 5, 2015, www.bostonglobe.com/metro/
2015/08/05/kennedy-library-sees-mass-exodus-new-and-veteran-employees/
FL43CXMIIGU397FzS1zwJL/story.html; "Saving the JFK Library for
Future Generations," *Boston Globe*, September 17, 2015, www.bostonglobe
.com/opinion/editorials/2015/09/17/saving-jfk-library-for-new-generation/
ohYstZxAcJ7MOtjga79RxL/story.html; Joan Vennochi, "Less Camelot,
More Truth Needed at JFK Library," *Boston Globe*, September 20, 2015,
www.bostonglobe.com/opinion/editorials/2015/09/19/more-truth-less-
myth-needed-kennedy-library/UnziUnU5U4al2KijoNOfoO/story.html; and
O'Sullivan, "Federal Overseers Postpone Search for Permanent JFK Library
Director," *Boston Globe*, September 24, 2015, www.bostonglobe.com/
metro/2015/09/24/jfk-library-unrest-delays-new-director/rTNICVMdw
Y5y4kngJqCDiL/story.html. For the letter to the editor on the library crisis
signed by scholars Ellen Fitzpatrick, Robert Dallek, Thurston Clarke, David
J. Garrow, Diane McWhorter, Philip Muehlenbeck, Timothy Naftali, and
David Nasaw, see *Boston Globe*, September 19, 2015, www.bostonglobe
.com/opinion/letters/2015/09/18/reports-conflict-jfk-library-raise-concerns-
historians-scholars/Iplr9tTuk48izMZTMLyVkJ/story.html. It's worth noting
that Heather Campion subsequently resigned her position as head of the
Library Foundation.

21 Schlesinger, *Journals*, 53–220; Sorensen, *Counselor*; Schlesinger, *The Letters
of Arthur Schlesinger, Jr.*, ed. Andrew Schlesinger and Stephen Schlesinger
(New York: Random House, 2013); Martin W. Sandler, ed., *The Letters of
John F. Kennedy* (New York: Bloomsbury Press, 2013). See also Stephen
F. Knott, "What Might Have Been," *Review of Politics* 76, no. 1 (Fall
2014): 661–70; and Thurston Clarke, "Why We Keep Writing about JFK,"
Washington Post, October 24, 2013, www.washingtonpost.com/opinions/
why-we-keep-writing-about-jfk/2013/10/24/de308c56-3765-11e3-ae46-
e4248e75c8ea_story.html.

22 See, for example, Warren Mass, "50th Anniversary of JFK Assassination
Spawns Attacks on Dallas 'Right-Wingers,'" *New American*, November 11,
2013, www.thenewamerican.com/usnews/item/16873-50th-anniversary-of-
jfk-assassinatiojn-spawns-attacks-on-dallas-right-wingers.

23 Lisa Fabrizio, "Enough about JFK!," *American Spectator*, November 27, 2013,
http://spectator.org/articles/56878/enough-about-jfk. See also Mark Moyar,
"JFK and the Seeds of Disaster in Vietnam," *Wall Street Journal*, November
1, 2013, A15; Justin Raimondo, "JFK, Warmonger," *American Conservative*, November 15, 2013, www.theamericanconservative.com/articles/jfk-
warmonger/; and Humberto Fontova, "The Cuban Missile Crisis: Kennedy's
'Victory'?," *FrontPage Magazine*, October 24, 2013, www.frontpagemag
.com/2013/humberto-fontova/the-cuban-missile-crisis-kennedys-victory/.

24 Patrick J. Buchanan, "Nixon and Kennedy: The Myths and Reality," *Taki's
Magazine*, November 19, 2013, http://takimag.com/article/nixon_and_
kennedy_the_myths_and_reality/.

25 Ira Stoll, *JFK, Conservative* (Boston: Houghton Mifflin Harcourt, 2013). See
also Stoll, "JFK, Conservative: It's Time to Re-Evaluate the Legacy of Our
35th President," *American Spectator*, October 2013, 22–24.

26 Robert Mason, "Kennedy and the Conservatives," in Hoberek, *Cambridge Companion to John F. Kennedy*, 225–39.

27 L. Gordon Crovitz, "Information Age: Exposing the Myth of JFK's Policies," *Wall Street Journal*, November 18, 2013, A15; Jeff Jacoby, "Would Democrats Embrace JFK Now?," *Boston Globe*, October 20, 2013, K7; George F. Will, "The JFK We Had and the Memory That Lives," *Human Events*, November 21, 2013, www.humanevents.com/2013/11/21/the-jfk-we-had-and-the-memory-that-lives; and Ronald Radosh, "The Right Stuff: Where Was John F. Kennedy on the Ideological Spectrum?," *Weekly Standard*, November 25, 2013, www.weeklystandard.com/article/right-stuff/767133. See also William Murchison, "How Times Have Changed Since 1963!," *American Spectator*, November 19, 2013, http://spectator.org/print/56655; Donald Lambro, "Rejecting Kennedy's Economic Legacy," *Washington Times*, November 21, 2013, www.washingtontimes.com/news/2013/nov/21/lambro-rejecting-kennedys-economic-legacy/?page=all; and Fred Barnes, "The Man and the Myth: Why Prudent Politicians Embrace the JFK Legacy," December 2, 2013, *Weekly Standard*, www.weeklystandard.com/article/man-and-myth/768044.

28 Rob Portman, "Leadership, JFK-Style, Means Doing the Hard Things," *Cleveland.com*, November 22, 2013, www.cleveland.com/opinion/index.ssf/2013/11/leadership_means_doing_the_har.html; and Ted Cruz, "Remembering JFK," *National Review*, November 22, 2013, www.nationalreview.com/article/364605/remembering-jfk-ted-cruz.

29 Sean Wilentz, "Another Master of the Senate," *New York Times*, November 21, 2003, A31; Greenberg, "JFK, Unapologetic Liberal: His Underrated Career as Ideological Warrior," *New Republic*, November 25, 2013, 8–9; Richard Reeves, "What John F. Kennedy Was – and Wasn't," *Los Angeles Times*, November 21, 2013, http://articles.latimes.com/2013/nov/21/opinion/la-oe-reeves-kennedy-legacy-20131121; and E. J. Dionne, Jr., "What We Lost 50 Years Ago with JFK," *Washington Post*, November 20, 2013, www.washingtonpost.com/opinions/ej-dionne-what-we-lost-50-years-ago-with-jfk/2013/11/20/efb7ad30-5220-11e3-9fe0-fd2ca728e67c_story.html. See also Paul Rosenberg, "Stop Calling JFK Conservative: The Right's Favorite New Lie Is Filled with Historical Flaws," *Salon*, November 3, 2013, www.salon.com/2013/11/03/stop_calling_jfk_conservative_the_rights_favorite_new_lie_is_filled_with_historical_flaws/; Nicholas Burns, "JFK's Resounding Impact," *Boston Globe*, November 21, 2013, A17; "Ask What You Can Do ...," *San Francisco Chronicle*, November 22, 2013, A16; Bernard von Bothmer, "The Right's JFK Myth: Now They Claim He Was Conservative," *Salon*, November 22, 2013, www.salon.com/2013/11/22/the_rights_jfk_myth_now_they_claim_he_was_conservative/; Shauna Shames and Pamela O'Leary, "JFK, a Pioneer in the Women's Movement," *Los Angeles Times*, November 22, 2013, www.latimes.com/opinion/commentary/la-oe-shames-kennedy-women-20131122,0,6922807.story; and Terry O'Neill, "JFK's Contribution to Women's Rights – and What He Might Want Us to Do Next," *Huffington Post*, April 26, 2014, www.huffingtonpost.com/terry-oneill/jfks-contribution-to-wome_b_4321030.html.

30 In addition to sources cited in the previous note, see those cited in the following note.

31 See Brinkley, *John F. Kennedy*; Dallek, *Unfinished Life*; O'Brien, *John F. Kennedy: A Biography* (New York: Thomas Dunne Books/St. Martin's Press, 2005); Dallek, *John F. Kennedy*; Dallek, *Camelot's Court: Inside the Kennedy White House* (New York: Harper, 2013); Sabato, *Kennedy Half Century*; Clarke, *JFK's Last Hundred Days*; and Sachs, *To Move the World: JFK's Quest for Peace* (New York: Random House, 2013). See also Dallek, "Kennedy's Legacy of Inspiration," *New York Times*, November 21, 2013, www.nytimes.com/2013/11/22/opinion/kennedys-legacy-of-inspiration .html?_r=0.

32 Bradford, *America's Queen*; Spoto, *Jacqueline Bouvier Kennedy Onassis*; Smith, *Grace and Power*; Leaming, *Jacqueline Bouvier Kennedy Onassis*; Hill, *Mrs. Kennedy and Me*, with Lisa McCubbin (New York: Simon & Schuster, 2013); Perry, *Rose Kennedy: The Life and Times of a Political Matriarch* (New York: Norton, 2012); Nasaw, *The Patriarch: The Remarkable Life and Turbulent Times of Joseph P. Kennedy* (New York: Penguin, 2012); and Caroline Kennedy, *Rose Kennedy's Family Album: From the Fitzgerald Kennedy Private Collection, 1878–1946* (New York: Grand Central Publishing, 2013). See also Peter Baker, "A Camelot Nostalgia Tour for Those Who Remember, and Those Who Don't," *New York Times*, September 1, 2013, A14.

33 See, for example, Mulvaney and De Angelis, *Dear Mrs. Kennedy*; Russo and Moses, *Where Were You*; and Dean R. Owen, *November 22, 1963: Reflections on the Life, Assassination, and Legacy of John F. Kennedy* (New York: Skyhorse Publishing, 2013). For excellent and comprehensive reviews of the scholarly literature on all subjects, see the relevant essays in Selverstone, *Companion to John F. Kennedy*; and Campbell Craig, "Kennedy's International Legacy, Fifty Years On," *International Affairs* 89, no. 6 (November 2013): 1367–78. See also Blight, Lang, and Welch, *Vietnam If Kennedy Had Lived*; John T. Shaw, *JFK in the Senate: Pathway to the Presidency* (New York: Palgrave Macmillan, 2013); Philip E. Muehlenbeck, *Betting on the Africans: John F. Kennedy's Courting of African Nationalist Leaders* (New York: Oxford University Press, 2012); Robert B. Rakove, *Kennedy, Johnson, and the Nonaligned World* (New York: Cambridge University Press, 2012); and Ryan M. Irwin, *Gordian Knot: Apartheid and the Unmaking of the Liberal World Order* (Oxford: Oxford University Press, 2012).

34 Alford, *Once upon a Secret*; Matthews, *Jack Kennedy: Elusive Hero* (New York: Simon & Schuster, 2012); Bill O'Reilly and Martin Dugard, *Killing Kennedy: The End of Camelot* (New York: Henry Holt, 2012); Greenfield, *If Kennedy Lived: The First and Second Terms of President John F. Kennedy: An Alternate History* (New York: Putnam, 2013); Neil Steinberg, *Hatless Jack: The President, the Fedora, and the History of an American Style* (New York: Plume, 2004); and James W. Graham, *Victura: The Kennedys, a Sailboat, and the Sea* (Lebanon, NH: ForeEdge, 2014).

35   James Carroll, "JFK Magazines Flood Newsstands," November 11, 2013,
     http://blogs.courier-journal.com/politics/2013/11/11/jfk-magazines-flood-
     news-stands/.

36   Ling, *Kennedy*, 257–59. In yet another indication of the country's enduring
     fascination with the Kennedy story, Hulu aired a 2016 miniseries based on
     King's novel – a run-up, no doubt, to the one-hundredth anniversary of the
     president's birth.

37   Vincent P. Bzdek, "Jacqueline Kennedy Book, 'Historic Conversations,'
     Reveals Candid First Lady," *Washington Post*, September 14, 2011, www
     .washingtonpost.com/therootdc/jacqueline-kennedy-book-historic-
     conversations-reveals-candid-first-lady/2011/09/14/gIQARTGFTK_story
     .html; Baker, "Camelot Nostalgia Tour"; Mark Feeney, "Framed in Darkness,
     and Questions beyond Answers," *Boston Globe*, November 21, 2013, A1;
     and Lynn Elber, "Film Recounts Outpouring of Grief to JFK's Widow,"
     Sanford Herald, November 16, 2013, www.sanfordherald.com/features/
     film-recounts-outpouring-of-grief-to-jfk-s-widow/article_64c661ab-5655-
     5f8d-8ded-8b52df99f24a.html.

38   David Abel, "A Display of Grief," *Boston Globe*, November 19, 2013, B1.

39   Adam Clymer, "Textbooks Reassess Kennedy, Putting Camelot Under Siege,"
     New York Times, November 11, 2013, 1; and Anthony J. Gaughan, "Bonus
     Column: Contrasts Continue to Feed Kennedy Fascination," *Des Moines
     Register*, November 22, 2013, http://pqasb.pqarchiver.com/desmoinesregister/
     doc/1460474404.htm/?FMT=FT&FMTS=ABS:FT&type=current
     &date=Nov+22%2C+2013 &author=Gaughan%2. See also Costas
     Panagopoulos, "Ex-Presidential Approval: Retrospective Evaluations of
     Presidential Performance," *Presidential Studies Quarterly* 42, no. 4 (December
     2012): 719–29, esp. 719–20.

40   Baker, "Camelot Nostalgia Tour"; Richard Reeves, "How to Rate a
     President," *Los Angeles Times*, November 21, 2013, A17; Barnes, "Man and
     the Myth"; and Peter Grier, "Why Is John F. Kennedy Still So Popular?,"
     Christian Science Monitor, November 21, 2013, www.csmonitor.com/USA/
     Politics/Decoder/2013/1121/Why-is-John-F.-Kennedy-still-so-popular-video.
     Readers who want an excellent overview of Kennedy's standing in public
     opinion cannot do better than Sabato, *Kennedy Half Century*, 406–18.

41   Daum, *Kennedy in Berlin*, especially 199–214.

42   "UK to Commemorate Murdered Kennedy," *PA News Feed*, November 17, 2013,
     www.standard.co.uk/panensfeeds/uk-to-commemorate-murdered-Kennedy-
     8945203.html; and "John F. Kennedy Remembered at Runnymede
     Memorial," *BBC News*, November 22, 1963, www.bbc.com/news/uk-
     engand-surrey-25049235.

43   "Exposition JFK 1963–2013," at http://expositionjfk-paris2013.com/en/
     content/6-exhbition and "Remembering John F. Kennedy," US Consulate
     General, Strasbourg, Blog, December 9, 2013, https://cyberambassadors
     blog.wordpress.com/2013/12/09/remembering-john-f-kennedy/. See also,
     "JFK Remembrance Day," US Embassy, France, undated, http://france
     .usembassy.gov/jfkremembranceday.html.

44 Adrian Bridge, "Berlin Remembers JFK," June 26, 2013, www.telegraph
    .co.uk/travel/news/Berlin-remembers-JFK/.

45 Peter Murtagh, "JFK Visit to Ireland Commemorated," *Irish Times*, June
    23, 2013, www.irishtimes.com/news/jfk-visit-to-ireland-commemorated-1
    .1439728. On Japanese remembrance of the late president, see the Associated
    Press story, "Japan Admiringly Remembers JFK 50 years later," *Japan Times*,
    November 22, 2013, www.japantimes.co.jp/news/2013/11/22/national/
    japan-admiringly-remembers-jfk-50-years-later/#.V)GkIvGi6ro.

46 Reston, "What Was Killed."

47 White, *Kennedy*, 136–38.

48 Johnson quoted in "Meaning of the Life and Death," *Current*, 8.

49 See Rorabaugh, *Kennedy*, xix–xxi for a brief but good discussion of the peri-
    odization issue and his own view of the Kennedy years as a transitional era.

50 For a history of nostalgia, see Jean Starobinski, "The Idea of Nostalgia,"
    Diogenes 54 (1966): 81–103; Fred Davis, *Yearning for Yesterday: A Sociology
    of Nostalgia* (New York: Free Press, 1979); and Clay Routledge, "The
    Rehabilitation of an Old Emotion: A New Science of Nostalgia," *Scientific
    American*, July 10, 2013, http://blogs.scientificamerican.com/mind-guest-
    blog/the-rehabilitation-of-an-old-emotion-a-new-science-of-nostalgia/. For
    some interesting approaches to the subject, see Svetlana Boym, *The Future
    of Nostalgia* (New York: Basic Books, 2001); Michael Pickering and Emily
    Keightley, "The Modalities of Nostalgia," *Current Sociology* 54 (November
    2006): 919–41; Susan J. Matt, *Homesickness: An American History*
    (New York: Oxford University Press, 2011); and Gary Cross, *Consumed
    Nostalgia: Memory in the Age of Fast Capitalism* (New York: Columbia
    University Press, 2015).

51 Davis, *Yearning for Yesterday*, 105–108.

52 Harrington, "View from the Left."

53 Boeth, "JFK: Visions and Revisions," and *Los Angeles Times*, "A Man Who
    Stirred Them."

54 "Ten Years Later," *New York Times*.

55 Dallek quoted in Doyle McManus, "JFK, a Presidency on a Pedestal," *Los
    Angeles Times*, November 17, 2013, www.latimes.com/opinion/commentary/
    la-oe-mcmanus-column-legacy-20131117.0.7161721.

56 Neal, *National Trauma*, 120.

Selected Bibliography

Although this bibliography is not exhaustive, it should offer the reader a good sense of the texts that have informed the narrative and theoretical framework of this book. In addition to many of the scholarly works I consulted, it lists newspapers and magazines, published primary sources, and unpublished sources such as the manuscripts and oral histories available at the John F. Kennedy Presidential Library and the National Archives. Individual files within the Presidential Papers of John F. Kennedy, as well as First Lady Jacqueline Kennedy's personal papers, are not listed here. These include the staff files of August Heckscher, Dean F. Markham, Timothy Reardon, and Pierre E. G. Salinger, among others, in the case of the president's papers; and Mary Gallagher, Pamela Turnure, and Nancy Tuckerman, in the case of the first lady's papers. References to these and other files, such as the White House Office Files or Social Files, can be found within the notes.

Archival and Manuscript Collections

National Archives of the United States

Historical Studies Division, Historical Office, Bureau of Public Affairs, Department of State. *The Funeral of President Kennedy and United States Government Actions, November 22–25, 1963*. Research Project no. 662, March 1967, DOS Record Number 1191001710094, Record Series Lot 71D411, S/S Files, National Archives II, College Park, MD.

John F. Kennedy Presidential Library

McGeorge Bundy Personal Papers
Chet Huntley Personal Papers
Papers of John F. Kennedy, Presidential Papers
Robert F. Kennedy Papers, Senate Papers, Series: Correspondence: Personal File, 1964–1968

Jacqueline Bouvier Kennedy Onassis Personal Papers
Evelyn Lincoln Personal Papers
David F. Powers Personal Papers
Arthur M. Schlesinger Jr. Personal Papers
R. Sargent Shriver Personal Papers
William Walton Personal Papers
Theodore H. White Personal Papers

Interviews from the John F. Kennedy Presidential Library
Oral History Collection

Derek C. Bok, interview by Vicki Daitch, November 19, 2002
Christine Camp, interview by Ann M. Campbell, November 24, 1969
Thomas P. Costin, interview by William J. Hartigan, April 5, 1976
William Voss Elder III, interview by Ronald J. Grele, December 15, 1965
Rowland Evans Jr., interview by Roberta W. Green, July 30, 1970
Paul B. Fay Jr., interview by James A. Oesterle, November 9, 1970
Barbara Gamarekian, interview by Diane T. Michaelis, June 10, 1964
August Heckscher, interview by Wolf Von Eckhardt, New York, December 10, 1965
Letitia Baldrige Hollensteiner, interview by Mrs. Wayne Fredericks, April 24, 1964
Claudia "Lady Bird" Johnson, Oral History Interview XLIII by Harry Middleton, November 23, 1996, Internet copy of original in the Lyndon Baines Johnson Presidential Library
Laura Bergquist Knebel, interview by Nelson Aldrich, December 8, 1965
Evelyn N. Lincoln, interview by Larry Hackman, William Moss, Sylvie Turner, and William Johnson, July 18, 1974
Frank Mankiewicz, interview by Larry J. Hackman, October 2, 1969
Godfrey McHugh, interview by Sheldon Stern, May 19, 1998
Theodore J. Musho, interview by Vicki Daitch, November 12, 2002
Lawrence F. O'Brien, Oral History Interview II by Michael L. Gillette, October 29, 1985, Internet copy of original in the Lyndon Baines Johnson Presidential Library
I. M. Pei, interview by Vicki Daitch, March 18, 1966
Pierre E. G. Salinger, interview by Theodore H. White, August 10, 1965
Walter Sheridan, interview by Roberta W. Green, June 12, 1970
Charles Spaulding, interview by Larry J. Hackman, March 22, 1969
John Stewart, Dan Fenn, William Moss, and Larry Hackman, interview by Vicki Daitch, April 16 and 17, 2004
Stanley Tretick, interview by Diana Michaelis, September 15, 1964
Nancy Tuckerman and Pamela Turnure, interview by Mrs. Wayne Fredericks, 1964
William Walton, interview by Meghan Floyd Desnoyers, March 30, 1993
John C. Warnecke and Robert Hart, interview by Tom Page, December 4, 1964
J. B. West, interview by Nancy Tuckerman and Pamela Turnure, 1967
Elmer Young and James Nelson, interview by Pamela Turnure, June 11, 1964

Newspapers and Periodicals

America
American Conservative
American Heritage
American Spectator
Atlanta Constitution
Atlantic
Boston Globe
Chicago Tribune
Christian Century
Christian Science Monitor
Cincinnati Enquirer
Cleveland Plain Dealer
Current
Dallas Morning News
Esquire
Life
Look
Los Angeles Times
Nation
New American
New Republic
Newsweek
New York Post
New York Times
People
Publishers Weekly
Redbook
San Francisco Chronicle
Saturday Evening Post
Saturday Review
Scientific American
Time
USA Today Magazine
US News & World Report
Wall Street Journal
Washington Post
Washington Post, Times Herald
Weekly Standard
Vanity Fair

Articles and Books

Abbott, James A., and Elaine M. Rice. *Designing Camelot: The Kennedy White House Restoration*. New York: Van Nostrand Reinhold, 1998.
Adler, Bill, ed. *The Complete Kennedy Wit*. New York: Citadel Press, 1967.

ed. *John F. Kennedy and the Young People of America*. New York: McKay, 1965.

ed. *The Kennedy Wit*. New York: Gramercy Publishing, 1964.

comp. *Kids' Letters to President Kennedy*. New York: Morrow, 1962.

ed. *More Kennedy Wit*. New York: Citadel Press, 1965.

ed. *Presidential Wit*. New York: Third Press, 1966.

Adler, Robert M. "The Public Controversy over the Kennedy Memorabilia Project." In *Archives, Documentation, and Institutions of Social Memory: Essays from the Sawyer Seminar*, edited by Francis X. Blouin Jr. and William G. Rosenberg, 225–36. Ann Arbor: University of Michigan Press, 2009.

Aldrich, Nelson W., Jr. "Saint Jacqueline and the Celebritariat." *Horizon* 21, no. 8 (August 1978): 23–33.

Alexander, Jeffrey C. "Toward a Theory of Cultural Trauma." In Alexander et al., *Cultural Trauma*, 1–30.

Alexander, Jeffrey C., Ron Eyerman, Bernhard Giesen, Neil J. Smelser, and Piotr Sztompka. *Cultural Trauma and Collective Identity*. Berkeley: University of California Press, 2004.

Alford, Mimi. *Once upon a Secret: My Affair with President John F. Kennedy and Its Aftermath*. New York: Random House, 2013.

Andersen, Christopher. *Jack and Jackie: Portrait of an American Marriage*. New York: Avon Books, 1997.

Anthony, Carl Sferrazza. *As We Remember Her: Jacqueline Kennedy Onassis in the Words of Her Family and Friends*. New York: HarperCollins, 2003.

Ariès, Philippe. *Western Attitudes toward Death from the Middle Ages to the Present*. Translated by Patricia M. Ranum. London: Marion Boyars, 1994.

Attwood, William. "Twenty Years after Dallas." *Virginia Quarterly Review* 59, no. 4 (Autumn 1983): 557–63.

Baldrige, Letitia. *In the Kennedy Style: Magical Evenings in the Kennedy White House*. New York: Doubleday, 1998.

Of Diamonds and Diplomats: An Autobiography of a Happy Life. New York: Houghton Mifflin/Ballantine Books, 1969.

Barber, James D. "Peer Group Discussion and Recovery from the Kennedy Assassination." In Greenberg and Parker, *Kennedy Assassination*, 112–29.

Barnes, Clare, Jr. *John F. Kennedy: Scrimshaw Collector*. Boston: Little, Brown, 1964.

Bartlett, Apple Parish, and Susan Bartlett Crater. *Sister: The Life of Legendary American Interior Decorator, Mrs. Henry Parish II*. New York: St. Martin's Press, 2000.

Bellah, Robert N. "Civil Religion in America." In *Beyond Belief: Essays on Religion in a Post-Traditionalist World*, 168–89. Berkeley: University of California Press, 1991.

Bernstein, Irving. *Promises Kept: John F. Kennedy's New Frontier*. New York: Oxford University Press, 1991.

Berry, Joseph P., Jr. *John F. Kennedy and the Media: The First Television President*. Latham, MD: University Press of America, 1987.

Berry, Wendell, and Ben Shahn. *November Twenty Six Nineteen Hundred Sixty Three*. New York: George Braziller, 1964.

Berthold, Carol Ann. "The Image and Character of President John F. Kennedy: A Rhetorical-Critical Approach." PhD diss., Northwestern University, 1975.

Bial, Henry, ed. *The Performance Studies Reader*. 2nd ed. New York: Routledge, 2007.

Binkiewicz, Donna M. "Culture from Camelot: The Origins and Goals of Arts Policy in the Kennedy Administration." *UCLA Historical Journal* 16 (1996): 103–30.

Bishop, Jim. *The Day Kennedy Was Shot*. New York: Funk & Wagnalls, 1968.

Blair, Joan, and Clay Blair Jr. *The Search for JFK*. New York: Berkley Medallion Books, 1976.

Blight, James G., Janet M. Lang, and David A Welch. *Vietnam If Kennedy Had Lived: Virtual JFK*. Lanham, MD: Rowman & Littlefield, 2009.

Bloncourt, Pauline. *An Old and a Young Leader: Winston Churchill and John Kennedy*. London: Faber, 1970.

Bowles, Hamish, Arthur M. Schlesinger Jr., and Rachel Lambert Mellon. *Jacqueline Kennedy: The White House Years; Selections from the John F. Kennedy Library and Museum*. New York: Bulfinch Press/Little, Brown, 2001.

Boym, Svetlana. *The Future of Nostalgia*. New York: Basic Books, 2001.

Bradford, Sarah. *America's Queen: The Life of Jacqueline Kennedy Onassis*. New York: Penguin, 2001.

Bradlee, Ben. *A Good Life: Newspapering and Other Adventures*. New York: Simon & Schuster, 1996.

Bradlee, Benjamin C. *Conversations with Kennedy*. New York: W. W. Norton, 1984.

Bradley, Richard. *American Political Mythology from Kennedy to Nixon*. New York: Peter Lang, 2000.

Brauer, Carl M. "John F. Kennedy Presidential Library and Museum." *Public Historian* 28, no. 3 (Summer 2006): 194–97.

Brennan, John F. *The Evolution of Everyman: Ancestral Lineage of John F. Kennedy*. Dundalk, Ireland: Dundalgan Press, 1968.

Brinkley, Alan. *John F. Kennedy*. New York: Times Books/Henry Holt, 2012.

"Kennedy in Retrospect." *New England Journal of Social Studies Bulletin* 41, no. 2 (Winter 1983–84): 7–15.

Brody, Richard. "Star Power: John F. Kennedy Welcomed Documentary Cameras, which Loved Him Back." *The New Yorker*, May 9, 2016, 6.

Brown, Roger, and James Kulik. "Flashbulb Memories." In *Memory Observed: Remembering in Natural Contexts*, edited by Ulric Neisser, 23–40. San Francisco: W. H. Freeman, 1982.

Brown, Thomas. *JFK: History of an Image*. Bloomington: Indiana University Press, 1988.

Bruno, Jerry, and Jeff Greenfield. *The Advance Man: An Offbeat Look at What Really Happens in Political Campaigns*. New York: Morrow, 1971.

Bryant, Traphes. *Dog Days at the White House: The Outrageous Memoirs of the Presidential Kennel Keeper*. With Frances Spatz Leighton. New York: Macmillan, 1975.

Butler, Thomas, ed. *Memory: History, Culture, and the Mind*. New York: Basil Blackwell, 1989.

Cameron, Elizabeth. "The John F. Kennedy Library Exhibit." *Wilson Library Bulletin* 39, no. 1 (September 1964): 63–65.

Cannell, Michael. *I. M. Pei: Mandarin of Modernism*. New York: Carol Southern Books, 1995.

Caro, Robert A. *The Passage of Power: The Years of Lyndon Johnson*. New York: Alfred A. Knopf, 2012.

Cassini, Oleg. *In My Own Fashion: An Autobiography*. New York: Simon & Schuster, 1987.

  A Thousand Days of Magic: Dressing Jacqueline Kennedy for the White House. New York: Rizzoli International Publications, 1995.

A Catalogue of Old, Used, Rare and Out-of-Print Books on John F. Kennedy. Washington, DC: Q. M. Dabney, 1975.

Catsam, Derek C. "Civil Rights." In Selverstone, *Companion to John F. Kennedy*, 540–57.

Cherry, Conrad, ed. *God's New Israel: Religious Interpretations of American Destiny*. Rev. ed. Chapel Hill: University of North Carolina Press, 1998.

Chidester, David, and Edward T. Linenthal, eds. *American Sacred Space*. Bloomington: Indiana University Press, 1995.

Christopherson, Edmund. *"Westward I Go Free": The Story of J. F. K. in Montana*. Missoula, MT: Earthquake Press, 1964.

Clarke, Thurston. *JFK's Last Hundred Days: The Transformation of a Man and the Emergence of a Great President*. New York: Penguin, 2013.

Coleman, Penny. *Corpses, Coffins, and Crypts: A History of Burial*. New York: Henry Holt, 1997.

Collier, Peter, and David Horowitz. *The Kennedys: An American Drama*. San Francisco: Encounter Books, 2002.

Comstock, Jim. *Pa and Ma and Mister Kennedy*. Richwood, WV: Appalachian Press, 1965.

Confino, Alon. "Collective Memory and Cultural History: Problems of Method." *American Historical Review* 102, no. 5 (December 1997): 1386–403.

Connerton, Paul. *How Societies Remember*. New York: Cambridge University Press, 1989.

Corry, John. *The Manchester Affair*. New York: G. P. Putnam's Sons, 1967.

Costigliola, Frank C. "'Like Children in the Darkness': European Reaction to the Assassination of John F. Kennedy." *Journal of Popular Culture* 20, no. 3 (Winter 1986): 115–24.

Cournos, John. *The Lost Leader*. New York: Twayne, 1964.

Cox, Richard J. "America's Pyramids: Presidents and Their Libraries." *Government Information Quarterly* 19 (2002): 45–75.

Craig, Campbell. "Kennedy's International Legacy, Fifty Years On." *International Affairs* 89, no. 6 (November 2013): 1367–78.

Crane, Diana. *Fashion and Its Social Agendas: Class, Gender, and Identity in Clothing*. Chicago: University of Chicago Press, 2000.

Cross, Gary. *Consumed Nostalgia: Memory in the Age of Fast Capitalism*. New York: Columbia University Press, 2015.

Crown, James Tracy. *The Kennedy Literature: A Bibliographical Essay on John F. Kennedy*. New York: New York University Press, 1968.

Cubitt, Geoffrey. *History and Memory*. Manchester, UK: Manchester University Press, 2007.

Dallek, Robert. *Camelot's Court: Inside the Kennedy White House*. New York: Harper, 2013.

    Flawed Giant: Lyndon Johnson and His Times, 1961–1973. New York: Oxford University Press, 1998.

    John F. Kennedy. New York: Oxford University Press, 2011.

    An Unfinished Life: John F. Kennedy, 1917–1963. New York: Back Bay Books, 2004.

Daum, Andreas W. *Kennedy in Berlin*. Translated by Dona Geyer. New York: Cambridge University Press, 2008.

    "Berlin." In Selverstone, *Companion to John F. Kennedy*, 209–27.

Davies, Douglas J. *Death, Ritual, and Belief: The Rhetoric of Funerary Rites*. 2nd ed. New York: Continuum, 2002.

Davis, Fred. *Yearning for Yesterday: A Sociology of Nostalgia*. New York: Free Press, 1979.

Davis, John H. *The Bouviers: Portrait of an American Family*. New York: Farrar, Straus & Giroux, 1969.

    Jacqueline Bouvier: An Intimate Memoir. New York: John Wiley & Sons, 1996.

Dobbins, Jim. *Dobbins' Diary of the New Frontier*. Boston: Humphries, 1964.

Donaldson, Gary A. *The First Modern Campaign: Kennedy, Nixon, and the Election of 1960*. New York: Rowman & Littlefield, 2007.

Durkheim, Emile. *The Elementary Forms of Religious Life*. Translated by K. E. Fields. New York: Free Press, 1995.

Eckert, Astrid M. *Institutions of Public Memory: The Legacies of German and American Politicians*. Washington, DC: German Historical Institute, 2007.

Erskine, Hazel Gaudet. "The Polls: Kennedy as President." *Public Opinion Quarterly* 28, no. 2 (Summer 1964): 334–42.

Exner, Judith. *My Story*. With Ovid Demaris. New York: Grove, 1977.

Fagin, Stephen. *Assassination and Commemoration: JFK, Dallas, and The Sixth Floor Museum at Dealey Plaza*. Norman: University of Oklahoma Press, 2013.

Fairlie, Henry. *The Kennedy Promise: The Politics of Expectation*. Garden City, NY: Doubleday, 1973.

Fanta, J. Julius. *Sailing with President Kennedy: The White House Yachtsman*. New York: Sea Lore, 1968.

Fay, Paul B., Jr. *The Pleasure of His Company*. New York: Harper & Row, 1966.

Fedosiuk, Polly Curren. *To Light a Torch: The Story of John F. Kennedy*. New York: Guild Press, 1966.

Fenn, Dan H., Jr. "Launching the John F. Kennedy Library." *American Archivist* 42, no. 4 (October 1979): 429–42.

Field, Douglas, "JFK and the Civil Rights Movement." In Hoberek, *The Cambridge Companion to John F. Kennedy*, 75–88.

Fine, William M., ed. *That Day with God*. New York: McGraw-Hill, 1965.

Fischer-Lichte, Erika. "Introduction: Theatricality: A Key Concept in Theatre and Cultural Studies." *Theatre Research International* 20, no. 2 (Summer 1995): 85–89.

    The Semiotics of Theater. Translated by Jeremy Gaines and Doris L. Jones. Bloomington: Indiana University Press, 1992.

Fitzpatrick, Ellen. *Letters to Jackie: Condolences from a Grieving Nation*. New York: HarperCollins, 2010.

Fleming, Dan B., Jr. *Ask What You Can Do for Your Country: The Memory and Legacy of John F. Kennedy*. Clearwater, FL: Vandamere Press, 2002.

Fox, Richard Wightman. *Lincoln's Body: A Cultural History*. New York: W. W. Norton, 2015.

Fries, Chuck, and Irv Wilson. *"We'll Never Be Young Again": Remembering the Last Days of John F. Kennedy*. With Spencer Green. Beverly Hills, CA: Tallfellow Press, 2003.

Frisbee, Lucy Post. *John F. Kennedy: Young Statesman*. Indianapolis: Bobbs-Merrill, 1964.

Gallagher, Mary Barelli. *My Life with Jacqueline Kennedy*. New York: Paperback Library, 1970.

Galloway, John, ed. *The Quotable Mr. Kennedy*. New York: Abelard-Schuman, 1962.

Gardner, Gerald C., ed. *The Shining Moments: The Words and Moods of John F. Kennedy*. New York: Pocket Books, 1964.

Garlick, Harry. *The Final Curtain: State Funerals and the Theatre of Power*. Amsterdam: Rodopi B.V., 1999.

Geer, Candy. *Six White Horses: An Illustrated Poem about John-John*. Ann Arbor, MI.: M & W Quill, 1964.

George, Alice L. *The Assassination of John F. Kennedy: Political Trauma and American Memory*. New York: Routledge, 2013.

Gienow-Hecht, Jessica C. E. "Nation Branding." In *Explaining the History of American Foreign Relations*, 3rd ed., edited by Frank Costigliola and Michael J. Hogan, 232–44. New York: Cambridge University Press, 2016.

    "'The World Is Ready to Listen': Symphony Orchestras and the Global Performance of America." *Diplomatic History* 36, no. 1 (January 2012): 17–28.

Giglio, James N., comp. *John F. Kennedy: A Bibliography*. Westport, CT: Greenwood Press, 1995.

    "John F. Kennedy as Domestic Leader: A Perspective on the Literature." In White, *Kennedy: The New Frontier Revisited*, 222–55.

    "The Medical Afflictions of President John F. Kennedy." *White House Studies* 6, no. 4 (2006): 343–58.

    "Past Frustrations and New Opportunities: Researching the Kennedy Presidency at the Kennedy Library." *Presidential Studies Quarterly* 22, no. 2 (Spring 1992): 371–79.

    The Presidency of John F. Kennedy. Lawrence: University Press of Kansas, 1991.

Giglio, James N., and Stephen G. Rabe. *Debating the Kennedy Presidency*. New York: Rowman & Littlefield, 2003.

Gillis, John R., ed. *Commemorations: The Politics of National Identity*. Princeton: Princeton University Press, 1996.

Gillon, Steven M. *The Kennedy Assassination 24 Hours After: Lyndon B. Johnson's Pivotal First Day as President*. New York: Basic Books, 2009.

Glass, Loren. "The Kennedy Legacy: From Hagiography to Expose and Back Again." In Hoberek, *Cambridge Companion to John F. Kennedy*, 240–49.

Glikes, Erwin A., and Paul Schwaber, eds. *Of Poetry and Power: Poems Occasioned by the Presidency and by the Death of John. F. Kennedy*. New York: Basic Books, 1964.

Goffman, Erving. *The Presentation of Self in Everyday Life*. London: Penguin, 1990.

Goldman, Alex J. *John Fitzgerald Kennedy: The World Remembers*. New York: Fleet Press, 1968.

⸻ ed. *The Quotable Kennedy*. New York: Citadel, 1965.

Goldzwig, Steven R., and Patricia A. Sullivan. "Post-Assassination Newspaper Editorial Eulogies: Analysis and Assessment." *Western Journal of Communication* 59, no. 2 (Spring 1995): 126–50.

Goodwin, Doris Kearns. *The Fitzgeralds and the Kennedys: An American Saga*. New York: Simon & Schuster, 1987.

Goodwin, Richard. *Remembering America: A Voice from the Sixties*. New York: Harper & Row, 1989.

Graham, James W. *Victura: The Kennedys, a Sailboat, and the Sea*. Lebanon, NH: ForeEdge, 2014.

Grainger, Roger. *The Social Symbolism of Grief and Mourning*. Philadelphia: Jessica Kingsley, 1998.

"The Grave of John F. Kennedy," *Architectural Record* 142 (December 1967): 128–30.

Greenberg, Bradley S., and Edwin B. Parker, eds. *The Kennedy Assassination and the American Public: Social Communication in Crisis*. Stanford, CA: Stanford University Press, 1965.

Greenfield, Jeff. *If Kennedy Lived: The First and Second Terms of President John F. Kennedy: An Alternate History*. New York: Putnam, 2013.

Guthman, Edwin. *We Band of Brothers*. New York: Harper & Row, 1971.

Halbwachs, Maurice. *On Collective Memory*. Edited and translated by Lewis A. Coser. Chicago: University of Chicago Press, 1992.

Hamilton, Charles. *The Robot That Helped to Make a President: A Reconnaissance into the Mysteries of John F. Kennedy's Signature*. New York, 1965.

Hamilton, Nigel. *American Caesars: Lives of the Presidents from Franklin D. Roosevelt to George W. Bush*. New Haven: Yale University Press, 2010.

⸻ *JFK: Reckless Youth*. New York: Random House, 1992.

⸻ "The Rise and Fall of Camelot." *New England Journal of History* 52, no. 2 (Fall 1995): 91–108.

Hanff, Helene. *John F. Kennedy: Young Man of Destiny*. Garden City, NY: Doubleday, 1965.

Hannan, Philip. *The Archbishop Wore Combat Boots: Memoir of an Extraordinary Life*. With Nancy Collins and Peter Finney, Jr. Huntington, IN: Our Sunday Visitor, 2010.

Hansen, Jodie Elliott, and Laura Hansen. *November 22, 1963: Ordinary and Extraordinary People Recall Their Reactions When They Heard the News.* New York: Thomas Dunne Books/St. Martin's Press, 2013.

Helfrich, Kurt. "Modernism for Washington? The Kennedys and the Redesign of Lafayette Square." *Washington History* 8, no. 1 (Spring/Summer 1996): 16–37.

Hellmann, John. *The Kennedy Obsession: The American Myth of JFK.* New York: Columbia University Press, 1997.

Henderson, Bruce, and Sam Summerlin. *1:33.* New York: Cowles, 1968.

Henggeler, Paul R. *The Kennedy Persuasion: The Politics of Style since JFK.* Chicago: Ivan R. Dee, 1995.

Hennessy, Maurice N. *I'll Come Back in the Springtime: John F. Kennedy and the Irish.* New York: Ives Washington, 1966.

Herken, Gregg. *The Georgetown Set: Friends and Rivals in Cold War Washington.* New York: Vintage Books, 2015.

Herndon, Booton. *The Humor of JFK.* Greenwich, CT: Fawcett, 1964.

Hersh, Seymour M. *The Dark Side of Camelot.* New York: Little, Brown/Back Bay Books, 1998.

Hertfelder, Thomas. "With a Whiff of Royalism: Exhibiting Biographies in American Presidential Libraries." In *Institutions of Public Memory: the Legacies of German and American Politicians,* edited by Astrid M. Eckert, 9–32. Washington, DC: German Historical Institute, 2007.

Heymann, C. David. *A Woman Named Jackie: An Intimate Biography of Jacqueline Bouvier Kennedy Onassis.* New York: Penguin, 1989.

Hill, Clint. *Five Days in November.* With Lisa McCubbin. New York: Gallery Books, 2013.

   Mrs. Kennedy and Me. With Lisa McCubbin. New York: Simon & Schuster, 2013.

Hinckley, Barbara. *The Symbolic Presidency: How Presidents Portray Themselves.* New York: Routledge, 1990.

Hobsbawm, Eric J., and Terence O. Ranger, eds. *The Invention of Tradition.* New York: Cambridge University Press, 1992.

Hodes, Martha. *Mourning Lincoln.* New Haven: Yale University Press, 2015.

Hoberek, Andrew, ed. *The Cambridge Companion to John F. Kennedy.* New York: Cambridge University Press, 2015.

Hodgson, Godfrey. *JFK and LBJ: The Last Two Great Presidents.* New Haven: Yale University Press, 2015.

Howe, Lawrence. "Now Playing at a Presidential Library near You: The Films of Presidential Museums." *Public Historian* 17, no. 1 (Winter 1995): 125–41.

Hoy, William G. *Do Funerals Matter? The Purposes and Practices of Death Rituals in Global Perspective.* New York: Routledge, 2013.

Hufbauer, Benjamin. *Presidential Temples: How Memorials and Libraries Shape Public Memory.* Lawrence: University Press of Kansas, 2005.

Hunt, Lynn, ed. *The New Cultural History.* Berkeley: University of California Press, 1989.

"In the News: Changes in Kennedy Library." *American Libraries* 5, no. 9 (October 1974): 465–66.

"In the News: Presidential Papers: ALA Units Discuss Public Ownership; Sites of Nixon, Kennedy Libraries Uncertain." *American Libraries* 6, no. 7 (July–August 1975): 402.

Irwin, Ryan M. *Gordian Knot: Apartheid and the Unmaking of the Liberal World Order*. New York: Oxford University Press, 2012.

"JFK Memorials Move Forward." *Architectural Forum* 120 (May 1964): 9.

John F. Kennedy: Catalogue of Books, Articles, Autographs, and Memorabilia. Austin, TX: Jenkins, [1964–65?].

John F. Kennedy Library. *John F. Kennedy: A Reading List*. Waltham, MA: Kennedy Library, 1974.

  The Kennedys: A Reading List for Young People. Waltham, MA: Kennedy Library, 1974.

John F. Kennedy Library Foundation. *Listening In: The Secret White House Recordings of John F. Kennedy*. New York: Hyperion, 2012.

John F. Kennedy School of Government. *The John F. Kennedy School of Government: The First Fifty Years*. Cambridge, MA: Ballinger, 1986.

Johnson, Lady Bird. *A White House Diary*. Austin: University of Texas Press, 2007.

Johnson, Lyndon Baines. *The Vantage Point: Perspectives of the Presidency, 1963–1969* New York: Holt, Rinehart & Winston, 1971.

Jost, Kenneth. "Presidential Libraries." *CQ Researcher* 17, no. 11 (March 16, 2007): 241–64.

Jovich, John B., ed. *Reflections on JFK's Assassination: 250 Famous Americans Remember November 22, 1963*. Bethesda, MD: Woodbine House, 1988.

Kammen, Michael G. *Mystic Chords of Memory: The Transformation of Tradition in American Culture*. New York: Knopf, 1991.

  In the Past Lane: Historical Perspectives on American Culture. New York: Oxford University Press, 1997.

Kaplan, Alice. *Dreaming in French: The Paris Years of Jacqueline Bouvier Kennedy, Susan Sontag, and Angela Davis*. Chicago: University of Chicago Press, 2012.

Kaufman, Burton I. "John F. Kennedy as World Leader: A Perspective on the Literature." In *America in the World: The Historiography of American Foreign Relations since 1941*, edited by Michael J. Hogan, 326–57. New York: Cambridge University Press, 1995.

Kearl, Michael C. *Endings: A Sociology of Death and Dying*. New York: Oxford University Press, 1989.

Kennedy, Caroline. *Rose Kennedy's Family Album: From the Fitzgerald Kennedy Private Collection, 1878–1946*. New York: Grand Central Publishing, 2013.

"Kennedy Grave Design is Disclosed." *Architectural Record* 137 (January 1965): 12–13.

Kennedy, John F. *Profiles in Courage*. New York: Harper, 1956.

  Public Papers of the Presidents of the United States: John F. Kennedy, 1961. Washington, DC: Government Printing Office, 1962.

  Quotations from the Scriptures. New York: Catholic Family Library, 1964.

  Why England Slept. New York: Wilfred Funk, 1940.

Kennedy, John F., Lyndon B. Johnson, Hubert H. Humphrey, and Thomas H. Kuchel. *Moral Crisis: The Case for Civil Rights*. Minneapolis: Gilbert Publishing, 1964.

Kennedy, Robert. "Mount Kennedy, II: A Peak Worthy of the President." *National Geographic* 128, no. 1 (July 1965): 5–9.

Kennedy, Rose Fitzgerald. *Times to Remember*. Garden City, NY: Doubleday, 1974.

Kessel, John H. "Mr. Kennedy and the Manufacture of News." *Parliamentary Affairs* 16, no. 3 (March 1963): 293–301.

Klein, Edward. *All Too Human: The Love Story of Jack and Jackie Kennedy*. New York: Pocket Star Books, 1996.

Knight, Peter. *The Kennedy Assassination*. Edinburgh: Edinburgh University Press, 2007.

Knott, Stephen F. "What Might Have Been." *Review of Politics* 76, no. 1 (Fall 2014): 661–70.

Konstantinou, Lee. "The Camelot Presidency: Kennedy and Postwar Style." In Hoberek, *The Cambridge Companion to John F. Kennedy*, 149–63.

Laderman, Gary. *The Sacred Remains: American Attitudes toward Death, 1799–1883*. New Haven: Yale University Press, 1996.

   Rest in Peace: A Cultural History of Death and the Funeral Home in Twentieth-Century America. New York: Oxford University Press, 2003.

Lasky, Victor. *JFK: The Man and the Myth*. New York: Macmillan, 1963.

Lattanzi-Licht, Marcia, and Kennedy J. Doka, eds. *Living with Grief, Coping with Public Tragedy*. New York: Brunner-Routledge, 2003.

Leaming, Barbara. *Jack Kennedy: The Education of a Statesman*. New York: W. W. Norton, 2006.

   Jacqueline Bouvier Kennedy Onassis: The Untold Story. New York: St. Martin's Press, 2014.

   Mrs. Kennedy: The Missing History of the Kennedy Years. New York: Touchstone, 2002.

Leeke, Jim. *Long Shadows: The Farewell to JFK*. Alexandria, VA: Attic Window Publishing, 2008.

Leuchtenburg, William E. "John F. Kennedy, Twenty Years Later." *American Heritage* 35, no. 1 (December 1983): 51–59.

Life Magazine. *John F. Kennedy Memorial Edition*. Chicago: Time, 1963.

Lincoln, Anne H. *The Kennedy White House Parties*. New York: Viking Press, 1967.

Lincoln, Evelyn. *My Twelve Years with John F. Kennedy*. New York: David McKay, 1965.

   Kennedy & Johnson. New York: Holt, Rinehart & Winston, 1968.

Ling, Peter J. *John F. Kennedy*. New York: Routledge, 2013.

Lipsitz, George. *Time Passes: Collective Memory and American Popular Culture*. Minneapolis: University of Minnesota Press, 1990.

Logevall, Fredrik. "Vietnam and the Question of What Might Have Been." In White, *Kennedy: The New Frontier Revisited*, 19–62.

Look Magazine. *Kennedy and His Family in Pictures*. New York: Cowles, 1963.

Lowe, Jacques. *The Kennedy Years*. New York: Viking, 1964.

   Portrait: The Emergence of John F. Kennedy. New York: McGraw-Hill, 1963.

Lowenthal, David. *The Past is a Foreign Country*. New York: Cambridge University Press, 1985.

The Heritage Crusade and the Spoils of History. New York: Cambridge University Press, 1998.

Lurie, Alison. *The Language of Clothes*. New York: Henry Holt, 2000.

Lurvey, Diana, ed. *The Kennedys: America's Royal Family*. New York: Ideal, 1962.

Lynch, Annette, and Mitchell D. Strauss, eds. *Changing Fashion: A Critical Introduction to Trend Analysis and Cultural Meaning*. New York: Berg, 2007.

Manchester, William. *Controversy and Other Essays in Journalism, 1950–1975*. Boston: Little, Brown, 1976.

The Death of a President: November 20–November 25, 1963. New York: Galahad Books, 1967.

One Brief Shining Moment: Remembering Kennedy. Boston: Little, Brown, 1983.

Marlin, William. "Lighthouse on an Era." *Architectural Record* 167 (February 1980): 81–90.

Marten, Paul. *Kennedy Requiem*. Toronto: Weller, 1963.

Martin, Ralph G. *A Hero for Our Time: An Intimate Story of the Kennedy Years*. New York: Ballantine Books, 1983.

Marvin, Carolyn, and David W. Ingle. *Blood Sacrifice and the Nation: Totem Rituals and the American Flag*. New York: Cambridge University Press, 1999.

Mason, Robert. "Kennedy and the Conservatives." In Hoberek, *Cambridge Companion to John F. Kennedy*, 225–39.

Matt, Susan J. *Homesickness: An American History*. New York: Oxford University Press, 2011.

Matthes, Melissa. "Assassination Sermons: Mourning JFK and Restoring Church Authority." *Journal of Church and State* 55, no. 2 (November 2012): 221–44.

Matthews, Christopher. *Jack Kennedy: Elusive Hero*. New York: Simon & Schuster, 2012.

Matusow, Allen J. *The Unraveling of America: A History of Liberalism in the 1960s*. New York: Harper & Row, 1984.

May, Ernest R., and Philip D. Zelikow. "Camelot Confidential." *Diplomatic History* 22, no. 4 (Fall 1998): 642–53.

Mayhew, Aubrey. *The World's Tribute to John F. Kennedy in Medallic Art*. New York: William Morrow, 1966.

McPherson, Alan. "Cuba." In Selverstone, *Companion to John F. Kennedy*, 228–47.

Meyers, Joan S., ed. *John Fitzgerald Kennedy: As We Remember Him*. New York: Atheneum, 1965.

Meyersohn, Maxwell, comp. *Memorable Quotations of John F. Kennedy*. New York: Crowell, 1965.

Mindak, William A., and Gerald D. Hursh. "Television's Functions on the Assassination Weekend." In Greenberg and Parker, *Kennedy Assassination*, 130–41.

Minutaglio, Bill, and Steven L. Davis. *Dallas 1963: The Road to the Kennedy Assassination*. London: John Murray, 2013.

Miroff, Bruce. *Pragmatic Illusions: The Presidential Politics of John F. Kennedy.* New York: David McKay, 1976.

Morrissey, Charles T., and Tracy E. K'Meyer. "An Interview with Charles T. Morrissey: Part I—'Getting Started: Beginning an Oral History Career.'" *Oral History Review* 24, no. 2 (Winter 1997): 73–94.

Mossman, Billy C., and M. W. Stark. *The Last Salute: Civil and Military Funerals, 1921–1969.* Washington, DC: Department of the Army, 1971.

Muehlenbeck, Philip E. *Betting on the Africans: John F. Kennedy's Courting of African Nationalist Leaders.* New York: Oxford University Press, 2012.

Mulvaney, Jay, and Paul De Angelis. *Dear Mrs. Kennedy: The World Shares Its Grief; Letters, November 1963.* New York: St. Martin's Press, 2010.

Nachant, Frances Grant. *Song of Peace.* Francestown, NH: Golden Quill, 1969.

Nasaw, David. *The Patriarch: The Remarkable Life and Turbulent Times of Joseph P. Kennedy.* New York: Penguin, 2012.

National Geographic Society. *The Kennedy Mystique: Creating Camelot.* Washington, DC: National Geographic Society, 2004.

Neal, Arthur G. *National Trauma and Collective Memory: Extraordinary Events in the American Experience.* 2nd ed. Armonk, NY: M. E. Sharpe, 2005.

Neisser, Ulric, ed. *Memory Observed: Remembering in Natural Contexts.* San Francisco: W. H. Freeman, 1982.

Nelson, Anna Kasten. "President Kennedy's National Security Policy: A Reconsideration." *Reviews in American History* 19, no. 1 (March 1991): 1–14.

Neustadt, Richard E. "Kennedy in the Presidency: A Premature Appraisal." *Political Science Quarterly* 79, no. 3 (September 1964): 321–34.

Newcomb, Joan I. *John F. Kennedy: An Annotated Bibliography.* Metuchen, NJ: Scarecrow Press, 1977.

Nora, Pierre. *Realms of Memory: Rethinking the French Past.* Edited by Lawrence D. Kritzman and translated by Arthur Goldhammer. 3 vols. New York: Columbia University Press, 1996–98.

Nowak, Martin S. *The White House in Mourning: Deaths and Funerals of Presidents in Office.* Jefferson, NC: McFarland, 2010.

O'Brien, Lawrence F. *No Final Victories: A Life in Politics from John F. Kennedy to Watergate.* New York: Ballantine Books, 1975.

O'Brien, Michael. *John F. Kennedy: A Biography.* New York: Thomas Dunne Books/St. Martin's Press, 2005.

O'Donnell, Kenneth P., and David F. Powers. *"Johnny, We Hardly Knew Ye": Memories of John Fitzgerald Kennedy.* With Joe McCarthy. Boston: Little, Brown, 1972.

Olick, Jeffrey K., Vered Vinitzky-Seroussi, and Daniel Levy, eds. *The Collective Memory Reader.* New York: Oxford University Press, 2011.

Onassis, Jacqueline Kennedy, and Arthur M. Schlesinger, Jr. *Jacqueline Kennedy: Historical Conversations on Life with John F. Kennedy, Interviews with Arthur M. Schlesinger, Jr., 1964.* New York: Hyperion, 2011.

O'Neill, William L. *Coming Apart: An Informal History of America in the 1960s.* Chicago: Quadrangle Books, 1971.

O'Reilly, Bill, and Martin Dugard. *Killing Kennedy: The End of Camelot*. New York: Henry Holt, 2012.

"Overrated & Underrated Americans." *American Heritage* 39, no. 5 (July/August 1988): 48–63.

Owen, Dean R. *November 22, 1963: Reflections on the Life, Assassination, and Legacy of John F. Kennedy*. New York: Skyhorse Publishing, 2013.

Pachter, Henry. "JFK as an Equestrian Statue: On Myth and Mythmakers." *Salmagundi* 1, no. 3 (1966): 3–26.

Panagopoulos, Costas. "Ex-Presidential Approval: Retrospective Evaluations of Presidential Performance." *Presidential Studies Quarterly* 42, no. 4 (December 2012): 719–29.

Parmet, Herbert S. *Jack: The Struggles of John F. Kennedy*. New York: Dial Press, 1980.

   JFK: The Presidency of John F. Kennedy. New York: Penguin, 1983.

   "JFK: Twenty Years Later." *New England Journal of History* 53, no. 1 (Spring/Fall 1997): 38–46.

Paterson, Thomas G., ed. *Kennedy's Quest for Victory: American Foreign Policy, 1961–1963*. New York: Oxford University Press, 1989.

"Pei Unveils New Design for Kennedy Library." *Architectural Record* 160 (July 1976): 39.

Perret, Geoffrey. *Jack: A Life Like No Other*. New York: Random House, 2002.

Perry, Barbara A. *Jacqueline Kennedy: First Lady of the New Frontier*. Lawrence: University Press of Kansas, 2004.

   Rose Kennedy: The Life and Times of a Political Matriarch. New York: Norton, 2012.

Peterson, Merrill D. *Lincoln in American Memory*. New York: Oxford University Press, 1995.

Pickering, Michael, and Emily Keightley. "The Modalities of Nostalgia." *Current Sociology* 54, no. 6 (November 2006): 919–41.

Pierard, Richard V., and Robert D. Linder. *Civil Religion & the Presidency*. Grand Rapids, MI: Academie Books, 1988.

Pietrusza, David. *1960: LBJ vs. JFK vs. Nixon: The Epic Campaign That Forged Three Presidencies*. New York: Union Square Press, 2008.

Pollard, James E. "The Kennedy Administration and the Press." *Journalism Quarterly* 41, no. 1 (March 1964): 3–14.

   The Presidents and the Press: Truman to Johnson. Washington, DC: Public Affairs Press, 1964.

Preston, Andrew. "Vietnam." In Selverstone, *Companion to John F. Kennedy*, 269–88.

Rakove, Robert B. *Kennedy, Johnson, and the Nonaligned World*. New York: Cambridge University Press, 2012.

Raymond, John, and Paul Ballot. *The Thousand Days: John Fitzgerald Kennedy as President*. Island Park, NY: Aspen, 1964.

Reedy, George. *Lyndon B. Johnson: A Memoir*. New York: Andrews and McMeel, 1982.

Reeves, Richard. *President Kennedy: Profile of Power*. New York: Simon & Schuster, 1994.

Reeves, Thomas C. *A Question of Character: A Life of John F. Kennedy.* New York: Free Press, 1991.

Rochette, Edward C. *The Medallic Portraits of John F. Kennedy.* Iola, WI: Krause Publications, 1966.

Rorabaugh, W. J. *Kennedy and the Promise of the Sixties.* New York: Cambridge University Press, 2002.

  The Real Making of the President: Kennedy, Nixon, and the 1960 Election. Lawrence: University Press of Kansas, 2009.

Rosenberg, Emily S. *A Date Which Will Live: Pearl Harbor in American Memory.* Durham, NC: Duke University Press, 2003.

Roth, James M. "Reclaiming Pieces of Camelot: How NARA and the JFK Library Recovered Missing Kennedy Documents and Artifacts." *Prologue* 38, no. 2 (Summer 2006). www.archives.gov/publications/prologue/2006/summer/camelot.html.

Rotter, Andrew J. "New Museum at the John F. Kennedy Library." *Journal of American History* 83, no. 1 (June 1996): 162–66.

Rubalcaba, Jill. *I. M. Pei: Architect of Time, Place, and Purpose.* Tarrytown, NY: Marshall Cavendish, 2011.

Rubin, Gretchen. *Forty Ways to Look at JFK.* New York: Ballantine Books, 2005.

Russell, G. Darrell. *Lincoln and Kennedy: Looked at Kindly Together.* New York: Carlton, 1973.

Russell, Jan Jarboe. *Lady Bird: A Biography of Mrs. Johnson.* New York: Scribner, 1999.

Russo, Gus, and Harry Moses, eds. *Where Were You? America Remembers the JFK Assassination.* Guilford, CT: Lyons Press, 2013.

Ryan, Mary. "The American Parade: Representations of the Nineteenth-Century Social Order." In Hunt, *New Cultural History,* 131–53.

Sabato, Larry J. *The Kennedy Half Century: The Presidency, Assassination, and Lasting Legacy of John F. Kennedy.* New York: Bloomsbury, 2013.

Sable, Martin H. *A Bio-Bibliography of the Kennedy Family.* Metuchen, NJ: Scarecrow Books, 1969.

Sachs, Jeffrey D. *To Move the World: JFK's Quest for Peace.* New York: Random House, 2013.

Salinger, Pierre. *With Kennedy.* Garden City, NY: Doubleday, 1966.

Salinger, Pierre, and Sander Vanocur, eds. *A Tribute to John F. Kennedy.* Chicago: Encyclopedia Britannica, 1964.

Sandler, Martin W., ed. *The Letters of John F. Kennedy.* New York: Bloomsbury Press, 2013.

Santa Cruz, Paul H. *Making JFK Matter: Popular Memory and the Thirty-fifth President.* Denton: University of North Texas Press, 2015.

Saunders, Doris E., ed. *The Kennedy Years and the Negro.* Chicago: Johnson Publishing, 1964.

Savage, Kirk. *Monument Wars: Washington, D.C., the National Mall, and the Transformation of the Memorial Landscape.* Berkeley: University of California Press, 2009.

Savage, Sean J. *JFK, LBJ, and the Democratic Party.* Albany: State University of New York Press, 2004.

"Say It with Trees." *American Forests* 70 (January 1964): 11.

Schechner, Richard. *Performance Studies*, 2nd ed. New York: Routledge, 2006.

Schild, Georg. "The Berlin Crisis." In White, *Kennedy: The New Frontier Revisited*, 91–131.

Schlesinger, Arthur M., Jr. *The Imperial Presidency*. New York: Houghton Mifflin, 1973.

   Journals: 1952–2000. Edited by Andrew Schlesinger and Stephen Schlesinger. New York: Penguin, 2007.

   The Letters of Arthur Schlesinger, Jr. Edited by Andrew Schlesinger and Stephen Schlesinger. New York: Random House, 2013.

   Robert Kennedy and His Times. New York: Houghton Mifflin, 2002.

   A Thousand Days: John F. Kennedy in the White House. Boston: Houghton Mifflin, 2002.

Schmertz, Mildred F. "Getting Ready for the John F. Kennedy Library: Not Everyone Wants to Make It Go Away." *Architectural Record* 156 (December 1974): 98–105.

Schmidt, M. Bernadette, comp. *The Trumpet Summons Us ... John F. Kennedy*. New York: Vantage Press, 1964.

Schneider, Nicholas A., comp. *Religious Views of President John F. Kennedy: In His Own Words*. St. Louis: B. Herder, 1965.

Schneider, Nicholas A., and Nathalie S. Rockhill, comps. and eds. *John F. Kennedy Talks to Young People*. New York: Hawthorne, 1968.

Schudson, Michael. *Watergate in American Memory: How We Remember, Forget, and Reconstruct the Past*. New York: Basic Books, 1993.

Schwartz, Barry. *Abraham Lincoln and the Forge of National Memory*. Chicago: University of Chicago Press, 2000.

   "The Social Context of Commemoration: A Study in Collective Memory." *Social Forces* 61, no. 2 (December 1982): 374–402.

   "The Reconstruction of Abraham Lincoln." In *Collective Remembering*, edited by David Middleton and Derek Edwards, 81–107. Newbury Park, CA: Sage Publications, 1990.

   "Mourning and the Making of a Sacred Symbol: Durkheim and the Lincoln Assassination." *Social Forces* 70, no. 2 (December 1991): 343–64.

Selverstone, Marc J., ed. *A Companion to John F. Kennedy*. West Sussex, UK: John Wiley & Sons, 2014.

   "Eternal Flaming: The Historiography of Kennedy Foreign Policy." *Passport* 70, no. 1 (April 2015): 22–29.

Semple, Robert B., Jr., ed. *Four Days in November: The Original Coverage of the John F. Kennedy Assassination by the Staff of the New York Times*. New York: St. Martin's Press, 2003.

Shannon, William V. *The American Irish*. New York: Macmillan, 1966.

   The Heir Apparent: Robert Kennedy and the Struggle for Power. New York: Macmillan, 1967.

Shaw, John T. *JFK in the Senate: Pathway to the Presidency*. New York: Palgrave Macmillan, 2013.

Shaw, Mark. *The John F. Kennedys: A Family Album*. New York: Farrar, Straus, 1964.

Shaw, Maud. *White House Nannie: My Years with Caroline and John Kennedy, Jr.* New York: New American Library, 1965.

Sheatsley, Paul B., and Jacob J. Feldman, "A National Survey on Public Reactions and Behavior." In Greenberg and Parker, *Kennedy Assassination*, 149–77.

Shenon, Philip. *A Cruel and Shocking Act: The Secret History of the Kennedy Assassination* New York: Henry Holt, 2013.

Shepard, Tazewell. *John F. Kennedy: Man of the Sea.* New York: Morrow, 1965.

Shesol, Jeff. *Mutual Contempt: Lyndon Johnson, Robert Kennedy, and the Feud That Defined a Decade.* New York: W. W. Norton, 1998.

Smelser, Neil J. "Epilogue: September 11, 2001, as Cultural Trauma." In Alexander et al., *Cultural Trauma*, 264–82.

"Psychological Trauma and Cultural Trauma." In Alexander et al., *Cultural Trauma*, 31–59.

Smith, Marie. *Entertaining in the White House.* Washington, DC: Acropolis Books, 1967.

Smith, Nancy Kegan, and Gary M. Stern. "A Historical Review of Access to Records in Presidential Libraries." *Public Historian* 28, no. 3 (Summer 2006): 79–116.

Smith, Sally Bedell. *Grace and Power: The Private World of the Kennedy White House.* New York: Random House, 2005.

Sorensen, Ted. *Counselor: A Life at the Edge of History.* New York: HarperCollins, 2008.

Kennedy. New York: Harper & Row, 1965.

Spoto, Donald. *Jacqueline Bouvier Kennedy Onassis: A Life.* New York: St. Martin's Press, 2000.

Starobinski, Jean. "The Idea of Nostalgia." *Diogenes* 54 (1966): 81–103.

Steinberg, Neil. *Hatless Jack: The President, the Fedora, and the History of an American Style.* New York: Plume, 2004.

Stewart, Charles J. "Catholic and Jewish Pulpit Reaction to the Kennedy Assassination." *Western Speech* 31, no. 2 (Spring 1967): 131–39.

Stewart, Charles J., and Bruce Kendall, eds. *A Man Named John F. Kennedy: Sermons on His Assassination.* Glen Rock, NJ: Paulist Press, 1964.

Stewart, John C. *Our Hero: John F. Kennedy.* Northport, AL: American Southern Publishing, 1964.

Stoll, Ira. *JFK, Conservative.* Boston: Houghton Mifflin Harcourt, 2013.

Stone, Ralph A., ed. *John F. Kennedy, 1917–1963: Chronology-Documents-Bibliographical Aids.* Dobbs Ferry, NY: Oceana, 1971.

Strousse, Flora. *John Fitzgerald Kennedy: Man of Courage.* New York: Harcourt, Brace & World, 1963.

Sumiala, Johanna. *Media and Ritual: Death, Community, and Everyday Life.* New York: Routledge, 2013.

Thayer, Mary Van Rensselaer. *Jacqueline Kennedy: The White House Years.* New York: Little, Brown, 1971.

Jacqueline Bouvier Kennedy. Garden City, NY: Doubleday & Company, 1961.

Thelen, David. "Memory and American History." *Journal of American History* 75, no. 4 (March 1989): 117–29.

Thomas, Evan. *Robert Kennedy: His Life.* New York: Simon & Schuster, 2002.

"To John F. Kennedy—Homage by Artists." *Art in America* 52, no. 5 (1964): 90–95.

Toscano, Vincent L. *Since Dallas: Images of John F. Kennedy in Popular and Scholarly Literature, 1963–1973.* San Francisco: R & E Research Associates, 1978.

Troy, Gil. "Jacqueline Kennedy's White House Renovations." *White House Studies* 1, no. 3 (2001): 395–402.

Tugwell, Rexford G. "The President and His Helpers: A Review Article." *Political Science Quarterly* 82, no. 2 (June 1967): 253–67.

Ulyatt, Michelle. "The John F. Kennedy Presidential Library and Museum as a Cultural Representation of the Public Memory of the President." *European Journal of American Culture* 33, no. 2 (June 2014): 117–30.

United Press International and Chase Studios. *John F. Kennedy from Childhood to Martyrdom.* Washington, DC: Tatler, 1963.

US Congress. *Memorial Addresses in the Congress of the United States and Tributes in Eulogy of John Fitzgerald Kennedy, Late a President of the United States.* Washington, DC: Government Printing Office, 1964.

US Library of Congress. *John Fitzgerald Kennedy, 1917–1963: A Chronological List of References.* Washington, DC: US Government Printing Office, 1964.

US Senate. Subcommittee on Public Works of the Committee on Appropriations. *Public Works Appropriation Hearing, Department of the Army, April 8, 1964, 88th Cong.* Washington, DC: Government Printing Office, 1964.

Van Buren, Abigail. *Where Were You When President Kennedy Was Shot? Memories and Tributes to a Slain President as Told to "Dear Abby."* Kansas City: Andrews & McMeel, 1993.

Valenti, Jack. *A Very Human President.* New York: Pocket Books, 1977.

Van Gelder, Lawrence. *Why the Kennedys Lost the Book Battle: The Untold Story.* New York: Award Books, 1967.

Van Rijn, Guido. *Kennedy's Blues: African-American Blues and Gospel Songs on JFK.* Jackson: University Press of Mississippi, 2007.

Vidal, Gore. "The Holy Family." In Vidal, *United States,* 809–26.

"The Manchester Book." In Vidal, *United States,* 804–8.

United States: Essays 1952–1992. New York: Random House, 1993.

Vilnis, Aija. *The Bearer of the Star Spangled Banner: In Memory of President John Fitzgerald Kennedy.* Translated by Lilija Pavars. New York: Robert Speller & Sons, 1964.

Walton, Richard J. *Cold War and Counterrevolution: The Foreign Policy of John F. Kennedy.* New York: Viking Press, 1972.

Washburn, Bradford. "Canada's Mount Kennedy, I: The Discovery." *National Geographic* 128, no. 1 (July 1965): 1–3.

Watson, Mary Ann. "An Enduring Fascination: The Papers of Jacqueline Kennedy." *Prologue* 19, no. 2 (Summer 1987): 117–25.

The Expanding Vista: American Television in the Kennedy Years. Durham, NC: Duke University Press, 1994.

Wenger, Kenneth R., ed. *John F. Kennedy Memorial Stamp Issues of the World.* Fort Lee, NJ: Wenger, 1970.

West, J. B. *Upstairs at the White House: My Life with the First Ladies*. With Mary Lynn Kotz. New York: Coward, McCann & Geoghegan, 1973.

Whalen, Richard J. *The Founding Father: The Story of Joseph P. Kennedy and the Family He Raised to Power*. New York: New American Library, 1964.

Whitbourn, John, ed. *Runnymede Memorial*. Ilford, England: Excel Press, 1965.

White, Mark. *Kennedy: A Cultural History of an American Icon*. New York: Bloomsbury Academic, 2013.

White, Mark J. "The Cuban Imbroglio: From the Bay of Pigs to the Missile Crisis and Beyond." In White, *Kennedy: The New Frontier Revisited*, 63–90.

  "Introduction: A New Synthesis for the New Frontier." In White, *Kennedy: The New Frontier Revisited*, 1–17.

  ed. *Kennedy: The New Frontier Revisited*. New York: New York University Press, 1988.

  "Apparent Perfection: The Image of John F. Kennedy." *History* 98 (April 2013): 226–46.

White, Theodore H. *The Making of the President, 1960*. New York: Atheneum, 1961.

Whittaker, James W. "Mount Kennedy, III: The First Ascent." *National Geographic* 128, no. 1 (July 1965): 11–33.

Wicker, Tom. *JFK and LBJ: The Influence of Personality upon Politics*. New York: Morrow, 1968.

  Kennedy without Tears: The Man beneath the Myth. New York: William Morrow, 1964.

Wills, Garry. *The Kennedy Imprisonment: A Meditation on Power*. Boston: Houghton Mifflin, 2002.

Wilson, John F. *Public Religion in American Culture*. Philadelphia: Temple University Press, 1079.

Winter, Jay. "The Generation of Memory: Reflections on the 'Memory Boom' in Contemporary Historical Studies." *Bulletin of the German Historical Institute* 27, no. 3 (Fall 2000): 69–92.

  Remembering War: The Great War Between Memory and History in the Twentieth Century. New Haven: Yale University Press, 2006.

Wiseman, Carter. *I. M. Pei: A Profile in American Architecture*. New York: Harry N. Abrams, 1990.

Wolff, Perry. *A Tour of the White House with Mrs. John F. Kennedy*. New York: Dell Publishing, 1963.

Wolffe, John. *Great Deaths: Grieving, Religion, and Nationhood in Victorian and Edwardian Britain*. New York: Oxford University Press, 2000.

Woods, Randall B. *LBJ: Architect of American Ambition*. Cambridge, MA: Harvard University Press, 2007.

Wortsman, Gene, ed. *The New Frontier Joke Book*. New York: MacFadden-Bartell, 1963.

Young, James E. *The Texture of Memory: Holocaust Memorials and Meaning*. New Haven: Yale University Press, 1993.

Zelinsky, Wilbur. *Nation Into State: The Shifting Symbolic Foundations of American Nationalism*. Chapel Hill: University of North Carolina Press, 1988.

Zelizer, Barbie. *Covering the Body: The Kennedy Assassination, the Media, and the Shaping of Collective Memory*. Chicago: University of Chicago Press, 1992.

"The Kennedy Assassination Through a Popular Eye: Toward a Politics of Remembering." *Journal of Communication Inquiry* 16, no. 2 (Summer 1992): 21–36.

"Reading the Past against the Grain: The Shape of Memory Studies." *Critical Studies in Mass Communication* 12, no. 2 (June 1995): 214–39.

Index

Turnure, Pamela, 45, 108
Tyler, John, 75

Ullman, James Ramsey, 134
United Kingdom
    honoring/remembering Kennedy in, 219
    reactions to Kennedy's
        assassination in, 58

Van Buren, Abigail, 24, 53
Vanocur, Sander, 113
Verdon, René, 38
Vidal, Gore, 40, 105, 111
Vienna Conference, 8–9
Vig'ah Corporation, 132
VISTA, 63, 66
Von Eckardt, Wolf, 147, 148, 150, 151
    on memorial grave design, 149, 150
    on Pei's design for Kennedy Library,
        163, 166
    and Warnecke, 148, 149

Wallace, George, 13
Walton, Bill, 84, 88
Walton, Richard, 180
Walton, William, 147, 161
    and design for gravesite, 146, 161
    and design for Kennedy Library,
        161, 163
    East Room's decoration, 82
    on modern monuments, 146
Warnecke, John Carl, 145, 151, 152, 156
    and Jacqueline Kennedy, 145, 149
    and memorial gravesite, 145, 151
Warren, Earl, 52
Washington, George, 124
Waters, Muddy, 122

Watson, Mary Ann, 172
Watson, Thomas, 160
Watterson, Joseph, 148
Wehle, Philip C., 75, 76
West Germany, reactions to Kennedy's
    assassination in, 58, 60
West, J. B., 45
Whalen, Richard J., 119
White House Historical Association, 29
White House Rose Garden, 23
White House: An Historic Guide, The, 29
White, Mark, 41
White, Theodore, 112, 226
    on Jacqueline Kennedy, 103
    and Kennedy's image in collective
        memory, 102, 105, 113, 169, 222
    and Kennedy's White House
        records, 175
Whittaker, James W., 134, 135
Wicker, Tom, 110, 117, 124
Wilder, Billy, 54
Wilentz, Sean, 212
Will, George, 211, 212
Williams, Big Joe, 122
Wills, Garry, 180, 181
Wilson, Harold, 136
Wilson, Joan Hoff, 207
Winterthur Museum, 22
Winterthur Program in Early American
    Culture, 22
Wortsman, Eugene, 123
Wrightsman, Charles B., 23
Wrightsman, Jayne, 22, 23, 27

Yarborough, Ralph W., 1, 98

Zapruder, Abraham, 216